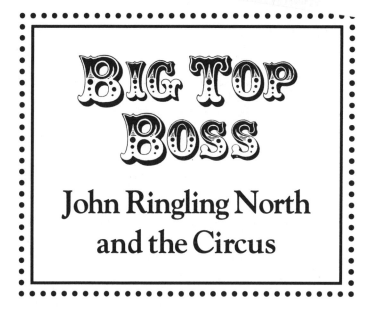

BIG TOP BOSS

John Ringling North and the Circus

David Lewis Hammarstrom

UNIVERSITY OF ILLINOIS PRESS
Urbana and Chicago

Library of Congress Cataloging-in-Publication Data

Hammarstrom, David Lewis,
   Big Top Boss: John Ringling North and the Circus
David Lewis Hammarstrom.
      p.   cm.
   Includes bibliographical references and index.
   ISBN 0-252-01901-6
   1. North, John Ringling, 1903–1985. 2. Circus owners—United
States—Biography. I. Title.
GV1811.N67H36 1992
338.7′67913′092—dc20
[B]

91-31440
CIP

Big Top Boss

To
Henry Ringling North

Contents

Illustrations follow pages 80 and 194

Ballyhoo and Thanks

He gave me the most magical day of my life. He also gave me one of the saddest. His daringly eclectic showmanship and the bohemian life he lived still fascinate me. That he was a hands-off producer made him that much more intriguing a figure. I always wondered just how he influenced the people he hired to design and direct his greatest shows on earth. And when, years later, I talked to some of those people, they wondered, too. He operated mysteriously from afar, much like one of his favorite aerialists, the serenely self-absorbed Pinito Del Oro, who seemed to swing high over the crowds in her own private sphere. So after years researching the enigmatic John Ringling North—yes, I'll say it—I still feel like someone slightly lost in the Land of Oz seeking a glimpse of the wizard beyond the mythical curtain that separates truth from fantasy.

I can tell you this much: the bold artistic impact that North had on the circus, however it was affected, is what sets his life apart dramatically. A lot of people can have love affairs like Mr. North did. And many souls with the means can sit up all night in suave cocktail lounges from here to Paris, sipping merrily on drinks. Mr. North is hardly unique for having done that. But how many people can reinvent the circus like he did? Before North, there was the Russian Anatoly Lunacharsky, who, following the Bolshevik Revolution of 1917, brought in—as would North twenty years later—the best minds in various other disciplines, from theater to ballet, to elevate the art of circus entertainment. Today, the same worthy cause has been courageously advanced by Guy Laliberte and his Canadian-based Cirque Du Soleil.

About that most magical of days . . . It was a very hot, very humid Thursday in early September 1955, the first—and only—time that I would ever see Ringling Bros. and Barnum & Bailey under the big top. The deep blue canvas stretched regally over a scrappy plot of land in Point Richmond, California, adjacent to a small yacht harbor in the calming distance. Long since paved over, the site today is a truck-to-train transfer yard for the Santa Fe Railway. Then it was—when at last that evening, following years of anxious anticipation, I entered the big top with ticket in hand for my own reserved chair on a Concello seat wagon—the most enchanted place on earth.

It was also a world excitingly in flux, stumbling and soaring recklessly down the road on the cutting edge of its own uncertain future. For you see, my introduction to the spangled empire of Mr. North was an appropriately ambivalent sampling of the magic and the madness and certainly the raging controversies that surrounded almost everything he did whenever he was aggressively in the background shaking things up. It was, I will admit, unsettling and yet strangely thrilling.

The act of creativity and change can feel very violent to the people whose values and traditions—whose livelihoods, even—it challenges. The souls who worked for Mr. North (more than one thousand on the payroll then) were forever threatened by the mere thought that at any moment he might suddenly decide to implement, with his usual cool detachment, some drastic new policy. By 1955 he was deep in the troubled throes of one of his most defiantly experimental periods. He had rounded up fifty-five elephants to parade around the hippodrome track in a lavish themed spectacle, "Mama's in the Park." And, in his ongoing efforts to sell the show more effectively in modern terms, he had set into motion what one disgruntled former press agent of his, complaining to a trade journal, dubbed a number of "dizzy directives." North was on a collision course with the Teamsters Union, about to picket the show. Only a few weeks before the Richmond date, three top Ringling managers had been fired on the Saint Paul, Minnesota, lot. Many loyal assistants followed them off. The air crackled with rumors of sinking morale and impending organizational doom.

After the show ended that night, I stood there in the cold, darkening shadows, the sound of seat wagons being hurriedly dismantled and tent poles dropping to the ground ringing through the air. I watched rough-looking men and sure elephants wrest wooden stakes from the earth, and I had the loneliest of feelings as it all disappeared back into a deserted space. Maybe it was a premonition inspired by my unsentimental uncle's having shown me that day an editorial in the *San Francisco Chronicle* predicting that this wonderful nomadic holiday would never return.

It didn't. Less than one year later, on July 16, while I watched the evening news on our family's first television set, a Dumont, there it was: pictures of the big top pitched over its last lot, Heidelberg Raceway in Pittsburgh, Pennsylvania, and news that John Ringling North had announced to the world that the tented circus was in his opinion "a thing of the past," that henceforth his shows would all be presented in auditoriums, ballparks, and outdoor stadiums. For a circus fan, this was the most depressing news imaginable. I felt as resentful as anyone toward the man who had taken away our dream world: the city of a thousand wonders that traveled by night on three sleek red and silver trains and erected its forty-odd tents over a new lot almost every day. Maybe North did not appear apologetic enough. Perhaps it was his overreported playboy image—the very antithesis of what it meant to be a real trouper, to be on the lot day in and day out, to be "with it and for it," as they said—that left him without fans. Even his seemingly blasé disregard for the old sunburst wagon wheels and baggage wagons, which now rotted away at the Sarasota quarters, came across as sacrilegious.

John Ringling North. The words became—and still are, I'm afraid—a painful reminder of the most traumatic day in American circus history. The dissident "forty-niners," members of the Ringling family who held the minority stock interests in the show, launched a fragile campaign to reinstate the canvas trappings and set things right again. At one point, I was drawn into the public-relations battle as a prospective young people's spokesman when Stuart Lancaster called me up from Florida to offer the position, with appearances on national television promised. What excitement and hope for this youngster! What a futile dream. Nothing ever materialized. Within years, the new indoor circus was making loads of money, and only the most diehard fans remained hurt and hostile on the sidelines, continuing to hope the tents would one day rise again.

Some thirty-five years later, model builders today construct miniatures of the glamorous North and Concello tent-show layouts, complete with seat wagons and the modern midway designs. Fans rave about the amateur movies of Ringling performances in the 1940s and 1950s (the glory years, they say) that are now being transferred to VHS recordings for commercial distribution, fragmented and poorly lighted as many of these historically rich films are. Somehow, the same fans have little to say when the name of the person who produced those shows is dropped, as if they were created *despite* him. As if, somehow, he really had little to do with it.

He had everything to do with it. The string of dazzling new departures over which North presided, partly in collaboration with his equally innovative general manager, Arthur M. Concello, merits a full and complete (and fair) account of his extraordinary life in the circus. Essentially, Mr. North hastened a movement that favored the genuine artist and theatrically progressive programs. The American public had long courted an infatuation with the circus *around* the circus, with the subsidiary freak shows on the midway, the exotic trappings of a gypsy world of clever charlatans and overhyped acts of humbug. Most of these tantalizing embellishments were added in the late nineteenth century as circuses grew in size and the competition between them became more intense. When William C. Coup, Dan Castello, and P. T. Barnum joined forces in 1870 to create the forerunner of the Greatest Show on Earth, the sideshows they carried were well supplied with Barnum's various dwarfs, bearded ladies, and assorted oddities and waxworks from his museum. The midway, typical of the day, was also rife with short-change artists, pickpockets, and con men, who paid the management a fee for "privileges" to work the crowds. To handle all the customers they so successfully attracted, within three seasons the Barnum triumvirate lengthened the tent, added more seats, and installed a second ring. They made the whole thing such a gargantuan delight that the public began to judge it by how much bigger, if not better, it looked every year.

Into this frenzied atmosphere entered John Ringling North's five ambitious young uncles, who were inspired by the high principles of their father, August Ringling, a humble harness maker and lover of the arts, to elevate the business in every way possible, from the quality of the performances they staged to a policy of fair dealing with the public that eliminated grift from the picture. No wonder it was relatively easy for John North to liberate himself from the costly tented operation. He had all along been mostly preoccupied with the main performance itself. To that end his best energies were directed, and to that end the thrust of this book is dedicated.

My research for this project commenced (certainly an interest in my subject did) when, in my childhood, I started cutting out newspaper articles and pasting them in scrapbooks. The very first items, in fact, are magazine photos of scenes from a movie then in the making, *The Greatest*

Show on Earth. A few years later, I discovered at Sawyer's newsstand in Santa Rosa, the town where I was being raised in Northern California, a publication called *The Billboard,* which covered in colorfully dramatic detail the circus business in the United States. Every week thereafter, I hurried down on Saturdays to Sawyer's, where a copy of the latest issue (soon with my last name scribbled in red pencil across the front page) was waiting in reserve for me. The stories were exciting to read because they vividly reflected the changing nature of the business. Some thrilled. Others disturbed. There were, of course, years of old *Billboards* that I had not seen dating back to the late 1930s, when Mr. North took over management of the show. These I viewed through a sad assortment of ill-maintained microfilm machines at the Los Angeles Public Library, not long before the electrical wiring system in that neglected facility nearly burned it to the ground. It was my mustiest research experience, and it took me as close as I could get to reliving the circus history, so integral to this book, that I had not been around to observe or read about.

Also consulted were back issues of *Variety,* examined principally at the San Francisco Public Library. Concerning my high regard for both journals— as they were then edited, I should clarify—I am reminded of what John Tebbel had to say about another trade journal in his book *Between Covers* (New York: Oxford University Press, 1987): "Although scholars do not like to think so, the trade journalism of the book business is the best source available.... The stories were written by skilled and informed professionals who were on the scene at the time and had access to sources, notably the men and women involved, whose firsthand accounts are otherwise simply not extant. When these trade sources are tested against other evidence, they are nearly always substantiated."

Many periodicals and newspapers were reviewed, a good lot of them at the Glendale Public Library, courtesy of Ed Shreely. Then there are all the program magazines and route books issued annually by the circus itself, these in my own modest collection, which contain a comprehensive listing of names, dates, logistical details, program lineups, season-end statistics, etc. The press agents who customarily prepared these records (some of them highly gifted scribes) could be as reliably informative in documenting Ringling history as they were prone to hyperbole and fantasy when they were on the front end working the ballyhoo.

Tape recordings of the musical scores and videocassettes of the actual performances (made from the transference of old 16mm movies) provide a wonderful window to the past. The late Dyer Reynolds kindly allowed me to make copies of his collection of tapes of the production music from 1950 through 1956. Since then, tapes of the entire Merle Evans scores, notably the 1950 and 1955 editions, have surfaced on the fan memorabilia market. A leading source of these rare video and audio materials is Mike Martin of Largo, Florida. His VHS offerings, made from film footage shot by Doug Morris, and another video, *Circus Resplendent*, the latter offered by Saebos Productions in association with the New Britain Youth Museum, have made it possible for me to examine and critique many acts that I never saw. It should be pointed out, however, that these films hardly encompass every act booked by North, and many of the acts they include are panned quickly by the camera, depriving the viewer of anything more than fragments of the performer's routine.

On the more scholarly level, of musty documents in misty archival regions available for examination, there are at present depressingly few. We are not, after all, dealing here with another P. T. Barnum, the journalist turned self-made "Prince of Humbug," who spent the greater part of his life writing, rewriting, and adding to his bloated autobiography. Neither are we dealing with a Hollywood mogul, the Samuel Goldwyn type who left behind a warehouse full of memos and telegrams and letters and notes, most of which he dictated, revealing in microscopic detail his every thought and wish on every film he ever made. We are dealing with the relatively silent John Ringling North, silent certainly in the sense of having authored so few letters and memos.

Consider that, thanks to Fred Pfening III, who made them available from his Pfening Archives, we can view the letters Mr. North wrote his first general manager, George W. Smith, over a four-year period. How many? A total of three. Waneta Sage-Cagne, museum archivist at the John and Mable Ringling Museum of Art, expressed to me how frustrating it was for her to discover, upon taking up the position in Sarasota, Florida, that documentation pertaining to John Ringling's life is so alarmingly scarce. Ms. Sage-Cagne allowed me access to the Henry North and Alden Hatch *Circus Kings* manuscript in its copyedited form, some interesting unpublished portions of which have helped enrich these pages.

Bob Ardren, coordinator of the Ringling Museum Circus Galleries, did his best on behalf of my cause. And historian Joe McKennon, a major contributor to the facility in past years, gifted me with a copy of his very interesting and relevant *Rape of an Estate*, which reprints the John Ringling will and which, sadly, details the sorry plight of neglected circus materials and exhibits on the museum grounds in Sarasota. Particularly missed is

the now-dismantled Back Yard Scene, which McKennon, with then cura-
tor Mel Miller, helped create—a truly enchanting re-creation of the older
tent-show era under a simulated twilight sky that simply had no equal in
any other historical institution. It is almost as if the spirit of North's
indifference to tradition plagues even this famous facility bearing his
family's name.

The world of the circus is demandingly physical, and the people who
inhabit this world spend precious few moments analyzing what goes on.
Fewer still write anything down. Who has the time? Tomorrow's town
weighs heavily on everybody's mind—always. How to get there. Where to
park. Whom to see for electrical and water hookups. There are the
unexpected repairs to props and equipment that absorb one's attention in
between. And there is the constant setting-up and tearing-down grind,
usually participated in by the performers themselves (unlike their counterparts in the other performing arts), whether by contract or habit. What the
public sees is a language overwhelmingly physical. John North's own
wandering lifestyle—his travels around the world in search of fresh talent
and his nocturnal pursuits—was to a degree true to the spirit of the circus.
And as articulate as he could be (he was, by all accounts, a superb
storyteller), rarely did he spend much time verbalizing over the business
that had made him famous.

Perhaps in his defense it can be favorably noted that he had little to say
in his defense. Are we the luckier for not having been left a book of his
memoirs? Something as self-servingly manipulative as what P. T. Barnum
foisted upon the public can lull even the devoted scholar into a dangerous
flirtation with a body of misinformation and half-truth for which few
verifying sources exist. Without an accounting from Mr. North, we are
forced to pay closer attention to more potentially objective voices, those
individuals who were close enough to the scene to understand it, but not
too close to our subject to fictionalize away the variable nuances, either
with too much friendly praise or too much biased criticism.

Enter the spoken word. In lieu of the dearth of dusty documents, there
is the interview, an unfortunately slighted function among a certain school
of historians. I personally do not think the interview is any less or more
valid than the so-called written record. After all, if people are by nature
unobjective, are we to look upon the papers they leave behind with any
less suspicion? Whom to believe in a world filled with vanity and deceit
where self-honesty is oh so rare? Whom, indeed. Sometimes, the interview is the only road to discovery. And sometimes, no matter how much

documentation is extant, certain significant events were never committed to paper but remain only in the minds of the participants. This being especially true along the sawdust trail, I have made every effort these past years to speak with as many people as possible who were involved with Mr. North or had a chance to observe him close up—while they are still with us. Without Phil Hall's having casually remembered, for example, the time when Art Concello took John North to task for the questionable value of his original music in the show (an incident, by the way, confirmed by Concello), a key turning point in the then souring relationship between North and Concello might have been lost forever.

So much of the circus lives in the memories of troupers. Most everyone I sought out was wonderfully cooperative in sharing recollections with me. To begin with, I am eternally grateful to Henry Ringling North, not only for the interview he granted, but for his having paved the way on my behalf to meet his illustrious brother, John, following a decade-long quest to interview the subject of my book. I am also indebted to Countess Ida von Zedlitz-Trützschler of Geneva, Switzerland, North's companion of many years, for her kindness in answering, through correspondence and conversation, my many questions.

Deepest thanks are in order, for the generous time each of them gave me—usually over a tape recorder—to John Ringling North II, Rudy Bundy, Dody Heath Soames, Bertram Mills (by way of a helpful Max Butler), Noyelles Burkhart, Michael Burke, Richard Barstow, Miles White, Harold Ronk, Irving Caesar, Antoinette Concello, Mary Jane Miller, La Norma Fox, Unus, Chita Cristiani, Cosetta Cristiani, Ken Dodd, Jackie Le Claire, Jane Johnson, Phil Hall, Daisy Hall, Art Cooksey, Chuck Burnes, Bambi Burnes, and William Perry. I should add that the caring assistance of Robert Mitchell led me to some of these people. The Ringling Lancasters, who held minority stock interests in the circus—Charles and his wife, Alice, and Stuart—were quite forthcoming and informative in explaining their side of the story.

In earlier years, I spoke with two of North's childhood chums in Baraboo, Wisconsin, now both deceased (as, sadly, are many of those listed above), Louis Nolan and Curtis Page, Sr. Additional information of relevance was gleaned from interviews in past years with Merle and Nena Evans, Karl Wallenda, and Floyd King. Miscellaneous queries directed to Don Marcks, Paul Wissler, Robert MacDougall, and Howard Tibbals were readily answered. In Los Angeles, Lynda Sauer and Gary Tavetian provided legal insights into the possible motives for various actions taken by squabbling members of the Ringling family during the litigious 1940s, particularly in the wake of the tragic Hartford fire. Also in Lotus Land, the interest and confidence of Kathleen Spendlove, my personal librarian, was an inspiration, as was the friendly encouragement expressed by members of the Clifford E. Vargas Tent of the Circus Fans Association of America, who warmly hosted me one evening in Anaheim shortly after I had embarked on the very first draft of this book. Up in Oakland, my good friend Liz Johnson offered encouragement, a sympathetic ear, and sensible advice along the way.

Among my most enjoyable hours devoted to this project were those spent in the company of Arthur M. Concello, North's principal manager, on and off, over the years. In this regard, surely luck was on my side. Mr. Concello fielded my every question in his inimitably trouperesque fashion, crusty to the core and always to the point, though with infinite patience and a touch of rare humor now and then. Doggedly unsentimental, yet he charmed me with a grittier vision of the circus in his reminiscing eyes. Back in California, whenever I called him up with yet another "Just *one* more question, Mr. Concello?" he readily reciprocated with his generous good nature. Ken Dodd deserves the warmest accolades of circus buffs everywhere for the pivotal role he played in helping secure Mr. Concello's permission to quote from his interviews.

The photographs that grace these pages, many being published for the first time, are here primarily through the courtesy of Timothy Noël Tegge of Los Angeles and photographer Ted Sato of Sarasota, who took all the wonderful pictures that bear his credit when he was Ringling's official photographer during three of its last seasons under canvas, from 1953 to 1955. Without their gracious cooperation, the book you are holding in your hands would not be nearly so handsome or tastefully illustrated. Many thanks also, for the use of private family photographs, to Countess Ida von Zedlitz-Trützschler, John Ringling North II, Rudy Bundy, and Dody Heath Soames.

Finally, as fate would have it, the manuscript in a more primitive stage fell innocently—"over the transom," as they say—into the hands of a university press, where an obstacle course of scholarly challenges lay in wait to test its factual authenticity and completeness. In heated response thereto, I have spent the last two years adding to, subtracting from, correcting and revising, clarifying and amplifying . . . adding to, subtracting from . . . For the expanded and refined text that such a process fosters, readers can thank the questioning editors of Champaign. They can thank the knowledgeable Tom Parkinson, a former editor of *The Billboard* and one of the first readers of my manuscript, who brought to my attention more errors of fact than I would care to be judged by and who offered many constructive suggestions for its further development. His invaluable feedback is gratefully acknowledged.

It is a very good time, I believe, to be bringing out this book, for we are luckily in the midst of a new golden age for the circus, certainly as we know it in the United States. American big-top buffs enjoy a wider array of circus troupes—from both near and far—and a greater depth in the artistry and directorial qualities of many of these companies than probably has ever been the case for any previous generation. May today's performers and directors be stimulated by the examples of innovation in these pages to seek fresh, ever more exciting visions of their own in helping to advance the life-affirming magic that is the essence of circus. It is an art from of inestimable power to challenge and celebrate the best that is in us. And so, *this* way to the big show, children of all ages . . . !

Big Top Boss

In Uncle John's Image

He jumped over silver bars and cables, ran around odd-shaped boxes painted with stars, stumbled onto clumps of damp, musty canvas. He giggled to the touch of a long, gray object way up there swooping down to scoop up peanuts that had been placed in his two tiny hands. He breathed in the rare aroma of sawdust, chased after hoops whirling in the sky and ladies dancing on horses. "Come back, Johnny!" his mother shouted, unable to contain his spirit that first spring morning when he was taken by hand down to the winter home of his uncles' circus. He wanted to keep running, deeper into the mysterious maze of strange, swirling colors and exciting new sounds.

He danced to the joy of discovery as he was taken back home, much against his will. What a magical place he had been to! And each time he returned, he ran farther and jumped higher over bars and cables, stood closer to the growling creatures in their cages that made scary noises. Most of the bigger people gave him things and let him have his way, and this favored status made it easy for him to think, at a very early age, that everything belonged to him and was there for his pleasure. Maybe so, for he was named after his most famous uncle, John Ringling, in whose flamboyant footsteps he would learn to walk, and thus he grew up believing he would one day ascend to the throne of circus power, never realizing all the tragedies of fate and residual family fights that lay ahead to vex his dream.

John Ringling North, that privileged child, was born in Baraboo, Wisconsin, on August 17, 1903, the first son of Henry Whitestone North, a railroad engineer, and Ida Ringling, the only sister among seven towering brothers. A family portrait reveals Ida to be a woman of demure beauty, slight build, and placid composure, with searching eyes. Surrounded by her parents, August and Salome, and brothers, she must have felt, if anything, unique. The exhibitionist nature of the business in which August Ringling's sons invested all their energies did not brush off on Ida, who remained passive on the sidelines, never expressing much desire to join the spangled parade. No doubt she deferred to her parents, who had always wished for their children respectable places in society and the arts.

Johnny North bore his mother's striking looks—his face calm and composed, his eyes searching, too. He was raised in the storybook atmosphere of Baraboo, centered peacefully in the wooded, largely German world of Wisconsin near the Dells, still an ideal summer resort. The tree-shaded streets of Baraboo and its picturesque town square—altered little in time—offer a haven from the meaner nearby industrial cities of Milwaukee and Chicago. They conjure up turn-of-the-century small-town charms associated with the old values.

Baraboo was a sleepy community, except for the bustling commotion at the Ringling winter quarters on the edge of town, a random assortment of barns and open spaces through which a small river winds its way. The site, historically preserved, is known as the Circus World Musuem. Each autumn the town was woken up by the clattering arrival of long red and silver circus trains, by dozens of wagons rolled off the runs and pulled by teams of horses down to the barns, by the mad music of elephants and tigers being coaxed into their winter stalls.

Just how the more conservative Baraboo residents dealt with this annual influx of gilded paraphernalia and surly roustabouts is debatable. Young Johnny North welcomed the magic with open arms. Indeed, the exotic sights and shrieks awakened him to his own destiny, to the essential difference in his life from that of other boys. John's childhood pals remember his liking to run down to winter quarters, there to watch the performers hone new routines, his Great Uncle Henry Moeller and staff bang old wagons back into shape and construct new ones. Every moment held out the promise of something unexpected. Johnny and a few of his pals were once held spellbound by a challenge between two top acrobats, Percy Clark and Johnny Rooney. Boasted Clark to Rooney, "I can go up, turn a somersault, and come down on a two-foot square." Bragged Clark in return, "Well, I can go up and come down on only my *footprints.*" Rooney flashed a few bills in his challenger's face. "Here's fifty dollars if you can!"

Percy went up, landed perfectly on his footprints, and Rooney made good on the fifty, just like that.[1]

The intimate access to this special world that John North enjoyed surely massaged his ego. It may also have imbued him with a sense of royal status as he compared his circumstances with those of ordinary lads his age. By the time he was seven years old, he could view all five of his uncles who had founded the circus, then in their undisputed prime: Al, Otto, Alf. T., John, and Charles. (There were two other brothers, Henry, now actively involved, and Gus, who died in 1907.) The next year, Otto, the King, as they called him, passed onto what troupers call the Big Lot. It would be another five years before Otto was joined by Albert, the next brother to pass away. So John was able to watch and study five of his uncles until he was thirteen years old. There was a lot to absorb, considering the many skills they had together amassed in their jolting conquest of circusdom.

Baraboo was proud of the Ringling success story and willing to turn its head, on occasion, away from the unromantic sight of itinerant roustabouts. The annual spring departure for the road tour was a source of relief to many townspeople. Louis Nolan, one of John's buddies, remembers, among other impromptu events, the birth of an elephant in the winter-quarters barns and the howling consternation of its mother, who soon killed it. "She tore things all to hell. You could hear her roaring all over town."[2] Another time, a large number of horses got loose and trotted leisurely through the streets in a light snowfall until circus hands corralled them.

Such was the excitement of Johnny's childhood. No wonder he emulated his uncles more than his own father, upon whom he may have looked with confusing disappointment. Henry Whitestone North was of humbler trade. By some whimsical accounts, he was woefully out of place in Ida's world. She sent her relatives into shock when she announced her intentions to marry him.

"He's nobody!" they reacted, horrified over her choice of mates.

Ida was adamant. "I'm going to marry this guy."

"No, you can't!"

"Yes, I can!"

Ida's steely independence suggests an inclination to separate herself even more from the gypsy world of the circus. Neither she nor her husband-to-be had plans to sign on as jugglers or bull handlers. Ida "practically eloped," according to family sources. "She was so much in love with the guy."[3]

The simple station in life occupied by Henry Whitestone, working on the Chicago and North Western line, contradicted his favored upbringing. He had come from an aristocratic English family that owned a six hundred-acre estate, Northbrook, in Galway, Ireland. It boasted an eighteenth-century manor house with spacious lawns, oak trees, fox-hunting stables. Henry's father, Samuel Wade North, was the son of Capt. William North, who served as an infantry commander during the Napoleonic Wars. Samuel Wade came to America at the same time the Ringlings were emigrating to this country. He stopped first in Montreal, where he lured a lovely seventeen-year-old girl, Mary Fahey, away from her convent and into matrimony. The newlyweds made their home in the village of Onalaska, near La Crosse, Wisconsin. Samuel was a dapper, well-heeled Irish gent who strolled the streets of the tiny town, graced with blanketed Indians, trappers, and farmers. He wore a cutaway coat, gray-striped trousers, and a lofty silk hat. He had never worked a day in his life, and on occasion he would line up his three sons to readmonish them, "You must remember that a gentleman never works."4

However, Samuel did not provide his sons with the means sufficient to follow his advice, although he did culture them with a knowledge of Greek and Latin and saw to it that their education exceeded that offered by most one-room schoolhouses. His youngest son, Henry Whitestone, was athletically inclined, short and strong with dark hair and olive skin. He was a good catcher for the La Crosse baseball team in the days when, instead of wearing gloves, the catcher held a hunk of raw meat in his receiving hand as protection against the ball's impact.

Needing a job, Henry landed employment with the railroad in 1891 and came to Baraboo, one of its division points. In his early thirties and still devilishly carefree, Henry Whitestone met Ida Ringling shortly after her high school graduation. The two fell hopelessly in love, to such a degree that they were able to sustain a decade-long courtship despite constant disapproval from Ida's parents and brothers. The problem was that Henry was a divorced man, and the Ringlings treated Ida, unlike her trouping brothers, as the family's one claim to propriety. Despite these oppressive expectations to contend with, Ida and Henry maintained steady, stubborn contact, meeting at various parties to which both were invited. They participated in amateur theatricals, which gave them further time together in the shadows. Their deep mutual affection endured, in the end overcoming its greatest test when Ida caved into family pressures and accepted an engagement to a much younger man closer to her age. He was exuberantly endorsed by the Ringlings, jubilant over finally having set Ida on the proper path. Invitations were in the mail, the house filled with wedding gifts, when who should suddenly sweep Ida off her feet, carry her clear to Chicago, and marry her once and for all? None other than the railroad man she loved so dearly. The year was 1902.

So traumatized was the family by this marital sabotage that they would have nothing to do with Ida for the next year, refusing even to acknowledge her presence on the streets of Baraboo when she passed solemnly by, her head held low. It is hard to imagine so complete a rejection, the details of which were provided by Ida's second son, Henry. He tells us how Ida scored a diplomatic coup by christening her firstborn John Ringling North, thereby playing to the blatant male chauvinism of her brothers. She was welcomed back into the family fold. Henry Whitestone North, the proud father, was at last accepted, too. Little Johnny was their passport.[5]

Ida's strong, willful nature and her taciturn, slow manner of speech rubbed off on John. To illustrate how humorless she struck some as being, on one occasion when she was enjoying a Sunday lunch with a circle of her relatives, niece Hester Ringling Sanford among them, the subject of extrasensory perception came up. Hester began by recalling a night when she woke up from her sleep and proceeded to write out a prediction that so-and-so had died. The next morning, to Hester's morbid surprise, her premonition was confirmed by the receipt of a telegram.

Other such tales passed around the table. Then it was Ida's turn.

"I know a story, too," she enthused. "We were moving, from up north to down south, and there was a portrait of my husband, Henry. I think he was in his railroad uniform. Now, after all of our things had been sent south to Sarasota, we had the packing company come in. They put the picture in a box, nailed it up, and mailed it south. Then I had this dream, shortly after, that there were eleven nail holes that had gone through the painting, . . ."

Ida had everyone's attention.

She continued: ". . . of my dead husband. It kept haunting me. I kept having this dream, and I couldn't wait to get to Florida to find out. Well, finally I got there. I rushed in. I told the workingmen to open the box. 'Open it immediately. I must see!'"

Another example of ESP, everyone around the table expected.

"They pulled the nails out, and opened the box . . ."

"Yes?"

". . . and there were *no* holes. There was nothing wrong in there."

A pause.

"The picture was perfectly complete."

A big dead hush fell over the room.

Ida's son, Henry, decided to break it. "Mother, that's the dumbest story I've ever heard!"

Everyone laughed. Not Ida.

"I don't see anything strange," she said, oblivious to the humor.[6]

"She was very literal," recalls Stuart Lancaster, who draws a parallel with her son John's personality. He acquired a very somber side, just like his mother, and moved through life often seeming to be detached from it, unable or unwilling to see the humor at a given moment. Those ever-searching eyes seemed poised on things far beyond the mundane. In a peculiar way, Ida's ability to remove herself from the circus, to stay outside it, affected John in like manner. Of course, Ida's detachment reflected the family's ambivalence over the very thing that had brought it into such good fortune. The Ringlings were not prepared to encourage, let alone condone, the thought of Ida's making a career of sawdust and spangles. Al Ringling's wife, Louise, a real trouper, had suffered the cold shoulder of Ringling rejection when her marriage to Al was belatedly made known. In those days, a woman who dared perform in tights and sequins was looked down upon, and Louise did it all, from charming snakes to riding horses. The family would have been horrified had Ida desired a similar fate under the big top.

So John had two decidedly domestic parents. It was his uncles who gave him the razzle-dazzle view of life, particularly his Uncle John, by far the most flamboyant of the clan. John Ringling was the youngest of the founding five and the cockiest, and in many ways he led the parade, always arguing for greater conquests and more power. When the brothers had barely completed their first season under canvas, in 1884, John Ringling talked them into letting him go out ahead of the show on the advance. He longed for the freedom to be his own person, to pursue opportunities up the road, including sexual diversions. He operated outside the more puritanical restraints of his brothers, even though they, too, indulged in the worldly pleasures.

John Ringling had been a clown in the show during its vaudeville days, a duty he grew to resent very quickly, much preferring the role of manager and advance man and the dignity and respect that went with it. He continued to badger his older brothers into more-daring business transactions, restless for the fame and fortune they all desired. Largely upon

John Ringling's urgings, supported by Otto, they eventually purchased the Barnum and Bailey show, reaping with it the undisputed status of American circus kings. Uncle John convinced himself he was the most responsible, and it went to his head. He began residing in Chicago hotels, looking back on Baraboo with disdain. He traveled the world in search of new acts. He became the circus king, overshadowing his brothers with the flair of a true impressario.

Young Johnny North, as Louis Nolan remembers, was first and foremost "Uncle John's pet boy."[7] He was the son his uncle never had, and he read the situation correctly: if he could prove himself capable, his powerful uncle would teach him the ropes and groom him to take over in his place someday. From John Ringling to John Ringling North . . .

John took gracefully to the idea. After all, there were precious few other potential heirs apparent. When it came to child rearing, the Ringlings were anything but prolific. Al, Otto, and John were all childless. Al, as one family member speculates, "had his belly full with all those brothers of his he'd helped to raise."[8] Otto, who never married, was thought to be a frugal, unloving man, while John's male prowess, ironically, yielded no offspring—at least none of legitimate record. Charles and his wife, Edith, bore two children, Hester and Robert, both of whom followed higher roads in life. Hester took up the call of teaching, as her mother had done, while Robert, musically endowed, pursued a promising opera career. John North's brother Henry, six years his junior, was an affable pal from the very start, amenable to playing a supportive role. A few years later, a sister, Salome, was born, and she, like her mother, never sought a role to play in the circus world.

John's boyhood chums give the impression that he conducted himself fairly normally as a young man growing up through the Baraboo school system. Although Louis Nolan thought him to be "very egotistical" at times, for the most part he found Johnny to be "more or less regular."[9] Curtis Page, another of Johnny's young sidekicks, who went on to edit the Baraboo paper, paints a convincing portrait of a rather levelheaded, self-assured young man. "John had a very good personality. He met people well. He was a lot of fun because he could do a lot of things. He was a fair athlete, he played football. He was good in all subjects. He had a good control of the English language and he wrote quite well. He had a good sense of humor. He learned to play an E-flat saxophone by himself. Before a few weeks were up, he was playing it really well. He had a lot of talent that his uncles had. He could dance the soft shoe. Most people liked him. There was bound to be a little jealousy on the part of some."[10]

Page recalls that North was not too selective in his choice of friends. He was, however, selective enough to get into a little school clique in seventh grade. It consisted of a group of seven boys ("the navy") and seven girls ("the army") who flaunted their self-appointed status with typical nerve. According to Louis Nolan, himself a member, they regarded the other three hundred or so pupils milling around them as merely being there "to fill up the seats." John could be as snobby as the others. "We didn't go around destroying things," says Nolan, "but God help those who didn't like us or who didn't treat us right. We could make life miserable for them."

This upscale gang in which John hung out flirted with civil disobedience on more than one occasion. In the charming Al Ringling theater, built by Al Ringling in 1915 to resemble, on a smaller scale, the great opera hall of Louis XIV's palace in Versailles, the kids could watch silent flicks for a nickel. They could also patronize the theater's ice cream parlor, a privately run concern. Its operator once accused them of stealing samples of his product, and since Johnny was one of those falsely charged, the man almost lost his license to his angry Ringling landlords. Louis Nolan, another of the kids held briefly under suspicion, remembers with a roar, "That was the *first* ice cream that we *hadn't* taken!"[11]

Johnny North was a live wire in the crowd, talented and ready to please. The girls, whom he adored, taught him how to dance. At a high school party during a period when the shimmy was outlawed, they all called for Johnny.

"Come on up and dance for us!"

Without reservations, he did a soft-shoe, at the end of which he shook himself the length of the floor. His classmates cheered him on.

John started composing his own songs in high school. At church, where he refrained from the profanities he had been picking up, since age eight, from canvas people, he directed the choir with convincing devotion for a spell. He was drawn to the religious pageantry, in which he wore red robes and carried a tall, golden cross while leading his singers into the chapel.

And while he displayed some acting talent as well, he was very much a career-minded circus Ringling, never taking his theatrical gifts to serious intent. Although John's grandfather, August, had once provided musical lessons for his sons, had imagined them pursuing classical careers, they had all disappointed him by choosing, instead, to spend their lives chasing a spangled dream. Alf. T. and Charles had maintained their musical interests to a passable degree, sometimes composing tunes for the pageants that opened the circus. John North's approach to art was similar. Most of all, he learned to appreciate the good life, to live from one big moment to the next. He was gregarious and easygoing, a gracious participant. Social life—and womanizing—would hold the same commanding interest for him that they did for his Uncle John. "He liked the girls well, and they liked him, too," says Curtis Page. Johnny courted through high school a girl named Katherine Wexler, to whom he remained fairly constant.

Ida had raised John and Henry in a small, conventional house. When Al Ringling died in 1916, the Norths inherited Uncle Al's mansion. For thirteen-year-old Johnny, the move was excitingly upward. Al's house was made of Lake Superior sandstone. The rooms within were opulently decorated: damask walls in the parlor and music room, authentic gold leaf on the kitchen ceiling, a dark-wood-paneled library. There were horse stables in the rear, a ballroom in the basement where the North brothers invited their best friends. On some Sundays, Ida baked a cake and had "the navy" over. Henry played pool and billiard games with the guys. John might be studying.[12] Later, they would climb into Uncle Al's Pierce Arrow with their mother and go out for a spin. When Johnny was allowed to drive it himself, he was nearly off the road as much as he was on it. His liability at the wheel was later rectified by the procurement of regular chauffeurs.

Those were wonderful days for a young boy to be growing up. "Baraboo was a unique little spot in the world," remembers Henry North. "It was about fifty years behind the times—even in those times—when I was a little boy. They still had fire wagons pulled by horses, and the farmers all came in with their wagons and horses. In the wintertime, when there was snow and ice, out came the big sleds. It was great fun holding onto those runners, sliding behind."[13]

The nephews of circus kings, John and Henry were naturally influenced toward ballyhoo. One of their first producing efforts was to present Minnie, one of many ponies they had been given to play with. The venue they chose was more noteworthy than the act, for Minnie was coached up the stairs of Uncle Al's house to the third-floor attic. When Ida heard a clomp-clomp-clomp from the ceiling and noticed plaster beginning to fall into her pots and pans on the stove, she promptly ordered Minnie's evacuation. Henry practically had to carry the thing down the stairs, the pony's abrupt exit being the most entertaining part of its curious exhibition.

In the spring, John played the entrepreneur, engaging a throng of kids to move a homemade tent around town and set it up on neighborhood lawns. The acts they offered were primitive, the main idea being to re-create the imagery of a circus on tour. One year they all dressed up as Roman gladiators, courtesy of the Ringling Bros. wardrobe department. "It was mostly moving the tent," recounts Page. "There was not much in the way of circus acts." A Ringling concessionaire, Sid Rubeen, sometimes supplied the boys, free of cost, actual circus pennants, whirlybirds, whips, canes, and funny hats. The boys borrowed clown props from winter quarters, such as a police patrol wagon, which they smugly hitched to a pony and drove all over town, the gong clanging loudly.

During the summer months, they were given the biggest thrill of all when they were allowed to ride the circus train for a couple of weeks. They rode either in Uncle John's private car, the Jomar, or Uncle Charlie's, the Caledonia, whichever happened to be hooked to the end of the train according to who was in charge. Especially built for John Ringling by the Pullman Company, the Jomar was "the longest private car in the world," with mahogany woodwork, brass chairs, a brass double bed; the Caledonia, decorated in rich reds and golds and with lace curtains, conveyed the older era. Both signified circus royalty. Ida loved riding the rails, too, as she had in her youth with her brothers. Yet she never stopped fretting over the dangers of dodging trains in railroad yards, ceaselessly warning John and Henry, "Watch out when you cross the tracks! Look both ways! Be careful!"

On the circus lots, Johnny got to know the stars of the show and was accorded a privileged access to the magical world of billowing white tops that most boys his age could only dream of. In the dressing tent of the great aerialist Lillian Leitzel, he joined other children for early-morning lessons. Leitzel became so enamored of Johnny's charms that he was able to liberate her from her many sullen moods by whispering a simple affectionate word or two into her ear.[14] Learning to cope with the circus's most celebrated star prepared John to deal with almost anybody.

The more involved he became in the show, the less attention he paid to his dancing and musical talents, treating them like so many hobbies to be tinkered with. John was more inclined to seize without reservation the opportunities offered him by his uncles to learn their jobs. When the John B. Rogers theatrical organization came through Baraboo to work with local high school talent, John is remembered for landing a part, then suddenly falling ill during rehearsals. Did he fear not being good enough, or failing to win an award? Receiving too little encouragement from the directors?[15]

"I think he had an ambition for the circus from the beginning," offers Curtis Page. "He wanted to be at the top always, so I'm sure his aim would be to run it. If he'd set himself a goal, he'd work very hard to reach that goal."

By then, John was well on his way. He had gotten his first circus job when he was not quite twelve years old. That was the summer he was allowed to go out with the show for more than a two-week vacation, and he didn't call in sick.

Ringling Roots

John North's first assignments with the circus showed that he, like his uncles, favored the business end of it over the lure of performing. That summer when he turned twelve, he received his first write-up in the press, *The Billboard* reporting that he was taking saddle lessons from the show's star equestrienne, May Wirth, arguably the greatest ever in her field. John enjoyed a brief infatuation with his vivacious mentor, which came to a halt when he sprained an ankle.[1] Out of it, he cultivated a love for the sport of riding, a pastime he would enjoy throughout his life.

The same historic summer of 1915, he became a revenue-producing member of the staff by hawking popcorn and lemonade. In circus parlance, he was a candy butcher, one who works the seats. It was an action job requiring agility in scampering up and down the portable grandstands, agility in balancing a tray containing the product while shouting, "POPCORN HERE!" or "HEY, GET YOUR COLD SODA POP!" This opened Johnny's eyes to the immediacy of the circus business, to how the money is pulled in through quick transactions as the show, ever moving forward, captivates an audience for a couple of hot, hectic hours.

John discovered a diverse mix of human beings, many on the fringes of society—from the bizarre sideshow characters, who hung proudly together in a kind of mock antisociety, to the drifting canvas men and roustabouts, who pitched the tents in the morning and struck them at night. He saw a cross section of humanity moving side by side, brushing elbows gently, each resolved in the certain knowledge that without the other—the artist, the stake driver, the horse handler—the whole thing would fail to go on.

John learned to respect this unique community in its perverse, poetic wholeness.

Did he indulge himself, too? Surely he was given tips from the pros on how to take advantage of a packed tent on a hot afternoon. Cashiering mistakes, innocent or not, were made and condoned. Customers reached over customers to toss a bill in the candy butcher's direction, still watching the show while calling out an order, determined not to miss the rider's somersault from horse to horse, that tumbler's spin off the springboard . . . over those elephants! Those clowns in the funny fire truck rumbling down the track, look! "LADIES AND GENTLEMEEEEEN! IF I MAY DIRECT YOUR ATTENTION TO . . . !"

This gray zone of salesmanship served as John's professional introduction to the circus, which he began viewing from two related though ethically disparate angles: the way his uncles *wanted* it run, free of grift, and the way it was, sometimes plagued with grifters bent on bending the rules. Short-change artists and their like never lasted very long, for the Ringlings loomed over it all with foreboding power. "There were so damn many of the brothers all over the place," commented Floyd King, "it was hard to get away with anything."[2]

The rather revolutionary ethics of the Ringling brothers (at least as advertised and, in the opinion of most people, actually implemented with rigor) were largely inspired and insisted upon by their father, August Ringling, a well-bred man of German ancestry. His grandfather and relatives founded and maintained a fine German publishing house during the seventeenth and eighteenth centuries. August's father, Frederich, was born in Dankelshausen, Hanover, in 1795. At eighteen years of age and following the example of his father and grandfather, Frederich enlisted as a soldier and fought under Wellington against Napoleon Bonaparte at the Battle of Waterloo. During the war, the seeds of future enmity in the House of Ringling were sown, for on the other side of the battle line stood a soldier named Etling, defender of Napoleon, who subsequently spent nine years as a prisoner of war in England. Etling's second daughter, Helena, married Nicholas Juliar, a Frenchman, and their daughter, Marie Salome, in turn, wed August Ringling.

Once peace was restored after Waterloo, Frederich returned to his native village, only to find that political unrest and insecure property rights had robbed his family of its considerable assets. He took up the trade of shoemaker, later enrolled at college to study chemistry. He was credited, according to the book written by his grandson, Alf. T. Ringling, with "devising a plan for making bread by means of the potato." The ingenious scheme addressed a grain famine that had swept Europe. Frederich's potato bread required so little grain flour that it could be mass-produced at a fine profit.[3]

Frederich married Rosina Baurmann and they had two children, a daughter, Wilhelmina, and a son, August, who was given a good education and taught the useful trade of saddler "for possible future necessity." Frederich feared his son might be dealt the same economic setbacks that he had suffered. And so it was. No sooner had young August proved his apprenticeship in harness making than a financial disaster, not detailed, overtook the elder Ringling, now past fifty years of age.

In search of better prospects, August sailed, in his twenty-first year, for America. He first spent a year in Canada, then moved farther west to Milwaukee, where he secured work at a large harness-goods manufactory. He was promoted to foreman in a few months' time, partly credited to the rapid ease with which he mastered the English language. August Americanized his family name to Ringling (it had been Rungeling, which sounded close), not realizing how well its more euphonious sound would serve his sons when they entered show business.

Meanwhile, August's father and mother, along with his sister, soon followed him to the land of opportunity. So did the vagaries of a checkered fate: in the early 1850s, a cholera epidemic visited Milwaukee, claiming the life of August's father, Frederich. His grief-stricken mother died within a few months. About that time, August, now age twenty-five, married into the line that had fought his father at Waterloo, taking Marie Salome Juliar, Etling's granddaughter, for his bride. Salome introduced the French blood in the Ringling family line, she having been the daughter of Helena Etling, a German, and Nicholas Juliar, the Frenchman. She also brought with her a top wagon builder—someone the future circus kings could handily use—in the person of Henry Moeller, who had married her sister, Helena.

Salome's father had been a weaver and vineyard owner. In his native village of Ostheim, Alsace, he was considered a man of property. He came to America in 1845 with his wife and five children, settling on a farm near Milwaukee. At the age of sixty-five, he tried volunteering, at the outbreak of the Civil War, to help defend the Union but was rejected on the basis of age, an insult to which he never reconciled himself. Nicholas maintained a fine physique and proud carriage into his twilight years, passing on in robust health at the then-remarkable age of eighty-four. Nicholas had taken delight in the theatrical ambitions of his grandsons, although he did not live long enough to see the tinseled empire they would build as full-grown men.

The Ringling boys had gotten the bug to start a circus of their own back in McGregor, Iowa, when on the banks of the Mississippi River one misty morning Dan Rice's Great Paris Pavilion Circus floated into town. The five brothers who later established their own show—Al, Otto, Alf. T., Charles, and John—were all there at dockside that dawn, so taken by the unloading that in later years they would treat the event as tantamount to a divine revelation. In *Life Story of the Ringling Brothers,* published in 1900, Alf. T. writes: "The sight of the spectacle had so affected the brothers that they stood riveted to the spot, clasping each other's hands in speechless ecstasy. When the last wagon had rolled slowly up the bank of the street, Al, with a sigh of relaxation, turned to Otto and said, 'What would you say if we had a show like that?' " Otto's reply, as recorded by Alf. T., was prophetic: "Well, I would say to the big man with the loud voice, who bossed the fellows unloading the big band wagon, not to swear like he did."[4]

And thus were uttered the first words of the Ringling press kit. The boys went forward, with a sense of their own destiny, to redeem the circus world from itself. However, in preparation for the epochal event, they started out in a small way, doing the things that little kids did. They presented panoramas, a popular diversion of the pre-moving-picture era, charging so many pins for admission. They purchased a broken-down goat named Billy Rainbow and had themselves a parade. They patched together makeshift little tents out of discarded carpets (once in a while out of their mother's curtains, not discarded).

The childhood follies were assembled while the father, struggling in his harness-making business, moved from town to town in a kind of on-the-edge flight from insolvency that curiously resembled the fragile nature of his sons' early amateur endeavors. When August Ringling moved the family to Baraboo in 1855, he took out an ad in the *Baraboo Republic:* "HO, FELLOW CITIZENS! GIVE ATTENTION TO THE ONE-HORSE HARNESS SHOP!" Response was initially so good that another ad followed one year later: "The ONE HORSE establishment will now, good friends, pass as a DOUBLE HORSE concern." Another two years and Ringling was encountering hard times. He sold out his stock and moved the family to McGregor.

Ringling taught his sons his own trade and saw to it that they were schooled in the arts and music. Otto read profusely. Charles and Alf. T.

learned to play the violin and clarinet. The boys attended church services and were groomed to be pillars of the community. They were more influenced, though, by their father's nomadic wanderings in pursuit of his livelihood. Certainly this was true of Albert and John, two bohemian spark plugs who refused to conform. Both gravitated to unconventional adventures on the open road. John, the youngest of the brothers, ran away from home more than once, a punk in his own time. Albert, the oldest, ventured into the outdoor-show world. He juggled a little, taught himself to balance a plow on his chin, worked in small tent shows in the summertime. He spent the winters doing regular jobs, one being for a carriage-making shop in the small nearby town of Broadhead, Wisconsin, where he would annually settle into a boardinghouse room with trunk and props and hang a trapeze swing from the ceiling for practice.

Al Ringling kept the childhood vision alive. On Saturday afternoons in Broadhead, he strung a rope between two trees down at the town square and walked it for the amusement of all who happened to come by, admission free. His big feature act was to cook himself breakfast up there on a tiny stove. Al developed into a good all-around performer, and he was well liked. He worked in vaudeville for Fred White, a Wisconsin ventriloquist. One summer he managed a small outfit bearing his name: the Hall, Long and Ringling Palace Show. One winter he took out his own variety troupe, the 4-Big-4 Show, and headed up the Parson-Roy Circus another summer. In the off-seasons, he often organized amateur revues.

On a spring day in 1882, Albert Ringling returned to Baraboo, ostensibly to visit the family. What he really had in mind was taking out a show with his brothers. The boys persuaded their father once and for all to accept the inevitable: they were born to entertain. August Ringling could only shake his head in disbelief and resignation. Show people were looked down upon by preachers and their congregations. And all the fine musical training his sons had received would end up where—in a circus band? In his book, Alf. T. only hints at any dissension, stating that his father "refrained from any act or word that might be taken by them as encouragement to their amusement plans. . . . In his own mind he had other than circus ambitions for his boys, but he refrained from urging these upon them."[5] What the elder Ringling did have some say in was the relatively moral foundation upon which the circus that would eventually bear his name was founded. He is said by some historians to have insisted upon a code of ethics rarely subscribed to by any of the successful tent-show proprietors of that day: Don't sucker the customer. Keep honest.

Led by Al and John, the boys were ecstatic. Al had it all figured out how they could pool their talents into a formidable collective and take the show world by storm. John was a natural clown, raring to go. Alf. T. and Charles could provide the music and do their acrobatic stunts. Otto, who could have gone either way, was lured into the fragile enterprise by being given control of the finances, a position he fancied. As for the remaining two brothers, August ("Gus") was not interested enough to be swayed and Henry was still too young to go out.

The Ringlings began by taking out winter hall shows. In 1882 they toured as the Classic Comic and Concert Company. The next season they lightened up under the title Grand Carnival of Fun. On May 19, 1884, in Baraboo, they opened their first circus under a six hundred-seat tent. The boys began in partnership with the ailing but once illustrious showman Yankee Robinson. Yankee passed on that summer, but not before predicting that his youthful associates "were the coming men." Prophetic he was. Within six years the boys were on rails; within eleven they staged an auspicious spring indoor opening in Chicago.

What is especially remarkable about the Ringling success story is that the brothers never signed a formal agreement among themselves. They never spelled out in writing the exact business relationship that held them so loyally together. From all accounts, they simply honored an unspoken pact of trust. Essentially, all matters were decided upon by a simple majority vote. To illustrate how true they remained to this policy, on one occasion when John Ringling was away, the other four were locked in a terrible debate at winter quarters over the proposed color scheme for a pageant that was being planned. Two were in favor, two against. The angry shouts and jeers could be heard over the screeching of wild animals in the adjoining barns.

"Okay," said Al, exasperated, "let's get someone to sit in John's chair and vote for him."

Sounded reasonable to the others.

Otto volunteered to search the grounds for a candidate. A few minutes later he brought in Henry Moeller, his uncle who built the wagons.

Moeller was dropped into the argument, and he wished he hadn't been. "I didn't know anything about specs," he later confessed to a close friend. "I didn't know anything more when they got through telling me than I did when I first went in there. Otto and I were great friends. That night, after all the arguing, I found out Otto wanted it a certain way. So I voted with Otto."[6] The following summer when the show was up in

Madison and Moeller was standing in the tent watching the spec (opening parade) go by, Al came over, put an arm around him and said, "Henry, how do you like your spec?"

In private, the brothers argued long and loud. In public, they carefully displayed a calm, united front. They accepted the greater force they comprised as a group. At the same time, they all fell into complementary management roles; thus the operation was adequately covered in all departments. Al assumed the reins of ringmaster and performance director. Alf. T. wrote advertising copy and press releases and designed the lithographs. Completely self-taught in these trades, yet Alf. T. won praise from the pros. King Otto, as they liked to call the largest of the five brothers, guarded the treasury like a Pinkerton detective. John, who was thought to have hated clowning despite his success at it—he wanted to be taken seriously, not laughed at—was taken very seriously when he took over the advance with a flair for making deals. Charles, a good sport, managed for a time the advance billposting brigades, leading his crews through some bloody victories against the opposition. That was a time when rival circuses fought viciously for valuable lithograph space on barns and storefronts. Later, Charles assumed control of all personnel and was loved by everyone, as was Al.

When they started opening each spring in Chicago, in 1895, the brothers were ominously close to competing directly with Barnum and Bailey's gigantic traveling hit, the Greatest Show on Earth. And when James A. Bailey—surviving his famous partner, the Prince of Humbug—toured the Continent for five years beginning in 1897, the Ringlings solidified their hold on the American public. Upon Bailey's return, they worked out plans to avoid facing each other in costly day-and-date battles. In 1905, Bailey sold them a half-interest in one of his properties, Forepaugh–Sells Bros. Circus, and shortly after he died the following year, the boys bought his interest from his estate.

At the height of their power, the Ringlings each sported a mustache and wore a Prince Albert coat. Their five stolid faces, arranged in various formations on billboard-size twenty-four-sheet lithographs, became household images throughout the United States. One winter, three of them, each bundled up in a fur coat, casually strolled into a car showroom in Milwaukee. The dealer told someone afterward that he thought they looked "sort of farmerish." They asked to be shown his Pierce Arrows. He complied, and after a few brief glances, one of the Ringlings said, "I'll take that one." Another Ringling said, "I'll take this one here." Still another, "I think I'd like that one over there." And so each of the brothers doled out the asking price of five or six thousand dollars in rolled bills.[7] They drove off in royal succession. For a moment, it was like childhood all over again.

These curious new circus titans who claimed that the customer is always right were held under a microscope by the entire show world. They were credited some years for bold innovations, criticized in others for failing to innovate. They were accused of guerrilla warfare and of trying to monopolize the business by rivals.[8] Their gingerly regard for the customer did not extend to their treatment of competitors. Led by the worldly John Ringling, deemed the most ruthless of all the brothers, the Ringlings fought their rivals with merciless vigor. Reviews of their shows ran the spectrum from orgasmic praise to indignation. They listened to their critics, ever sensitive to their image, ever ready to adapt. They rarely stood still, their progressive spirit vividly conveyed in the following ad, no doubt conceived by Alf. T. Ringling in anticipation of a mighty battle with Barnum and Bailey. The place was Saint Louis, the season 1895:

> The Up-To-Date show! It has arrived! The show that stands on its own merits. Does not divide—Uses no other name than that of its proprietor. Sails under no false colors—Borrows nothing from the past—Gives you the energy and results of the actual living present—Is too big—Too modern—Too generous—Too broad—Too liberal—Too prosperous—Too great to seriously notice the petty insinuations of concerns that cannot keep up in the march of progress, and disdainfully holds in contempt the ridiculous, ill-tempered, undignified, fearbegotten, whimsical prattle of disgruntled, outclassed, overshadowed and overwhelmed would-be rivals.

It was a wildly active era that would eventually take a toll on family unity. The winning formula, based on the dedication of the five to a childhood vision of success, did not sustain itself so well in the later years when the brothers, looking for new conquests, expanded their holdings beyond their own show. A year after James A. Bailey's death, in 1907, the Ringlings purchased the Barnum and Bailey title for less than a half-million dollars, taking advantage of a financial depression. At one time or another, they had three circuses on the road. The dazzling collective achievements alienated the five original founders to a degree. Henry Ringling was brought into the fold and made manager of the Ringling show. Albert had a falling out with the others and threatened to withdraw and start his own Al Ringling Circus.[9] He was dissuaded from desertion by being given operational control of the Forepaugh-Sells title, a fifty-car show that had lain dormant for a couple of seasons. Struggling to keep three different circuses out, the Ringlings were in virtual competition with themselves. It was even too much for the booking genius of John Ringling, taken to task by observers for "glaring routing errors." Forepaugh-Sells lasted two tours. And in 1919 the brothers combined their two major properties into one entertainment giant, Ringling Bros. and Barnum & Bailey.

By then, all but two of the brothers had passed on. Otto was the first to go, in 1911; Al followed in 1916, Henry in 1918. Then the death of Alf. T. at age fifty-eight, shortly before the show's New York premiere in 1919, left a real void in the House of Ringling. The intellectual of the group, Alf. T. was a smart balancing force. Now a simple majority vote was a thing of the past. Only John and Charles remained, and the strange bickering that ensued between the two brought internal hostilities and differences of opinion out into the open. It also set the stage for a residual battle that would be played out between their respective heirs for years to come.

The contrasts between John and Charles Ringling were classic, if not amusing. While John grew more aloof, preferring to cultivate his international reputation and scout new acts abroad, Charles, as much adored by everyone as Al had been, stayed back on the lot to oversee the day-to-day activities. He was warm and compassionate and had ample time for everyone. His grandson, Charles Ringling Lancaster, remembers as a child being impressed by how open Uncle Charlie was to suggestions from anyone, including youngsters, for improving the show. "He was meticulous about everything. He never was sloppy, and he always made everybody—down to the last canvas worker—feel that he was a personal friend."[10]

A diplomat in dealing with subordinates, Charles once approached their boss canvas man, Jimmy Whalen, on Whalen's profanity after having kindly endured it for some time. Whalen had a habit of addressing his men as "you sons of bitches." The Ringling in charge was ever so tactful. "Ah, Jim," began Charles, "you probably know that we have a standard of importance here on the lot, and we don't have rough language, because, well, we wouldn't mind it ourselves, but, ah, we got to put a soft pedal on it. So, will you try holding it down, and get another name for your boys? And everything'll be fine."

"Yes, sir, Mr. Ringling," replied Whalen.

As Charles was walking off, he overheard Jimmy crying out, "Okay, come on, *sons!* And *you* know what kind of sons I mean!"

Charles would advise a performer to leave out a hazardous trick from an act when harsh weather made the ring surface dangerous. John Ringling would more likely protest its omission, coldly insisting that every item under contract be presented. And so on. In their personal lives, the two brothers got caught up in petty rivalries to outdo each other, largely because Mrs. Charles (Edith) Ringling pushed her husband along to hold his own. John Ringling erected an opulent mansion on Sarasota Bay, Ca'd'Zan. Charles followed suit not long after with a huge house of his own a few hundred yards away, in design closer to Colonial than to the Venetian palace in whose gaudier shadows it stood. One got himself an expensive yacht; so did, of course, the other. Both built banks in Sarasota. One would have been sufficient for the restful Florida fishing community in which the two remaining Ringlings resided during the winters and eventually quartered their circus.

And with that, family politics polarized into two divisive factions, with John Ringling North clearly on his Uncle John's side and Robert Ringling standing firm with his father, Charles. The various heirs who held a minority stock interest stood by, more or less intimidated by the two remaining circus kings, between whom a growing rift revealed a sad if somewhat humorous picture of the darker side of success. And those who observed it carefully might have foreseen the strange, volatile future that lay ahead for anyone bent on seizing the reins of power once they were up for grabs.

Heir Unapparent

In the best of times, John Ringling had such affection for his two nephews, John and Henry North, and their mother, Ida, that he willed them his residuary estate: all of his assets, excluding Ca'd'Zan and the art museum, which he bequeathed to the state of Florida. Ida and John North were named coexecutors in an early Ringling will, while John and Henry and their cousin Randolph Wadsworth were designated trustees for the state of Florida. Later, at John North's suggestion, his uncle cut the residuary estate into two parts, leaving only half of it to Ida so that she could avoid high inheritance taxes, the other half in trust to Florida as a funding source to maintain the art museum and grounds and increase its collection.

Ringling treated his nephews as his own offspring, especially after their father died in 1920, when John was seventeen, Henry eleven. He paid tuition for both at Yale University. At one time or another he fondly introduced Henry to friends as "my son who goes to Yale."[1] Henry did graduate, having impressed Professor William Phelps of the English Department, an avid circus buff, as his "most promising student."[2]

Uncle John gave the boys plenty of jobs in the circus and showed them the ins and outs of trouping. With his encouragement, young Johnny North advanced up the midway to more important positions, all the while making himself generally useful, as true troupers were expected to be. Henry, six years younger than John, was thrilled one summer to discover his older brother riding by in the street parade (the free daily ritual staged to drum up consumer interest) as a Napoleonic hussar.

John's Uncle John wanted to toughen him up for the harder, more grueling side of circus life. And for all his labors, he received typically spartan Ringling wages. He was elevated to a job on one of the advance-advertising cars. The menial grind of lithograph posting drove Johnny into a panic. Hastily he feigned an illness in the family "requiring" his immediate return home. Shortly afterward, he was put on the front door to monitor ticket-taking activities—forever fraught with under-the-table rackets—and was so resented by the veteran staff that, according to brother Henry, a plot to discredit John's scruples was hatched. He was accused by implication of stealing several hundred dollars from a ticket man's wallet. Only after North called in the Burns Detective Agency to investigate the allegations did the "lost" money suddenly reappear.[3]

Then installed in the red wagon, John learned to count the money and make daily bank deposits, a task he relished. One day an old Baraboo school chum, Curtis Page, showed up on the Minneapolis lot, hoping to make contact. North, open as always to the flimsiest excuse for fun, invited Nolan to join him for a late lunch. They took off in Nolan's automobile for a restaurant uptown. North had with him a buldging leather briefcase.

"Oh, Curtis," he said, "I got to stop off at the bank first."

Page escorted North into the bank, where the latter stepped up to a window and dropped off about fourteen thousand dollars, all in small bills.[4]

Johnny enjoyed mixing business with pleasure more than anything else. He did make a half-hearted attempt at higher education, first enrolling at the University of Wisconsin with his mom's blessings, where he was pledged to one of the best fraternities, Psi Upsilon. He spent most of his spare time, in Nolan's words, "getting acquainted with the ladies very rapidly." After a year of this, John was next sent off to Yale, compliments of Uncle John. He pursued an undergraduate program of study in—of all subjects—physics, possibly inspired by the academic reach of his grandfather, Frederich, who had studied chemistry. In his freshman year, 1922–23, he took chemistry, English, French, history, and mathematics. His sophomore year, 1923–24, was devoted to economics, English, French, geology, and history.[5]

He roomed alone the first year, lived in Stabeck the second. One of his classmates was Rudy Vallee, who credits John with teaching him how to tap-dance and who called the Class of 1926, of which John was a member, "the greatest theatrical class ever to graduate from Yale." John never made it to the cap-and-gown finals. He was decidedly more interested in sporting a Rolls-Royce and a mistress, neither condoned on campus, than matriculating.[6] Whatever grades he earned, the registrar's office at Yale adamantly refused to release them for this book, stating that, per official policy, not until seventy-five years after North's departure from college can they be made public. He evidently took advantage of his lessons in French, a language that, along with German, he learned to speak fairly well.

At the end of his junior year, in 1924, and upon reaching his twenty-first birthday, John went home to Baraboo to collect a twenty thousand dollar legacy from his late Uncle Al, now due. During the visit, Johnny and Curtis Page drove down to Devils Lake in a Dodge sedan, where they met Jane Connelly of Connellsville, Pennsylvania, who was in the area visiting her aunt, wife of the Ringling family physician, Dr. Dan Kelly. John, quickly smitten, couldn't take his eyes off the pretty Jane. He offered her a lift back to Baraboo. She was flattered. They all got into the car and took off. The roads were icy, the driver just a tad anxious. En route the vehicle careened around a slippery bend in the road and overturned. Curtis and Jane were only bruised. John was thrown out the door and pinned under the auto, where he came precariously close to suffering major injuries. As they waited for help, Jane got down on her hands and knees and prayed aloud—successfully—for Johnny's safe rescue. When he was finally pulled out from under the wreck, John declared, "*That's the girl for me!*"[7] They were married within a few weeks, and John was relieved to have a reason not to return to Yale. Seems the university did not allow married students, either.

The newlyweds took their honeymoon in style, John's twenty-thousand-dollar inheritance paying the way. Jane went along with John for a couple of frustrating years, unable to enjoy, beyond the novelty of a first season, life in a circus-train berth. And in the off season, Johnny was so busy hawking real estate to suckers for his uncle, or running off to who-knows-where to do who-knows-what, that Jane soon realized the mistake she had made. They were separated in 1927, legally divorced a few years hence.

John's primary passion invariably reclaimed his soul. Traditional marriage had not a chance against all the glittering distractions he chose to worship. The world ahead was filled with adventure, with fast days on the move, drum rolls and crashing cymbals, the approving shouts of the crowds, the late-night parties, cocktails with the rich and famous, rendezvous with beautiful women. Johnny wanted the circus in life. Most of all, he wanted *everything* that his Uncle John had.

With the passing of Charles Ringling in 1926, John Ringling alone now ruled the monarch of American amusements. Ringling Bros. and

Barnum & Bailey was then in its undisputed heyday, never more glamorous or successful. The show played to more than a million people during a three-and-a-half-week opening spring stand in Gotham. Tickets went for as much as $3.30. On the road, fifteen thousand souls jam-packed the sprawling canvas amphitheater twice a day to cheer on the big top's biggest names: the Flying Clarkonians, Con Colleano, May Wirth, Lillian Leitzel, Bird Millman, the Yacoppis, Hillary Long ("The Human Monorail"), Pallenberg's Bears and Alf Loyal's Dogs, Jorgen Christiansen working sixty-nine liberty horses in a single ring, the whole dizzifying affair rousingly underscored by the galops and marches and whirling waltzes of maestro Merle Evans and his "famous concert band." The Greatest Show on Earth was just that.

"It is the standard circus, the all-satisfying circus," proclaimed the Ringling scribes. "America turns to it for its amusement. Novelists write of it, journalists depict its varied phases, and magazines give pages upon pages to the wonder of it. America's foremost cartoonists have toured with it that they may catch and picture the joy of it. Painters draw upon it for inspiration . . . and now these titans of the tented world have united their greatest and grandest features into one, all-eclipsing institution."[8]

John Ringling's circus raked in the profits, as did his many lucrative outside interests. A shrewd investor, Ringling snatched up short-line railroads as in a game of Monopoly, acquired Oklahoma oil fields and Sarasota land. With his friend Tex Rickard, the boxing promoter, and a group of New York investors, he helped build a new Madison Square Garden on Eighth Avenue between Forty-ninth and Fiftieth streets. By 1930, *Fortune* magazine would rank him "the best millionaire alive," reporting on his "superb" attire, his magnificent Fifth Avenue home and his Venetian palazzo in Sarasota, his steam yacht and his private railroad car. "He bought $50,000 worth of statues from the Metropolitan Museum, has collected more square yards of Rubens than any other private individual on Earth."[9]

Ringling's crowning achievement was the art museum and his personal residence, Ca'd'Zan, constructed at a cost of $1.5 million. He and his wife, Mable, had traveled the Continent on countless crossings to collect great works of art. Ships arrived from Europe bearing exotic materials that Mable had procured: English veined marble, tens of thousands of Barcelona red barrel tiles for the roof. She was known to have desired "a pretentious mansion, to fit their social status."[10] Most would agree that Mable got what she wanted. Dripping with opulent decor and a glorious mishmash of furnishings from slightly divergent origins, the structure has struck more than one student of architecture as being aesthetically excessive, if not grotesque. In overall design, most experts agree, it was modeled after the Doge's Palace in Venice. It also bears the eccentric flair of its original occupant, for the roof is outlandishly topped by a tower vaguely resembling one on the Madison Square Garden of the time, far from vintage Venetian.

Contained within are thirty rooms and fourteen baths, fitted with carved and gilded furniture, rare tapestries and paintings, marble floors and columns. The doors are carved walnut, the bathtubs made of marble, with gold-plated fixtures. A great hall, two and a half stories high, features a black and white marble floor arranged in checkerboard design. The ceiling rises to a skylight of colored glass. A huge stone fireplace and a four thousand-pipe organ complement the space. A marble balcony on the second floor surrounds three sides of the hall and allows access to the bedrooms.

On riotous Saturday evenings at Ca'd'Zan, among a host of famous faces who showed up now and then, were Will Rogers and Flo Ziegfeld, Diamond Jim Brady and humorist Finley Peter Dunne, New York politician Jimmy Walker, tobacco man R. J. Reynolds. This was the world into which John Ringling North was baptized. All around him was flamboyance and wealth and glib merriment, cigar-smoking tycoons, and quirky, free-spirited artist types coming and going. He and brother Henry could run upstairs to play billiards in the attic game room, replete with ceiling portraits, painted by Ziegfeld's set designer of, among others, Uncle John and Aunt Mable. They could take the elevator back downstairs to see what was happening in the main hall or run out onto the variegated terrace for a swim in the pool or go down to the dock where Aunt Mable's Venetian gondola was moored, waiting to take visitors for a cruise on the balmy moonlit bay.

Music filled the air. Laughter and gaiety bubbled over. Success by association imbued young Johnny with a sure sense of his own destiny. He patterned himself after Uncle John, absorbed as much wordly advice as he could get. And during the better days, Uncle John imparted to his nephews plenty of his views on a whole range of topics, from running a circus to chasing the fair sex. In one of his heady moods, he clued John and Henry in on the art of "'tishing the girls" in places of ill repute, where a lady expected a big wad of bills. So as not to ruin the "temporary illusion of romance" by broaching any sort of payment, Uncle John told them how he would wrap a twenty-dollar bill around a clump of tissue paper. When this was inserted in the woman's garter, along with her being treated to a bottle of wine, it resulted in the favors he sought. Ringling was also adept at smuggling ladies of the evening into his Chicago hotel rooms, slyly circumventing the watchful eyes of prudish night clerks."[11]

Besides paying Johnny fifty dollars a week for circus work, Ringling also gave him more lucrative opportunities in other fields. He took Johnny into his real-estate dealings and made him the sort of a salesman most people try to avoid. During a Florida land boom in the twenties, John North was handed a satchel of deeds—some even for lots that were not under water—and peddled them to unsuspecting strangers at a cruel markup. The sales blitz earned him ten thousand dollars some months, but then the bubble burst. In another line, Johnny took a crack on his own at the stock market, going to work as a customer's man for the New York firm of J. R. Schmeltzer. He was affable as he could be, and clients flocked to him for hot tips in a hot lounge atmosphere. In two days Johnny took in twenty thousand dollars. He rented a swanky apartment on East Sixty-fourth Street and had interior decorators from Macy's fancy up the place.

His confidence and bank account bolstered, John still preferred the call of the calliope to the din and jingle of Wall Street. In the fall of 1929, he and an old college classmate were making plans to take out a small circus with veteran show owner Charles Sparks, who the year before had sold his own Sparks Circus and now wanted to get back into the business. Henry North believes this projected venture was the first serious attempt on John's part to involve himself in circus management. The move much pleased his Uncle John, who liked and respected Charles Sparks and who welcomed another show on the road that would go up against the circuses operated by his principal rival, the American Circus Corporation.

Then came the October stock-market crash. A lot of good ideas were thrown into disarray, the prospective North-Sparks partnership included.[12] John returned to work for his uncle's circus shortly after Wall Street laid its celebrated egg. A durable source of income was what he needed, and he gladly accepted fifty dollars a week again, this at a time when Uncle John was starting to lose his grip but good. The nephew's dreams of one day taking over management of the show now seemed tantalizingly close to realization. Moreover, when John looked around to check out other potential heirs apparent to the throne, the field appeared wide open.

Robert Ringling, John's cousin, posed little threat. Gifted of voice and encouraged by his late father's own love of serious music, Robert had pursued opera, beginning at Northwestern University in Evanston, Illinois, where his parents maintained a second home. Robert left the university early to study voice and began performing as a concert baritone in 1922. The following winter he was signed by the San Carlo Opera Company to tour the United States. Robert's father sent him to Europe for further training, and while in Munich he was heard by the directors of the Chicago Civic Opera Company and given a contract. His tenure with that group lasted for several seasons. He possessed a fine, very strong voice and could learn roles within twenty-four hours' notice. Unfortunately, his powerful presence did not extend below the waist, where he had become crippled from a broken pelvis he suffered during his early teens while playing sandlot football. He was laid up in a hip cast for months and was off his feet four years. He grew accustomed to a soft existence, the family giving in "to his every whim."[13] The injury left him with short, stunted legs, and thereafter he always walked with a limp.

Other than Robert, six years older than his cousin John North, there was Richard Ringling, the only son of Alf. T., who had married Aubrey Black. Richard was a bright, witty companion, on the flaky side, who boasted that he took to booze and cigarettes at the enterprising age of twelve. At one brief juncture, Richard owned and ran a billiard parlor on Broadway, attracting a horde of streetwise types to the premises. Richard had little motivation to stick anything out other than his overindulgences. His proud father, once hoping to instill the bug in him, gave Richard a circus complete with staff. In order not to offend the Ringling brothers, Richard steered clear of using the family name by calling his little show the R. T. Richards Circus. Richard lacked gusto, pushed mostly on by his dad's hopes, and his fledging tenter soon folded. He was next set up on a Montana ranch, another gift from dad that failed to show a profit. After his father died, Richard started borrowing money from his Uncle John, in whose sinking debt he was ill prepared to exert himself as one of the major shareholders he had become through inheritance.

Henry Ringling's son, Henry II, was left without any financial shares in the show; he showed little interest in its operation anyway. As for Gus Ringling's three daughters—Mattie, Alice, and Lorene—they stayed submissively on the sidelines.

So John North had every reason to feel secure in his heir-apparent position. What he could not have understood so well, however, was that the subsidiary role he played to Uncle John placed him in a vulnerable spot. In good times, the rapport between them flourished. When adversity struck the older Ringling, it was another story. Ringling's troubles began in the spring of 1929 when he stood up officials of Madison Square Garden, failing to attend a meeting they had called at which the contract for the circus's following spring run was to be settled. Ringling had been at odds with his landlords over a new clause they wanted to insert in the agreement; it would give them the right to preempt circus performers on certain Friday nights for boxing matches. At their wit's end over Ringling's stormy, stubborn resistance to the idea (he protested, rightly so, that Friday nights were some of the most profitable performance times for the circus), they caved in to the American Circus Corporation, awarding its owners, Jerry Mugivan, Bert Bowers, and Edward Ballard, the date for one of that group's biggest properties, the Sells-Floto Circus.

John Ringling was shocked and outraged when he woke up to what had transpired in his surly absence. And he found himself at the manipulative mercy of Bowers, Ballard, and Mugivan, who had egged him on only the previous year to take out an option to buy them out for $1.8 million. Now Ringling was compelled to act on the option as the only way for rescuing the lost Garden date, and he had to accept the much higher rental rates. To consummate the costly sale, Ringling borrowed money from Prudential Bond and Mortgage Company. It was a sweeping business transaction, turning John Ringling, to quote *Variety*, into "the unopposed owner of the entire circus field."[14] A heap of personnel and paraphernalia—five more circuses, three hundred additional railcars, dozens of tents—came under his blasé, overconfident control. "My kittens," he called them.

The Garden crisis surmounted, a few weeks later tragedy befell Ringling's beloved wife, Mable, who had been suffering from a complication of diabetes and Addison's disease for several years, unbeknown to her husband. The two were out boating on Sarasota Bay when the rig caught fire. Already ill from the primitive kidney treatments to which she had been painfully subjected, Mable suffered severe burns and died shortly afterward, in June 1929. John Ringling was beside himself with grief, so deeply had he loved and needed her. She had kept John happily engaged in the social and cultural worlds, had given him the marital stability he needed, all the while overlooking his furtive affairs with European sensibilities. A balancing force in his life, if Mable had lived, she may well have dissuaded him from the reckless, counterproductive decisions he made during the critical ensuing months.

It was no time to be acting infallible or pompous. That fall came the stock-market crash of 1929, nothing that visibly affected Ringling at the outset. Reeling with insecurity over the loss of Mable (his personal crash), he rushed into a second marriage with a widow some twenty years his junior, Emily Haag Buck, whom he had met one summer night in 1930 at a fast casino in Monte Carlo. John Ringling watched Emily, a gambler of evident means, drop thirty-two thousand dollars in one giggling spree. He married her on December 30 the same year, a few days after arranging a fifty-thousand dollar loan from his bride-to-be. The two proved instantly incompatible, with Emily constantly entertaining her frivolous friends and hangers-on at Ca'd'Zan, much to John's eternal annoyance. One night, fed up with Emily's bobbing about the main hall from one dizzy guest to another, Ringling cried out, "By God, Emily, light *somewhere!*"

Nothing went right anymore. Ticket sales for Ringling's circuses took a nosedive as the Great Depression set in and people had less money to spend. Business was so disastrous during the 1930 tour that the Ringling show considered dropping all road matinees. Scarcely had there ever been more than a few hundred souls inside the big top in the afternoons.[15] John Ringling took a few precautionary steps—such as shelving the Sparks and John Robinson titles—but he didn't protect his assets nearly enough. Stubborn and arrogant, he dragged his feet on making interest payments due on his Prudential note. What mostly bothered him was the increasing intrusiveness of Edith and Aubrey Ringling, who held, respectively, the shares of their late husbands, Charles and Alf. T. Ringling. Together, the two ladies owned a majority interest in Ringling Bros. and Barnum & Bailey, and they were growing leery of the show's descent into insolvency.

Then came yet another setback for John Ringling: in the spring of 1932 he suffered a stroke. Acting on his doctor's advice to take it easy for a while, he took retreat at the Half Moon Hotel at Coney Island, owned and operated—as was one of the island's principal amusement parks, Dreamland—by his good friend Samuel Gumpertz. The two men had been planning to develop a permanent circus attraction near the famous Brooklyn boardwalk. Gumpertz had proved himself as a carnival man and procurer of freak-show novelties after dabbling in various aspects of show business since he started out as a nine-year-old acrobat. He ushered and acted and sang, went from press agent to producer of kinetoscopes, the primitive forerunner of the motion picture. He produced stage shows as well and invested wisely in real estate. The attractions that flourished under his aegis ran the gamut from Eugene Sandow the strong man to Harry Houdini the magician. He is said to have given theatrical giant

Florenz Ziegfeld his start. For a time he scouted strange people for the Ringling sideshows. However, the strangest thing Gumpertz brought onto the Ringling midway turned out to be himself.

While John Ringling lay low at the Half Moon Hotel, another interest payment came due on the Prudential note, now reduced to a million dollars, and it went into default. That caused Edith and Aubrey to huddle with the ambitious Gumpertz, whose credentials made him a likely candidate to run the circus while Ringling recuperated. Dancing to a similar thought, Gumpertz had shrewdly bought the Prudential note by organizing his own syndicate of backers, corporately titled Allied Owners and New York Investors. That made him a partner in kind with the two Ringling widows, and in July 1932, John Ringling, hardly recovered from his stroke, was issued a cold-blooded ultimatum by the new note holders. They threatened to throw Ringling Bros. into bankruptcy over the defaulted interest payment and assume control themselves unless Ringling agreed to their terms: the circus would be incorporated in Delaware, and Allied Owners would receive 10 percent of the stock as a bonus for its participation. The remaining 90 percent of the stock would be divided evenly between the three heirs: John Ringling, Edith, and Aubrey. In addition, Ringling would be required to pledge his personal assets, including all of his Rubens originals, until the outstanding note, assumed by the new corporation, was paid.

Worse still, John Ringling's attorney of many years, John M. Kelly, was now advising Edith and Aubrey, whom he regarded as adversaries, and for a time John stumbled along without professional counsel. He surrendered almost completely to the Allied Owners proposition, getting it to agree to a concession whereby he was able to form the Rembrandt Corporation, to which he deeded his coveted art collection, thereby insuring the paintings against individual liquidation. Stock in the corporation was put up as part of the collateral demanded by the creditors. At the next stockholders meeting, Ringling was elected titular president, his salary reduced from fifty thousand dollars a year to one-tenth that amount. Gumpertz was appointed general manager; Edith, Aubrey, and John Kelly were made vice-presidents.

Given Ringling's illness, the new organization appeared entirely plausible, and the trades played up the ongoing close friendship between the recuperating circus king and the man from Dreamland now managing the circus in his place. John Ringling was thunderstruck by a revelation to the contrary, however, when, arising out of his negotiations, begun about a year later, to bring the Cristiani bareback-riding family to America in 1934, he received a caustic telegram. It warned him that if he did not quit taking part in such talks—indeed, from involving himself in the operation of the circus—"we will hold a stockholders meeting and turn you out."[16] It was signed by Sam Gumpertz.

"I guess Gumpertz was ambitious and saw a chance to get some power in the circus," reflects Henry North. "I think he wasn't very faithful to his old friend, John Ringling, whom he'd known for many years. I think my uncle mistakenly put too much trust in him. And when temptation—which would tempt many—got a hold of old Sam, why he took advantage of it, and moved my uncle out and himself in."[17]

Left to twiddle his thumbs, Ringling grew suspicious and paranoid. He initiated divorce proceedings against Emily Haag Buck, and she promptly countersued, seeking repayment of her fifty-thousand dollar loan to him. Federal tax men plagued Mr. Ringling with a lot of embarrassing questions and eventually mounted a case against the circus for admission-tax evasion amounting to millions of dollars. As well, John and his late brother Charles were suspected of personal income-tax fraud (they had once expressed themselves as believing all such governmental deductions to be unconstitutional). More agents showed up on the well-worn doorstep of Ca'd'Zan from Sarasota County and the state of Florida, seeking payment of long-overdue property taxes.

Wherever he turned, the beleaguered showman encountered someone either wanting to use him or bring him to task for past wrongdoings. In fact, John Ringling became so resentful of his dissenting relatives who occupied the two houses just a glance north of his, believing they were the cause of his problems, that he erected a fourteen-foot-high wall on the edge of his property line to shut them out of view. "I thought, 'Gee, that's pretty picky,'" recalls Alice Lancster, who lived in one of the houses with her husband, Charles, whose mother, Hester, was Charles Ringling's daughter. "John Ringling didn't like our kitchen noises and smells drifting into his yard, especially if he and Mable were entertaining. His house, mind you, was a long ways away. So he had the wall extended much higher, which in later times, after he was gone, started to tip and be a danger. And we were afraid it would fall on our kids. Hester called the museum and said, 'Please take that wall extension down before it falls on my grandchildren!'"[18]

John Ringling saw these people as self-pampered dilettantes living off the fat of Ringling riches. Even when John and Henry North approached

him now, their motivations, too, were suspect. Young Johnny was starting
to use his full name, which some feel rankled the uncle. As when an
understudy takes over a role and starts to shine as brilliantly as the star,
Ringling began to resent his nephew's act-alike ways. The nephew's role
model was a man whom many thought to be unscrupulous and tyrannically
egocentric. While the elder Ringling could rationalize away his own ruthless nature, he is sure to have resented it in others, certainly in a nephew
appearing to move in on his waning power.

North had managed Uncle John's real-estate interests, but during John
Ringling's last three years on this earth, he and his nephew saw less and
less of each other. Whatever the source of friction between them was, it
exploded in May 1935 when Ringling hastily summoned an attorney to
his New York hotel suite to prepare a codicil to his will. He wanted
to revoke any and all of his estate previously bequeathed to the Norths.
The amendment was drawn up on hotel stationery and signed in a stormy
rage by Ringling. He could not wait. Offers Stuart Lancaster: "He wanted
to get rid of John North totally. He wanted him the hell out of the picture.
It was pretty obvious."[19] Yet, curiously, the codicil failed to remove North
and his mother as coexecutors, a possible oversight that left the feuding
family in a muddle and the legal system profitably engaged over what John
Ringling had really wanted.

What could have set Mr. Ringling off? Several incidents point to a
motive. For one, Johnny North and his mother brought an attorney to
Uncle John in an effort to provide him with much-needed legal advice in
the wake of the mounting lawsuits he faced. He was not too impressed
with the counsel offered, especially not with the security deposit requested
up front to cover expected legal fees. In fact, Ringling suspected he was
being set up by another set of greedy relatives. The lawyer whose services
he rejected eventually wound up behind bars for criminal conduct.

Another incident in which John North supposedly disillusioned his
uncle began when in early 1934 they needed to raise fifty-five thousand
dollars due on the Allied Owners note and avoid bankruptcy proceedings
against them. Stashed away in Ringling's New York apartment (from
pre-Prohibition days) were four hundred cases of bourbon. The nephew
proposed selling three hundred of them to raise the cash, and the uncle
agreed. "Hell, yes! We need the money, Johnny!" They set a price per case
at around forty or fifty dollars, in effect operating without a wholesale
liquor license. According to circus man Floyd King, Johnny sold the
whiskey at an even higher price to a friend in the liquor business, pocket-

ing the difference for himself. A couple of weeks later, the buyer called to order more liquor and reached John Ringling. "I don't have my notebook with me," said Ringling. "What did you pay me before for this?" Replied the clandestine client, "I paid you seventy-five dollars per case."

That sad little revelation, as Floyd King understood it, caused the rift. "John Ringling knew exactly what he paid for it, so he got very hot at John Ringling North, as the story goes, and they separated. The last two or three years of John Ringling's life, his two nephews didn't contact him at all. He wouldn't let them come around anymore."[20] Consistent with the fallout were reports to the effect that Robert Ringling, of all people, had joined up with the circus in 1934, at the special request of his Uncle John, to "help manage the show."

If John Ringling did intend to rid himself of the Norths altogether but had been ill served by an inept lawyer, he had plenty of time during the last eighteen months of his life to discover and rectify the oversight. In *Circus Kings*, Henry North states that his uncle confided to a "mutual friend" that he had "torn up the codicil."[21] Another possibility is that Uncle John simply wished to retain his crafty nephew as executor while depriving him of a fortune he might easily squander away. He had observed young Johnny to know how fast money went through his hands and how much better he performed when his shoulder was to the circus wheel and the wages were low.

Henry North also maintains that it is unfair to judge his uncle harshly those last years. "I've never blamed our uncle for cutting us out of the will, because our uncle was a very sick man, and he was subject to influences. We knew what he really felt about us. There is no use having any hard feelings or regrets after the facts. You can't change them. He cut us out of the will, but, on the other hand, he still showed his confidence in us. He left my brother as executor, and me as one of the trustees."[22]

Uncle John spent his last waking hours dreaming of a return to power. He talked to acts, promising some a place on the bill when he had no right to. At the New York opening in 1936, he stormed about the premises, angrily criticizing everything about the show, including some of the posters that had been designed and printed under his old regime. Gumpertz virtually kicked him out of the Garden.

Back in Sarasota, he sat in his Rolls-Royce for hours on end, staring blankly into space as birds chirped by, searching his failing mind for a way out of his dilemma. He once confided in his great-nephew, Charles Ringling Lancaster, "Oh, Sonny, it's awful to get old, and things aren't like they used to be."[23] He rarely had more than a few hundred dollars in his bank account, yet he refused to charge admission to his art museum. At the end of each day, he would be given the parking fees that had been collected, hardly enough to pay for household expenses and the back wages owed his servants, who constantly threatened to walk off. Ringling jealously guarded his paintings, railing at the mere suggestion that he put a few on the market to raise cash. "I don't *sell* paintings," he bellowed. "I *buy* them!"

When the U.S. government scheduled an auction for December 9, 1936, to sell off some of John Ringling's possessions as a way of addressing their claims against his estate, the ailing showman made a final bid for a comeback. He got all dressed up and took the next train up the coast to New York City. He contacted his old cronies on Wall Street, hoping to arrange a loan that would stave off the auctioneers and also put him back in charge of the Greatest Show on Earth.

Uncle John was on the verge, so he thought, of such a deal when he fell ill with pneumonia. On the morning of December 2, he passed quietly on, the last of the Ringling brothers to go. At his side were his sister, Ida, and his estranged nephew, John.

When an anxious group of potential heirs gathered to hear the will read, they were fairly stunned to learn that virtually everything had been left to the state of Florida (Ida North's legacy had been reduced to a piddling annual payment of five thousand dollars). Everyone had expected Ca'd'Zan and the art museum to be so disposed of, but how had John Ringling envisioned a state government getting involved in the circus business?

Nephew Johnny had to wonder what it all meant. He had been left with nothing, but he was still—incredibly—named a coexecutor with his mother. Or was he? Suspicions to the contrary soon surfaced. The Norths had a tenuous mandate on their hands to represent the vast estate holdings, which included a 30 percent stock interest in the circus. And sensing what a challenge to his precarious authority the mounting opposition might pose, Johnny wasted no time in taking the initiative. This was the moment he had been planning for all his life, ever since he first ran around clumps of musty canvas and chased after ladies dancing on horses and hoops whirling in the sky, ever since, as that little boy, being crowned with the sublime notion that it all belonged to him. The one thing that John Ringling North had no trouble acquiring and acting out was the air and attitude of ownership.

Gargantua on Parade

Having been left with not a penny by his uncle, John North, now coexecutor of the estate, was left with only a legacy of woes. In some eerie way it seemed as if Uncle John were saying, "Okay, take my abysmal situation and see what *you* can do with it."

Straddled with a will that prohibited liquidation of the estate's most valuable assets and faced with a sure fight to remove him as executor, John had to walk a tightrope of skilled diplomacy. Too abrasive and he would bring more heat upon his flimsy position, easily contested in a court of law. Too weak and he would fail to gain the credibility needed to prove his usefulness to the state and to his family. North assumed authority in a disarming manner, drawing upon his real-estate experience on Uncle John's behalf and his tenure on Wall Street in making friends and deals. He was tough and tenacious, driven by a burning desire to run the circus, as he all along had dreamed he would one day do. And managing the estate, which held John Ringling's circus stock, gave North a base of power.

He spent most of 1937 reacquainting himself with estate matters and began meeting with state and county officials, who were anxious to settle numerous liens against it. As well, there was a horde of creditors at the door: circus suppliers, the U.S. government, even Emily Haag Buck, John Ringling's former wife, seeking the repayment of her fifty thousand dollar prenuptial loan. The federal government was suing for thirteen million dollars in back taxes. Undaunted by the magnitude of it all, John acquired a meticulous knowledge that impressed Florida officials immensely when he later testified on his own behalf before the legislature. He was given fine accounting assistance by James A. Haley, who had served his uncle in a similar capacity and who would, a few years hence, wed Aubrey Ringling, Alf. T.'s widow.

Some of the politicians with whom John met viewed his station as a fluke of inept will writing and refused friendliness or cooperation. He knew they were planning to oppose his tenuous executorship in court. Others could be wined and dined, and some were not above taking gifts in return for future support, according to more than one of John's dissident relatives, gleefully content to report such unseemly conduct: "As executor of the estate, he passed out all kinds of treasures from the house. Like, there was a liquor supply in the basement, and he passed out all kinds of things to state officials and local officials. So that he got all kinds of concessions, and that's the way he finally got control of the show."[1]

The family's biggest concern, of course, was the circus itself, the source of cash flow for a growing list of Ringling heirs. They fretted collectively over the fear of its slipping completely out of their hands, leaving them each at the mercy of having to find ordinary jobs or stand in daylong breadlines. Many were addicted to the easy life their legacies made possible. Moreover, they did not enjoy the idea of the show's being run by outsiders or their indebtedness to Gumpertz's Allied Owners and New York Investors, whose note was a million dollars from being paid off. The depression might go on for years, and a few bum seasons could drive the whole concern into foreclosure.

This depressing state of affairs was next taken up by John, whose strategy was a plan (similar to what his late uncle's had been) to buy off the Allied Owners note and return control of the show to family hands. He boarded a train for New York. Setting foot in the Big Apple, he spent more than two hundred dollars on a fancy suit to fit the occasion. He went to Manufacturers Trust Company, where he looked up a friend, Harvey Gibson.

"Hi, Johnny!"

"I need to talk to you."

"What do you need?"

"I need a million dollars."[2]

John made a persuasive case for the loan. Not only would it enable the family to take the circus back under its wings, it also would get the collateral out of hock so that the estate's assets could be disposed of. John placed his own contingency on the transaction: if he couldn't get his relatives to let him run the show, he would not consummate the deal. Gibson said yes.

Next, Johnny addressed Aunt Edith and his cousin Aubrey, who together held a majority of the circus stock.

"I have a plan to save the circus," he announced.

They listened.

"Look, if I get this loan off your backs, will you give me a contract to run the show for five years?"

Although Aunt Edith saw in Johnny many of the same detestable qualities she had so resented in her late brother-in-law, John Ringling, she was won over by North's determination and by the financial urgencies of the moment. She concurred, and Aubrey went along.

John Ringling North had at last reached the throne of Ringling power, or so he thought. The family breathed a collective sigh of relief. Everyone felt good about everyone. Robert Ringling even put his "opera career" on hold (a rather lame sacrifice, actually) to volunteer his services for the cause of a Ringling rejuvenation. "GUMPERTZ EXPECTED TO RESIGN," rang a *Billboard* headline in November 1937. "FAMILY MEMBERS ARE IN D.C. NEGOTIATING WITH THE FEDERAL GOVERNMENT ON THE QUESTION OF BACK TAXES...THEN EXPECTED TO GIVE ATTENTION TO THE NOTE WITH THE NEW YORK INVESTORS." *Billboard*'s next issue reported that North was in New York "cleaning up final details of the important transaction prior to the corporation's annual meeting."[3]

His power base broadened to include a semblance of authority over the family, North now focused his energies on the next edition of the circus. At the outset he was limited in what he could do, inasmuch as the upcoming season's acts had already been signed, the basic format laid out. And think what evil thoughts he might about Sam Gumpertz, the Coney Island showman had steadily guided the show back into the black, adhering faithfully to the traditional Ringling format of a fast-moving lineup consisting of some twenty-odd displays, each presenting as many as seven individual acts in the three rings and four stages under a cavernous six-pole tent. The program still listed many stars seen during the last days of John Ringling's reign, and it was preceded by a ponderous opening pageant of gaudy if predictable frills.

After several lackluster seasons through the mid-1930s, business had suddenly taken off in 1936. Likewise, overflow houses in 1937 put piles of green bills back in the red wagon's coffers. Sixteen thousand customers had jammed the tent one afternoon in Bridgeport, Connecticut. During four shows in Kansas City, Missouri, fifty-five thousand souls had poured through the turnstiles. Houston, Texas, drawing more than eighteen thousand people on a Monday night, was declared the "greatest circus crowd in history" by press agent Roland Butler reporting to *The Billboard*, if he can be believed.[4] (Butler listed the next-best business day as that accorded the show's 1933 jubilee appearance in its birthplace of Baraboo, Wisconsin.) Fall turnouts in Texas and Oklahoma towns broke all Ringling attendance records, according to Sam Gumpertz. Circus fans hold fond memories of the durable and satisfying "Gumpertz era."

North was hardly taking in hand a foundering enterprise, even though, in a burst of take-charge enthusiasm, he promised the press, "We intend to operate the show as the Ringling brothers did. We have plans for making it a much more valuable show. We believe it has many undeveloped possibilities and it is our intention to develop them to the fullest."[5]

A fresh broom sweeps clean, whether dust is present or not. North did reveal in his first year as producer a showmanly flair that promised a new era. His Broadway leanings made him especially critical of the so-called spec, the opening parade. The token efforts at lavishness that Gumpertz had frugally authorized were starting to look threadbare and repetitive. They might have evoked oohs and aahs from an audience reacting more to the thrill of just seeing the show commence, but the time-worn costumes were forgettable, the content bland. Gumpertz's last pedestrian effort was titled "India." Before that, he had paraded his "Durbar of Delhi" around the track for four seasons in a row. Bandmaster Merle Evans was amused by a long dragon that was supposed to be the centerpiece of one of them. "Gump got this big piece of canvas, there were holes in it, he had someone paint it to look like a dragon, and strung it over a bunch of canvasmen."[6]

Working with the roster of acts he inherited (most of them quite good, some tops in their respective fields), North decided the best he could do at this late hour was dress up the show in a more stylish and modern vein. To that end he engaged one of legitimate theater's most sought-after costume designers, Charles Le Maire, who had worked on the Ziegfeld Follies and *George White's Scandals* and would later enjoy major acclaim in Hollywood. They came up with a fetching-enough idea for a pageant titled "Nepal," conceived to be a thematic lead-in for the entrance of Frank ("Bring 'em Back Alive") Buck, whom North signed only two months before the New York opening, on April 8, at the astounding salary of one thousand dollars a week. Buck was given a private car, too. At the peak of his popularity as a modern-day Livingston or Stanley, the safari hunter was figured to be a big draw and got top billing. His engagement signaled the return to the Ringling fold of big-cage wild-animal acts, not seen (other than Clyde Beatty's appearances at the New York and Boston indoor dates) since 1926, when Charles Ringling disbanded them. The affair was appropriately ballyhooed in the circus magazine:

> "NEPAL," enacting the story of the Royal Welcome afforded the Jungle King upon his triumphant return from Malaysian Wilds by the Maharajah of Nepal and His Court, introduces to Ringling Bros. and Barnum & Bailey spectators
>
> BRING 'EM BACK ALIVE
> FRANK BUCK
>
> Internationally Renowned Adventurer, who has led scores of Hazardous Expeditions in Remote Fastnesses, where only the Most Intrepid Dare Set Foot. To Secure Rare Live Animals for The Greatest Show on Earth, as well as the Foremost Zoos Throughout the Civilized World. "NEPAL," a new art form in the circus, is the longest step forward taken by the Big Show since the last talking clown chuckled himself into Spangleland's Valhalla."[7]

North tapped deeper into the jungle theme by responding to a Brooklyn woman wishing to sell him her pet gorilla, Buddie, and in so doing the young showman honored a regular circus tradition of presenting rare and exotic animal attractions that could be hyped dramatically. Since Henry North's nickname was Buddy, he had good reason to propose an alternate show-biz name for the ape, not wanting to be the constant butt of same-name humor. It was pure ballyhoo genius that inspired Henry to suggest the fiendish name Gargantua. It alone conjured up chilling visions of supernatural brute force. The public's imagination was ignited.

Gargantua had been raised in his native West Africa and one day took refuge—so the story goes—in the arms of a couple of benign missionaries. Unable to convert him, they sold their heathen pet to Capt. Arthur Phillips, commander of an African trading ship, the *West Key Bar.* Gargantua won a free trip to America. After he docked in Boston, one of the sailors, angry over having been discharged by Captain Phillips, in a fit of revenge tossed some nitric acid into Gargantua's face. The ape ended up with a theatrically menacing look. Phillips unloaded him on Gertrude Lintz, a Brooklyn animal fancier. She took loving care of her unique little pet until one stormy night when, having grown quite big by now, he jumped into bed with her. That's when the brothers North, then living in a New

York hotel, were fatefully brought into the picture. Mrs. Lintz invited herself into their suite with two motives: liberation from a maturing nightmare and profitable gain to be made off a deal with two up-and-coming circus moguls eager to prove themselves.

The gorilla's gut-grabbing name stirred Ringling's press chief, Roland Butler, to some of his most effective story writing and poster art, which paid off in more free front-page publicity than anyone had expected. Butler played into the King Kong hysteria, yet never directly drew a parallel between the two bigger-than-life beasts. "THE WORLD'S MOST TERRIFYING LIVING CREATURE...A HORRIFYING NIGHTMARE VISION OF WHAT MAN MIGHT HAVE BEEN," proclaimed Butler's rhetoric. "WITH A SMIRK OF CRUEL CALCULATION AND A SADISTIC SCOWL ON HIS HUGE BESTIAL FACE, THIS PERNICIOUS PRIMATE DEFIES CIVILIZATION FROM BE-HIND HEAVY STEEL BARS OF THE STRONGEST CAGE EVER CONSTRUCTED."

The secret shipment of Gargantua to Sarasota from Miami was closely guarded, the press tantalizingly deprived of so much as a single glimpse. A special wagon built by Bill Yeske, a forty-year Ringling veteran, was air-conditioned by John's friend Lemuel Bulware of the Carrier Corporation in Syracuse, New York, whose firm's creation of the descriptive term "jungle-conditioned cage" earned it the Advertiser's Award in 1938. The interior approximated the atmosphere of Gargantua's native Congo, pro-duced by humidifiers and thermostatic controls, all carefully monitored, according to the press kit.

When photographers were finally allowed to shoot the sneering brute behind bars, they dodged scraps of food hurled at them in scowling protest. Johnny had part of a coat sleeve torn off (and came close to losing an arm) when Gargantua tried to grab hold of his new owner. Then there was the attack on the star's keeper, Richard Kroner. Both close calls received prime coverage by the fourth estate. Gargantua made the cover of *Life*, and Henry North contributed a wry piece to the circus magazine, alleging to trace Gargantua's genealogy. "Can Gargantua beat Gene Tunney?" (the retired and undefeated world heavyweight boxing champion), col-umnist Arthur Brisbane asked. North's capricious gorilla was perceived as possessing a "malicious moronic mind," and he liked to play games. A ball tossed his way would invariably be thrown back, underhanded, now and then directly into the pitcher's head. He engaged in tug-of-war duels, holding his own against five or six humans panting at the opposite end of the rope, other times jerking them suddenly off their feet with a facetious tug.

Another good move by North was to transfer the Cristiani family of bareback riders to the Ringling show from one of its subsidiary outfits still on the road, the Al G. Barnes–Sells-Floto Circus. A rousing troupe of top equestrians from Italy, they lit up the ring with thundering gusto and startling, well-polished tricks. Interestingly, they were about the last act that Uncle John had booked before getting the bum's rush off the lot from Gumpertz.

The show premiered in New York City on April 8, 1938, before a near-capacity crowd. Critical reactions were upbeat. *The Billboard* led the way with front-page headlines:

AUDIENCE ASTOUNDED BY DRESSING OF BIG SHOW'S '38 PERFORMANCE
OPENING SPEC, "NEPAL," REAL SENSATION
JACOBS, LIONS, CRISTIANIS, BUCK
AND GARGANTUA ARE OTHER BIG LURES

The Billboard reviewed the program as differing "but slightly from that offered by Sam Gumpertz and the New York investors in 1937." What it really jumped to was the costuming: "Magnificent to say the least. . . . It is the sensational opening spec, tabbed 'Nepal,' and wardrobing throughout that make it a standout version of the 'Greatest Show on Earth.' "8

Homemade films of the show under canvas, now historically revered, show "Nepal" to be a bold departure from the tired pageants of the recent past. Something very new was in the air—the smart gait of the participants, the high-stepping attitude of the showgirl majorettes, the swirling plumes, the confident thrust of it all down the track. Something new, indeed. Le Maire's designs made an impact, *The Billboard* scribe noting:

> One astounding result is that there is a revolutionary improvement in color blending; eye filling effects are frequent and there is achieved every benefit of circus sparkle and tinsel without any of the gaudiness that could be called by the name of cheap by those without a modicum of kindness. "Nepal" is truly a thrilling ambulant spectacle—from the girls who lead the way deftly twirling batons, down through the wild animals that are led and carried, and winding up with Buck waving greetings from his howdah, his colorful entourage and the troupe of about 50 bengal lancers.

Variety agreed, with added pleasure expressed for the Wallendas, who stopped the show, and for the jungle stud in the jungle-conditioned cage: "If he survives the season, Gargantua should ensure a fortune to the show. He's the toughest so-and-so who ever hit the lot."9

As the show world was about to discover, so was John Ringling North. Buoyed by solid first-effort results, John's euphoria ended three nights later when he found himself, along with a few loyal Ringling veterans, pushing Gargantua's wagon around the sawdust and helping to rig the acts after a walkout by two hundred workingmen left the circus handless. North now faced yet another crisis: the growing clout of labor movements in depression-dazed America. The specter of his Uncle John's last luckless years continued to haunt him.

Shakespeare's Roustabouts

The circus world that John North grew up in was a paternalistic one, built on a caste system with strict rules governing everything its employees did—or supposedly did—on and off the lot. Most performers, including married ones, were separated on the train, where the men shared double berths, the women likewise. As strange as it may seem now, every effort was made to keep the unmarried sexes out of social contact at all times. The ballet girls were forbidden to associate with single men, warned not to stop in hotels "at any time." And they had to register each night in their sleeping cars no later than 11 P.M. "The excuse of 'accidental' meetings on Sunday, in the parks, at picture shows, etc., will not be accepted."

Women were instructed to avoid "flashy, loud style" in their dress. In the dining tent, according to Henry Ringling North, they wouldn't let you in "without a jacket and without a tie on the hottest damn day you ever heard of out in Iowa in July. . . . You went into the cookhouse properly dressed, you damn sure did when Ollie Webb was running it."[1] The Ringlings were clearly in control. Part of what they offered their performers, managers, and department heads was the sheer prestige of working for the Greatest Show on Earth.

For the thrill of being a part of that mysterious world that moved by night, employees were given a decent weekly wage, not always as high as what some other shows gave, doled out each Friday inside the dressing top, as the dressing tent was called. They would say, "The eagle shits today!" A guy would sit down at a small table, and everybody would line up and be paid in cash. Jackie Le Claire's father once told him, "If they don't pay the first week, they're going to have twice as hard a time paying the second week, so you might as well get away from that."[2]

Ringling Bros. and Barnum & Bailey, the one enduring exception, always paid. And like every other tented operation, it paid as little as it could get away with. The show employed at least three times as many common workingmen as it did performers, and it depended on a cheap manpower pool to move its tents and wagons down the road. Typically, the drifters it was able to attract would show up one day, maybe answering a local ad, maybe responding to the colorful arrival of the trains. They'd sign on, penny poor, respond like cattle to orders, go along with the drudgery long enough to get a first stipend and blow it on booze. Most of them, a few weeks later, would disappear into the night, not with the circus. They had scarce motivation or skills, lacked discipline, although a few worked their way up to become respected bosses. One crop was replaced with another. The turnover went on.

Ironically, these muscular itinerants were exactly what the show needed, for they were easily exploitable and they accepted the lowest of wages. They were also a continual source of unrest to the management, so easy was it for former convicts and dangerous misfits to infiltrate their ranks. When the trains rolled into Sarasota each November at the end of the tour, the town cringed at the influx of these characters, those who had stayed on for winter-quarters work and were now being set free in the rich resort community.

As the Great Depression of the 1930s deepened, the country was racked by a nasty political debate centered on the morality of capitalism, a system then seen as having failed the American people. This hastened the rise of labor unions. "Capitalist exploitation!" shouted protesters, raising their placards over the main streets of America. Not even was the hurly-burly world of the circus exempt from suspicious examination. How were its workmen treated? What wages did they earn? How long were their hours? What were the conditions under which they toiled?

Whether any such questions were actually asked, the Ringling show tried answering them. Its press agents concocted such reassuring ditties as the following, attributed to Frank Braden in the 1936 circus magazine:

if you ask a circus workingman about the hardships of his life, he'll likely—if he is an old timer—snort: "Hardships! Hardships with this show! Nothing to that, at all, unless it's around 100 degrees in the shade c⁻ the lot's knee deep in mud." . . . They eat the best three times daily and they eat all they want.

Their food's the same as the big boss eats, too, they'll add. What's more, every man jack of them has a berth in a show sleeping car. . . . Early rising circus fans who meet the first section of the show trains see the working forces in the sleepers attached to that train pulling out 3:30 a.m., and they are apt to overlook the fact that the majority of men aboard were able to turn in around 7 p.m., in the last town; that is, if they were so inclined. . . . The Big Show, with its trains rolling out of an exhibition stand at convenient intervals, is able to systematize its gigantic routine of heavy tasks with clock-like precision, so that every worker knows when and how to get his proper amount of sleep.[3]

Written when Sam Gumpertz was in charge, these pieces reflect his sensitivity to the labor upheavals engulfing the nation. Several circus-related crafts had already organized. The International Alliance of Billposters, in existence for many years, took out a large ad in *The Billboard* in spring 1937 to tout its success in signing agreements with eleven shows, including Ringling, and to point a wary finger at eight other circuses still holding out. The American Federation of Labor (AFL) also got into the act. In May that year, the burgeoning, AFL-affiliated American Federation of Actors (AFA), a truly bizarre conglomeration of both performers and roustabouts run by an old Shakespearean actor, Ralph Whitehead, brought the nervous Gumpertz to the bargaining table. He agreed to some hefty pay hikes, to go into effect the following season, which upped the common worker's minimum monthly wage to sixty dollars. Whitehead heralded his contract coup in a full-page *Billboard* splash, anxious to sign up other circuses, only a few of which he did in due course.

The historic pact was another of the myriad burdens that Johnny North inherited when he entered the picture. What riled Johnny more than anything about the pact was that it had been authorized by Sam Gumpertz, the man who in his mind had betrayed his Uncle John. Neither was he prepared by family indoctrination to accept the idea of anyone other than a Ringling deciding who got paid what. Not that he was unwilling to do business with organized labor. In the spring of 1938, John inked a new contract with the American Federation of Musicians, long organized on the show, which stipulated a weekly pay increase of $2.50. This brought the base wage for each musician up to $42.50, the bandleader's to $65.50. John further agreed to employ a minimum of twenty-six men, and to give each an additional daily stipend of $3.50 during the New York engagement at Madison Square Garden.

By custom, show hands were paid the lower winter-quarters rate during the indoor stands in New York and Boston, the reason being that the more strenuous daily set-up and tear-down chores did not commence until the Brooklyn date, where the circus began its under-canvas tour. Ralph Whitehead may not have been fully aware of this tradition when he signed the agreement with Gumpertz. At any rate, a day or so after the show opened its 1938 season at the Garden—and some say in response to Whitehead's insistence on full wages immediately—John matter-of-factly made it known that he would not be honoring the higher wages agreed to until the tented tour got under way. In fact, what Whitehead had in his hand, argued circus attorneys, "contained no particular stipulation for work at winter quarters and indoor dates."[4] The show had signed a separate contract creating a seven-dollar-a-week minimum for off-season work, and it was this rate John intended to pay at the New York and Boston stops.

Whitehead cried foul play and raised the specter of a massive walkout. Were he to make good on his threat, he would be violating the new contract, which prohibited lockouts and strikes and which stipulated that the parties must submit their grievances to arbitration. Either side could legally request it with a ten-day notice. North accused the union of bad faith. He told reporters Whitehead had accepted his invitation to discuss the issue in Sarasota the previous winter but never showed up. Whitehead accused North of a squeeze play and blamed the whole fiasco on "dissension in the Ringling family."

At the urging of circus officials, Mayor Fiorello La Guardia agreed to meet with the feuding parties the following morning (Wednesday) in an effort to help them settle their differences, providing that a strike called for Tuesday evening was canceled. The rigid and tyrannical Whitehead, a frustrated actor now experiencing a semblance of respect in the labor field, openly defied the arbitration clause in the contract he had signed. He stood North up, and he was about to stand Mayor La Guardia up. "Too late!" he declared, as if delivering his lines from center stage while the first-act curtain fell.

That evening there were few hands around the arena to set up the animal cages. Fred Bradna, the equestrian director, described the unprecedented standoff in his excellent book, *The Big Top:* "I was just preparing to line up spec, which was to open the show, when the director of personnel, Pat Valdo, informed me that the handlers had refused to work, and Mr. North had refused to meet their demands. 'What will we do?' I inquired. 'The boss says we show,' Valdo answered. Show we did."[5]

John took the microphone to apologize to the audience for the incon-
venience, then uttered his now-famous salutation, "I welcome you to the
greatest show on earth!"

And with that, a wobbly, sometimes abbreviated make-do program
unfolded. "Nepal" was presented without elephants or horses. Frank Buck
came in on foot. "A cheer went up," writes Bradna, "different from any I
have heard. It was a show at once of defiance and triumph."

Volunteers poured out of the seats onto the hippodrome track to lend a
hand. There were so many that some had to be politely turned back.
Photographers flooded the arena, flashbulbs going off everywhere. It was
difficult for patrons to see all of the acts. A long-standing feud between the
two top equestrian troupes, the Loyal-Repenskys and the Cristianis, was
put on hold so that each could assist the other. Clown Charlie Bell and his
tiny dog filled in with a solo spot while amateur handlers herded the
elephants up from the basement. And so it went, professionals and
volunteers working side by side to erect the safety nets for the flying acts,
remove pachyderm dung from the rings. When it came time for Gargantua's
cage to be rolled around the arena, those putting shoulder to wheel
included John and Henry North and the star flyer, Art Concello, wisely
sewing the seeds of a future association with North.

"After the performance," recounts Bradna, "Johnny North was black
with dirt, and his hands were burned with rope friction. But on his face
was a triumphant smile. He had done what his uncles would have done."[6]

The strike edition ran for two more performances the following day. By
then, North and Whitehead were talking to each other before the New
York Mediation Board, presided over by Arthur S. Meyer. It took them
eight hours to arrive at a compromise agreement that affirmed the terms of
the original contract and created a minimum scale of forty-five dollars a
month for the indoor dates in New York and Boston. The show now
operated under three contracts: the five-year pact covering canvas dates,
the one covering winter-quarters pay, and the new one-year deal for
indoor rates.

Prop hands returned to the job, but the endless bickering among
personnel over the union deal and all its ramifications kept the company
in turmoil. Many performers resented having to pay union dues. Others
didn't want to join at all. Most regarded as ridiculous and unworkable the
lumping together of roustabouts and performers into the same affiliation.
Frank Buck, refusing to sign on, thought he didn't belong in either category:
"I'm not an actor. I'm a scientist." Old-guard Ringling employees added

their resistance: "We don't see why we should pay dues to an organization that spends it on unnecessary strikes against the show that pays, feeds, and keeps us through the season."[7]

Disappointing business kept North on edge. He was forced to collect dues from performers who resented paying them, accused by the union of not collecting from everyone. He asked Whitehead for further pay cuts because of a drop in business, intimating the show might return to the barn if they were not granted. Whitehead thought a bluff was on the table and stood firm. Rumors spread through the Brooklyn lot, where the new sixty dollar minimum was to go in effect, that North was not going to pay it, causing a second walkout shortly after the Saturday evening performance. Two hours later, North having pledged to honor the agreement, the strikers went back to work.

The season ahead was to prove the most disastrous in American circus history. Several shows had already folded, and others were hurrying across the Canadian border in search of better turnouts. The Ringling ticket wagons were bringing in about twelve thousand dollars a day, compared with twenty thousand dollars in better times. John continued pressing Whitehead for pay cuts in the neighborhood of 25 percent, and Whitehead, refusing to compromise, kept telling reporters, "They'll keep the show open and pay regular wages."

John took his concerns directly to the workingmen, whom he assembled in the main tent between shows. He stepped onto a raised platform in the center ring and spoke about the crippling depression and the thirteen million people it had left unemployed. "These, gentlemen, are not normal times. . . . To start with, I will say in all honesty, that it is without pleasure that I have asked you to take such a reduction in your wages, but much of necessity is often without pleasure." He spoke of the tremendous expenses incurred in operating so large a circus, and ended with a call for cooperation: "I'd like to think that it might mark a return to that old order of things."[8]

The speech failed to win the desired cooperation. John had tried his hand at diplomacy and time was running out; he couldn't afford to jeopardize the family's regained control of the show. The all-important New York and Boston dates had been played, where the bulk of the profits was realized, and public sentiment in the union issue seemed tilted in John's favor. So he decided to take the upper hand and risk an early closing. He let nearly two hundred hands go in Lima, Ohio, another sixty in Fort Wayne, Indiana. What he got in Toledo, Ohio, when sixty-eight baggage handlers deserted the train, leaving seventeen sliced air hoses behind, was malicious reciprocation.

The horse men said they were only following their boss off the lot, he having declared in exasperation, when he went to the red wagon asking to be paid off, that he could no longer control them. When the trains pulled into Erie, Pennsylvania, the next morning, federal agents were at the yards to probe acts of vandalism. Unfazed by the violence, two days later in Rochester, New York, John delivered an ultimatum: either the workers accept his proposed 25 percent pay cut or the show would head back to winter quarters. Since nobody walked during the next two days, John cleverly posted a second message that is a gem of self-deluded manipulation: "To all employees: The management wishes to thank you for the prompt action you have taken in accepting the 25% reduction in pay, which acceptance has resulted in the show not closing today.... The moment you decided upon this course, surmounting an impending crisis, you won the profound respect and admiration of every showman in the amusement world. You have proved once more the truth of the time-honored phrase, 'The show must go on!' "

When a trade reporter asked John to clarify what he meant, he replied, "We posted a notice two days ago that the circus would close if the reduction was not accepted. Since all employees were working today, I assume they have accepted this reduction."9

It didn't wash with Whitehead, who was beside himself over the audacious ploy. The union leader, still believing North to be part bluff, told all hands to keep working until the show reached Paterson, New Jersey, where the next pay envelopes were to be handed out, to see for sure if the cut was actually implemented. It proved too long a wait for the infuriated Whitehead, however, especially given the show's appearance, only two days away, in Scranton, Pennsylvania, a strong union town. Needing as sympathetic a setting as he could finagle, Whitehead decided to call a strike in Scranton after the opening show on Wednesday afternoon.

For the first time in its fifty-four-year history, Ringling Bros. stood still as the result of a walkout. Now Whitehead could accuse North of violating their contract's negotiation and arbitration clauses. Union members gathered at Adlin Hall, the atmosphere charged with anti-Ringling hysteria. Whitehead addressed the crowd with oratorical frenzy.

"Did you accept the twenty-five percent cut?"

"NO! NO! NO!" they yelled back.

"Should we strike?"

"Yes! Yes! Yes!"

"We're on strike?"

"WE'RE ON STRIKE!"

They sent word of their decision to the circus and invited North to address the meeting. They waited for an hour, and still no response. Whitehead kept the troops in the hall. "If North is not a fool, and I don't think he is, he'll come over here!" They waited in vain another half-hour. Union officials made several more attempts to reach North. They were not to have the satisfaction of his company.

His own anger boiling over, John was talking to the press, letting off steam, expressing his extreme displeasure over the ludicrous AFA agreement. "This contract is . . . something I inherited when I shoved Gumpertz out of the picture last December."[10]

In the Casey Hotel with brother Henry, he drafted his final offer: If the workers were not on the grounds by 1 P.M. the next day and fully prepared to accept the cuts, the tents would be struck and sent back to Florida.

Some four thousand customers already seated under the big top for the night show were given refunds and sent home. By 11:30 P.M., both sides still refusing to budge, the circus decided against trying to tear down and move on to Wilkes-Barre, the next day's stand.

The Ringling tents stood deserted for four days as tension between the circus and the strikers mounted. John and Henry remained behind police protection at the hotel. They were given little sympathy by Scranton's liberal mayor. The times favored the plight of the workingman, and Whitehead was in as much glory as he had ever known on the stage, orchestrating with rare bravado his union's jeering resistance to the North ultimatum. A corps of loyal performers willing to make compromises was handily outnumbered by the rabble of common workers, the majority of whom had not been with the circus for more than a few weeks or months. Anyone wishing to question Whitehead's rationale was ridiculed and refused the platform.

Nonetheless, North won encouraging wage concessions from his own people—not, of course, authorized by Whitehead. Frank Buck went along with a slashing 75 percent cut in his salary, down to $250 a week. Henry North accepted $75. Art Concello circulated a petition signed by 250 performers stating they wanted to accept the pay reductions and see the show go on. Members of other unions on the show were of the same mind. Ninety-six of the performers, convening on their own to take a vote, endorsed the pay cut 83 to 13. Whitehead called the results a mockery and gathered the entire performing staff together the following day at Adlin Hall, where the issue was discussed in a more hysterical atmosphere. And against the pleas of circus management, Whitehead refused to allow a secret ballot. An open vote was taken. The performers now backed the union.

North offered to open his books to the AFA. Whitehead wanted an audited version, which North said he could not supply. Edith Ringling pleaded with a group of workers gathered in the big top on Saturday afternoon. "Please think long and hard before putting the Greatest Show on Earth off the road."[11] The heart-felt ovation she received did not translate into concessions from the union. Whitehead cried to reporters, "I'm sick and tired of standing back quibbling for peace. Now we'll take it to the National Labor Relations Board." The only agreement he and North were able to make was for the striking workers to dismantle the show so it could be returned to Sarasota. The circus promised to make good on all back wages owed and to incur other union-related expenses, including Whitehead's own bills and the Adlin Hall rental. North had already housed and fed the strikers during the Scranton standoff, true to the paternalistic ways of the circus.

The trains did not leave town until after Monday morning, when the circus was able to withdraw the necessary payoff cash from local banks. En route to Florida, a stop at the Potomac yards in Washington, ostensibly to water the animals, lasted for several dramatic hours. Circus fans held their breath in hopeful speculation: why hadn't orders been given to move the train farther south? Why hadn't the horse cars been diverted to Peru, Indiana, where the baggage stock was ordinarily wintered? While reporters milled about the train, being shown the slashed air hoses and asking questions, others wondered out loud whether a reorganization might be in the works. They took heart when John and Henry North arrived at the train shortly before midnight, having motored down from New York.

The North brothers went into a huddle with key executives. What they discussed is not known, but rather than stay on the road, John more likely saw an opportune moment to exploit public sentiment in his favor. He could blame the early closing on unreasonable union demands. At the same time, any public hostility he might be able to generate against Whitehead would only improve his future bargaining position with the man. When he and Henry emerged from the conference, it was announced that the canvas would be kept damp by repeated waterings along the route, then rolled out to dry in the Florida sunshine.

The cars rattled out of the Potomac yards amid an outpouring of save-the-circus fervor brilliantly orchestrated by Melvin D. Hildreth, by profession an attorney and by hobby the president of the Circus Fans Association of America. *The Billboard* printed his thoughts on the matter:

> "I am sick at heart. . . . the awful part about the whole affair is that the Ringling show has always had the highest standards. And in its relation with labor it stood at the forefront. Never was there any redlighting on that show. Never was there any skimping of meals, cheating of employees. And yet that is the circus that had to suffer. . . . At the Potomac yards, I watched the train leave for Sarasota. Words cannot begin to describe the sadness of the picture. It is very difficult for me, too, to understand why an actors union should be controlled by roustabouts who seldom know what it is to serve even one circus season."[12]

Hildreth made good sense. *Variety,* commenting on the unlikely marriage of actors and workers, reported that the show had issued two thousand three hundred Social Security cards the previous tour to the various men who came and went to fill some three hundred jobs in the "drifter classification."

Editorials around the country lamented the forced closing. "Surely, if there was ever a time when the country needed the cheering influence of the circus, it is now," wrote the *Beaumont* (Texas) *Enterprise.* "It moved in some glamorous orbit of self sufficiency, divorced from the realities of life," observed an editor in the *Springfield* (Massachusetts) *Union.* And from the *New York Times:* "The show will only go on at union rates. The animals are willing, the freaks are willing, the performers are willing, but the union is adamant. . . . Is it the beginning of the end of the big top?"

Once free of Whitehead's wrath, North moved fast to repair a damaged season, sending out his lead acts to appear with the Ringling-owned Al G. Barnes–Sells-Floto Circus. Gargantua and company joined with the smaller outfit in Redfield, South Dakota, temporarily retitled "Al G. Barnes–Sells-Floto Circus presents Ringling Bros. and Barnum & Bailey's Stupendous New Features."

John moved shrewdly in contrary directions, which befuddled his AFA antagonists into submission. He appointed McCormick Steele, a Yale classmate and former New York State Labor Department official, to the newly created post of personnel director. He brazenly made it known that the show would henceforth be a strictly nonunion, open-shop affair. Ralph Whitehead retaliated from afar, calling for a national boycott of all

Ringling shows and dispatching a motley of pickets to the Al G. Barnes lots. Judge Joseph A. Padway, Whitehead's general counsel and an adviser to the AFL, issued a terse warning: "It is possible that John Ringling North believes he has thereby broken the back of the AFA circus division. The fact remains that Mr. North does not realize the effectiveness of his contractual obligations. . . . He will find that when he attempts to reopen the circus on an open shop basis, the law will be there to stop him."[13]

John turned the charm on with other labor leaders in the American Federation of Labor and with the National Labor Relations Board. His hybrid circus out west was drawing good-enough crowds, the smaller forty-five-hundred-seat tent an easier venue to fill with customers. Boycotts staged by chapters of the Central Labor Union in Omaha, Nebraska, and Jefferson City, Missouri, failed to dampen consumer interest. On Labor Day in Wichita, Kansas, AFL officials invited John to join their parade and he gladly complied, sending forth several circus wagons bearing pro-union placards. At a celebration that afternoon, he told the gathering, "It afforded me deep pleasure to show in this small way my esteem for organized labor in Wichita, and for the American Federation of Labor everywhere. . . . We feel that we are continuing an era of good feeling and understanding, by cooperating with the AFL."

He didn't look so bad after all. The circus played September dates in Oklahoma City under the auspices of the Central Trade and Labor Council, a public-relations gesture that paid off handsomely and prompted two local labor leaders, Walter Nelson and Leonard Dickerson, to question the AFA's agenda. They said they were convinced that organized labor could never be applied 100 percent to the circus business. "The turnover in common labor of the circus is tremendous, and the bookeeping and auditing work is staggering, to say nothing of social security tax duties."[14] As Art Concello would remark years later, "the circus was an animal labor didn't fit into."[15]

Meanwhile, Ralph Whitehead was on his way, so he thought, to meet with North during the show's Houston, Texas, dates October 10–12. North refused to see Whitehead, telling the press, "I have absolutely nothing to discuss with him." William Green, president of the AFL, and several of his associates got Johnny's attention instead. They conferred at the Rice Hotel. A "most pleasant feeling" existed between all parties. They were treated to the best seats in the tent at a Tuesday night performance of the circus, and they enjoyed themselves so much they stayed on for the aftershow.

Whitehead was not seen at the circus. He left Houston more uncertain and cantankerous. Now his priorities were changing: he wanted some kind of a contract with Ringling only so that he could approach his next organizing target, carnival workers, with authority. By the time he caught up with North on December 13 in New York, he was a virtual beggar willing to sign most anything just to salvage his vanishing credibility. A round-table discussion brought together the two North brothers, Robert Ringling, William Dunn, circus attorneys Leonard Biscoe and John Reddy, Ralph Whitehead, and Dan Hurley for the AFA. Also in attendance were two reps from the AFL, Matthew Woll, a vice-president, and Judge Joseph Padway, whose participation was a key factor in North's agreeing to talk. Woll had given prior indication that he favored divorcing common labor from the AFA jurisdiction. Moreover, his conservative style was said to supply a check to North's Irish temper, "close to the boiling point," while William Dunn had a similar civilizing effect on Whitehead's "militancy."

The outcome of the meeting gave North an impressive edge. The compromise agreement they reached carried a duration of only one year and ordered a whopping 25 percent reduction in the workingman's wage (the exact decrease North had held out for). It excluded department heads from membership and reestablished the closed-shop pact with AFA, guaranteed separate meetings for performers and workers, and insured against lockouts or strikes. Whitehead's union newsletter made no mention of a single compromise. Trade journals termed the contract "a clear victory" for the circus.[16]

That it was. The paternalistic Ringling show had reclaimed the edge over the common canvas man. Johnny North, proving himself as tough a so-and-so as Gargantua, had broken the union's back, and in so doing he had given the finger to old Sam Gumpertz, signer of the now defunct deal. His uncle John should be resting easier.

The Lady Who Wouldn't

For the time being, at least, John had subdued his union enemies like Clyde Beatty taming cats in the big cage. He had come out of it the winner, and he acted as if he didn't have a labor-related care in the world. Maybe he didn't, since he had shrewdly set into motion a number of labor-movement counterforces that eventually would deflate Whitehead's power base. The AFA chief, while chasing North through the 1939 season for cooperation, faced a drive within his own ranks, led by the San Francisco local, to oust him for mismanagement of funds. In September the AFA lost its jurisdiction over performers to the American Guild of Variety Artists (AGVA) and was left with only the roustabouts to represent.

Whitehead reemerged the following spring under the more appropriate title Circus, Carnival, Fair, and Rodeo Union, with a charter granted by the AFL. North refused to do business with him, arguing that he lacked majority representation. Whitehead made a feeble attempt to picket Madison Square Garden, his lines crossed by AFL executives. He took his case to the U.S. Department of Labor, getting it to investigate the show for possible violations of the Wage and Hour Act. All the while, another union was springing into existence, this one from within the Ringling organization; it was called the American Federation of Outdoor and Indoor Circus and Carnival Workers. It was started by, among others, Ray Milton, the show's trainmaster, and Lloyd Morgan, who pledged to serve as officers without pay and exclude from voting membership managers and department heads such as themselves. North welcomed its formation, for it helped further erode Whitehead's claim to legitimacy. Finally, the National

Labor Relations Board entered the picture, declaring Whitehead's group the rightful bargaining agent. Trade ads heralded the decision:

THIS MEANS THERE IS ONLY ONE UNION THAT CAN PROTECT YOU. THE RINGLING SHOW WILL NOT INTERFERE WITH ITS EMPLOYEES RIGHT TO COLLECTIVE BARGAINING.
THE RINGLING SHOW WILL NOT DEAL WITH THE AMERICAN FEDERATION OF OUTDOOR AND INDOOR CIRCUS AND CARNIVAL WORKERS.
THE RINGLING SHOW WILL NOT RESTRICT ANY EMPLOYEES FROM JOINING ANY UNION AFFILIATED WITH THE AMERICAN FEDERATION OF LABOR.
WORKERS, SOONER OR LATER YOU WILL JOIN THE CIRCUS, CARNIVAL, FAIR AND RODEO UNION, SO YOU MIGHT AS WELL JOIN NOW.[1]

Lacking a consistent work force, however, with which to solidify a viable membership base, Whitehead lost momentum and within a couple of years was out of business. It was now up to the American Guild of Variety Artists to corner North, and it brought this off with agonizing hit-and-miss success. John would hold out a tentative promise to agree to something supposedly negotiated, dole out dues for his performers, then drag his feet again until shoved into another corner and threatened with legal action.

He liked getting his way. Not quite thirty-five years old when he began running the show, John was soon donning a derby hat in dashing style, as his uncle had done, strutting across the lot with cane in hand, cigarette holder to the mouth, head cocked upward. No challenge was too difficult for him, nobody's game beyond his ability to understand and outmaneuver. On the personal front, he expected the same results. His relationships with women had been mostly of the playboy-mistress sort. He was used to getting what he wanted without romantic folderol. And disregarding his uncle's admonition against taking up with one of his own employees, John decided he had to have the show's star equestrienne, Chita Cristiani.

She rode in the family act, which had come over from Italy and had been on the Ringling payroll four years, appearing with a couple of its subsidiary circuses, Hagenbeck-Wallace and then Al G. Barnes–Sells-Floto. When 1938 came around, John transferred the Cristianis to the Ringling-Barnum unit and started paying Chita a lot of attention. He hardly realized that in reaching out to Chita he would be going up against a very proud family that viewed his motives with well-founded suspicion.

The Cristianis were a close-knit bunch of crack riders who stuck together in the passionate Italian spirit. They presented probably the greatest group act of all time. Belmonte's stunts, Lucio's twisting somersault from horse to horse, Cosetta's sassy high kicks, Chita's ballet—all left the critics panting with praise. Their coming to America marked John Ringling's last big booking coup. He had seen them perform in London in 1933 and, true to form, uttered not a word of interest but sent over his agent, Pat Valdo, to offer a contract and hash out the details. Though the act then consisted of but five riders, the entire troupe—with groom, secretary, relatives, and all—numbered about eighteen. So eager was Ringling to engage them that he consented to pay the passage for everyone, a deal insisted upon by "Papa" Ernesto Cristiani.

The troupe opened at Madison Square Garden in 1934 and that night was threatening to return to Europe because Pat Valdo had not made good on his promise to give them the center ring. They were assigned one of the end rings, while a regular Ringling staple, the Loyal-Repenskys, took the central spot. The fuming Cristianis (nobody could do it better) got perfect sympathetic cooperation from their horses, which, according to Chita, "were not used to the side ring" and flat-out refused to canter therein. "When we got to turn around to jump on the horse," she says, "we don't see no horse!" The animals were wandering up the track, some trying to crash the middle ring.

One of the brothers got Pat Valdo up against a wall, grabbing him angrily by the chest. "You promise us main ring! Put us in center, you say! This is no good, we're going back!"

Valdo may have made such a promise, speaking for John Ringling, when he booked the act, then may have been given contradictory orders by Sam Gumpertz, who was on the scene managing when he presented it. Valdo pleaded with the family for patience and promised in the alternative to make them stars in the Hagenbeck-Wallace outfit. They said okay to the transfer, which lasted for two years, after which they were moved to the Al G. Barnes–Sells-Floto Circus for another two.

The Cristianis were prone to temperamental outbursts when things did not go their way. On one occasion when the big-top crew repeatedly had been putting too much water on the sawdust, making it slippery for the horses, the Cristianis staged a colorful protest. Triumphantly they entered the tent and marched into the ring, where they bowed, promptly turned around, and proceeded to walk back out, not one of their horses having been put to use.

"You are crazy!" shouted Alfredo Codona, the legendary flyer, who, in his retirement, had turned equestrian director.

"We are not crazy!" Chita yelled back, siding with her brothers and sisters. "We want respect!"[2]

Most of the time they got it, as John was about to learn when he first approached Chita, no pushover, assuming she would be an easy conquest. She had been attracting hordes of suitors, favoring a few of them with token interest, collecting scads of gifts in the process and staying comfortably out of trouble. One of her obsessed admirers was journalist Paul Gallagher, whom she admits "never had any sex appeal for me." He began writing stories about the family, some published in the pages of *Esquire*. One described Chita as riding a horse "like a virgin." He penned a story, "The Gigannis," based on the family, that was optioned by MGM for a screenplay but never made into a film. Another caller was the Al. G. Barnes head ticket seller, Harry Bert, who on one costly date took the entire family out for dinner, footing the bill himself, so that he could hold Chita's lovely hand on the sly.[3]

North wanted to hold her hand, too. He made his overtures late in the 1938 season after the labor strike, when he and his best acts joined the Barnes show. Now in a more relaxed frame of mind, John, twelve years older than Chita, sent her a message of interest via a mutual friend. Chita was flattered by the inquiry, for John North was *the* up-and-coming boss man, considered a catch by any showgirl. Chita sent off a favorable reply and reported to Papa on this new development. Papa was wisely on guard. He had come to the States warned about women who were "stolen away" by shifty men like those portrayed in western movies. Overly protective, he feared the worst possible scenario in which his dear child was being set up for a quick roll on a casting couch—or trampoline.

"So Johnny wants to meet you?" he said. "Very well, but he's got to meet *two* daughters."

Papa insisted on a strict 11 P.M. curfew—sometimes he might extend it an hour—and the observance of rules designed to keep his daughter out of the casual-mistress category. Chita's sister, Cosetta, acted as escort. Lucky for Cosetta, John's brother, Henry, then technically separated from his wife, was available to round out the cozy little entourage. So the foursome went double dating in high style. "It was easier for me," says Chita, "and enjoyable for Cosetta."

Not so much for John. The first date proved Papa Cristiani's instincts right. John got into Chita's dress and tried pulling it up.

"You take down that dress right now!" she demanded.

He did.

That issue settled, John saw Chita as a long-term goal. He proved to be a good sport, and the four had fun crashing night spots in the larger cities. When they were in New York, they went to all the "in" places. They spent some time at the World's Fair. They went shopping together for fun. John revealed a side of himself rarely, if ever, witnessed by the circus community. He loved to sing and dance, of course, loved to be at the center of late-night revelries. Chita and Cosetta had a ball being seen with the two famous brothers. Indeed, the family enjoyed the heightened status it brought.

Official chaperon Cosetta lived up to her position, once coming to her sister's defense in a German restaurant in Greenwich Village. A sailor had been harassing Chita for a dance and had grabbed hold of her arm in a move to sweep her off her feet. John and Henry were off in the restroom. Cosetta took a deep breath, walked up to the sailor, and knocked him cold to the floor, after which she and Chita made their exit.[4]

Another time, Henry faced the fists of a drunk who had stumbled over his feet and wanted revenge. Chita took the matter into her hands, sending the rowdy buffoon flying over two tables. Henry's mouth dropped open in amazement. "Nothing to worry about, Buddy," said Cosetta, aware of her superior strength and pluck.[5] Then there was the time they sent Henry ahead to reserve a table. When they got there, they found him *under* the table, slightly smashed.

Johnny preferred topping off the evening by doing a solo dance, climaxed with a wild yelp and a leap to the floor into a spectacular split. One night, his pants split, too. He took hold of a nearby tablecloth, flung it around himself, and made an exit. Cosetta couldn't wait to get back to the train to tell Papa about that. She loved reporting on the evening's high points, adding a little embellishment here and there, so vivid was her sense of fiction.

When John was in London visiting the Bertram Mills Circus in the winter of 1938, the Cristianis were there performing with it. Then far from committed to just one man, Chita was entertaining the gift-laden overtures of Lord Astor's son, David, who was running his father's newspaper. He sent her flowers every day, took her out to dinner, showered her with lovely jewels. She was a bit smitten by Astor and found John's reaction ambivalent. He was furious when he learned of the royal flirtation, yet flattered to think that his competitors for Chita's hand came from such high circles.

The following spring, after the Ringling show had settled into its New

York run, John got so frustrated with the elder Cristiani's infernal restraints that late one night the two had it out, some say over a telephone call Johnny made to Chita at three in the morning, pleading with her to come to his hotel. "I must see you now, please!"

Papa came on the line and confronted North like an errant son.

"I'm the boss of this show," replied Johnny, at the end of his manly tether. "I can keep her out if I want."

"She has to work tomorrow!" screamed her angry father.

"If she doesn't want to work, she doesn't have to!"

"Says who?"

"Me!"

"You might be the boss of the circus," said Papa, "but you're not the boss of my family. She's got to be home to do the act. That's what she gets paid for."

Once more John struck out, deprived of the outlet his lusty nature sought. He was thwarted and yet too sexually driven to give Chita the romance she wanted. A hug here, a pinch there, a stolen kiss are things she would gladly have accepted. John could not make the transition into the sensual zone of courtship that hovers on the hint of consummation. After Chita's first rebuff, he became stilted. Soon he was treating her like a saint, gently kissing her on the cheek as one kisses a little child. Not more. Not less. Nothing tantalizingly in between.

"I not only love you," he uttered, "but I *worship* you!"

Chita was baffled, not bewitched or bothered. "He had very little romance in him," she offers. "I'm the romantic type, and he would kiss me without even putting his arm around me. I thought there was something wrong."

So did Chita's mother, who distrusted North so much that he was afraid to come near her. "I'll meet you at the door," he would tell Chita when the two arranged a date. Usually, Chita and Cosetta were sent home, after their evenings out with the North boys, in a limousine, compliments of the circus.

Though John worshiped Chita, he did not enjoy her taking the spotlight away from him, another of his quirks she found dispiriting. Men would naturally give her the eye, and John resented being an appendage to someone else's aura. Chita puts it this way: "John liked horses, he loved music and he loved to play the saxophone. Most of all, he liked being John Ringling North. Other people looked at me. He didn't like it. Most men are proud of their girl, but he wanted to be the center of attention."

She put aside her reservations at first, so much did she enjoy going out with the top man of the big top. She and Cosetta were taken to the best places, and she had something all other girls envied. "That's probably why I dated him."

Their relationship lasted through the better part of the 1939 tour. Whenever John came onto the lot, he usually headed straight for the private Cristiani dressing tent. He would take a seat in front of it and sit there in a trancelike state, satisfied to be near the girl he loved and couldn't have. All the while Chita was running in and out, doing her acts and handling the costumes. She thought it a little weird that Johnny "would just ignore everything else and sit there for hours."

The hours went by and nothing happened. There was always that blasted curfew getting in the way. One night the girls were visiting the boys in John's private car. It was getting close to the exit-for-home hour and the train was rolling. They knew they had best be back in the family car—five coaches away and no passageway through the train. They waited for the train to stop somewhere along the way so they could jump out and make haste up the tracks. Finally, that moment came.

"Come on, Chita!" cried Cosetta.

The girls flung themselves down the stairwell like two Cinderellas at the stroke of midnight, John and Henry following. Together they ran nervously ahead, suddenly encountering the splintery wood ties of a bridge.

"Watch out!" one of them yelled. "There's water down there!"

John slipped between two of the ties and nearly fell through. Henry and Cosetta reached down, each grabbing a part of his clinging body. They managed to pull him back up while Chita watched in horror. The next morning, the two coaches were no longer separated by other cars on the train. They were now connected end to end, though still without a direct passageway between, ironically symbolic of a union that would never be consummated.

John made a proposal of sorts, placing on Chita's finger a medium-size diamond ring. She wore it for a spell, never intending to marry him. She had grown wary of John's stubborn self-centeredness. He professed a dislike for children. He had not a kind word to say for man's best friend, not even for brother Henry's Great Dane. He told Chita it had taken him ten years to "get rid" of his first wife, who was a Catholic, not realizing that Chita was of the same religion. What little intimacy they had achieved was ruined when John challenged Chita with an ultimatum.

"When we get married," he announced, "you'll have to forget about your family."

Chita was thunderstruck.

"Me forget about my family?"

"Yes, I'll take you to Europe and you'll have to change your name, too. I'll buy you the title of countess. We'll do it right."

"Forget about my family? You got another guess coming."

"You think about it, Chita. . . . "

"Think about *what?* I only have one mother and father. I only have one family. Why separate from my family?"

John had nothing to add.

Chita had long since concluded she would never give her hand to a man so adverse to the idea of having children. She loved children. She loved family. As for her flamboyant boyfriend, she didn't love him at all.

Preparing for his last exit, John boasted that he would go to Europe and find somebody "very important."

The two parted company on amicable terms.

Of this intriguing romance, little has been said by way of rumor or report. Henry North dismisses it as "a nice little flirtation," although in *Circus Kings* he refers to John's having "loved another circus girl" (not giving her name) in connection with giving his own version of the bridge incident.[6]

In another book, *The Cristianis*, its author, Richard Hubler, gives the affair prime coverage. He contends that Chita was stringing John along all the time and quotes her as saying, "I wanted to hang onto him, but I didn't want to marry him." Hubler figured the relationship "gave the Cristianis a stranglehold on contract talks and circus approval throughout the world, as long as their eldest daughter was tied up with North. They applauded themselves on the coming match."[7]

Chita denies Hubler's account, pointing out how the family was much in demand (it was) and did not need her dalliance with North to gain or sustain ideal work arrangements. In fact, if North's negotiating attitude toward his star bareback riders had been contingent on Chita's treatment of him, he could easily have let their contract lapse at the end of either the 1939 or 1940 seasons, which he didn't. They continued to perform with John's circus for three more years.

Chita simply came to her senses about John and realized how incompatible they would be. She did not stay with the Ringling show but went off to work with other branches of the family at spot dates elsewhere.

So concluded the lone chapter in John's life in which he tried getting close to a performer on his payroll. He had learned his lesson; Uncle John was right. Never again, as far as anyone knows, did he involve himself with a Ringling showgirl. In fact, the souring outcome of his experience with Chita Cristiani, if anything pushed him away from further personal involvement with the circus crowd. He became that much more detached and aloof, that much more suspicious and insecure.

John went off to Europe to book new acts and to search for that very important somebody. Chita was left with the distinct feeling, perhaps all too true, that her former boyfriend loved only himself.

Brotherly Bombast

Just as John had boasted to Chita he would do, he came back from Europe with someone special. She was Germaine Aussey, the French film star, now wearing an engagement ring. Henry took more than a second look at her shapely figure (which in later years he compared with Marilyn Monroe's) and her greenish-blue eyes and long, flowing auburn hair. What a catch!

John discovered Germaine during a Paris blackout on Christmas Eve 1939. Eager to prove his manhood once again and anxious to cap his success with a glamorous marriage, he courted her persuasively. No doubt the early proposal she accepted was hastened by her desire to flee France, which was about to be invaded by the Nazis. The two were married in Philadelphia on May 11, 1940, the very month that Hitler's army ringed the Eiffel Tower. The ceremony was auspiciously quiet, John having quashed his press department's plans for a rice-over-sawdust affair with the wedding party mounted on white horses. He said his love for Germaine would not tolerate such vulgarity.

The newlyweds flew to Sarasota on a honeymoon, then returned to Philly, where the circus was now playing, to begin married life aboard the Jomar, which John had just had refurbished to rejoin the train. They entertained any number of local and national celebrities en route. There were plenty of cameras to pose for, nearly always with lions, tigers, and clowns to pose with. Harry Firestone, Jr., paid them a visit in Akron, Ohio. Mike Todd came aboard in Lincoln, Nebraska, to travel with the honeymooners. John was the perfect gentleman in the company of selected friends and famous people. During the Philly stand, he took pride in presenting a loving cup to Ellis Gimble (the department store mogul), who had sponsored circus parties for thousands of underprivileged children the past twenty years.

For too much of the journey, though, Germaine rode the Jomar alone, while John was off making deals or booking talent. The smaller towns offered her no diversion. She once confided to John Murray Anderson, then directing the circus, that she felt no better off than M'Toto (Mrs. Gargantua), for both occupied air-conditioned compartments on the train and both had once been photographed on the beach at Deauville.[1]

At the end of the tour, John and Germaine took up winter residence at Ida North's white Worcester house on Bird Key, a small island in Sarasota Bay only five minutes from the center of town, reachable by a causeway that Uncle John had built. Ida had lived there since 1932, and John and Henry had spent many off-seasons with her. The quaint two-story house was surrounded by coconut palms, its long driveway flanked by rows of Australian pines. All kinds of birds chirped and nested in the tree-covered vicinity. Millionaires lived in other houses leisurely spaced on the island.

It was a kind of paradise away from the everyday world, though Ida's place hosted a gaggle of lively relatives, old and young, there being an ample supply of bedrooms, it seemed, for all. In one slept Henry North and his wife, Ada Mae; in another their son, John Ringling North II, and his nurse; in another John and Germaine. There were rooms for Salome, the North brothers' one sister; her husband, Dick Wadsworth; and their two children, Ducky and Salome. Additional quarters took care of the Jomar's French chef, Charles, and his two assistants, an Italian butler, and Germaine's personal maid, whom she brought over from France. A nearby cottage housed the gardner, kept busy tending the manicured lawns and formal gardens, on the exterior of which the more natural vegetation grew wild and free.

Ida was a wonderful hostess who fostered an around-the-clock party mood. Fond of gourmet meals, she prepared them often, sometimes usurping her own chef's duties or bossing him about in a condescending way. He once ejected her from the kitchen, chasing her out with a carving knife. Ida cooked and played bridge most of the day, then stayed up half the night playing poker. Dinner was served around 9 P.M. Everyone gathered in the large main hall, casually attired, downing cocktails and trading jokes.

The one exception was Germaine, who swept down the staircase in Parisian frills, a floating anachronism in the gregarious Ringling household.

She had known too self-centered a life to appreciate sharing it with so many others. They, in turn, found her a tad stiff. Another of her quips hinting at disillusionment was made to a columnist: "I didn't marry a man, I married a whole family."[2]

Worse still, John's late hours rankled his new bride to no end. The Norths rarely retired before 4 or 5 A.M., the hour at which she had been accustomed to rising for 8 A.M. movie calls. She loathed the frivolous, never-ending card games and retreated instead to her room upstairs, where she brooded over John's having such good times without her. She also played second fiddle when a crowd of smart New York artists and directors convened downstairs in high spirits to plan a new edition of the circus. Seen among them, at one time or another coming and going, were John Murray Anderson, Miles White, George Balanchine, cartoonist Peter Arno, Norman Bel Geddes, and guests like Heywood Broun, Monte Woolley, and Charlie Baskerville, there just for the fun of it. Ida loved the creative ferment of it all, the heated, healthy arguments over ideas, so much did they remind her of similar sessions engaged in by her brothers back in Baraboo when they planned and ran the show.

More bystander than participant, Germaine may have been biding her time, waiting for the war to end and Paris to be liberated so she could go home and resume her film career. While the marriage lapsed into a polite form of mutual disinterest, John proceeded blithely on his way, marching to his own drummer, eternally loyal to his one abiding mistress: the circus. He was forging new directions for the Greatest Show on Earth, taking on the status quo with attention-getting gusto. What was so wonderfully ironic was the sense of humor that came out of John's early showmanship. The marketing of Gargantua had something to do with this. The brute had become such a hot conversation piece that John decided to ship him off to London in December 1938 for an appearance with the Bertram Mills winter circus. John followed on the *Queen Mary,* and the two had a ball putting on English curiosity seekers. North's celebrity ape earned a full page ad in *The Billboard* upon his return to the States—a not too flattering portrait of Gargantua growling at the reader, under which was printed a primitive handwritten note (presumably his own scrawl), saying, "Yah, I yam the only one in showbizness who don't read *The Billboard.* . . . Wanna make sumpin' outta it?"[3]

The glib ballyhoo epitomized the refreshing shift away from the old-fashioned wild-animal melodrama to something more satirical. And when John later tried hooking up Gargantua with a mate in the form of M'Toto, a more demure-sized gorilla that he purchased from a Havana housewife, he in effect launched a gold mine of publicity that thrived on the ever-intriguing question: will they or won't they? The long-reported courtship of the two apes—Mr. Gargantua forever spurning his bride's advances—kept them a box-office hit for as long as they both lived. It was a marvelous move, and nobody has tried claiming credit for it or suggesting that John got the idea from someone else. The new-style circus that was evolving was an extension of John's puckish personality.

"We're going to swing out," he told reporters in 1939, outlining planned innovations in color, form, lighting, costumes, and staging, all about to be given a radical face-lift. The positive 1938 reviews gave John confidence in his producing instincts. Moreover, the 1939 show would be completely his own. Treating few elements of the circus as sacred—other than the ongoing need for top artistry—John took a critical look at every phase of the operation, from the size, shape, and color of the tents to the content and staging values of the program. He moved across the lot like a self-ordained reformer, upsetting a lot of die-hard traditionalists in his path.

Closely behind him came brother Henry, the good-natured diplomat, ready always with a shoulder for the offended to cry on. "Many people thought that John was haughty, that he was unfriendly, that he was unattractive, that he was dictatorial," says Jane Johnson, who served as executive secretary to both brothers. "I suspect he was all of those things. Who had a better right to be, because he was a genius. He definitely had vision. Henry was the practical one, the one who could soothe things over if John went traipsing through saying, 'We're going to do this, we're going to do that. We're going to change this.' Buddy would say, 'Ah, that's all right, we'll do this gradually. My brother John has a wonderful idea. This is going to be very good for you.' "

She was struck by the depth of their dedication: "I had never seen people work the way those boys worked. Every waking hour they were thinking of that circus, thinking of ways they could improve it. . . . John would think things fast and he'd talk to his brother. He would have wonderful ideas. His ideas were big. And if they weren't practical, the boys would work it out together."[4]

Henry provided the perfect complement for his bombastic brother, much as Uncle Charlie had done for Uncle John. Henry was accessible to everyone, and with a warm, friendly pat on the back. After being jilted once, Henry took his tears to Cousin Hester. "Why doesn't she like me?" he sobbed. "I'm really a very sweet guy."[5] Indeed, he was sweet enough to stand happily in John's shadow. It is hard to know how much of what they did was actually thought up by Henry. The glory went either to John or to the brothers as a team. Henry had come up with the brilliant name for Gargantua. How many other things had he casually proposed in his marathon brainstorming sessions with brother John? He was the more literate and sensitive of the two. He showed John unstinting loyalty, and in return he was allowed ample participation. Jane Johnson saw them as duplicating in spirit the working philosophy of their uncles: "They would confer. They worked just like the original Ringlings brothers, worked as a team. They talked things over at night. If they had letter writing to do, Buddy would do the dictating."[6]

"Pure brotherly love" is how Rudy Bundy describes their relationship. A columnist commented, "The most astounding wonder is the brotherly affection of the North brothers for each other. When you see John—wait two feet and you will see Buddy. No secrets barred between these two. . . . Whenever one praises the show, the answer is, 'You will have to give my brother credit for that.' Heaven or earth, hell or brimstone can never come between the two North brothers."[7]

Henry idolized John. Whatever his own aspirations may have been, he put them aside to push for John's success. Henry was valuable, too, as a symbol of family control when John was gone and he stayed on the lot. And he worked well in public relations. One can only speculate to what degree he consciously shaped his role in order to compensate for John's shortcomings.

The circus format they inherited was timeworn, and they wanted, quite naturally, to make a mark of their own, not just say, "Look, we're in charge." John desired to upgrade the production values and achieve more intimacy between audience and artist. He viewed the cavernous six-pole tent—nearly six hundred feet long with fifteen thousand seats, three rings, and four stages, plus dozens of interior quarter poles—as a dinosaur of bigger-than-ever mania. Never mind the rapture of circus fans who superficially judged the stature of a circus by the number of railcars, the sheer volume of grandstand lumber carried, or the total number of seven-act displays on the bill. Even the public at large was conditioned to count elephants and tents.

In the afternoons, sunlight crept through the canvas, canceling any special lighting effects that might be tried. At night, the lights were barely adequate. The acts used their own costumes, creating overall a mishmash of random color schemes. Worst of all, patrons seated in the cheapest general-admission sections, located at the far ends of the tent, were offered a blurred view, at best, of what transpired in the center ring.

John thought the show was top heavy in paraphernalia and lacking in artistic focus. Of course, such criticism has been applied to any circus that dares present more than one act at a time. John was never that conservative. He intended to preserve a cherished American tradition. He only wanted to streamline the concept and develop it more along theatrical lines.

First to the scrap heap were two redundant king poles. A four-pole tent—shorter by two hundred feet and with three efficient rings remaining—would be quite sufficient. Charles Le Maire, given the job title "Ringling's carte blanche circus redesigner," was brought back in 1939 to design another show. He caused a mild uproar in the canvas department when he casually issued a so-called ultimatum from his Sarasota hotel suite: "Tent poles must go! The more poles a show has the more dissatisfied customers it also has, potentially." Old-timers, who included the number of tent poles in the category of prestige matters, were infuriated. Henry North had to assure everyone, as good as the idea might be, that it would not be implemented for some time.

Working in a less-controversial area, North and Le Maire decided to add box seats around the center sections, a gesture directed at the rich with money to spend. And by reducing the length of the tent, they would be giving their humbler patrons in the end seats a break by bringing them closer to all of the action. Consequently, another item for the museums were the four stages that routinely had been used to fill up the old six-poler. It meant fewer areas of expected action to fill, fewer acts to book, and fewer railroad cars needed for transport.

Le Maire specified a deep-blue shade of canvas, gold king poles, silver quarter poles—another departure that rankled the old guard. How could anything other than white canvas be called a real circus tent? The artistic benefits, however, were well reasoned. The improved lighting effects being planned could now be enjoyed in the matinees, too, for the darkened tent would keep the sunlight from interfering. A customary cluster of lights around the center poles was replaced by individual metal poles equipped with lamps and placed at intervals around the track. Spotlights and color tints were ordered. The bandstand and back-door areas were enhanced with neon-style borders. Blackouts between numbers were devised. It mattered not to John how many hundred poles might encircle the hippodrome, how many grandstand stringers and jacks he could boast in his inventory. What he cared about was the color and rhythm, the clarity and impact of the performance itself.

Comfort under the big top, never much to advertise, was another issue he and Henry addressed: how to combat scorching-hot Iowa afternoons. Air-conditioning the tent was not a completely original notion. Two years earlier, it had been tried out on Charles Hunt's Eddy Bros. Circus, a small truck show. Hunt was persuaded by Charles J. Meher to install one of his air-cooling units on a pole near the reserved-seat section. It had a fairly refreshing effect on the immediate area.

To accomplish the same in a vastly larger tent, the Norths brought in their own engineering experts. Eight specially built wagons were equipped with air-cooling apparatus and placed around the perimeter of the tent. The cooled air was pushed through canvas tubes that stretched from the wagons to sixteen openings in the tent's roof. If everything worked, there would be no more customers fanning themselves frantically with circus magazines or slurping through melted snow cones for relief. So be it if concession sales dropped. Johnny was no longer a candy butcher, anyway.

The Norths moved so fast that they developed a reputation for bold, innovative departures almost overnight. In truth, the circus had been evolving for years, but at a much slower pace. When Sam Gumpertz was in charge, he started replacing the old sunburst wagon wheels, which city officials were claiming damaged their streets, with pneumatic tires. He created a pillared aluminum marquee for the main entrance, decidedly more modern looking. Thinking of his employees' well-being, Gumpertz added a hospital car to the train, and he had come up with the idea for a canvas covering that extended from the dressing tent to the back door of the big top, thus ensuring performers a rain-free trek between changing costumes and playing to the house.

The colorful opening pageants, too, had long been a mainstay on the program. If naysayers wanted to complain about the ones now being presented, they could be reminded of such epics, produced by Ringling Bros. in the teens, as "Joan of Arc" or "Cinderella," the latter requiring 1,370 performers (mostly costumed roustabouts) and 735 horses—a likely overstatement that, nonetheless, proves the point. As innovative as they were, almost everything the North brothers did was rooted in some tradition, however embryonic. It was their courage to transform things dramatically, using the best creative minds available, that made the difference.

In *Circus Kings,* Henry provides this rationale:

As we saw it, the mood of the American people was vastly different in the thirties from what it was in the rip-roaring twenties. Then they had felt themselves hurtling forward into a future of irresistible progress. So they looked fondly over their shoulders at a seemingly serene past. Progress had been stopped dead by the depression; and the zest had gone out of living. The mood was now one of *Weltschmerz,* world-woe. The past was thoroughly discredited by the hardships of the present. In their stagnation, people looked, not too hopefully, to the future. They sought a 'new deal,' a Brave New World.[8]

That is what John and Henry were about to give them under the big top.

Dream Seasons

The 1939 show opened with a Le Maire–designed spec, "The World Comes to the World's Fair." Then came such arresting new features, all making their American debut, as England's tightwire comic, Hubert Castle; the Pilades from Italy, who performed somersaulting leaps over massed elephants; and high-wire thriller the Great Arturo. Returning for well-deserved encores were the Cristianis, the Flying Concellos, Terrell Jacobs, Pallenberg's Bears, aerialists Albert Powell and Torrence and Victoria, dressage rider William Heyer, and other reassuring names. Another new headliner, Rosello, caused the biggest stir with his startling "Man in the Moon" routine aloft. Unfortunately, he fell to serious injuries the second night out, losing his grip while descending to the ground at the completion of his turn. He was gone for the season, the show's twenty-six thousand dollars worth of advertising paper invested in his promotion down the drain.

Reviews were generally excellent, only *Variety's* Jack Pulaski finding the leaner program to be somewhat shy of adequate thrills. "The Ringling outfit," he reported, "has been geared for lower operating nut than last season . . . by replacement of name turns. Show seems to be up to form with lapses here and there."[1] Pulaski was tickled by the talk of Gargantua's "British accent" (supposedly acquired during the gorilla's winter stint in London) and loved Rosello, the doomed aerialist. *The Billboard* buzzed over the revised Ringling format, acknowledging that while the show had been bigger in past years, it had "never uncorked so much entertainment voltage that has been so easy to watch and enjoy."[2] From the *New York*

Times came an inconclusive write-up, the unbylined writer mostly amused by the artificially dispensed aromas of lilac, honeysuckle, and tea rose that "hissed into the air" over the sawdust. Publicist Frank Braden had informed the reviewer that the idea of perfuming the circus had been tried out on the road during the previous summer tour. Another novelty that charmed the *Times* was Lulu (Albertino), "the lady clown," whose appearance marked a debut for the distaff side in the traditionally all-male clown alley. Lulu paraded in spec as a Scottish bagpiper and turned up later in greasepaint.

The scribes up in Boston registered unqualified approval, knocking the program only for excessive length. And once the tents went up for the canvas tour and all the new physical changes could be appraised, critics gave it a thumbs-up endorsement. The improved sight lines clicked on the public-relations level, as did the new lighting effects. Could the same be said of the "air conditioning," reported to work "in fits and starts"? From Jane Johnson: "It really didn't cool the tent. You can't cool a tent. It was helpful but it became very expensive and it meant extra wagons and extra men. If it had worked it wouldn't have made any difference because the circus was making money."[3] The public eagerly embraced the idea of sending cool air into the tent, maybe more so than exotic scents, even if its impact was negligible. Reports varied confusingly, *Variety* at one point figuring the innovation had "helped considerably to strengthen revenue." Or was it Gargantua's accent that did the trick? It is difficult to pinpoint the specific reasons why crowds line up to buy tickets. By season's end, the Norths had an encouraging profit on their hands, the press and public affectionately on their side.

The 1940 edition took John's ideas a few steps further. Le Maire was thanked, paid off, and sent on his way. In his place came Max Weldy, famed designer of the Folies-Bergère, who created the colorful, overly formal spec "The Return of Marco Polo." What distinguished the show more than Weldy's imprint were twelve new acts, several of them showstoppers, each listed in the program under a prominent FIRST TIME IN AMERICA headline. Topping the group was Alfred Court, a beguiling, mild-mannered Frenchman who worked a magnificent spread of animals, including black jaguars, black panthers, pumas, African and Indian spotted leopards, a mountain lion, and a Siberian snow leopard. He had brought to the United States fifty-two animals in all, and his gentle technique of control—avoiding the sound and fury of whip, gun, and chair—made audiences enamored of him.

Other standouts on the bill were single-trapeze swinger Elly Ardelty, a wow of a looker who sold her act, and juggler Massimilliano Truzzi, whose rapid-fire style rivaled that of the late Rastelli. Douglas Whyte scored well with his basketball dog stars. Dressage exponent Roberto de Vasconcellos cut a dashing figure in the saddle. The Cristianis were as wonderful as ever, as were the never-disappointing Yacoppis, still with Ringling after a decade, piling up impressive five-man-highs from springboard takeoffs. Rounding out the list of newcomers were the Ritters, Rola Rola, Adrianna and Charly, and the Akimotos in the acrobatic sphere; the Lopez Trio and the Wolthings in the aerial category. Critics fell uniformly into line with praise, and the entire production was televised by NBC on April 25, a first for the circus. Johnny was roasted by the Dexter Fellows Tent of the Circus Saints and Sinners Club of America.

Crowds flocked to Madison Square Garden, where business was termed a "dream record" by the experts, even more impressive considering that the run did not span, as was usually the case, Easter week, with its built-in box office enhancement. Thousands were turned away up at Boston after a slow start suddenly soared in the wake of cheering notices. Other cities along the route delivered overflow turnouts. The public responded with glee, one Atlanta fan declaring, "This has got the old circus beat a mile!" Salt Lake City drew twenty-five thousand people in one day. Old-timers compared business to the Roaring Twenties. The bookeepers concurred, calling it the best season since 1929.

John and Henry North were acclaimed by the press and credited by trade observers for giving the circus world a new set of standards to live by. "The North bunch has the punch and push that made the Ringling brothers a household name," wrote one fan to *The Billboard*. From Justin Edwards, a press agent, came the prediction their work would be "watched with great interest and no doubt heralded a new era for the circus, regardless of the tearful protests of the die-hards."[4]

In the shadows of the Ringling revolution, other shows looked even more tawdry and out of date. A raft of articles published in *The Billboard*, written by both pros and fans, addressed the need for improved standards. One was titled "Circus at the Crossroads," another "Is Circus Really Slipping?" Eugene Whitmore summed up best what a lot of people who lived in the present were saying:

> The paying customers are not particularly bothered by whether a show has 70 or 200 cars of lumber. What the customer—the cash customer—wants

is a show that will keep his heart pounding a little faster, and which will at least a few times during an evening, give him a good belly laugh. The North brothers aim to offer just such a show, and if, when the trains pull out of Sarasota, there happen to be two or four or six or even ten cars more or less, I do not believe they care. . . .

They say, I have heard at least a dozen times, that the riding was the best ever seen in the Ringling show. Yet the Cristiani family has been around for several years. The truth is that many people are really seeing the superlative riding of that great circus family for the first time—they have had too many things to divert their attention. Now that they have the Cristianis to watch, they really watch them and enjoy them. And we submit that the Cristianis are enough for anybody to watch at one time.

When we begin to analyze all the things the North brothers have done, we realize that it was high time for action. . . . There is showmanship on the Ringling show today that there never was in my time, and I haven't missed a Ringling or a Barnum show, or the combined show, since the big feature was a horse that went up in a balloon.[5]

Those were days of unpredictable excitement. Next to the creative forefront came industrial designer Norman Bel Geddes, who had just enjoyed major success at the 1939 New York World's Fair with his Futurama, seen by twenty million people. Geddes came up with plans for a modernized midway: the sideshow banners to be redone in current poster art; painted panels depicting jungle scenes to be placed above, below and between the animal wagons in the menagerie top; the dens to be better illuminated within.

Geddes became as disenchanted as Le Maire had over the maze of tent poles obscuring customer views. The canvas department was again thrown into a tizzy when the designer unveiled his own visionary concept: a poleless tent suspended from exterior cables strung between four massive towers. Geddes proposed constructing a smaller prototype version of the tent as a place in which to exhibit "Mr. and Mrs. Gargantua the Great," the newlyweds about to embark on their first tour. The air-conditioned cages occupied by the respective spouses would be placed back to back—allowing them mating contact should they so desire—three levels of walkways installed in front, affording patrons an intimate glimpse of the hairy honeymooners.

Slated to rise the following season, if all went well, would be a big top without poles, thirty-two times larger than the prototype tent. The intriguing Geddes blueprints were reproduced in an issue of *Popular Science*.

And in the circus magazine, the lead article, "The Sky's the Limit" described Geddes as being "fired by the enthusiasm and vision of John Ringling North."6 A photograph of the two shows John examining Norman's models for the proposed new physical layout. Dressed in a pin-striped suit, his handsome faced composed in quiet confidence, John looks as impressively—and gracefully—in control as he ever would.

Geddes was also given the performance to design, and his ideas helped take it closer to a more unified work. He infused the principal spec, "Old King Cole and Mother Goose" with elements of humor, and it appeared as the fifth display on the program, marking the first time in the show's history that spec did not come first. Max Weldy stayed on the payroll to costume the aerial ballet, "Birdland," featuring Elly Ardelty, whose compelling beauty and selling power, now well appreciated by all, merited top treatment. Two other production numbers were woven into the show: an equestrian slanted romp, "Evening in Central Park," and another first of sorts for the Ringling show, a grand finale. For the latter, trapeze star and teacher Art Concello assembled a line of fifty-six women to appear in patriotic attire. The finale replaced a part of the show certain to be lamented by some of the diehards: the customary Roman hippodrome races, which had always brought the performance, at least theoretically, to a rousing finish.

The format into which the show was still evolving was no doubt influenced by the rising popularity of ice shows, a new form of entertainment that emerged in the late 1930s, in which various solo skating turns were interspersed with lavishly costumed ensemble numbers. Then, too, it was another step forward for the three-ring circus, extending itself artfully beyond the old swinging-ladder routines and multi-equestrian displays.

In consultation with Geddes on the tenuous subject of dance under the big top, John and Henry decided late one January night that they just had to have Albertina Rasch, the prima ballerina who had choreographed a string of hit musicals, among them the Ziegfeld Follies and more recently the current wow, Gertrude Lawrence's *Lady in the Dark*. She said yes to the offer and was soon down in Sarasota's spring sunshine figuring out a few basic steps that could be learned and executed, in a generally upright posture over sawdust, by a class of showgirls better noted for acrobatic stamina than dainty footwork.

Plenty pleased with the roster of artists he had signed in 1940 and faced with the difficulty of scouting new acts abroad during the war, John decided to bring most of them back. He counted on the new production trappings and the pizzazz of his biggest individual stars—the Cristianis, Truzzi, Alfred Court, Ardelty, and the Yacoppis—to create the expected thrills. This Norman Bel Geddes version of the circus opened in New York City on April 7, 1941. Madison Square Garden was ablaze with a kaleidoscope of colors: sawdust tinted reddish pink in the outer rings, white in the center, blue on the hippodrome track; bunting draped liberally from the rafters in hues of blue, green, white, and silver.

The stark changes were received by the critics with a mixture of awe and apprehension. "Now it looks more a spectacle than circus—more Broadway in the Ringling show than before," commented Jack Pulaski in *Variety*, reasoning that since new European acts were impossible to come by, it was "logical to make the performance a sight show." He greeted "Old King Cole" as "the most ambitious parade yet in a circus," cheered the retirement of the hippodrome races and aftershow concert, dubbing it "an obsolete aftermath that hasn't meant anything for years."[7] *The Billboard*'s reviewer much favored the new layout, writing that it "teems with color, novelty," with reservations about Truzzi, for "missing tricks more often than he accomplished them" and overextending his stay in the ring, and for the pitifully few chances given the clowns to strut their stuff.

Business took off like wildfire, shows at Madison Square Garden averaging 11,000 paying visitors each. About 600,000 people spent an average of two dollars per ticket, easily swelling the total gate to an all-time high during the twenty-eight-day, fifty-five-performance stand. "What practically everyone agrees," reported *The Billboard*, "is that it's the best costumed, best lighted, and best presented circus in the big show's history."[8] (The old Garden had seen healthy turnouts, too, but seated fewer than 10,000 spectators, compared to the new setup's 14,500 chairs.)

The season was a ticket-selling sizzler, and once the tents went up, the restyled Geddes midway added to the sales pitch. As skilled an architect as he was, though, not all of Geddes's ideas proved workable. The six twenty-seven-foot steel pylons he placed on the entrance grounds—between which were strung bunting and banners—each weighed a depressing sixteen hundred pounds. They may have enhanced the midway, but they did not enhance the morale of the workingmen assigned to lug them off and on the wagons. Then there was the new menagerie tent, made of red canvas, which had the nauseous effect under a beating sun of making the people inside it look yellow and sickly.

Inside the blue big top, now seating around eleven thousand—the reserved sections rising twenty-one rows, the blues twenty-four—customers were greeted by smartly outfitted ushers in dark blue pants with gold and red stripes, baby blue gold-braided jackets with red trimmings, white dickeys, and blue pearl hats. The show was a revelation of all things new and glorious under the sun, inspiring its publicists to proclaim that "the spirit of big top fiesta seizes the circus goer the instant he or she sights the lot."[9]

Everybody wanted to experience it. The brothers North had created a total environment rooted in the lure of circus and yet elevated to a startling new level of visual enchantment. In Philadelphia, every perform-ance was a turnaway. The sideshow there enjoyed its biggest week ever. Overflow houses greeted Ringling in Ohio cities, where often thousands were "strawed" at the ends of the tent, a sea of patronage covering most of the track and necessitating the elimination of parts of the program. Fifteen thousand souls jammed the tent in Springfield, Massachusetts. Several thousand more were told, "Sorry, no more room." Cleveland drew sixty thousand in four showings, Detroit seventy-four thousand in four days. The circus played to a record-breaking twelve turnaway night crowds in a row on its way west through New England and upper New York state. Best-ever gates were logged in Chicago. A stop in Denver, as told by Henry to the trades, netted the largest advance sale ever and the largest advance for any show ever to play the Mile-High City, the largest one-day sale, and the largest audience, a seemingly impossible feat, considering that the tent might seat thirteen or fourteen thousand in an overflow situation and that the previous record crowd, reported at Houston in 1937, was alleged to be eighteen thousand people.

Newspaper reviews along the route enthused over the "Old King Cole" spec, the new animal-cage motifs, the air-conditioning effects, and the music. Acts drawing the most praise were the Cristianis, as usual; the Shyrettos; Truzzi; Ardelty; Hubert Castle; Roberto de Vasconcellos; the Fernandez troupes; and all the flying routines executed by the Concellos, the Randolls, and the Comets. Arthur Court's exhibition was whimsically diverse: lions, tigers, and bears cavorting in one ring; a similar contingent plus black jaguars and Great Dane dogs in another; black and spotted leopards, pumas, cougars, panthers, jaguars, and ocelots in the center. In toto, the twenty-one-display program packed a lean, tight wallop.

"RINGLING BROTHERS HEADED FOR BIGGEST SEASON IN SHOW'S HIS-TORY," rang one trade headline. "RINGLING BROS. GETTING TOP COIN IN 58 YEAR HISTORY," screamed another. Business almost everywhere was reported at overcapacity. San Francisco and Oakland were certainly no exceptions, and a ten-day run in Los Angeles netted a nifty $230,000, drawing 120,000-plus customers and giving thousands more the "Sorry, no more seats" sign on Saturday and Sunday nights. Straw was placed on the track to accommodate more overflow crowds as the show swung eastward, back toward the Florida fall. Closing in Miami on November 22, the tour was declared "the best ever."[10]

Indeed it was. John had to be thrilled. He and brother Henry had realized the sort of dream season that all troupers long for but few ever have. To be sure, business benefited greatly from the burgeoning wartime economy, which put amusement dollars into the pockets of Americans once again at work. And yet all circuses on the road did not reap the same golden harvest. What gave Ringling the edge? Showmanship spelled the difference. Mr. and Mrs. Gargantua the Great. Norman Bel Geddes. Albertina Rasch. Smartly attired ushers. Alfred Court and Truzzi and the Cristianis. Mother Goose. Thin, promising shafts of cool air trickling down upon a public willing to believe in a fine idea yet to be perfected.

Nobody dared question the vision of John and Henry Ringling North at this towering moment in their lives. The glory they had earned was theirs to savor, though with it came added temptations. While John's success gave him more leverage in dealing with the state of Florida, whose attorney general had launched a campaign to oust him as estate executor, it also increased his self-confidence to a dangerous degree. And if the darker events during this period (to be detailed shortly) have been withheld, such is out of respect for the crowning achievements of the moment and out of a desire not to detract from the glowing aura of that triumphant 1941 season, a watershed in Ringling history.

From his toddler days forward, John North loved fancy attire. (Courtesy of Countess Ida von Zedlitz-Trützschler)

North's classbook photo, Yale Class of 1926. (Courtesy of Alfred C. Mohr, class secretary)

North at the construction site of the 1939 New York World's Fair. (Courtesy of John Ringling North II)

Long before TV nature shows, Americans thrilled to the sights and smells of exotic creatures in the circus menagerie tent. (From the collection of Timothy Noël Tegge)

Photogenic Gargantua the Great, North's single most publicized attraction. (From the collection of Timothy Noël Tegge)

Tiger, tiger, gently through the hoop. (Photo by Ted Sato)

Unloading the trains at dawn: sunburst wagon wheels and rubber-tired trucks symbolize modernization during the North era. (From the collection of Timothy Noël Tegge)

North, left, with Art Concello and William Curtis at a 1948 Sarasota publicity bash for the new Concello-designed seat wagon. (From the collection of Timothy Noël Tegge)

The delightful Doll Family, at Sarasota winter quarters in the 1940s, charmed sideshow crowds for many years. (From the collection of Timothy Noël Tegge)

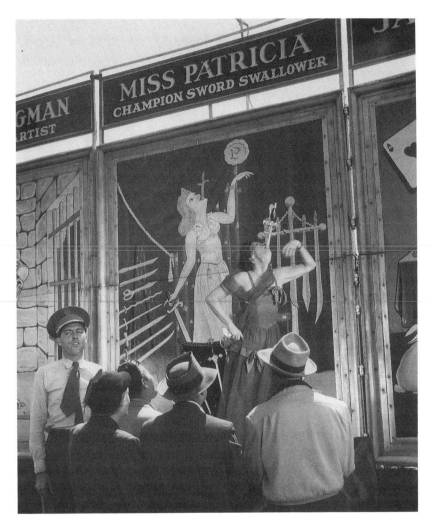

The old circus: a sword swallower makes a pitch for patronage at the sideshow. (From the collection of Timothy Noël Tegge)

Aerial star Pinito Del Oro, seen here with her husband and assistant, was one of North's favorite performers. (From the collection of Timothy Noël Tegge)

Unus, "Talk of the Uni verse," first appeared on the Ringling show in 1948. (From the collection of Timothy Noël Tegge)

High-wire soloist Josephine Berosini, a star of the 1954 edition. (Photo by Ted Sato)

Francis Brunn, ranked among the greatest jugglers of all time. (From the collection of Timothy Noël Tegge)

Art Concello, left, with North, circa 1948, photographed for a shirt advertisement. (Photo by Maxwell Coplan, from the collection of Timothy Noël Tegge)

The brothers North: John, left, with Henry in 1954. Frank McClosky, right, was made their general manager that year. (Photo by Ted Sato)

Sawdust and serenity: the big top in its reigning glory on a Washington, D.C., lot. (Photo by Ted Sato)

Elephants in Tutus

Success grants the eccentric more freedom, drives the social climber higher. John's accumulating credits were exceptional: enthusiastic reviews, sensational box office, the marvelous Gargantua ballyhoo, an attractively revamped big-top setting and performance, control of the show back in family hands.

Florida officials were suitably impressed, some giving John the political backing he needed to seek his goals. "We long for the day when you can control and own the circus stock," said Nathan Mayo, secretary of agriculture.[1] Even John's opponents had nice things to say. He was complimented on his astute handling of the circus by Judge W. T. Harrison, when ordered, along with his mother, to post a joint one hundred thousand dollar bond guaranteeing their proper performance as coexecutors of the estate (they were accused of misappropriating Oklahoma oil interests for themselves). Not liked enough, though, by the state attorney general, still seeking to have their executorship ruled invalid by the courts. All the while Johnny ran ahead, exploiting every chance to increase his political clout in state-government circles and enhance his producing image.

If at times he came off as brash and unfeeling, more preoccupied with business decisions than human needs, he had the devotion of his brother, Henry, to lend the reassuring impression that he respected family ties, too, that down deep he was a caring person himself. Part of the reason for John's growing aloofness was his natural inclination to delegate power to his underlings, another of the many traits inherited from or patterned after his famous uncle. Easy to do or not, it was imperative that he trust in those beneath him, given the overwhelming demands made on his time by matters of the estate, the haggling with various union leaders, and by his own penchant for night life.

John scarcely had time to fuss over all the details that went into the making of a circus program, from how to arrange the acts (whom to spot where and when) to the fine-tuning of costume coordination. Although he involved himself in production meetings and passed informally on costume sketches (rarely countering the designer's intent), John did not hover over his staff to any degree. He spent far more of his time (a habit of necessity he would expand in the years to come) touring abroad in search of new acts for the Greatest Show on Earth. Once booked, they were entrusted to Fred Bradna and Pat Valdo for general supervision, Max Weldy for costume fittings, and the directors and choreographers for placement in the ensemble numbers and tips on how to fake it as dancers.

John's mode of hiring people rarely included conventional formalities. When he decided, acting on a capital suggestion from Henry, that Arthur Concello would make an ideal manager, he first dispatched Henry to feel Art out. Art told Henry he wanted to hear the words from John himself. Even then Art did not immediately agree to the job offer. He held out for a while, seeking the best of all possible terms. Concello was still a top flyer, both he and wife Antoinette turning triple somersaults with aplomb. And he was managing half a dozen flying troupes, three of them with Ringling. He trained countless flyers at his own special school in Bloomington, Illinois. He took in royalties from all this.

North kept badgering him to take the job. Concello's frustrating indifference provoked a bold gesture from North, usually a miserly negotiator: "Take *any* salary you want!" Concello was now pacing Madison Square Garden with a managerial air. Meanwhile, John called George Griffin, the show's treasurer, based in Sarasota, and told him to appease Concello without question. "Anything he wants, it's okay." Art didn't take a paycheck for a month or two, but for all intents and purposes he was running the show. Finally, he called up Griffin.

"Ah, say, ah, how much money does North get?"

Griffin reluctantly gave the manager-designate the figure.

"Well, let me see," said Concello, "Ah . . . I shouldn't take more than North."[2]

Griffin agreed.

Concello named his salary, the exact amount North was being paid, and with that he became general manager of Ringling Bros. and Barnum & Bailey Combined Shows, Inc.

John was that bohemian in many, many ways. A born producer, he placed examplary trust in his managers and directors. He drew his reputation from what they, rather than he, had to offer. This made him equally vulnerable to bad direction and bad advice. There was the embarrassment of a half-baked Wild West shindig, produced by John for the New York World's Fair of 1939 and 1940, titled "Cavalcade of Centaurs." John was asked by the fair president, Grover Whalen, to concoct a "gigantic horse show." Even before it went into rehearsal, such as it was, John complained to the press that he had been pressured into the chore by Manufacturers Trust Company, those New York bankers who had lent him the million dollars he needed to put the family back in control of the circus.[3] Why John resented the assignment, which offered the promise of additional glory and profit in the New York spotlight, remains a puzzle. Perhaps he knew from the outset that Wild West shows were passé. He had already disbanded his own from the circus aftershow. Here it was again, rearing its dusty head in another venue, taunting him to make it relevant to the times. How?

John took the easy, sleazy way out. He signed on a disparate group of riders: Cherokee Indians cheaply secured from Oklahoma; *charros* from Mexico City; Argentine gauchos; a friend of his, Bill Sterling, former head of the Texas Rangers, who rode horses mainly for pleasure; a bunch of Kentucky horsemen; an Arabian sheikh from the Middle East; and sixteen women, hired from a local model agency to create the coup de scandal. One of them asked for details. "You'll ride around naked on a horse," replied John.[4]

What he puckishly envisioned was a mounted Lady Godiva chorus. The budget approved for all this was twelve thousand dollars a week, with a thirteen-week guarantee. When Whalen heard of the nudity, however, he promptly canceled the sheikh's appearance and had his light men devise ways for focusing their wattage onto the grandstand, away from the ladies; he was unable to dissuade North from dignifying his risqué review. The two gentlemen soon weren't speaking, and Whalen forbade North from publicizing the event. With muted fanfare, it opened one night. Hours before, a nudity ban had been imposed on the show, but John counseled one of his models, Ann Wilson, to the contrary. The stage was set for a wild surprise.

In the premiere were Mayor La Guardia, dwarfed under a stately

Stetson hat, and Whalen himself, sporting a pencil mustache, both astride ancient cow ponies. Following was Wilson, who in full view of the crowd tossed aside, first her Indian blanket, then a handkerchief and feather tied around her head. She now rode au naturel, the two politicians ahead of her horse looking back over their shoulders in gawking disbelief. The next morning, Johnny was called on the carpet by Whalen and relieved of his duties. The show went on in censored form, attracting little interest from fairgoers.

There wasn't much comedy. There weren't many good riders. The best feature was thought to be the closing number, in which the sixteen girls galloped gigglingly around the track, according to *The Billboard,* "in little more than blond prop tresses."[5] Max Weldy supplied the scant garments, Pat Valdo stood by as personnel consultant. Whalen downplayed the travesty, which bore little relevance to the fair's reaching theme, "The World of Tomorrow." The unwanted offering was quickly dubbed a turkey, losing ten thousand dollars a week.

Maybe John was ahead of his time. In conception, the crazy patchwork of amateur and ethnic riders and galloping burlesque queens seems hilariously slanted for a more hip, high-camp audience that did not yet exist. Or it may have been just the wrong forum in which to unleash it. John walked away from the fiasco fully dressed and collected his weekly $750 stipend for the guaranteed thirteen-week period. He did not take the flop any more gracefully than he had resisted undertaking it in the first place. Fair officials, he asserted, had refused to stand by him. He said it made him sick "to see the show with my name on it sacrificed because of amateur efforts, mad showmanship, and disorganization."[6] Whalen had also been left with a sick feeling. He substituted in John's place John Krimsky, who couldn't find a way for redeeming the show. The ingredients for workable fair entertainment just weren't there.

Another embarrassment John suffered concerned an alleged attempt on his part to ban his performers (those under contract to appear in the 1940 edition) from participating in 1939 winter Shrine Circus dates produced by Orrin Davenport. The edict, as it was termed, appeared on a placard posted at the Sarasota quarters and supposedly led performers to fear that their contracts would never be renewed again if they sought work with Davenport. As reported on by *The Billboard's* Leonard Traube in his feisty column "Out in the Open," Davenport, who by custom had rented equipment and animals from the Ringling organization, decided not to and was thus "made a leper from whom everyone in the seasonal employ of the Ringling corporation must shy." Traube lashed out at the North boys, calling them "the poobahs who run the show," labeling their tactics "totalitarian," their corporation "soulless." Comparing them to their uncles, he wrote, "The Norths had better count 10 before they get mad and decide to scrap the sound business principles and employer-employee relations built up by their forebears lying in revered graves."[7]

Two weeks later, a letter from Henry North addressed to the editor of *The Billboard* was printed in Traube's column. In it, Henry rebutted any so-called edict or placard containing such as "absolutely untrue." And he claimed that no such policy had ever existed or ever would. Nonplused by the diatribe of his critic, Henry quipped, "I am sure that you will agree that we should not be open to any severe criticism for not going to your Mr. Traube in connection with rehiring acts." He did leave himself open for an easy counterattack, which Traube was ready to issue in a subsequent column, by pointing out, "It is clearly stated in our performer's agreement with contractors that the show wishes to some extent to influence the type of work and place of exhibit to be done by contractors while under contract to the circus."[8]

The alleged edict erupted into a bitter controversy that would haunt John until his dying days. For the first time, he faced real animosity from members of his own organization as well as from the press. Whether or not he intended to follow through on such a threat—real or implied—was difficult to prove. Was an artist's contract allowed to expire because of her playing a Davenport date or because her act had lost its appeal before Ringling audiences? It was never considered a good practice to engage the same acts year after year, and John, in particular, affected some seasons a greater turnover in personnel than his predecessors had done, preferring as he did to offer the public shows infused with novelty. "John didn't like it," comments Art Concello. "He'd bring acts over from Europe. Give 'em thirty weeks work. They'd go to Detroit [for a winter circus]. The customers would come to us the following season, saying, 'I saw that act with Shrine!' "[9]

Nonetheless, circus artists became angered over the edict, and Henry faced the thankless task of assuring them, to the contrary, that no such warning had been made. One disgruntled employee, name withheld, wrote a letter to *The Billboard*, arguing, "It is quite obvious that the ruling *was* made, and in most cases abided by, otherwise how come all those regulars who play the Shrine dates year after year cancelled so suddenly?" Referring to the dismal 1938 tour, the writer asked, "Does he [North] remember the unlimited loyalty of the performers when he asked us for our help to move the show [Barnes-Ringling], and how we worked putting it up and taking it down that *his* business might survive? Is that gratitude? . . . These are some of the problems we would as performers like to have John or Henry North answer, but unfortunately, like those of us who had to cancel Mr. Davenport's [Shrine] dates to save our necks, we must keep our mouths shut."

In fact, a 1939 agreement form stipulated that "from the date of this contract through the beginning of the season, person will not appear in [a] New York circus." That left virtually the entire field open in every other American city.

If John's initial threat was as forbidding as some thought it to be, he diplomatically retreated, thereafter making it impossible to draw a direct link between an act's working an off-season date and its being barred, as a result, from ever ever again appearing under his aegis. Over the years, many of John's top—and favorite—artists played the Davenport winter circuit and still returned to work again for him. In fact, two acts signed for the 1942 season, the Wallendas and Roland Tiebor's Seals, both fit this category. Tiebor joined the show a few days late in New York, having just motored in from a Shrine date in the late spring.

The controversy did raise the curtain on a seemingly colder and more heartless side of John which called to mind a similar streak in John Ringling. Like uncle, like nephew. John was learning to distance himself from the company, maintaining contact with only his top managers and production people. He moved deeper in his all-night social worlds outside the circus. He loved the New York scene, loved associating with and being noticed in the presence of celebrities and artists. He was drawn to them, as were they to him. He attended Broadway shows, hummed the music of Porter and Kern and Rodgers, enjoyed staying up half the night at the Stork and 21 clubs. He courted the company of witty, smart-acting people, dilettantes or doers, using his power and prestige to lure them to his table.

He had the charm and money to engage the show world's best creative minds. His remarkable success with Norman Bel Geddes stirred his restless imagination. He wanted more. He saw the circus rings and the hippodrome track encircling it as his own personal canvas and himself as its Picasso. In this sense, Johnny was quite different from Uncle John, who expressed little such inclination, content to see the same format preserved year after year. Johnny was a powerful creative force in his own right, driven by an almost unconscious need to surprise his audiences continually.

The relationship with Geddes was good, and John remained open to further suggestions, feeling the format still had a ways to go. In what direction, who might say? Miles White, who had been hired by Geddes to design the costumes and who would shortly come into his own doing the same for a new musical by Richard Rodgers and Oscar Hammerstein II, *Oklahoma!* remembers feeling slightly unimpressed with Albertina Rasch's contributions and wondering to his superiors whether they might do better.[10] As White saw it, Rasch worked basically with a line of ballet girls for production frills and the concept was limiting, so the next year he suggested they bring in a director like John Murray Anderson (for whom White had already worked), who might introduce a more theatrical concept. Through Geddes, Murray Anderson was engaged. Actually, much of what Anderson contributed in his first year as circus director extended a format that was by then well into development. What he did inject into many of the specs he staged, sometimes very effectively, were elements of comedy and drama, which made them that much more interesting.

In *Out Without My Rubbers*, Anderson recalls North's approaching him one summer night in 1941 when the circus was playing in Los Angeles. Would he be interested in staging the next year's edition? Murray was invited to attend the current show, which he found to be "a rather shopworn affair," not a surprising critique for a director of his ego. He easily convinced himself, no doubt, no matter what the show's present quality, that he could make it better.

Thus hired, Anderson arrived for rehearsals the following spring in Sarasota, where his sense of humor, described by some as wicked, had a field day. He was shown about the Ringling estate by Henry. The two were examining a Rubens original in one of Uncle John's galleries when Henry's Great Dane puppy mistook it for a fire hydrant, lifted a leg, and sprayed the masterpiece. Murray was shocked. "It proves his appreciation of art," said Henry.[11]

Perhaps the strangest directorial chore Anderson faced was the staging of a ballet for elephants, an idea John said he had come up with during a visit to Budapest in the pre-Axis days. He had persuaded George Balanchine, the well-known Russian dancer, to choreograph it through a plea presented by Anderson. In turn, Balanchine got on the telephone to recruit a reluctant Igor Stravinsky, noted twentieth-century composer of serious music, for the score.

"Igor," began Balanchine, "how would you like to compose a ballet for some circus elephants?"

"Elephants?"

"Yes."

"How old are they?" asked the maestro.

"Oh," replied George, thinking it over, "well, they are young elephants."

"All right, if they are young," replied Igor, "perhaps I can do it."

John arranged through correspondence with Stravinsky for a fee even lower than the modest one he originally proposed. What John got, however, was a lead sheet of sixteen bars—without harmonies or orchestration. For these, plus a few more notes needed to extend the modest melody line, John ended up putting out much more money. Stravinsky held his own.

Murray Anderson reveled in the Ringling rehearsals, for they gave him an audience of sometimes thousands: the people who paid money to visit the winter quarters. Among the more illustrious who came and went in the early spring to take in the workouts were familiar faces from all over the world: the Sitwells from England, Edith in a great Gothic cloak, her nose pressed against the glass of Gargantua's cage; Schiaparelli from Paris; Drew Pearson and his wife; Edalji Dinshaw all the way from India, his socks held up by golden garters, each bearing an eighteen-carat diamond; Mrs. Oliver Jennings; the John Alden Carpenters, regular Stateside fans.

Murray cast himself in the starring role, badgering the girls like the perennial Forty-second Street director. "Elephants never forget; showgirls do!" he roared, playing gleefully to the grandstands. And he flaunted his penchant for nicknaming the performers and staff. Dressage rider Marion Seifert was "Miss Horse," young Miles White "the Eccentric," Johnny North "the Eagle," Pat Valdo—whose knowledge of the big top Anderson respected—"Mr. Circus." There were far more abusive names, such as "The Cockroach" and "Alcoholics Anonymous."[12]

Over in the elephant area, George Balanchine, a much calmer sort, consulted with the bull man, Walter McClain, on how to make the pachyderms look more balletic. The master found his charges to be true professionals. "Elephants," said Balanchine, "are no harder to teach than ballerinas." Came time to join the two. George told the girls to assume graceful positions in the trunks of their mammoth partners. A few slipped out prematurely, falling onto the sawdust with shrieks. Observing their failure with tact, George suggested, "Try landing on the balls of your feet."

Another celebrity who roamed the grounds was cartoonist Peter Arno of *New Yorker* renown, asked by Johnny to draw for the circus magazine. Arno's contributions were classic. One depicts a luckless aerialist clutching faithfully the shoes of his partner flying above him, not realizing they are no longer attached to his partner's feet. Another portrays a wild animal trainer and his beasts taking refuge in each other's arms as they view, in horror, a tiny mouse in the middle of the ring peering up at them innocently. On the cover are a couple of dancing elephants, one in a tutu coyly resisting the fond embrace of one in brief shorts. The theme of 1942's show was "Gayety." Nothing was considered too sacred for spoofing, not even the wedding of two famous gorillas made the brunt of the humor in "Bridal Bells Ring Out in Clownland."

John's circus of comedy introduced to American audiences the gifted aerial direction of the celebrated genius and French-acclaimed Barbette, a Round Rock, Texas, native who made it big in Europe as a female impersonator on the single trapeze. Barbette was hired through Murray Anderson to arrange the webbing routines for a thirty-six-girl aerial ballet featuring the still-fetching exploits of Elly Ardelty. Another ingenious specialty they created was an enormous balloon figure, "Harry, the Five Story Clown," complete with a contingent of smaller figures, "The Spare Parts," known by such names as Dippy, Dottie, General Nut, Handy Andy, Mme. Lula Flu-Flu, Muscles, Nervy Nat, and King Zula. It would sadly never see the light of a performance, the huge object being too large and cumbersome for the roustabouts to handle with dispatch. John ruefully reminisced over this number for many years, referring to its deletion from the program as one of his biggest disappointments.[13]

The twenty-four-display layout opened in New York on April 9 and sent most of the critics into orbit. "The most sumptious, yet witty, fast stepping and often gripping performance the circus has given us in many seasons," wrote Frederick Woltman in the *World Telegram*.[14] Commented Jack Pulaski in *Variety*: "There is a snap in the performance that is in tune with the war times. . . . It actually lives up to the 'Greatest Show on Earth' billing. . . . It is still the circus, but it attains a higher standard than heretofore."[15]

John T. MacMans of *PM* agreed: "Although nothing new has been added in the death-defying way, the Greatest Show on Earth is greater than ever this year. It is more colorful, better costumed, and better displayed than ever before. . . . It is certainly the first and only show in the world ever to collect under one roof four such illustrious showman as Norman Bel Geddes, John Murray Anderson, George Balanchine and Gargantua."[16] The *New York Times* termed it "a show of extraordinary beauty . . . a circus with the pastel quality of a child's dream." In what might be the only circus review of its kind ever, the *Times* writer raved, raved, and raved about the production numbers to the surprising extent of virtually ignoring all of the actual circus acts themselves. Every float and contingent in the inspiring "Holidays" pageant was described in detail. "Ballet of the Elephants," judged "breathtaking," was also given a full and convincing account.[17] Another *Times* scribe, the esteemed theater critic Brooks Atkinson, took in a performance, too, and added a second endorsement in the form of a Sunday-edition feature story. Commented Atkinson: "It was high time to modernize the circus. . . . What they have given us is the handsomest and fleetest circus of—well, call it the ages. . . . It is drenched in blue sawdust, which gives it a feeling of restful splendor, and the pastel costumes are modern and beautiful. By varying the lighting Mr. Anderson has broken up the sheer mass of the spectacle and directed attention to the most breathtaking events."[18]

Others wondered whether the circus wasn't straying a bit off course. "The circus has gone intellectual," observed the *New York Post*.[19] Robert Sylvester in the *News* called it the "most ambitious modernistic production to date. Some parts of it even look like a night club."[20] Nor did the elephant ballet tickle everyone, *The Billboard* judging it "one of the big hits of the show . . . a sensation when viewed from all aspects,"[21] and *Variety* making but brief mention of it while labeling the Stravinsky score "weird" and "out of place."

The music was a little more than odd, certainly for a circus at the time and certainly for the big ears of the dancing pachyderms, who, in the opinion of bandmaster Merle Evans, "didn't like it much."[22] The strange harmonies of "Circus Polka," as it would later be named, were foreign to them, and they would respond by trumpeting "in unison," according to Murray Anderson, his narrative recollections suspiciously colorful.

To keep the bulls in sync with Stravinsky's mad beat, their handlers were instructed to poke them along. This didn't work very well because the handlers were just as unsure of the erratic rhythms. The circus ballerinas held their own on the two stages they danced over between the three rings of tutu-clad pachyderms. Balanchine's wife, Zorina, had made a guest appearance opening night, dancing in tandem with the principal pachyderm, Modoc. The "Corps de Ballet" was in proud form. Soon after, the precarious formations began to resemble a Peter Arno cartoon come true.

Unhappily for John, the season ahead was nothing to take as lightly.

His flair for novelty had once again mesmerized New Yorkers, who stood patiently in long lines all day long at the Garden to buy tickets. Then adversity entered the picture in a series of problems' and complications and, finally, in a tragic fire that amounted to an unheeded omen.

Into the Net

In a way, John's season of woes began during the 1942 New York engagement when, six days before opening night, he fired his general manager, George Smith. Art Concello, who succeeded Smith, remembers that Smith had a drinking problem and that North felt uneasy trusting the show to Smith's hands while he was away for extended periods. A stern letter by Henry North to Smith confirming his termination stated, "It is useless for me to go into detail recalling to you the various times that you have been warned that a persistence in your neglect of duty would result in your discharge from our service, or to recall to you the chances you have had and the great expense we have gone to."[1] In fact, since taking over the running of the show in 1938, the North boys had made a concerted effort to help Smith straighten himself out, and they had put up with a lot on occasion.

During the 1938 labor strikes while he was evidently intoxicated on the Atlanta lot, Smith, a onetime union organizer, actually took sides with the labor antagonists against the show he was being paid to manage. "Last night, while people's clothes were burning and circus property was being destroyed, you stood outside the circus car and made wise cracks," John wrote Smith the next day. "I know that when you are yourself that is the last thing in the world you would do. I make this suggestion to you for your own good, and for the good of the organization: that you start drinking only two highballs a day or go back to those coca colas which you were drinking last winter in Sarasota. The manager of the circus should be admired and respected at all times."[2]

The Norths had nurtured Smith along for another three seasons. Finally, John either could no longer deal with the problem or he saw superior management material in Art Concello. Nonetheless, George Smith had a strong following and was generally held in high regard by the Ringling family, having worked his way up the Ringling ladder since starting out as a kid in the cook house with the Forepaugh-Sells show, then managed by Al Ringling. Because the press was not told why Smith was abruptly dismissed, its reports tended to imply a lack of good cause for the action, and this cast considerable doubt on the management style of John North.

Another unsettling incident at Madison Square Garden that spring was a violent altercation between Roberto de Vasconcellos and another dressage rider, Arthur Konyot, allegedly over Konyot's son's being given the center ring (in the program, Vasconcellos was listed in the center spot). A nasty fight left Vasconcellos with head injuries and brain damage. Following a long recovery period, he transferred to another show and filed suit against Ringling for failing to protect him from Konyot, about whom he claimed to have warned the management. The circus filed a countersuit seeking to enjoin Vasconcellos from performing elsewhere until the expiration of his contract. The matter was settled out of court, and the undaunted equestrian returned in later years to be featured many more times on Ringling sawdust.

The road tour was plagued with more problems. On the last day of the Philadelphia stand, the musicians, their contract with the show having expired the previous night, went out on strike. North refused the $2.50-per-week raise they demanded. Merle Evans, the bandleader, was caught between his musicians and the management. He decided to back his men on the picket lines, although he assured the press that they were all "perfectly satisfied" with their present salaries and work conditions but were forced to stage the protest. "We wanted to play today, but the union refused to let us."

John and Merle exchanged cordial words while the one passed the other on his way to and from the grounds. Henry North told a reporter that his brother had written to the union president, James Petrillo, offering to sit down at a bargaining table but had not received a reply. If John was so interested, it is odd how cynically he reacted to the sudden walkout. He expressed little or no concern for the band's future once it stood him up. John made snide references to the full houses his show was continuing to draw, evidently unaffected by the vacated bandstand. He boasted that recorded music, in lieu of live musicians, was working out just fine and that on June 4 in Philly, when phonograph records were spun, the circus drew "the biggest cash business" in its history.[3]

Part visionary (taped music would one day come into its own), part negotiator, John flatly stated that the circus and sideshow bands would not be carried "for the remainder of the season and possibly for future seasons." As if his insolence weren't sufficient, one of John's spokesmen added, "The musicians proved to us that we could get along without them and we are convinced."

Perhaps they were right. The elephants managed to go forward in their dirt-stained tutus to the strains of a recording of "Dance of the Hours" from *La Gioconda*, which sounded similar enough to the Stravinsky original, not yet released on wax. Jane Johnson had heard the piece one morning on the radio. She rushed down to the lot and told Henry about it. "It sounds just like the elephant ballet!" Excitedly, they called the station for the title and label, then made a tour of music outlets in search of a copy. They found one and played it that day. The trumpeting elephants approved.[4]

The worst of all troubles occurred in Cleveland, Ohio, on August 4 when one of the dancing pachyderms and a twenty-year veteran, Ringling Rosy— along with three other bulls, Kass, One Eyed Tribly, and Wallace Rose—fell victim to a fire that swept the menagerie tent. One worker speculated that sparks from a passing locomotive had fallen on the canvas. Police arrested Le Mandria Ford, a sixteen-year-old who had boastfully confessed that he and another worker, both recently fired by the circus, had set the menagerie ablaze to get even. In subsequent court hearings, however, the youth's contradictory statements, encompassing both confession and denial, and the testimony of psychiatrists recommending that he be committed to a home for the feebleminded left the judge convinced that he had no case to try.

The tent was destroyed within three minutes. Forty animals died, including the four elephants, thirteen camels, nine zebras, two giraffes, four lions, two tigers, a couple of midget burros, three Indian deer, two brindled gnus, an ostrich, a puma, and a llama, altogether valued by North at over two hundred thousand dollars. Walter McClain marveled that forty-one of his elephants had been spared. Gargantua and M'Toto were miraculously saved, too, the canvas above them doused with water and dropped onto their wagons to form a protective covering while workers fought to pull them out from under the flames.

The devastated troupe added a few replacement animals (a giraffe was lent by the Toledo zoo) and moved on. Business remained generally excellent, except for the Chicago date, where temperatures below forty degrees kept customers away in droves. Those who endured the weather sat on their seats shivering beneath blankets, while the showgirls shivered in their tights. A curiously inept booking decision, for never had the circus played Chicago so late in the year.

Another major problem adversely affecting the show was the onslaught of World War II. The distant fighting cast a pall on the American landscape. The circus was now moving under the graces of a special wartime agency, the Office of Defense Transportation (ODT). There were fewer hands to help set it up and tear it down. Four hundred Ringling personnel had by now enlisted in the armed services, and more were planning to do so at season's end. To reduce the need for manpower, some dates were extended by a day or two, although the extra shows did not always pay for themselves. Yet despite late arrivals, bad weather, and the crippled work force, the season was justly declared "one of the best ever." The route book indicates that 4,120,000 people saw the circus during the 425 performances it gave in the 104 cities it visited, covering 13,008 miles to reach them all before heading back to Sarasota in late fall. That represents an average per-show attendance of nearly 10,000 souls, a record any showman in any facet of the entertainment industry would envy.

Even Sam Gumpertz, now operating director of Hamid's Million Dollar Pier in Atlantic City, had good things to say: "The circus is doing a marvelous business this year. It goes to show the public still wants it. . . . As long as there's a world, my boy, there will be a circus."[5]

For the second year in a row, a dividend was declared at the end of the tour. The remainder of the Manufacturers Trust Company note was paid off to the tune of six hundred thousand dollars. Still left in cash reserve was a sum well exceeding a million dollars. Feeling more secure than ever in their appointed posts, John and Henry announced their intention to keep the circus on the road throughout the war years. They handed to each of their employees this statement, which was reprinted in the year-end route book:

> The management of the Ringling Bros. and Barnum & Bailey Circus thinks it timely and fitting to state its policy and hopes for the future at this critical period in our national history. Through letters from many individuals, wide editorial comment from the nation's press, and direct expression from

the country's Army, Navy, and political leaders, it has been made clear that the public wants the Greatest Show on Earth to carry on during war time. We plan to make next year's show bigger and better than ever in quality and spirit if not in size. . . . D.C. officials have been most sympathetic and cooperative. . . . President Roosevelt personally has expressed his appreciation of the fact that the show is going on. Hard and trying days are ahead of us, but such prospects have never before chilled the American spirit or stopped American Initiative, and we feel that as long as those two qualities are alive, the American Circus, too, will roll on.[6]

Roll on it did, and nearly into oblivion when John's relatives decided they could run the show better than he. John's great success and increasingly bohemian lifestyle had become a source of envy and resentment for his Aunt Edith (Mrs. Charles Ringling). Edith was a strong, assertive woman whose association with the Ringling brothers had given her a slightly imperial complex. The daughter of a pastor, she married Charles Ringling in 1887 when she was eighteen years old and traveled the "mud show" circuit with him during the summer. She became a schoolteacher and proved a tough, inspiring taskmaster at the chalkboard. She was a prolific reader, she exulted in the outdoors (sometimes stayed up half the night hunting or fishing at age eighty), and she was a good musician on the euphonium and the cello. She played the piano well enough to accompany husband Charlie on his Stradivarius violin or the viola. They installed a piano in their private car, the Caledonia, and made music together over the rails.

On circus lots, "she moved through the crowds with unbelievable speed for anyone, let alone an old lady," remembers her grandaughter-in-law, Alice Lancaster. "You just couldn't keep up with her."[7] Edith's decisive vigor provided a fine complement to Charlie's softer nature, and when the latter got caught up in all the petty rivalries with his brother, John Ringling, it has been said that Edith was the one who goaded him to hold his own. After Charles died in 1926, Edith grew more hostile toward her tyrannical brother-in-law, who then carried on as if he alone owned the circus, which he didn't. By virtue of inheriting Charlie's interest, which amounted to a third of the stock, Edith became a key player. And in friendly collusion with Aubrey Ringling, who held another third of the stock, she and Aubrey supervised the removal of John Ringling from power, when he became too ill to carry on, and the appointment, in his place, of Sam Gumpertz.

If this went to her head, Edith was not the first Ringling to suffer from a misleading sense of self-importance. "She thought she was a tremendous business woman," as Alice Lancaster tells it, passing along a story to illustrate. When Edith got the urge to build a dock along the edge of her bayside house (as John Ringling had once done), she boasted to a contractor that she could predict precisely what his estimate would be to do the work. He decided to defer to her quote as being correct and was awarded the contract. He later went all over town telling people he could have done the job for a lot less money, "but I figured it was worth four thousand dollars for her to be right!"[8]

Edith was secure in her illusions. She dominated and spoiled her two children, Hester and Robert, and their offspring. They were an intelligent, educated, and rather witty bunch of people. Robert practiced singing almost daily, his vocal chords taking herculean flight over the grounds. "He had a terrific voice. You could hear him for half a mile," remembers Hester's son, Stuart Lancaster, then a budding actor who organized the respected Palm Tree Playhouse in Sarasota.[9] At dinner they rarely spoke about the circus, a subject fraught with conflicting alliances and emotions. Robert talked about opera, Stuart the theater, and Hester (a teacher, like her mother) about their shopping sprees and social fetes. Sometimes museum patrons accidentally wandered into their house, believing it to be a part of the Ringling estate. On one occasion, thirteen-year-old David Lancaster was confronted by an eccentric woman. He politely asked if he could help her. "No," she said, "I'm one of the originals!" David looked up at her in disbelief and stuck out his belly. "Oh, yeah? I'm originaler!"[10]

Behind all the pretty chitchat, the days of endless pleasure, and the family-subsidized quasi careers, Edith Ringling wanted something more real for Robert, especially when his mediocre opera career began to fade. She began building a case against John Ringling North—against his evident disdain of circus traditions, his flamboyant lifestyle, and his high-handed tactics. He reminded her of his Uncle John, so similar were the two, and Edith reacted in the same competitive manner, pushing Robert to exert himself in circus management as she had once pushed his father. There were plenty of controversial issues connected with the season just past upon which Edith could base an anti-North campaign: the debatable firing of George Smith; the cavalier indifference of John's administration to the striking musicians; the increasing flux of New York artists hired to restyle the program, seriously questioned by some critics; and letters supposedly received from fans around the country asking for a return to "the good old days."[11]

It was the perfect moment, Edith decided, for she and Robert to stand up and set things right. She had, back in late 1941, entered into a pact with Aubrey Ringling, called the Ladies' Agreement, binding them to vote their stock together. This guaranteed them control of the show's destiny. Now they were in perfect accord and well prepared to knock Johnny North off his feet at the upcoming board of directors meeting in January 1943.

Up to that moment, John had been trying to swing a deal with the government whereby the show would play army camps and USO facilities on a nonprofit basis and conduct war-bond drives. John assumed that such an arrangement would waive any restrictions the Office of Defense Transportation might otherwise impose on the movement of the show trains. It had already been requiring permits and had threatened to curtail or ban altogether the movement of circus and carnival trains. John also assumed that, with government backing, the necessary canvas and rope materials would be easier to obtain. Brother Henry's own account portrays John as being fearful of another tragic fire like the one that destroyed the menagerie tent and so many animals in the season just past. Although there are no known records of this specific issue being raised at the 1943 board of directors meeting, Henry has made this concern gravely clear. "Oh, my God, we were terrified all the time. We were understaffed. We had fire watch constantly under the tent. We were on the lookout for everything, of course. Those were perilous times."[12]

Whatever matters were actually discussed at the special board meeting in the guise of rational decision making, they would hardly conceal the personal feuds that seethed below the surface. Before going into the meeting, North confided to Concello that he was about to be ejected from his post.[13] As is generally known, John made his proposal that the circus be toured under the auspices of the U.S. government or be kept back in winter quarters on a caretaker basis for the duration of the war. A silence followed, after which Edith and Aubrey, voting their stock together, "voiced disgust with John's ideas and management."[14]

The final decision came down to whether the circus should be operated as usual. Surprisingly, William Dunn, a Manufacturers Trust Company vice-president who had been in John's camp, cast the deciding vote in favor of keeping it on the road. (Dunn realized that come April, when John's five-year contract to run the show expired, the two ladies would remove him anyway.) Sensing the inevitable power shift, John resigned and his cousin was elected president and chief operating officer of the corporation.

"ROBERT RINGLING TO HEAD RINGLING BROTHERS" rang a headline in *The Billboard*. [15] The circus world was stunned. The story reported the family to be "strong for the old guard." George Smith, who had been supervising the movement of army shows for the government, was rehired to manage, this constituting his "third excursion back into grace." Robert Ringling was on his way to New York to confer with James Petrillo of the musicians' union, determined to get the band back onto the bandstand. And the Loyal-Repensky troupe of horse riders was reinstated on the program to replace the departing Cristianis.

Also to be revived was the six-pole big top. That little thought was given to the added burden the additional equipment would place on a depleted staff suggested a kind of reckless naïveté. Edith, Aubrey, and Robert thought only of the emotional significance of their actions, aimed at pleasing an imagined multitude of fans who would instantly acclaim their true Ringling heritage. They wanted to set themselves apart, as visibly as they could, from the peculiar Mr. John North, middle name not spoken.

A Fire He Didn't Start

Johnny was on the outside now—powerless, not too confident, and barely solvent. He had almost no income to his name, his fees as coexecutor of the estate kept to a minimum by suspicious Florida officials. Some observers of the scene, Merle Evans among them, recall John's suffering through a very difficult period, at times virtually bumming rides around town or borrowing dollars and dimes for taxi fare.

Sadly symbolic of his plight, John's marriage to Germaine Aussey, what little meaning it held to either, was finally put to rest when Germaine announced their separation in 1943. The rumor mills hinted that the husband had been deserted because he was a playboy who had let the circus slip through his fingers and that as a result the lush matrimonial benefits were no longer there for the wife. Germaine had the class to resent this openly in a letter to the press in which she asserted: "I have married Mr. North for love and not for the glamour of the circus. . . . I like this country, and the prospect of living in it with the man I loved appealed to me."[1] Her thoughtful rebuttal could not conceal her basic incompatibility with John's self-centered lifestyle. (The two did remain good friends; Germaine remarried and settled on Long Island. In later years, every spring John would send out his Cadillac to pick up Germaine and her children and bring them to Madison Square Garden in New York to enjoy a new edition of the circus from the producer's private box.)

During these humble times, John drew closer to Rudy Bundy, whom he had met on New Year's Eve in 1940 at the Lida Sarasota Casino. He and Henry had approached the bandleader for the name of a tune he had played that evening. A frustrated musician of sorts, John was naturally drawn to Rudy, a professional who had arrived in Sarasota only three days before, having worked such places as the Bigson Hotel in Cincinnati and the Henry Grady Hotel in Atlanta. For Sarasota, a community then of ten thousand people, a big band was a major event and Rudy was accorded celebrity status. He and John hit it off.

Rudy was one of the very few people who ever got close to John, close enough, at least, to penetrate his well-controlled facade. Of course, the two had a strong mutual interest to share. And Rudy's soothing, easygoing ways gave John a substitute for his brother, Henry, who was off with the navy participating in the North African and Italian invasions. The two palled around almost constantly for a time, right after John was deposed by his relatives. "That's when we got together," Rudy remembers.[2]

Many nights John would end up at the casino or at another venue Rudy worked down on lower Main Street, the Manhattan, and after hours they would go to Ida's house on Bird Key or to John's private car out at winter quarters. They could go on for hours talking about big bands of the era. When Rudy bought himself a house on Lido Beach, he would have John over and would cook for him and they would sit up half the night drinking. There was also wine to indulge in from the Prohibition-days stock in Uncle John's infamous cellar.

"He drank slow," explains Rudy. "He didn't drink all the time. He was a good drinker. And he wasn't one that was gulping it down. If you take one hour to drink a drink, why you lose most of it before you start on the next one."

John liked to jam on the saxophone, and there was always an opening in Rudy's band. How good a musician was he? In Rudy's tactful opinion: "Well, like all college guys, if they played a little, they played."

Rudy wasn't too well heeled himself. Shortly after he opened at the casino, it went into receivership and he was given the opportunity by one of the note holders—of all people, Sam Gumpertz—to keep the doors open and run it himself on a rent-free basis. For several years, Rudy etched out a modest living from the sale of drinks and a small cover charge.

The two began considering alternative business ventures. John's desire to open his own nightclub led them like scavengers one bright morning down to St. Armand's Circle. John pointed to a boarded-up building that had once housed his uncle's booming real-estate firm. He stomped through a thicket of weeds to kick the door in, and they squinted eagerly for a view of the interior. It was not what they expected to find: dusty and old, the floorboards creaking, not too much room. Rudy wondered.

"I know," beamed John, as they walked away, "let's open a nightclub at the John Ringling Hotel!"

Now *there* was an idea, Rudy thought.

"I don't know how many people we'll pull in," John chuckled. "Heck, if nobody comes, you and I will sit down and drink all the drinks ourselves."[3]

Thus was born, in 1944, the M'Toto Room (named after Gargantua's bride), a cozy little space operated for nearly ten years by Rudy. The hotel manager, a chap who retired in the early evening, was happy to have Rudy run the room, which he did with charm and grace. He cut his group down to around six or seven men, still figuring it "a big band for then." The M'Toto Room swayed to the lilting strains of Bundy's dance music, John sometimes joining in with his sax.

The evenings were lively in a small-town sense, and those who hung around late enough might get a rare glimpse of John North's gregarious nature. After two o'clock he would usually invite a few souls—mostly good-looking women—to stay on for additional drinks into the wee hours. Phil and Daisy Hall, who got to know John this way, often just showed up at his urging to supply the dance floor with two warm bodies. For this they were given some drinks and sandwiches.

The Halls recall the congenial host John was: "He'd be the bartender. And he was very kind. He could be very gallant. He was very nice to the people that worked for him. He liked pretty women around, and he appreciated the girls who did the acts in the hotel. He was always very polite. I've never seen him get out of line with anybody around the show."[4]

Phil and Daisy never saw John use his position for sexual gain, an impression that only confirms his known policy (notwithstanding the Chita Cristiani flirtation) of not getting involved with showgirls in his employ. "He chose his women outside of the circus," offers Daisy, "and they were always like starlets, very beautiful."

John's many evenings at the M'Toto Room, and at the other night spots around town, merged one into another like an endless succession of slowly sipped drinks through a blur of hazy sunsets and missed sunrises. He had little, in fact, to look forward to. He once told Rudy, "I'll never go back to the circus until I own fifty-one percent."

The thought of his running the circus again seemed remote at that point. His relatives had assumed management of the show in a successful way. The 1943 tour was a big, profitable winner. If John dared look into the current edition of the circus's program magazine, he would discover the lead story, "Circus by Ringling," heralding the achievements of the other Ringlings and he would find, probably not to his surprise, that the board of directors listing, which had deprived him of his full middle name in 1943, now left out his middle initial as well. Why not? According to the peculiar logic of the circus publicity department, John North was not a Ringling at all.

The "good old days" were on the rebound in the form of a public-relations blitz approved—if not launched—by Edith and Robert to hype themselves as being destined to run the circus. Press chief Roland Butler was cheered to contribute. "Ringlings All" headlined one of his yarns, "A Ringling Son Has Taken in Person His Rightful Place in the Circus Sun" another. Butler's rhetoric alluded to a virtual family resurrection: "Created by Ringlings, run by Ringlings and personally staged by the circus president, Robert Ringling, this year's show sweeps into a still more 'circusy' groove, to the delights of the millions who prefer their tanbark tonic straight." A deceptive reoccurring theme was clear: control of the show was back in the hands of real Ringlings, and the traditional big-top fixtures, things for which they stood—six king poles, white canvas, stages between the rings—were the stuff of true circus, causing old-timers to exclaim, "The Big Show's itself again!"[5]

Top press agents—and Roland Butler was about the best of them all—exert remarkable influence over the way things are perceived by the public and press. Butler's ballyhoo played well to the trades, *The Billboard* joining his bandwagon with a strong sendoff for Robert Ringling. "It will probably take another season or two before the circus really goes back strictly to its own and traditional sphere, unaffected and uninfluenced by non-circus showmanship. That is what Robert Ringling and his ballyhoo associates have in mind when they tell the national public these days that old features are back. . . . Some other romances and attachments being clung to, of course, until the delicate question of complete and unadulterated parting can be approached with care, grace, tact and grade A diplomacy, Robert Ringling gives every indication of being the kind of person who will make the transition smoothly."[6]

Ironically, the kind of circus these self-proclaimed "Ringlings All" brought to New York in 1943—and what they continued to produce the seasons following—slavishly imitated the production concepts of Mr. North. Cousin Robert stuck with Murray Anderson through his first year at the producing helm, partly because the Broadway stager's two-year contract included the 1943 opus and he had already collected two-thirds of his fifteen thousand dollar fee. Max Weldy, another North appointee, was hired back into grace as production manager. Weldy seemed willing to do most anything just to stay on the Ringling payroll, and his flexibility would pay off in the long run.

Ironically, Robert boasted to costume designer Miles White, whom he unsuccessfully tried to retain, "We're gonna make this an old-fashioned circus. None of this expensive highfalutin Broadway look!"[7] Whereas Johnny had gone to the ballet world for some of his direction, Robert turned to Radio City Music Hall for his, thereby hiring one of its top dance captains, Lauretta Jefferson (nicknamed "Jeffy" by Anderson), to choreograph the production numbers. It was a good move, for Jefferson won solid respect from the showgirls, and she mounted, in collaboration with Anderson, the superlative "Changing of the Guard," an ensemble effort conceived by Robert Ringling, involving the girls and the elephants. Spectacular in its precision pacing and form, the number is still talked about to this day by everyone who was in it or saw it. It was so enthusiastically received that it was justifiably revived three seasons in a row.

Robert's creative staff actually delivered five production numbers (one more than North had been producing per show): a nostalgic opening pageant, "Hold Your Horses!"; a second walk-around spec, "Let Freedom Ring," with costumes by the noted Billy Livingston; an aerial ballet expertly routined by another returnee, Barbette; and the finale, "Drums of Victory." The old closing hippodrome races and aftershow concert were not among the revived "great traditions." Nor did Robert's allowing women's briefs to slip tantalizingly below their navels conjure up the innocence of a yesteryear supposedly being reaffirmed. The overly scant costumes led to another first for the show: Boston censors, aghast over the sight of Shirley Lindemann being whirled about an elephant's trunk in binkini and bra, ordered her whirled out of the performance.

In fact, Robert was so obsessed with pulchritude for its own sake, that young Jackie Le Claire, who worked in clown alley with his father, Jack, while aspiring to be an aerialist as well, had to go in drag to win a spot in one of the aerial displays. "You could not have sold Robert Ringling on a male aerial act," recalls Jackie, whose female impersonation did not click on hot sawdust settings, where his makeup would melt away. During Jackie's one in-drag season, he also stood by as a "female" understudy for the "Changing of the Guard" number, but never appeared. "No one thought I was a drag queen," he said. "They thought I was a bull dyke."[8] Jackie thereafter stuck to clowning, a genre in which the genders can be easily and humorously mixed without provoking sarcastic catcalls.

To his credit, Robert Ringling got the musicians back into their uniforms and playing again, although he caved in to the unfriendly demands of James Petrillo, consenting to a basic pay raise from $47.50 a week to $54.00. Robert was the first to present the show with an intermission, something that drew raves. And believing that the acts would sell themselves on their own merit, Robert curiously cut out all announcements one season. A speechless ringmaster merely stood by with whistle in hand to cue the performers on and off. On the more generous side, Robert, Edith, and Aubrey donated many seats (set aside at each performance) for war-bond purchasers and admitted literally thousands of servicemen free along the route as the North brothers had started doing the previous season. In some cities, such as Detroit, a third show was added—usually at 10 A.M.—to accommodate the guys in uniform, as well as wartime workers who labored on round-the-clock shifts. In 1943 alone they were credited with more than one million dollars in war-bond sales.

Critics were quick to notice, however, a continuation of the more modern staging format started by North. Others were none too impressed by Robert's penchant for solo action, favored either for artistic integrity or economic necessity or both. Whereas the show had normally presented ten or more displays, each containing three to seven acts, in simultaneous performance, Robert offered only seven in 1943, five in 1944. The puzzling emphasis on single turns made the extra stages he had reinstated seem anachronistic. Why the enlarged spread of canvas—and the additional performing areas—for a program that was closer to the European style? Robert's vision of circus was unclear, unconvincing.

He was ideally suited to stage a one-ring circus, and that is what he did. It was called "Spangles," a summer program created in 1943 to keep Madison Square Garden occupied at a critical time when Garden officials feared their facility could be seized by the government for use as a storage depot during the war. Another reason was to thwart a rival big top being set up by the bohemian showman Larry Sunbrock, who had intended to compete against Ringling's regular spring run but encountered resistance from local agencies demanding that he use flameproof canvas.

"Spangles" was a beautiful show, staged in front of a cyclorama that spread across the Garden, reducing the seating area by roughly half and creating a theaterlike atmosphere. Lauretta Jefferson did an exemplary staging job, with Henry Kyes—pulled from the Ringling band—directing the music, Billy Livingston delivering the costumes, Bert Knapp an original score, and A. A. Ostrander the set pieces. Old-timer Charles Sparks managed the company, and Irma Carter served in the novel role of ringmistress.

A line of twenty-five girls helped introduce and enhance the acts with posturing and choreography. True to European custom, vendors were not allowed in the arena. A number of Ringling artists (including Elly Ardelty, the Kimris, and Roland Tiebor's Seals) appeared on the bill, some returning to the main show to be replaced by others.

Audience reactions were upbeat. The reviewing force typed out only so-so notices. One scribe wondered whether the show didn't contain "too much theatre." The production closed on August 17 to make way for the resumption of boxing matches. Its two-month, fifty-five-show run had attracted an average house of three thousand customers. Plans to tour it as an indoor venture in the fall and winter never materialized, and "Spangles," a highly respectable first effort, slipped away into the history books.

Like it or not, it was the big, booming Greatest Show on Earth that pulled in the money-making crowds, and Robert Ringling never quite felt comfortable in the canvas arenas. Once in Washington, D.C., Mary Jane Miller shared her happiness with the boss. "Oh, isn't it wonderful to be under the big top again!" Answered Robert, "Oh, no, no! I'd much rather be inside the buildings around the stage. This is *dirty* out here!"[9]

He was a weak administrator to begin with, on the wishy-washy side, a nice-enough guy who had never been around his family's circus that much. Merle Evans thought he was plain terrible in the way he played favorites.[10] When Robert first won his post, he called up Karl Wallenda, nervously seeking technical advice. "Karl, I'm in trouble. You got to help me. I'm going to take over management of the circus, and I don't know the first thing about it."[11] The man directly under Robert in authority was James Haley, there by virtue of his recent marriage to Aubrey Ringling. Haley had served both John Ringling and John North as the estate accountant. Operationally, Robert and James hired back the veteran general manager George Smith to run the show, and he still suffered the distractions of his drinking habit.

Many of Robert's moves made little sense. He approved the addition of eleven cars to the train, needed to haul a larger menagerie and big top across the country, this at a time when there wasn't sufficient help to set up and tear down the show in its current size. Robert trusted his authority, perhaps too carelessly, to a number of seasoned department heads, for not all of them exercised appropriate caution, given the precarious circumstances under which the show now operated. The understaffed organization grew ever more vulnerable to any number of likely mishaps. In Philadelphia, for example, a fire broke out on the sidewall of the dressing tent. Luckily, it was caught and extinguished within minutes.

If the possibility of fire was not a constant source of concern and vigilance, it should have been. A spring tradition those years, shocking as it now seems, was to lay out the new canvas in the Sarasota sun and waterproof it. This was accomplished by mixing melted wax and gasoline to form a paraffin substance, sprinkled onto the canvas and swept into the fabric. Thus was created a potentially flammable nightmare waiting for the tiniest spark to set it off.

Came a two-day stand up in Hartford, Connecticut, on July 5 and 6, 1944. The grounds were barely large enough to contain all of the forty-odd tents. The big top had been squeezed into a tight spot partly surrounded by shrubbery. There were but two fire hydrants available. A couple of men assigned to fire watch had veered away from their posts. The sun was blazing hot, and by the second day of the run the scorching canvas hung ominously in the humid air, a brittle sheet of gasoline and wax ever so close to ignition. Eight thousand people were sitting beneath it, the opening wild-animal displays in action. The Wallendas, next on the bill, had climbed up the tiny rope ladders to assume position on their high-wire pedestal when a great round of applause erupted and the animals started exiting through the connecting chutes that ran from the rings, across the hippodrome track, and out through the sidewalls to the wagons in the backyard.

"We were all in the dressing tent," recounts Jackie Le Claire. "It was very hot and we could hear the band very well. They were driving the animals out of the arena, they were doing a reprise of this original Faust music. And they got into this boom, boom, boom!—and all of a sudden, we heard this crescendo of voices coming up, things getting louder, and we suddenly became aware that something was amiss."[12]

The big top was in flames. Terrified patrons were scattering in all directions, some running out under the sidewalls, others fleeing out the back end and through the dressing top. The unlucky ones on the front side (where the animal chutes crossed the track) stumbled helplessly between them and were trampled over by the rush of oncoming bodies. Throughout the initial mayhem, Merle Evans heroically led the band through "The Stars and Stripes Forever" until burning quarter poles began falling in its direction.

Within seven minutes, the tent was in ashes. One hundred sixty-eight souls—mostly women and children—lay dead or dying in cruel disarray on the front side. The twisted remains of the seating structures and animal cages resembled a blackened battlefield. And what quickly emerged in the tragic aftermath was a sort of morality play in which the actions of survival and judgment sadly contradicted accepted norms of human behavior. The young victims had been pushed aside by hysterical adult men scuttling for their own safety. Most people had escaped so easily that a few dared return while the tent was still on fire, hoping to retrieve personal items left behind. One woman who refused to leave her seat had to be knocked unconscious and carried out. Not one circus employee died or was hospitalized, and only a few suffered minor burns. Many of them grabbed scores of children, tossing them out through the sides of the tent, and all refused medical help until the injured and dead could be treated. (The only victim they were unable to identify was a young girl, who became known sympathetically to the world as "Little Miss 1565," the name on her gravestone, derived from the number given her at the morgue. Nearly fifty years later, she was finally identified as Eleanor Emily Cook, thanks to the results of a nine-year investigation launched by Hartford police Lt. Rick Davey, whose interest in the matter turned to obsession. In March 1991, Eleanor's death certificate was amended to bear her actual name, and on June 22 the same year she was reburied alongside her brother, Edward, another Hartford fire casualty, in the family plot at Southampton, Massachusetts.)

What went wrong and who was to blame? Local law enforcement officials, aided by National Guardsmen, the Connecticut State Police, and detachments from nearby army bases, ringed the lot with an incriminating air. Fire detectives combed the grounds for evidence. A few observers claimed the blaze had begun either at the men's donicker (an outhouse) or at the front end of the big top and that it must have been set off by a lighted cigarette or match.

Inspectors eventually pointed to the controversial mixture of gasoline and paraffin that had been used to waterproof the tent. Responding from his home in Evanston, Illinois, where he had been during the debacle, Robert Ringling argued defensively that the holocaust could have been prevented had the circus been granted access by the government to wartime priority fireproofing materials. He said the sailmakers who sewed his tents were the same ones who supplied canvas hospital shelters for the armed forces.

What had been going on behind the scenes, however, casts some doubt on Robert's sincerity. The family had grappled with the issue informally. Robert's sister, Hester Ringling Sanford, had warned him and their mother repeatedly about the obvious dangers. And when she got news of the fire via teletype in Chautauqua, New York, where the family was summering, she nearly fainted. "I knew it would happen! I knew it would happen!"[13] By one family account, fireproofing the canvas was possible but Robert junked the idea.[14] If it had been impossible to come by, as Robert strongly implied, why had Art Concello, then operating the Clyde Beatty Circus on the West Coast, been able to fireproof his tents earlier that spring in compliance with orders from the Los Angeles fire marshal's office?

Hartford prosecutor S. Burr Leikind arrested five circus officials—James Haley, George Smith, Leonard Aylesworth, Edward Versteeg, and David Blanchfield—on charges of manslaughter and released them all on bail pending a formal hearing. Coroner Frank E. Healy found them "guilty of such wanton and reckless conduct, either of commission or omission, wherein there is a duty to act, which makes them criminally liable for the deaths." Evidence gathered by the coroner was chilling: Aylesworth was charged with deserting his post, having gone to Springfield, Massachusetts, to lay out the next lot and leaving no one in charge in his absence; Versteeg with "utterly failing" in his duty to distribute and place in position the fire extinguishers in his charge, which could have stopped the fire at its origin; two others, William Caley and Samuel Clark, with having left their fire-watch posts; Blanchfield with placing his trucks and wagons so closely around the tent as to imperil the lives of people using its exits. The maximum penalties were one thousand dollar fines and fifteen years' imprisonment.

To his credit, Robert Ringling took fast, sensible action in seeing the circus through the crisis. He backed a plan proposed by William Dunn, a member of the board who had played a key role in Ringling finances, that pledged every penny of the show's future earnings to pay off all fire claims settled through arbitration.[15] He set up an office in Hartford, staffed by Roland Butler and Herbert Duval, to foster good public relations and gave the Red Cross a ten thousand dollar check for its help in treating burned victims. Robert salvaged the remainder of the season by playing in open-air stadiums and ballparks, dubbed by one scribe "the topless show." Before the first outdoor date in Akron, Ohio, Robert took microphone in hand under the piercing August sun and conducted final rehearsals. Evidently, he thrived on adversity.

So did his cousin, John North, who, in the words of Alice Lancaster, "was jumping with joy."[16] Back in Sarasota, John saw his own salvation in the ashes of Hartford. He felt little sympathy for his relatives, now struggling to survive a catastrophe, for they had pushed him brazenly aside two years earlier and refused even to acknowledge him as one of the family. John was determined now to put the Ringling back in his name. Dissidently poised, he refused to vote for the Hartford arbitration agreement, backed by every other member of the board. He later denied under oath that he wanted to liquidate the show's assets in bankruptcy court and evade liability, although he failed to reveal the course of action he would have advocated. He had also opposed Robert's plan to tour the circus for the remainder of the 1944 season in open-air venues.

John's most audacious move was going to the Hartford trial to appear as a voluntary witness for the prosecution. He proceeded to rebut defense attorney William Hadden's argument, concurred with by Robert Ringling, that the circus operation would be "desperately jeopardized" in the event the defendants, facing possible jail terms, were not allowed to continue with it. John testified that none of the men was irreplaceable and announced that he was considering a mismanagement suit "on behalf of the corporation" against certain individuals now heading the circus.

In the eyes of Judge William J. Shea of Hartford Superior Court, John proved a credible witness. The defense was denied its motion for suspended sentences on the argument that "if the circus cannot go on tour it cannot meet the claims of relatives of the victims." The trial lasted but a few days, and the sentences handed out by Judge Shea surprised even the prosecution. Smith and Aylesworth got two to five years; Haley, one to five; Versteeg, Clark, and Caley, a year each. David Blanchfield was dismissed for the "apparent honesty of his testimony," he having admitted he did not consider his services to the circus irreplaceable. Smith and Aylesworth were granted a stay until the following July so that they could help prepare the show for its initial canvas dates.

John seized every opportunity to further his goal. He filed his lawsuit seeking to oust the management and demanding reimbursement to the circus of $2.5 million, at that time the estimated total of fire claims (they reached $4 million). In return, John was sued by those currently running the show for "resorting to every measure possible to force the present management out . . . and failing this, endeavoring to wreck the circus so that he would be able to take control."

His most effective move was to play on James Haley's hatred of Robert Ringling. Haley blamed Ringling for letting him take the rap and for not defending his usefulness to the circus more forcefully at the trial. Should Robert, upon learning of the fire, have gone to Hartford and assumed full responsibility as the circus's highest-ranking official? He didn't, and he was ordered to testify at the trial under an interstate subpoena. Haley, now brooding behind bars, could debate the question in his mind for days on end. No matter what common sense may have told him, in his heart he felt betrayed. Robert never sent James a letter or visited him in jail.

By contrast, Johnny North, whose testimony also had helped send Haley to the slammer, then had the good sense to try visiting him there. No matter how much Haley resented North—he refused to see him at first—the two shared a mutual contempt for Robert Ringling, and when James finally agreed to talk to John in the warden's office, he was courted persuasively. Jim wanted to enjoy some real power and prestige as the president of the circus, something he had never experienced as a glorified flunky to his condescending brother-in-law, Robert Ringling. John wanted authority to produce the show, an activity which would bring him back into the limelight while he wheeled and dealed further in an effort to gain the elusive 51 percent control of the beleaguered circus. By the time Jim was released from prison, Christmas Eve 1945 (he got out early on good behavior after serving eight months and seventeen days), the two men had a working accord. The stage was set for an audacious power play.

All Eyes on the Courtroom

In his strategic favor, John could now benefit by the onus of Robert's failed administration in the wake of the Hartford disaster and by his own comparatively superior management and producing record. He also found himself in the middle of a host of nasty intrafamily squabbles, various relatives seeking revenge on one another for anything from imagined or actual betrayal to the pettiness of simple misunderstandings. Of course, the central conflict sprang from Jim Haley's perception that Robert Ringling had refused to defend him adequately at the Hartford fire trial. This, Haley reasoned, led to the year he had spent in jail.

The long-standing rivalry between cousins John and Robert only worsened. These bickering Ringlings became the talk of the weekly trades. When John started making a lot of noise about taking steps to regain control of the show, Robert quipped to a reporter from *Variety*, "I'd sooner see the show sold out of the family hands than have North get control."[1]

As the 1946 board of directors meeting approached, John and Jim were two individuals not at odds with each other. No matter what their personal differences, they were a force to be reckoned with; were they to vote their stock together, they could easily pull the strings. However, that would require the necessary cooperation of Jim's wife, Aubrey, who actually held and voted the Haley stock. Curiously, she had her own very different agenda at first. She had sought Henry North out with an offer to run the circus. (Actually, it wasn't a bad idea. Henry had been successfully associated with his brother, John, in running the show when the latter first took it over in 1938; he was known for having made his share of valuable suggestions; and, most of all, he was generally well liked and respected by almost everyone in the family.) One of the peculiar conditions Aubrey set down, according to Henry, was that he help her "get rid of John."[2] Henry would have nothing to do with such a thought. He understood that Aubrey and Robert had an agreement whereby neither would talk to John without the other present.

On the other hand, a condition that Jim Haley had set down with John over their agreement to work together was that Henry would have nothing to do with the show. It seems that Henry had written Jim a "caustic letter" (contents not disclosed) from North Africa. Then, shortly before the 1946 stockholders' confab in April, Jim and Robert nearly came to blows in a nasty row. Aubrey was conspicuously absent from the meeting, reportedly because of illness. Husband Jim, voting her stock by proxy, collaborated with John on a daring power play that amounted to mutiny. Together, they elevated Jim to the position of president and John to the first vice-president's chair and downgraded Robert to a virtual unemployed free-lance opera singer. And for this they landed a wry front-page *Billboard* headline: "ROBERT RINGLING SHUSHED."[3]

At the meeting, Robert and Edith roared their disapproval, first declaring that Haley had no right to vote his wife's stock by proxy. That argument didn't get them anywhere, so they contested the vote as a direct violation of a pact entered into between Edith and Aubrey in 1941, the Ladies' Agreement, which bound them to vote their stock together. Since Edith was clearly on her son Robert's side and Aubrey (by proxy) in John's corner, the split vote was illegal. Edith and Robert were smugly ignored by North and Haley, who rose from the conference table and proceeded out the door, leaving the governing body of Ringling Bros. and Barnum & Bailey Combined Shows, Inc. in a shambles. That night at Madison Square Garden, Robert assumed his usual position at the Fiftieth Street ramp, acting as presidential as ever. Eyeing him from across the sawdust floor was another man also acting presidential, James A. Haley. The bitter residual fires of Hartford burned brightly in their eyes, and this was but a preshow to the bizarre spectacle of family politics and courtroom capers that lay ahead. As Mary Jane Miller puts it, recalling all the Ringling wranglings around and through which performers and staff had to cope, "we'd laugh. We'd say, 'Well, who's our boss this year?' Or 'this *day?*'"[4]

Given the chaos he had helped to create, John North now enjoyed at least as much authority as anybody else, and he maximized the opportunities at hand to reassert and make visible his deft producing talents. In fact, it was in his optimistic nature, as Henry would later note, that he immediately began to run the show as if he alone owned it. He had the backing of James A. Haley, the disputed new circus president. And if Robert wished to wage a court battle, so be it. John and Jim stood firm on shaky ground, firm enough to sustain the illusion of authority. Robert, physically outnumbered, gradually caved into to their brazen takeover, especially when faced with threats of harm (he would later claim) and refused access to the backstage area and the circus office at the Garden.

John fostered the image of control and decision making. He took a critical look at the current edition of the circus, which Robert had produced and which had won mostly approving nods from the reviewers, and he made a few cosmetic improvements. Merle Evans was encouraged to replace a stilted, classical score composed by Deems Taylor for the "Toyland" spec. This he immediately did—and with much relief—by using instead some Victor Herbert melodies that addressed the theme in a more popular vein. At the same time, John reached into his own trunk for a beguiling fox-trot that he himself had composed, "Paris." Evans liked it enough, or was smart enough, to arrange the tune and play it during the Wallendas' act. "Paris" got a more-than-decent reception and gave John enough confidence in his melodic gifts to consider, in future years, foisting more of his original music on the show.

John lifted the ban on all announcements, letting Arthur Springer, the ringmaster (dubbed by one trade reporter "Sphinx Springer"), utter a total of six words during each performance: "Con Colleano!" "Justino Loyal!" "The Wallendas!" And in response to growing criticism that the Ringling show was becoming too solo-act oriented, John publicized his disagreement with the Robert Ringling policy by sending Pat Valdo to scout additional acts around the country, the stated reason being "to bolster a noticeable weakness in the program." They may have rearranged the running order slightly to reduce the number of single turns by merging them into more multidisplays. There wasn't really much they could do at this point other than plan for a fuller complement of action in the future, which is exactly what John would end up doing in the most flamboyant fashion.

Perhaps the shrewdest of John's moves was to rehire the famous Ringling clown Felix Adler, who had been dismissed under Robert Ringling's tenure, allegedly for making winter dates with circuses in the Midwest. Ironically, John's dramatically publicized reinstatement of Adler amounted to his condoning an activity he had once been criticized for prohibiting.

Whether or not John ever did, the political circumstances now favored his taking the very opposite position; he knew when to be pragmatic. Adler was as tickled to reclaim his old spot in clown alley as audiences were to see him.

The show, by some accounts, was significantly changed for the better by the time it got to Chicago. Writing in *The Billboard*, Pat Purcell expressed pleasure and surprise, finding the program "almost startlingly different. . . . They have removed most of the operatic touches and swung it back to circus, and it was evident that the cash customers like it. All the hands around the show seem to be having a fun time, indeed."[5] In America's tough crossroads city, never to be taken for granted, the SOLD OUT signs went up every night, with turnaway crowds the rule rather than the exception. The circus drew 155,000 people in nineteen shows; 1946 wound up a big, walloping winner. Competing with seventeen other tent circuses on the road that year, Ringling reported the biggest year financially in its history. A million-dollar profit was turned over to the Hartford-fire receiver, Edward Rogin. North and Haley had pulled off an impressive success.

Crowned once again with the aura of a top producer (even if he had merely revised and revamped another man's work), John was in a heady frame of mind. That fall, he set sail for Europe, announcing at his New York departure, "I hope to book an entire new performance." He also made it known that John Murray Anderson was coming back to stage the show again, a move the frugally inclined Haley had resisted, believing it would add unnecessary production expenses to the books. John also talked Miles White into returning. White had assisted Norman Bel Geddes with costume sketches when the latter staged for North. Now the young designer enjoyed his own Broadway credits, costuming for, among others, Rodgers and Hammerstein. Barbette joined again as well to create an aerial splash, "Can Can." Esther Junger was signed to choreograph and Albert Johnson to provide the artwork, while Arthur Springer, promised more verbal latitude, renewed his contract to blow the whistle.

Gone from the Ringling fold were Billy Livingston, Florence Baker, Robert Barnhart, and Fred Erwingo, hired by Robert Ringling and now let go by North for his own favorites. Gone, too, were the outstanding acts of Lalage, William Heyer, and the Wallendas, who would never again be seen with the Big Show. Karl Wallenda's close relationship to Robert Ringling ("my dear friend") cost him dearly when John took over. Perhaps John could not bear the sight of Karl, too much a symbol of Aunt Edith's and

Robert's old regime, but of all times for such ill-productive behavior! This was the moment in circus history when Karl was perfecting and ready to unveil the single most sensational aerial attraction ever seen in any circus anywhere: the stupefying seven-high pyramid walk. He proposed doing it for John but was still ignored. "He wouldn't even listen," says Karl. "I was too much friend caught in a feud. Very bad situation. I think Johnny North never forgave me that I was too good friends with his biggest enemy he had, Robert Ringling. They never talked, nothing. The minute Johnny North came in there, I knew he didn't like me."[6] Wallenda started his own show, and within ten weeks it was bankrupt. A circus rarely succeeds on the drawing power of a single act.

John's three-month talent search through Holland, France, Belgium, Switzerland, Italy, England, and Scandinavia was a smashing success, even though he confessed upon his return to the States, "Believe it or not, I tried to book a lot of acts that didn't show the slightest interest in trying to get to America. Some I did book had to be persuaded hard." North said he had avoided Germany altogether, not only for "patriotic reasons," but because to get an act signed and out of the American Zone would have necessitated a three-way clearance involving the army, the State Department, and the local German government. The British and French zones were avoided, too, for twice the red tape was required, while the Russian sector, reported John, was "hopeless as a source." Confining his attention to the other countries rife with jugglers and tumblers, he gobbled up just about every troupe within reach and brought back to the United States forty new acts. In comparison, the previous year's edition had premiered but three. Never before in its history had the Ringling show engaged anywhere near so many new performers for a given season.

John's brilliant bouquet of fresh talent included Konselman's Polar Bears, the bareback-riding Bostocks with Marion Seifert, such aerialists as the Merions, the Corsimars, the Idalys, Lola Dobritch, Chrysis De La Grange, the Joanidis, the Great Reverhos, the Bontas, the Medinis, the Cybas, and the Thommens. There were four flying trapeze groups in a single display (something Robert had started), two of them—the Esquedas and the Sambiassis—making their American debut. On bicycles came the Fred Harrys, the Goetschis, and the Mathis Duo. With juggling clubs came the Malletts, the Chiesas, and the Perzoffs. And one acrobatic assemblage showcased five new troupes: the Boginas, Rachellis-Borgianas, Asia Boys and Wong Geng Fo, the Robenis, and the Cathalis. The list of new entries went on and on. It was the year when Harold Alzana first held Americans spellbound with his high-wire antics after reaching his rigging aloft via an inclined wire. The year Rose Gould thrilled millions with her fantastic midair maneuvers, all performed from a rope held perilously at the ends by two male partners positioned above her high over the center ring—a solo well worth soloing. It was the year when Natal—"Man or Monkey?"—stormed the audience to hilarious effect. The year when Rhodin's Bears, Armand Guerre's Sea Lions, and Vargas's Chimps were first seen on Ringling sawdust.

Stager John Murray Anderson laced them all together with charming spectacles: "The Royal Ascot," an equestrian outing that featured "Europe's most distinguished emissaries of haute école horsemanship and dressage," included among whom were Claude Valois and Jose Moeser; "The Wedding of Cinderella," the principal pageant brought to a climax by the star's journey to the ball—around the hippodrome track, naturally—on the most gorgeous of golden-leafed floats; the aerial ballet of Barbette; and the grand finale, "Elephantasia," to which Miles White lent, through his costumes, an air of mysterious enchantment. Photographers from *National Geographic* were given free reign at the Boston Garden spring engagement. Some of the fine color plates they shot graced the pages of the magazine's March issue the following year.

Pink sawdust was spread over the arena floor, and carefully designed ring curbs and carpets bore the unmistakably fine Miles White imprint. The program overflowed in novelty while achieving the singular aura of a unified event. It was all of a piece, and it sent critics into euphoria. "You've never seen anything like it," sang Robert Williams in the *New York Post*. "The Greatest Show on Earth merely lived up to its lofty label, so much so it left its own press agents groping for words." Roared Walter Winchell, "This circus out big-tops them all!" The *Harold Tribune*'s Howard Skidmore wrote, "The show that unfolded had even veteran performers agape. The result is an international congress of circus elite such as has not been seen since before the war."[7] Pat Purcell reported for *The Billboard*, "The new acts drip with color. . . . The Alzanas, Rose Gould, the Idalys, and Chrysis De La Grange all rated their feature spots. The production numbers were out of this world . . . solid circus all the way."[8]

Variety fell into line, deciding that "the foreign thrill acts and 'The Wedding of Cinderella' make the Ringling circus better than ever."[9] All the reviews were upbeat, none issuing any particular qualms. "If you want to develop a rip-roaring case of jingled nerves," stated the *Brooklyn Home News Report*, "the circus which opened in the Garden last night is your dish." Sighed showman Billy Rose, whose endorsement charmed John greatly, "I'm glad to see the 'Greatest Show on Earth' is again the greatest show on earth."[10]

Business at Madison Square Garden skyrocketed accordingly, the last sixteen shows selling out in advance. The entire performance was televised twice before a total estimated TV audience of 325,000, up markedly from the 25,000 people who viewed it on the little magic box the year before. "Produced by John Ringling North" were magical words once more. If anything, John worked best in a state of flux, when his job could be snatched away from him at any moment. His position was never more insecure than now.

During those turbulent months, John spent about as much time consulting with his attorneys and making courtroom appearances as he did walking the midway or searching for new acts. He was forced to defend the takeover that he and Haley had engineered against the legal efforts of Edith and Robert Ringling to regain their controlling positions. The family waded through a thicket of litigation and esoteric judicial pronouncements that almost defy human understanding. In contesting the 1946 meeting, Edith's attorney argued that Karl D. Loos, who was present, had held the power to decide how the women should vote in the event that they could not agree, or to adjourn the meeting for a period of two months to allow them further time in which to hash out their differences. Loos, in fact, had pressed for an adjournment but was blithely ignored by North and Haley, the latter voting his wife Aubrey's stock by proxy, another allegedly illegal action. The issue went back and forth on the litigation front.

In December 1946 a Court of Chancery judge, Vice-Chancellor Collins J. Seitz, upheld the Loos decision for adjournment and ordered the stockholders to undertake a new election on December 10 in Wilmington, Delaware, in the presence of a neutral attorney, Daniel L. Herman. Seitz believed that the directors, now acting with "explicit knowledge" of their rights, might be more inclined to abide by the rules. John feared the outcome of such a meeting and had his attorney postpone the vote indefinitely by filing an appeal with the Delaware Supreme Court. When that body finally addressed the matter in the summer of 1947, it upheld the Court of Chancery ruling that the Ladies' Agreement was "valid and enforceable." It declared that effect should be given to a rejection only of those votes (cast in the infamous 1946 meeting) representing Aubrey

Haley's shares. This meant that the election of six of the officers—including John to the post of first vice-president—could stand. James Haley lacked sufficient votes, so his position as president was voided.

Thus Robert Ringling obtained an order from the Court of Chancery restoring him to the presidency and enjoining the others from interfering with his management. He took over on June 6 at Washington, D.C., where the show was playing. Ringling was escorted to the Oklahoma Avenue and Benning Road showgrounds by Dan Gordon Judge, his attorney, and William Dunn. Also present on the lot, each guarding the impression of power, were James and Aubrey Haley, Secretary-Treasurer J. R. Griffin, and John Ringling North. The tense, ever-changing game of Who's in Charge Today? became an in joke within the industry. "Situation here was odd," reported one of the trades, "with various Ringlings and Norths all occupying quarters on the circus grounds and keeping an eye on each other."

Only two weeks later, at the special board meeting ordered by the courts to take place in Delaware, Robert's brief stint in the saddle toppled when his mother, Edith, and her voting partner, Aubrey, again could not agree on whom to vote for. Karl Loos, their legally appointed arbitrator, opted to bind their votes. He favored Aubrey's way of thinking, which naturally favored her husband, James. This put North and Haley back on top, Haley as president and North in the newly created post of executive vice-president and chairman of the executive committee. Robert Ringling was tossed a first vice-president slot. All but for the addition of William Dunn to the board, as now constituted it was virtually the same as it was in the aftermath of the disputed 1946 election. The new executive committee implemented a radical change of policy, stipulating that all future decisions would have to be made by a unanimous rather than a majority vote, a hilariously impractical goal considering the divisive makeup of this eccentric governing body.

Once more all Ringling employees heaved a collective sigh of relief, feeling another reprieve from the endless Ringling wranglings. A correspondent from *The Billboard* took a pulse of company morale a fortnight later: "Browsing around the lot, one gets the impression that peace and harmony reign as far as the management is concerned. James A. Haley is much in evidence as the president. But vice presidents Robert Ringling and John Ringling North were not in sight. There was a feeling, however, that the employees were not worried about whose back to scratch, and it has been quite some time since they could go about their tasks without that worry."[11]

In reality, a frantic struggle was taking place off the lot for 51 percent control of the show, the principal players being cousins John and Robert. In balance was the 30 percent stock held by the John Ringling estate, over which John and his mother, Ida, still presided as coexecutors, having shrewdly fended off attempts by the state of Florida and their relatives to remove them. (A lower court finally ruled that John Ringling had not intended to include a clause in his codicil terminating the executorship of his sister or nephew.) By this time, the Norths had reached settlement with all the creditors holding liens against the estate, which in total amounted to about two million dollars.

Florida officials, anxious to settle the estate, still faced, then, about $2,000,000 in debts: the fees they owed the Norths (in the neighborhood of $1,000,000), another $640,000 to the attorneys, and other miscellaneous outstanding claims. The money could conceivably be raised by the sale of certain estate holdings, which the state had no intention of holding on to, appraised as follows: Sarasota real estate, $2,000,000; Oklahoma oil interests, $800,000; three hundred shares of circus stock, $500,000; miscellaneous properties, $100,000. The total amount, $3,400,000, may have been inflated for sale purposes. Nonetheless, John wanted all these assets, especially the circus stock, very badly, and he had the inside track in many ways, from his winning image as a circus producer to the relationships he had built with state officials. As far back as 1942 he had been given signals by the state that it might cooperate in negotiating a sale with him. Remember Nathan Mayo saying, "We long to see the day when you own the circus"?

In 1946, Florida Secretary of State R. A. Gray had suggested they try peddling the three hundred shares of circus stock to the present stockholders—not to any one Ringling in particular, because, as he figured, another Ringling family squabble might "pave the way for some fine negotiations." Right he was. John came forward with a $500,000 offer, included with which was his pledge to forfeit all the executor fees and expenses owed him and his mother and to assume any outstanding liens against the estate. In return, he would receive the circus stock, the Oklahoma oil and Sarasota land, both lucrative sources of long-term capital gain. John's package stipulated that the state would agree to drop its pending suit to remove him as executor.

Then came—guess who?—Robert Ringling, in tandem with his mother, Edith. They also offered $500,000, seeking roughly the same terms, except for a clause requiring that the state continue its suit to remove John as executor. Both bids were rejected, although Gov. Millard Caldwell had recommended the acceptance of John's. There were voices in the Florida legislature urging the Cabinet to court bids from outside the Ringling family, too. About a year later, John returned with a modestly adjusted offer of $550,000, not enough to sway the Cabinet. Then came, from a bigger league, a bona fide Texas oil tycoon who dangled $1,200,000 just for the Florida real-estate holdings. This time it was John who stood in the way, presumably exercising executor powers of his own to nix deals.

John quickly followed with a third offer, topping the Texan's by a mere $50,000. Cabinet members saw a bargain at last. Under the terms of John Ringling's will, the money they collected could be set aside to pay for upkeep of the art museum, Ca'd'Zan, and the grounds, as well as to pay for future art acquisitions. Once more, by doing business with John, they would be wonderfully free of all the executor and attorney fees—to be incurred by the Norths.

John got the "yes" he desperately wanted. He agreed to pay $200,000 upon signing the deal, the remaining $1,050,000 to be delivered in ninety days. Thus he now held the 30 percent stock from the estate plus his own 7 percent. To underwrite this sweeping transaction, he organized a syndicate, Ringling Enterprises, consisting of himself, his mother, and two of their attorneys, Leonard Bisco and Sydney Newman. The syndicate's purchase left Bisco and Newman holding 40 percent (120 shares) of the circus stock, which John wanted himself in order to advance his quest for a controlling interest in the show. He proposed purchasing these shares from the two partners and they debated the stock value to determine what John owed them. John argued that the 300 shares were worth no more than $450,000. The attorneys said $500,000. "Okay," countered the anxious John, "let's toss a coin to see if it's $400,000 or $500,000." They consented and the wrong toss cost John $40,000, since he ended up having to pay Newman and Bisco $200,000 instead of $160,000 for their 40 percent share. John and his mother mortgaged nearly everything they owned to raise the capital.

Now John was only 14 percent in stock shares away from the coveted 51 percent control he sought. There are many conflicting accounts of how he acquired these shares. The most interesting is offered by Stuart Lancaster, who insists that a teeterboard battle for power between John and Edith at the next board meeting played out like a cliff-hanger until the final moments.[12] The Haleys were in a position to play a deciding role because they could sell either faction the necessary shares to give it the controlling edge. James Haley was no longer on John's North side. The two had had a falling out earlier in the year over a difference of opinion about John Murray Anderson's usefulness to the circus. Haley hated the costly production expenses that came with Anderson's involvement; John refused to let the director go. So Haley realigned himself with the Edith Ringling branch of the family, and he much favored selling out to them because of his admiration for Robert's son, James, an eager apprentice who showed some executive promise.

But there were several strong factors in John North's favor that probably helped him persuade his Aunt Edith to put the brakes on her campaign. John had a superlative track record running the show. Robert, a semi-invalid, had suffered a stroke that summer. Another grave concern for Edith was John's mismanagement suit against the circus, still fermenting in the courts, one judge having upheld it. John is thought to have won Edith's agreement to vote with him by pledging to drop the suit and promising to make Robert chairman of the board for life at an attractive salary. Reason may have prevailed. By no account did the Haleys stand in the way. Aubrey had grown weary of the pivotal position she occupied between her two bickering cousins. The sale of the Haley stock went as follows: 140 shares to John for $194,444.48; 175 shares to Robert for $243,055.55. This left John with an accumulated total of 510 shares; Robert and Edith with 490. The Haleys walked away with a profit of $437,500.00.

In John's camp during those final hectic weeks was Art Concello. John told Art by telephone in August that he was getting control and that he needed about a hundred thousand dollars to complete the down payment required on his purchase of the estate holdings. Art was promised his management post back, so he took immediate measures to divest himself of his interest in the Clyde Beatty Circus, which he owned and had been running during his absence from the Ringling banner. Art sold the circus to Beatty, whose dream it had all along been to run it himself. Art then raised the one hundred grand John needed and handed it to him—in cash. Others who came up with more money for John—and who were given, as a result, positions with the show—included Harry Dube, who published the program, and the Miller brothers, who sold concessions.

North and Concello spoke again by telephone in mid-October. "Be in Atlanta," North instructed him. "We're gonna take over."[13] On October 27, Concello showed up on the lot with his top men from the Beatty show,

known as the "sneeze mob." Their entrance down the midway was grim
and abrupt. They took over the physical operation the moment they
arrived. George Smith, the manager, was promptly relieved of his duties
and paid off. The atmosphere turned like that. The transition was so
unpleasant that the Haleys walked off the Atlanta showgrounds in a
visible huff, followed by reporters of "a break in friendly relations" with
North. When questioned by a reporter about the incident, John replied,
"James Haley is, to the best of my knowledge, still president. No written
resignation has been submitted by him."[14] Only the formalities remained.
When the Haleys departed the Atlanta lot—past Art Concello, past his
tenacious cronies, who now called the shots—they took with them the last
vestiges of the older Ringling order. Gone forever was the comparative
innocence attached to a more staid, morally regulated era.

John consummated his purchase of the necessary Haley-owned stock at
a special board of directors meeting held three weeks later. Saturday,
November 15, 1947, was probably the most exhilarating day of his life.
That is when, as reported by the trades, he acquired a 51 percent interest
in Ringling Bros. and Barnum & Bailey Combined Shows, Inc., making
him the first person ever to control its destiny singly. He faced the future
with a wonderful sense of his childhood dreams. The circus was now his,
as all along he had naturally assumed it should be. To celebrate, John
threw an all-night party at the M'Toto Room. Cases of vintage champagne
and beluga caviar by the bucketload were dispensed generously to the
guests, many of them impromptu crashers off the Sarasota streets. John's
conquest was theirs for the toasting.

The following spring, when rehearsals were under way out at winter
quarters, there occurred an incident that best characterizes the new and
ultimate career that John had finally established for himself. At the M'Toto
Room one hot, packed, but merry evening, two clowns, Art Cooksey and
John Reilly, who had been unable to attract a waitress to their table, went
up to the busy bar, put down some money, and bought themselves drinks.
They then turned to a gentleman dressed in a tuxedo and said, "Excuse
me, boy, would you carry those two drinks over to our table." Replied the
astonished gentleman in puffed-up defiance, "I *beg* your pardon. *I* am
John Ringling North!"[15]

North and Concello

As has been shown, John was a delegator, preferring to paint the broad strokes and let others fill in the details. When he first took control of the show in 1938, his brother, Henry did a lot of the groundwork, complementing George Smith, whom they had inherited and kept on as general manager. Then there was Art Concello, appointed by the brothers to manage the 1942 season. Next came James Haley, with whom John shared the power for a brief though prosperous period, from the spring of 1946 through the fall of 1947.

Now Art was back on the scene, having come to John's aid with the cash he needed to complete his stock purchases and gain 51 percent control. Another thing Art had to offer were the designs for an ingenious new labor-saving seat wagon. The extreme difficulties faced by the circus in maintaining manpower made these wagons all the more appealing. John wanted them—another reason to make Art the manager.

Outwardly, the two were oddly dissimilar: John with his royal airs, Art the cigar-chomping man of the midway. John was on the short side (five-foot-eight). Art was shorter. John hobnobbed with the rich and famous, Art with the rich and infamous—all the unseemly characters who plied their dubious trades in the shadowy world of canvas tents forever on the move.

Inwardly, the two were more similar than most people realized. Both possessed a tough, tenacious nature. Both viewed the world existentially. Neither held anything connected with the circus as particularly sacred. A key difference between the two, some will say, is that Art was even more ruthless than John. Both admired the strength in the other. In Art, not only had John found someone to mind the store, he also came upon a workable friendship—someone to go drinking and woman watching with, at least in New York, when both were around the show during the spring engagements. In the end, John paid dearly for the services—professional and social—Concello rendered so well. In John's absence from the lot, Art established what *The Billboard* would one day call "his empire within an empire."[1] He amassed tremendous power. Somebody had to control it, to be sure. Concello points out, "The head of this thing was never there. He didn't want to know nothing." The only thing John did want to know, when he called up a couple of times during the tour to inquire tersely about it, was that the books were in the black. North's attitude could be summed up in five words: "Bring me a good statement."[2]

What is more remarkable is the almost unconditional trust that John placed in Art; at least he gave the illusion of complete confidence—and faith—in Concello's executive abilities. Art excelled under these circumstances, and it would appear that he, in turn, passed on to his own underlings the same degree of confidence, trust, and latitude. He took as his number-one priority the on-time operation of the show and developed a sterling reputation as a master big-top mover. Among those who have praised Concello's organizational genius, there is the English impresario Cyril B. Mills, who calls him "probably the best circus manager the world has ever seen."[3] Concello has said that "twenty good bosses" was the key to moving the tented circus on time. And he stood behind them just as John stood behind him. He much preferred letting each department head solve his own problems and handle his own complaints. "Otherwise," as he has said, "the boss ain't got no control."[4]

Perhaps the split-second timing that Concello had perfected as a top-flight trapeze star (he was one of only a very few in his time to do the triple) left him with a chronic abhorrence of late arrivals and sluggish setups. Concello constantly looked for ways to speed up the logistics while cutting down on labor and equipment. The inevitable transition from horses to horsepower, by now completed, was a policy he had helped to hasten. Of tractors pulling wagons, Concello has said, "They don't eat a thing until you turn them on."

Art replaced the heavy stand-up sections of the animal exhibition arenas with wire-mesh enclosures, which gave the roustabouts a break and offered audiences a superior view of the acts. Another relief for the workingmen were aluminum poles, added during those first North-Concello years, as were special cranes attached to the trucks, which made the loading of large rolls of canvas so much easier. The train itself, which had lengthened to 108 cars by 1947, an all-time high, was reduced to 90 cars in 1948, 80 in 1950, then down to 70 in 1951. Permission was obtained from the Federal Communications Commission to use walkie-talkie units on the show, which facilitated better communication between department heads. There was even a machine to "guy out" the tent (tighten the side ropes). Everything Art could think of to reduce the work force was tried. He had a true passion for tent-circus logistics.

His greatest invention of all was the seat wagon, which he designed. John ballyhooed it with all the hoopla he had given Gargantua. The lead story in the 1948 circus magazine described one of these mechanical marvels:

"It's on wheels—
It unfolds like an extension bridge table—
It grows chairs, Duran upholstered—It is the portable
Circus Bowl.[5]

Concello's design furthered the evolution of a more primitive seat wagon that canvas boss William Curtis had developed for use in the Hagenbeck-Wallace show, although Concello claims never to have seen a Curtis wagon. Whereas the Curtis design held eight tiers of chairs, Art's contained eighteen. Structurally, the two models were quite different. The Concello concept was a stroke of superb planning. His love of airplanes no doubt influenced the efficient engineering. First, the sides of the wagon folded out, then the entire seating surface tilted downward toward the front end. At that point, additional carry-on floor sections were attached to extend the level to the ground. The chairs remained permanently attached to the floorboards and were easily swung into upright position. There was room on each side of a center aisle for a row of seven cushioned chairs. The wagons transported equipment, and each contained a small private compartment at the rear, where star performers dressed. Those not so favored got into their costumes on the ground between the wagons—on the back side of the tent. Department bosses and workingmen rested in similar accommodations beneath the wagons placed on the front side (the side to which, by custom, performers play).

Concello took his design to Louis Hagen's Hagen Manufacturing Company in Memphis, Tennessee, and got a price quote of about two hundred thousand dollars for an order of eighteen units. North loved the idea, but, having just mortgaged everything he owned to buy the circus stock, he was in no position to sponsor the construction. So he challenged Art to furnish the funds needed, which Art did, and in so doing John fell that much deeper into his friend's debt. That's not all. Art exacted royalty payments from the circus for his patent on the design in the amount of twenty thousand dollars annually for ten years.

The first wagons to roll out of the Hagen plant were treated like prima donnas expected to steal the headlines. At a gala spring unveiling in Sarasota, performers and staff occupied the seats of one, the front aprons left off to allow reporters and photographers a view of the understructure. Modoc, Ringling's famed elephant who had starred in the Stravinsky ballet, stood on the aisle and raised her trunk approvingly over Art and Johnny, who stood together on the first steps, smiling confidently. It was a proud moment for the two daring innovators, and it marked the beginning of a unique era rich in Ringling history, an era as wonderful in the dazzling transformation of the show's very appearance on a lot as it was in the spectacular circus performances that took place under the big blue tent. Produced by John, managed by Art.

When the seat wagons were put into use that summer, they proved to be an absolute hit in all but (ironically) the most important category: comfort. The chairs were of modest size, the rows placed too close together for sufficient legroom. Concello was short enough not to notice. Patrons of moderate to tall stature sat with a cramped feeling. Moreover, the floor was not level underneath them, but part of a continuous descending grade. The portable circus bowl did not draw raves. A few customers expressed pleasure; according to firsthand reports in *The Billboard*, "some squawks were voiced," although not to the point of requesting refunds.[6] Comparisons with the older-style grandstand, with its flat floorboards and higher elevation from one row to the next, did not help. Duran-upholstered comfort? In a claustrophobic context . . .

Mechanically, the wagons were a marvel to watch in the assembly stages, each being quickly pulled into its appointed position in the tent, the sides soon after beginning to tilt upward, the front declining forward. The crankshafts buzzing, the clattering of seats being slammed into position—such rare industrial music under the big top. They were relatively safe (a minor mishap occurred up in Syracuse, New York, when one of the aprons at the front end gave way and dropped about four feet to the ground, causing minor injuries to three patrons), and they required far less manpower than the old jack-and-stringer type of seats. The show gave only six late matinees during the entire 1949 tour. Two of the wagons were rented in the spring of that year to the Boston Red Sox training camp. In the winter of 1953, the entire fleet (about twenty-eight wagons) went to McDill Air Force Base near Tampa to seat the audience at a five-hundred-mile stock-car race.

Privacy was only a sometime thing for the performers with less clout and the showgirls who had to dress on the ground between the wagons. There were instances when a wagon was not spotted in correct alignment to the next and the patrons sitting on the edge could glimpse down through the loose canvas partitians to review the natural goings-on below, where the performers bathed freely out of buckets. "Wonderful!" recounts Daisy Hall, remembering her years as a North Starlet when she dressed below a Concello seat wagon: "We used to have the announcer of the show peeping over, watching all the girls take their baths. And then, there was a little dwarf that used to crawl underneath in the back and watch the girls take their baths. Then the girls would really get naughty. Sometimes between shows, somebody'd be taking a bath, and we'd have the tent flap down, and they'd throw somebody out without their clothes on, into the backyard. . . . All that kind of fun."[7]

If anything, Art was highly amused by these racy scenes inadvertently made possible by his brilliant new invention. He had his girlfriends. He liked walking the lot—just as cocky as Johnny but a little more down to earth. He pinched a few behinds here and there, whenever he could get away with it. The power he wielded drew plenty of willing participants into his lap. While it would be unfair to say he slept on a casting couch, neither did he refrain from the friendly overtures of a showgirl seeking better opportunities for herself. Art could do just about anything he wanted to do. John was rarely around, leaving Art with nobody but himself to account to. On the lot, Concello was known as "Little Caesar." His word was final. He had, as he calls it, "the yes and the no."

Concello's ethics were not always a simple matter of yes or no, at least not as Mary Jane Miller remembers them. A very fine all-around showgirl, Miller had advanced into featured aerial acts, and she remains embittered by her experience with Concello concerning a spot in one of his flying acts. Miller started training with Art's wife, Antoinette, a superb flyer and the first woman to do the triple. Miller hoped to join the act the following season. Art liked what he saw and said yes.

Miller, a tough cracker herself, broached an ever so delicate subject with the boss.

"What about money?"

Said Art, "We'll take care of that in New York."

Came the spring opening at Madison Square Garden. Mary once again raised the subject of subjects. Art acted dumb.

"What do you mean?" he said.

Miller reminded him of their past conversation.

"Listen," he began, oblivious to any promises made, "I have girls that'll *pay me* to go up there!"

"Okay," said Mary. "I quit."

She took her grievances to Frank McClosky, directly under Concello in authority. He was sympathetic, but there was nothing he could do. Antoinette was so upset about the whole thing that she told Mary, "I'll pay you myself if you go up."

Miller, trouper that she was, went on without pay. "Tell Art I'm doing it for you, Antoinette, not for him."[8]

Art reflected John's tougher, amoral side, and when he and John's good friend Rudy Bundy met in 1949, there was no contest. John had offered Rudy a job with the circus when the nightclub business was no longer profitable enough for the bandleader. Rudy accepted, believing he would be placed in charge of something. Much gentler by nature than Art, to whom he was told to report, he did have the guts to tell him, "Don't put me anyplace where I have to steal money to make a living."

Concello thought for a moment, there being few options left from which to choose. "Okay, Rudy, why don't you go over and stand in front of the sideshow there and see what's going on. I'll let you know."

Rudy stood on the midway without much purpose, not willing to work the rackets built into most of the available jobs. Every once in a while, he would check back with Concello.

"Let's see," answered the boss, "I haven't figured out anything yet, but I'll let you know."

Rudy never did much more than baby-sit the glossy banner lines depicting strange people. The 1950 route book lists him as the sideshow's personnel director. After two years of inactivity, standing there in the shadows of the sneeze mob, he quit. "Everybody knew John Ringling North put me there," he says, "so they were a little afraid of me, afraid I was going around to find out what was going on."[9]

What *was* going on is called skimming, the siphoning away of money from the red wagon, where it rightfully belongs, into the pockets of racketwise operators. Concello, the circus godfather, condoned these practices for a cut of the take, of course. And his sneeze mob consisted of as many veteran Ringling men as it did the guys he brought with him off the Clyde Beatty lot.

There was the rehashing of general-admission tickets, turned back by ticket taker to seller to be sold again; the unreported sale by ushers of reserved seats inside the big top to customers wishing to upgrade. Phil Hall, who started on the show as an usher in 1943, was shown the ins and outs by an older pro who had been around for some time. One day Hall was told to begin allowing customers into a section of seats the show had not yet begun hawking to the public. "We'll just take the money," said Hall's senior.

"But they haven't broken the section yet," protested Hall, worried about repercussions.

"Well, they're going to. It's going to be a big house. Come on."

Between themselves, the two ushers pocketed two or three hundred dollars by admitting patrons into the section. Then came George Smith, the general manager himself, down the track with a roll of tickets in hand for the very seats now occupied.

"What are these people doing in there!" he roared. "Get them out!"

There was actually little Smith could do at that point, unless he dared risk antagonizing the public. For all the people in the chairs knew, they had been properly seated. "It was a fait accompli," says Hall, noting how vulnerable the circus was during the war years to what scarce help it could find. An usher caught doing the same thing in the older days might be fired. Not now. "My guess is they always figured the people had to make a dollar, and they needed the help."[10]

Concello faced a similar dilemma when he took over in the late 1940s: how to keep employees around on subminimum wages. He tolerated the petty rackets, making sure he got a fee for the privilege granted. When it came to dealing with the public, however, the customer was never victimized. Concello was adamant in upholding this Ringling policy, although short-change artists would try infiltrating the lot now and then. "If they caught up with you," says Hall, "they'd fire you. They didn't want to disturb the public. Concello was strict about that. Rehashing tickets didn't disturb the public; it cheated the show itself."

Another scam that cheated the show was the sale of tickets to a seat wagon that was reported to the front office as having been left behind at the train for repairs. This meant the red wagon refrained from selling tickets for the numberd chairs on that particular wagon, while the ushers

inside the tent pocketed extra cash by making their own personal transactions. Then, too, the staff made hay whenever overflow crowds had to
be seated on straw placed on the hippodrome track. It was a bonanza for
the Ringling scalpers. Art Concello himself was arrested once in San
Diego, California, and made to sit in a sheriff's office for two hours on
charges of having allegedly sold the big top beyond its legal capacity. While
he waited for his legal aduster ("the fixer") to come down and get him
released with an acceptable payoff, all he could say in his defense was how
hard it was to deny admission to throngs of women and children.

To keep a sizable work force around, a number of illegal activities were
tolerated. Drinking and gambling among workingmen thrived in the
"G-Top" (also known as the "Blue Room"), where an endless succession
of ushers, ticket sellers, roustabouts, and the like went with what little
money they had honestly earned to squander it away on frivolous addictions.
The buzzing little center of illicit pleasure, located in the backyard, served
two purposes: to get most of the money paid out by the show back into the
show (into the hands of the managers, that is) and, as aerialist La Norma
Fox so convincingly puts it, "they sort of liked for them to do it. That way
they were broke all the time and couldn't leave the show. They were
drifters. They would always try and find a better place to go. This way,
they never had enough money."[11]

Not only that. The broke canvas men would trudge haplessly up to the
red wagon for an advance, payable as an automatic deduction from his
next paycheck—minus 50 percent interest. "You always had to watch your
rigger," says Mary Jane Miller, "because the moment they got paid they
bought their wine and would get drunk."[12]

Despite all the artistic North frills, it remained a tough world moved by
a tough breed of characters. If the show did not condone the bootleg sale
of alcohol, which kept these itinerant hands near their posts, it risked their
wandering off in search of a liquor store and never returning. The G-Top
was certainly not Concello's invention, he has noted without apology,
referring to its presence (a small fifteen-by-fifteen-foot tent) in the backyard
ever since he first went to work for the circus. And as for its adverse effects
on the competence and morale of the staff, Concello would argue that
without the G-Top he couldn't keep his good bosses around, either.[13]

Some historians have held (perhaps overlooking the complete picture,
perhaps not) that there was a time when the Ringling show did not
condone such activities. What happened under the new North-Concello
regime at least represented a shift in imagery away from the older concept

of a more ethically regulated atmosphere. The Mafia mentality behind Concello's management style did attract a host of unsavory types to the lot. Where there was money to be made under the table, there were con men to do it.

Symptomatic of these changes was a bizarre spectacle of violence in the center ring during a 1948 matinee. Aerial star Chrysis De La Grange, at the completion of her turn in Barbette's "Monte Carlo Aerial Ballet," was confronted by another performer, sway-pole artist Kalsh Alberty, who slugged her in the face. Police hauled both down to the station, where Alberty was charged with assault and battery and later released on two hundred dollars bail. The reason for the argument was never revealed.

Little did the crowds realize that the seat wagons they occupied straddled two alien worlds: the performers on the one side dressing below in the wagons and the spaces between them; the workingmen on the other side, loitering about in the shadows, crap games in session, empty bottles strewn about as the show went on. Two of the most dangerous so-and-sos ever to hit the lot were a couple of brothers who arrived during the 1950 season after serving jail terms for a Brink's robbery. One of them took an instant liking to Daisy Hall, a single showgirl (by then the old rules banning contact between showgirls and the staff no longer applied). Daisy did not suspect the guy's dreadful background at first, so she went out with him on a date or two. Quickly he became infatuated, declaring his intention to marry her, a feeling not mutually shared.

He started calling her Maggie in his erratic rages while under the influence. He terrified her in a New Orleans lounge, where he had taken her after the show, by threatening to kill her if she continued resisting his proposals. When he adjourned to the restroom, Phil Hall, then a good friend of Daisy, hurried her out of the club. Later, Killer Kane, another friend of Daisy who had served time in prison, came to her rescue. Kane had words with Daisy's mad pursuer, warning the thug, "If you dare touch her *or* Phil, I'll chop your goddamn arm off!"

Daisy also could have reported her fears to Dummy, a bigger-than-life hulk, unable to speak a word, whom Concello had brought with him off the Beatty show. Whenever Phil was harassed by one of the sundry goons who attached themselves to the underbelly of the circus, he would go see Concello, his good friend. This would result in a visit by Dummy to the offending party. Dummy's big hand went up in the person's face and the message was clear:

"Don't do that."

No, don't.

Did anyone defy Dummy's wishes?

Never.

"It was like a damn movie," says Hall.

What were these types doing around the show anyway? "They were ushers. That's the type the show was starting to attract."[14]

John was shielded from most of this unpleasantness by Art, even though he is likely to have known what was going on. It enabled Johnny to spend more time abroad searching for new talent and living his charmed life. John came around the show so infrequently that he had to rely on Art, and this meant putting up with policies he may have disliked privately. When the two became embroiled in an argument—which was very seldom—Art would invite John to come back and manage things himself, without Concello. "If you want to do it your way, stay here and do it your way."[15]

Art could be every bit as belligerent as John, and he began to seize more control by exploiting John's need for a single person to mind the store while John was incessantly away. Insiders wondered where the power struggle might lead. In the words of one, "I think Art always figured that he could outdo somebody and end up with the show himself."[16]

To what extent the so-called Concello scams cut into the profit margin is difficult to estimate. Another profit-reducing factor was the skyrocketing cost of a North-produced circus, laden with opulent trappings and a surfeit of newly imported acts. Whereas the show handed a $1,000,000 check to the Hartford-fire receiver at the end of 1946, North now tried getting off with annual contributions of one-tenth that amount. Following such a payment in 1948, the officials in Hartford protested. John relented with a second check for $100,000. He wasn't nearly the good sport that his relatives had been in complying with the Hartford arbitration agreement. After the 1950 tour, John agreed to a lump-sum final payment of $690,612.43. This was the balance due on claims that had totaled $3,946,535.70.

Nineteen forty-eight was a very good year. Despite a crippling coal strike early in the season that threatened the movement of circuses and carnivals via coal-burning railroads, the Ringling train kept on rolling. En route to New York, the cars were attached to regular freight trains, then switched in Washington, D.C., to electrified lines. Big crowds waited in the Big Apple. On the West Coast, the circus turned away thousands of customers nightly at the new Cow Palace in San Francisco, a venue it did

not originally wish to play. Ringling agents had their eyes on a vacant tract
of public-utilities land in the city's North Beach area. Only after being
thwarted with red tape at city hall did they agree, instead, to book the
Cow Palace for eight days. The arena was bombarded by turnaway crowds,
and never again did Ringling officials desire to play anywhere in San
Francisco but that rather drab structure on foggy, windswept Geneva
Avenue, situated ideally close to nearby railroad yards. San Franciscans
never experienced the curious frustration of viewing the Greatest Show
on Earth from a Duran-upholstered chair on a Concello-designed seat
wagon.

Turnaway houses greeted the show in many other cities, it was that
kind of a year. Publicist Frank Braden went to town describing the season
in a route-book piece titled "Bulls Eye for Big Bertha." Braden's account
began thus: "Spectacular has been the Big Show's season of 1948—
spectacular in its triumphal coast-to-coast tour, in its mighty operation, in
its phenomenal grosses and in its never-to-be-forgotten performance."[17]

So far so good. North and Concello had little to worry about, or so it
appeared. Except that the future is forever changing. They were quickly
thrown on the defensive because of opposition mounted against them in
1949 by Cole Bros. Circus, the new owner of which, Jack Tavlin, acted like
he wanted to run Ringling off the road. A nasty series of day-and-date
battles between the two shows erupted. John and Art spent a heap of
money on extra advertising and WAIT posters, encouraging potential customers in cities booked by both circuses to WAIT FOR THE BIG SHOW. John
became so obsessed with his raging competitors that, according to trade
reports, he ordered Concello to route the show back to California for the
second year in a row (something never before done) just so he could stay
ahead of the Cole show on the West Coast and "smash it" out of existence.
At stops where Ringling had been predated by Cole, business suffered
accordingly. In Harrisburg, Pennsylvania, for example, where Cole Bros.
drew seven thousand five hundred customers, eight days later the Ringling
visit yielded about twice the patronage, still far from capacity takes. Ringling's
attendance records dropped that year. Cole's were worse. Tavlin elevated
veteran Cole Ticket Department official Frank Orman to manager in
midseason, but the show headed to the barns in early October with no
profits to speak of. The Cole title was acquired the following season by
Chicago ice-show magnate Arthur W. Wirtz and his Chicago Stadium
corporation.

Cole's new owner vowed to unseat North and Concello in the circus world. And his hiring of William ("Hopalong Cassidy") Boyd as a feature attraction provoked North into rare humor. That year North had imported Leon de Rousseau, who did a backward somersault drop from a fifty-foot tower to the ground, so John had Rousseau appear in cowboy attire and introduced as "Dropalong Placidly."

Wirtz presented a more menacing threat by booking his circus into large city arenas and baseball stadiums (all of which he partly owned), where he could play to potentially larger crowds. He opened the 1950 tour in his own Chicago Stadium. In New York that summer, the Cole show performed in Yankee Stadium, drawing one turnout of forty-seven thousand persons. After ten weeks of indoor dates, Wirtz put the show under canvas, beginning in Philly, where Ringling had played two months earlier. Business was light. On the whole, Wirtz did not do so well in many spots, failing to draw the kind of reviews or word of mouth needed to fill up the seats in any engagement beyond an opening-day rush. After scoring a few publicity points and raising North's and Concello's adrenaline, the Chicago impressario retired the show in mid-August. He brought it out again briefly in 1951, long enough to suffer a poorly patronized Chicago opening, and called it quits for good. A once-popular circus (favored by some fans even over Ringling) disappeared altogether from the sawdust trail.

Johnny and Art breathed easier. The two-year rivalry took its toll on their attendance. The 1949 route book recorded that the circus played to 3,473,000 souls that year—down sharply from more than 4,000,000 customers it entertained during the 1942 season; it drew even less, 3,179,000, in 1950. It can't all be blamed on the Cole competition. Society was changing in the aftermath of the war; people were responding to new forms of entertainment. Television was here. Movie business soared. The Grand Free Street Parade was headed for the museums.

For the gracious time being, John North and Art Concello accepted their moderate returns with an air of optimism. The reviews ranged from good to excellent. Many a house was filled to overflowing. And they moved forward in a strange kind of unspoken collaboration, creating together a circus world quite different in tone from the one before. Behind the scenes it was grimmer, out front and in the performance more sophisticated and surreal.

John preferred the surreal, so close were his sensitivites to those of an Impressionist painter. For a few glorious years, he drifted through a dream, playing the role of circus king to the hilt, posing for cameras, being seen at chic night spots around the globe. He never worried much about Art, back there someplace on the lot, moving through the shadows of flapping canvas and rumbling wagons, counting out a wad of bills, collecting more privilege payoffs, stuffing them all away in his personal assortment of cookie jars.

Neither had a worry in the world.

Jet-Set Johnny

He moved through Europe in his custom-built Cadillac, moved from city to city in search of yet more new acts. In the front seat sat Henri, his chauffeur, and next to Henri was Umberto Bedini, his Italian booking agent and consultant. He slept in the backseat, his girlfriend beside him, the shades usually drawn. They might be on their way to audition a bicycle troupe in Copenhagen or off to check out a juggler in Madrid. They knew that wherever they ended up, the evening would be topped off with a lavish sampling of the best local cuisine, after which they would spend half the night around drinks in some suave cocktail lounge. Another day, another party. Maybe another act signed for next year's edition of Ringling Bros. and Barnum & Bailey.

In a sense, he never grew out of that little boy back in Baraboo, jumping over silver bars and running around big red wagons, being given lots of wonderful things by his uncles and the people who worked for them, and in his mind thinking that whatever he wanted was his to have. Only now, he owned it all, and he took a lifelong delight in having the circus provide for his every amusement and pleasure. Abroad scouting for tomorrow's stars, or in the States just being in the States, he indulged himself in the finest restaurants and hotels, and rarely without a beautiful woman by his side. This was the life his Uncle John had known and the life John North was determined to live. In Paris, he put up at the Ritz (usually his center of operations), and went on menu-sampling sprees at all the hot spots: Maxim's and the Larue, Fouquet's, L'Escargot, Le Relais de la Belle-Aurore, and La Tour d'Argent. Then he transferred his attention to the famous spa, Baden-Baden, relaxing there in the enervating mud to "take the cure." He would down liebfraumilch rather than the sulfur waters, which he detested, and, when the baths bored him, spend time blowing away on his saxophone.[1]

His dress sartorially refined, John avoided ostentation for its own sake, yet he was a sight pictorially: a homburg hat, cane or umbrella, gloves, and buffed shoes. He was determined to perpetuate his Uncle John's persona in every way he knew how, and in so doing he was the actor who became the part he played. When not in the backseat of an automobile being cozy with whomever, John presented a regal face to the world. He was the bon vivant of the big top, the affable yet distant circus king who favored a handful of "friends" and smart acquaintances, mostly from the privileged realms of high achievement or high society. Dick Barstow, commenting on the royal airs John affected, is reminded of the princess who slept on seventeen mattresses and could still feel the presence, under one, of a single pin.

"He had the bearing of a very European-style gentleman," offers Phil Hall, whose friendship with Art Concello enabled him to observe North close up on a couple of telling occasions. "He was very theatrical, and he played the part well. And he never lowered those things. He put on that posture all the time. He played the part of a prince, and yet I think there was always a veneer of pretentiousness about John because he wasn't a prince."[2]

John's tinseled aspirations were partly a reflection of his family's elitist attitudes. Many of the Ringlings strove through art to assert a sense of superiority—as if to compensate for the comparatively low esteem in which circuses were held. As if, almost, the initial reservations of August Ringling over his sons' tent-show ambitious continued to haunt the family. The name Ringling never stood for ballet or theater or symphonic music; it merely stood for circus. Another possible reason for John's overidentification with high society was his father's simple job on the railroad. Did John suffer from an inferiority complex because of this? Stuart Lancaster believes he did.

Whatever he suffered from would be difficult to trace behind all the layers of pretense. John rarely disclosed his innermost fears or wishes. The newfound success he enjoyed in partnership with Concello extended his reputation across the Atlantic into the more prestigious European circus world. He extracted so many first-rate performers from abroad that the name Ringling Bros. and Barnum & Bailey conjured up visions of fame and fortune in the land of opportunity. John's talent-finding travels from circus to circus epitomized the wisdom of American know-how on the move. That was a time when the United States stood for the highest standards in numerous endeavors, from automobile design and washing machines to motion pictures and record players. The name John Ringling North stood for spectacular performances under the big top, laden with top talent from across the ocean. His developing mystique captivated the show world. He was naturally photogenic (a handsome presence in beer ads), though not a lively interview on radio or television, so monotonic was his manner of speech. In the private company of friends, he exuded a quiet charm. He seldom dominated the conversation, and many who enjoyed his companionship cannot recall his ever uttering a single profane word. In Dick Barstow's estimation, he was "a lady's gentleman and a gentleman's gentleman."[3]

He loved telling stories in the vein of a well-traveled raconteur, mostly about the goings-on of the rich and the famous whose paths he had crossed. He shied away from intellectualizing over abstract ideas. Phil Hall was with John and Art at the Copacabana in New York, John having returned from Italy, where he attended the 1951 world premiere in Venice of Stravinsky's opera *The Rake's Progress*. Hall, a music lover who later served as executive director of the Sarasota-based Asolo Opera Company, was anxious to know what John thought. The critique offered in response was hardly articulate. "I just don't think it was that good a work," said John, leaving it at that.[4]

He had attended the opera because it was the place to be seen. John's kind of music was simple Irish tunes and early American folk songs that he could snap out on his fingers. He liked playing the spoons, too, and he enjoyed patronizing Broadway musicals and light operas. "I wouldn't presume to talk to him too much about classical music," says Hall, "for he never really mentioned it."

Neither did John relate well to serious topics of the day, not, at least, in the presence of his circus associates. He had little to say about politics, and if he subscribed to a political party, he never mentioned it with much conviction. John was not drawn to petty gossip, either, unless it involved the changing fortunes of some famous acquaintance of his. And on matters of art, he displayed a natural sensitivity to aesthetics, although he rarely, if ever, verbalized about it much.

What John is mostly remembered for dwelling on were wines and cuts, places to dine, and important people. He dropped names with relish, and he adored the companionship of those from high places. For him, socializing in style was the ultimate pleasure. He lapped it up at every chance, music, drink, and chatter his perpetual jet-set high. He could handle every drink in a bartender's manual. And to keep his internal distresses in check, John kept a supply of Pepto-Bismol inside his coat pocket at all times, which he consumed with slavish devotion. Once out of it and panicking abroad, he telephoned another consumer in the States, Bing Crosby, who had fifteen cases flown to him the next day. Then John had to hire a lawyer to get it through French customs.[5]

The Ringling impresario drew celebrities to his table, such figures as J. Paul Getty, Sr., who became a good friend; the French Impressionist Vertés; world-class actors; and noted authors. He spent countless hours in drinking camaraderie with Ernest Hemingway, the two compatibly attuned to escapist pleasures. Others answered the call, of course, simply because John was something of a curiosity to behold and here was another excuse to indulge in good company.

Then there were times when John's late-night invitations did not fall on grateful ears. Columnist Robert Ruark was startled out of his sleep at 4 A.M. over a phone call from Mr. North, merrily inviting him to tea. The place was Havana, where the circus was playing a December engagement at the Sports Palace. It inspired a caustic column by Ruark, cynically describing the circus man as someone who ought to be locked up in a cage and displayed in his own show. Ruark reported that Hemingway himself had once chosen "two plane crashes and two wars over constant association with Mr. North." What really annoyed the columnist was John's seemingly indestructible youth and vigor as he passed his fiftieth birthday: "He bears no scars to show for his nocturnal prowlings in the jungles us poor, timid folks are afraid to approach. . . . This character continues to look like a candidate for a high-school debating team. My poor battered face has more seams, lumps, puffs, broken veins and oddly assorted chins than any one of Mr. North's clowns, but John has a complexion like Miss Rheingold and the stamina of a chorus girl."[6]

John's health amazed even the medical world. Each winter, he checked into the Mayo Clinic for a thorough exam. He was routinely released with flying colors, the doctors terming his exemplary condition incredible in view of the strenuous schedules he kept. A bundle of restless, thrusting energy, he was forever going back and forth between the United States and Europe. Of course, it was business that ostensibly took him abroad and justified the thousands of miles he covered in search of new talent.

The many compelling artists John engaged set him dramatically apart from other showmen, even from his own uncles. No one before John who produced the Ringling show came close to matching his overall record for the number of new acts imported season after season. Dick Barstow called him "an impressario but not a pitchman."[7] Indeed, John left the ballyhoo mostly up to his press agents, headed by the vociferous Roland Butler. Given John's generosity as a showman, they were easily inspired, as evidenced by this trade ad taken out shortly after the 1949 season began:

> The Big Show's in Madison Square Garden—and all's right with the world.
>
> In this, its 75th year, the Ringling Bros. and Barnum & Bailey Circus has electrified New York with the beauty of its ensemble productions, its abundance of sensational acts, its amazing speed and its wide-angled appeal.
>
> NOW IS THE HOUR OF JOHN RINGLING NORTH.
>
> His 1949 edition of the Greatest Show on Earth, accorded highest acclaim by press and public, is the talk of New York, as it soon will be the talk of the nation.[8]

In the eyes of many, John's endorsement of an act meant the ultimate in global validation. Indeed, he alone occupied a place in popular culture as the only circus talent scout ever to become famous for it. Interviewed for a profile piece in the *New Yorker*, Pat Valdo, another top judge of talent, declared John "the best circus scout this circus ever had, and I mean better than all four of his uncles put together."[9] Indeed, North achieved such respect in this field that he was portrayed in the 1956 film classic *Trapeze* as a force for inspiration. The North character shows up in several key scenes, checking on the progress of Tony Curtis in his quest to catch a triple somersault. At one point, Curtis's flying partner, played by Burt Lancaster, goads him on to try for the elusive feat just one more time by yelling, "John Ringling North is down there! Let's show him some *real* circus!"

Also in 1956, when John's prestige and visibility were at their highest levels, he was invited by the editors of *This Week* magazine, a Sunday newspaper supplement, to answer this question submitted by a reader: "What is the greatest single circus attraction you ever saw?" John's insistence on giving credit to a number of personal favorites ("incomparables in each class") fleshed out a fine two-page feature story. He was high on: Rastelli, the young juggler ("could juggle anything he could lift—china vases, flaming torches, knives—and in incredible quantities"), who died suddenly on the eve of his debut with John's show; Charlie Rivels, "the magnificent Spanish clown," whom John was never able to sign. "He was in essence a highly gifted trapeze acrobat who shaded his daring into laughter." John described a Rivels aerial routine that was patterned after Charlie Chaplin "the greatest clown turn I ever saw." In the trained-animal division, he nominated another act that never made it to his circus, a whimsical troupe of musical pigs that played xylophones, horns, bells, piano, and bass drum. They only got to appear in this country before inspectors from the U.S. Department of Agriculture promptly impounded them for foot-and-mouth disease.

In John's opinion, Alfred Court ranked as the greatest wild-animal trainer. "He was a master stylist . . . not in the pyrotechnical manner of the trainers who fire guns and shout and crack whips. . . . His animals were at all times in magnificent control. . . . He got precise response with quiet mastery." John praised Unus, "the most sensational equilibrist by far," spoke with affection of both P. T. Barnum's big animal star and his own ("Who can decide between Jumbo and Gargantua?"), tipped his hat to the legendary flyer Alfredo Codona. Finally, he paid the warmest tribute of all to his all-time overall personal favorite, Lillian Leitzel, who performed one-arm springovers from a rope, going in a continuous circle upward, often for 150 or 160 revolutions, once twirling around 239 times without stopping. "The spectacle of the dainty and lovely Lillian, twirling like a human pinwheel, high in the top of the tent, may never find its equal as long as there is a circus anywhere."[10]

About John's talent scouting style: he combined a great amount of pleasure with a small amount of work. He did not see many of the artists booked under his aegis until they opened the following spring in New York at Madison Square Garden. He often relied on the word of his agents. Other times, he might book a troupe because another show owner whose track record he respected was after it, too. The English circus owner Cyril B. Mills delivered many fine acts into John's hands in this fashion when the two crossed paths each year while both were canvassing Europe for new headliners for their respective shows. Mills operated the Bertram Mills Circus, established by his late father, for over thirty years until he closed it in 1966. And since he presented only short winter seasons, any act that signed with him could also sign with Ringling, whose tour did not conflict.

"In the early postwar years," recounts Mills, "I often met JRN and his agent Umberto Bedini in Scandinavia, which was good talent hunting ground for us both. I was not allowed by the Variety Artists Federation [Equity] to employ any ex-enemies and JRN was able to buy animals seized by the Swedish government against Nazi debts incurred in the purchase of war materials. During later years we met all over the Continent and there were occasions when Bedini and I went to the circus either in JRN's Cadillac or my Mercedes Benz."

The two owners attended a few circus performances together, but North did not discuss his personal reactions to any act with Mills. "It is not done for circus directors to pass verdicts on the likes and dislikes of one another," says Mills, "but I noticed he booked several acts which had a lot of girls, and I think he did this because the girls did an act and also had to appear without extra pay in production numbers and specs, and therefore they cost him less than American girls who only worked in production numbers."[11]

John took in very few matinees, partly because he slept so late, but more important, as Mills has helpfully pointed out, because of a policy by many of the smaller outfits abroad (from which future stars were discovered) to cut corners at the early show. Fewer spotlights were used, performers dressed in second-drawer costumes, and the companies that operated seven days a week gave them time off during certain afternoon shows. While they were doing this, it would have been most embarrassing to the owners had an important foreign director, such as North, decided to attend unannounced. John's principal agent, Bedini, took in the matinees in any event and reported back to the boss over a leisurely dinner.

A precious few of the acts that John engaged made little sense to hardly anyone at all, they were either so bad or so oddly out of place. Cyril Mills questions the wisdom of North's hiring two mediocre German nightclub entertainers, Rolly-Arry, to do their comedy singing act, *solo*, in his center ring. (*Variety* judged them "overlong and not very amusing.") It can be safely surmised, since John was more daringly inclined than his conservative agents to take a chance with an unusual act, that he himself saw and signed Rolly-Arry. Another questionable novelty that John would place his contractual faith in was a mere child xylophonist, Mister Mistin, whose placement on the Ringling bill in 1953 never made sense to Mills, either.

A risk taken to heart, nonetheless, North more actively pursued artists whose greatness he knew of, or those who resisted the initial offers of employment advanced by his agents. He wanted so badly to sign the vivacious young Irish juggler Veronica Martel that he called up her uncle at three in the morning.[12] Martell, one of only two Irish turns ever to work for North (the other was the wonderfully amusing Stephenson's Dogs), eventually signed. As were so many of the offerings that John went after, Martel's routine was very novel and very refreshing, the high point being her juggling a large number of small balls against the floor.

North could be vulnerable to a fast-talking performer who promised great things and dangled an expensive price tag. A low-wire walker once caught his attention in this way, insisting that he was worth five or six hundred dollars a week. North was so impressed with the performer's come-on that he decided to travel all the way up to Circus Scott in Sweden, where the man was next engaged to appear, just to check him out. The performer proved to be "no good," as remembered by John, recounting the fruitless quest.[13] A contract offer did not follow.

When he became involved in contract talks, John's easy demeanor turned cool and stern in the face of stiff negotiations. He offered piddling terms at first, held out for gradual concessions grudgingly consented to. According to some, he was every bit as unscrupulous as his Uncle John had been in luring artists to the States with visions of streets paved with gold.[14] Elly Ardelty was given assurances that did not come to pass. She had wanted to bring her rigging man over with her, to which North supposedly replied, "Okay, don't worry; we'll take care of that." It didn't turn out that way, though. The diminutive aerialist, billed as "The Russian Bird of Paradise," brought over only her large theatricalized bird cage. It was used by Barbette as the centerpiece in a spectacle in which all the North Starlets were dressed as cats. Ardelty had to rely on the Ringling roustabouts, under whose careless handling the prop became a bit too realistic. "She was just a darling little creature out there," recalls Jackie Le Claire. "They'd pull her up in this bird cage. . . . Sometimes that thing had been left in the horseshit, cowshit, and who knows what else. She'd have to sit in there and be delicate and graceful."[15]

Another wonderful star John discovered, at first relegating her to an end ring, was La Norma Fox, the pretty and vivacious Danish flyer. La Norma does not report any devious tricks on North's part. In fact, she never actually saw him until she opened with the show in New York City. True to John's quieter approach, he saw her, was impressed, then sent Bedini to inquire after her interest. La Norma feels that the extreme height at which she worked her act in Paris when John caught it is what impressed him the most. The package deal Bedini offered her included a place in the show for her husband, Andre Fox, to present his twelve liberty horses.

Sometime after her premiere at Madison Square Garden, La Norma was finally met by John, just in passing. "He was a very very pleasant gentleman," she recalls. "Very friendly, very nice. A very mild-mannered person."

Did he ever compliment her act?

"If he did, I don't remember. I don't think he got into much conversation with people. But he was friendly. He never walked past you without giving you a nice smile."[16]

A more colorful story, suspiciously unorthodox, concerns how John came across one of his great finds, Pinito Del Oro. As told by Robert Lewis Taylor in his book *Center Ring,* John discovered the lovely aerialist with a band of roadside entertainers in southern Spain. The two retired, at John's invitation, to a gypsy cave on the outskirts of Murcia, where a contract was drawn up and signed. But according to an account Del Oro gave *American Weekly* while performing with her father's Gran Circo Segura in Seville one night, she was spotted by a scout from the Ringling show and signed to a contract.[17]

How was Unus signed? According to his own account, North suffered many obstacles in his campaign to win over the celebrated soul who stood on his forefinger. The act was out of this world before it was, years later, duplicated by second-rate imitators. John drove all over Spain in a rented car in search of Unus, arriving in Granada and Barcelona just after, in each city, he had left. North finally caught up with him in Madrid, again after his engagement was over. Without ever having actually seen Unus perform, John immediately went to work on the equilibrist.

"You would like to go to America?"

"I don't know," answered Unus, coyly blasé. "I have heard it is not so good."

John talked faster than he usually did, painting a glowing picture of the opportunities ahead. Unus's assistant, Viva Asgard, was more receptive, and John played to the glow in her eyes. Unus remained indifferent to the idea while Asgard embraced it with increasing zeal. John talked on. A contract was laid on the table.

"I don't know," said the performer.

"We should sign it. We should go over there." said the woman.

"Okay, sign whatever you want. I don't care."

The sketchy document was signed by Asgard. John assumed he had next year's star under assignment.

Such hollow confidence. When John was up in Belgium a few months later, where Unus was performing his act on top of a light tower, he invited him to dinner to confirm the arrangements. By then Unus had come to his senses over the "ridiculous" terms of the contract that his assistant had signed. He was not about to join Ringling Bros. Circus for such an insulting compensation, a fact conveyed to North through icy disinterest.

John was beside himself. "You are to be in New York!"

"I won't go for this contract," protested Unus.

"You *must!*"

"Too little."

"You signed the agreement."

"I did not!"

"If you don't go," threatened John, "I'll stop you from working Europe."

"Go ahead," said the amazing equilibrist, now on both feet and headed for the door.

"You can't do that!"

He did.

John didn't clean his plate that evening. He spent the next few days haggling over terms with Unus. Bedini went back and forth between the two. Unus finally relented with a proposal that would guarantee him optimum treatment—or else. "Listen, Mr. North," he said. "I have so much. Performer has to pay his trip. Now if I come and I don't like it, you have to put in contract you will pay my way back to Europe again."[18]

John agreed. At a moment's notice, Unus could turn his back on America's biggest big top and leave it without the star attraction it would be investing thousands of dollars to advertise. In the headliner's own words, "North sent the word ahead to his staff: 'Now comes a man, his name is Unus. Give him everything he wants. Everything. Don't hesitate, because he's the one, he will turn around and go away.'"

A king's treatment he received. The hype accorded Unus—this from his billing in the circus magazine—paid tribute, however, to his new employer as well:

Flushed with a Succession of European Triumphs, but Shy of An American Venture, Only John Ringling North's persuasion Brings to America for the First Time the Upside-Down-Gravity Defying, Equilibristic Wonder, the Debonair, Incredible

UNUS

The Man Who Stands on His Forefinger[19]

The effort paid off in tremendous prestige to North and the circus, if not in consecutively sold-out houses. In *The Billboard*'s estimation, Unus was given more news space and radio time than any performer had ever received. He was not given a single pay raise, however, during the three consecutive seasons he appeared in Johnny's center ring. Unus departed the Ringling payroll in 1951 in search of more profitable bookings with indoor circuses. He and John did stay in friendly touch. In fact, when Unus represented the Ringling show at Dwight D. Eisenhower's 1952 White House inauguration as a personal favor to John, he was actually then a Shrine Circus superstar. He had come off one indoor date to play the White House and had to leave before the festivities were over to make another Shrine engagement the following day.

The one-finger stand performed with suave, mystical control by Franz Furtner (Unus's real name) was a wow of a stunt, slightly outside the realm of true artistry, so good that it seems almost blasphemous to hint at a hidden device cleverly concealed within the sleeve.

Interestingly, for the most part John did not devote himself to such clever exploitations. Gargantua and Unus were two sterling exceptions, the one a menacing creature capable of widespread destruction and the other an acrobat possessing seemingly superhuman balance. Both were illusory, and John usually settled for acts of indisputable skill. Among his further finds the next four seasons from 1948 forward, were the riding Zoppes with Cucciola, superlative juggler Francis Brunn, the Canestrellis on unsupported ladders, the Zavattas on the bounding ropes, Claussen's Bears and Peterson's Jockey Dogs, dressage riders Cilly Feindt and Lilian Wittmack. In the air were the Geraldos and the Rodry Brothers, the Platos, the Similis, Miss Mara and the Great Morituris, and Alma Piaia and the Three Margas. There was La Norma Fox and Pinito Del Oro, Miss Loni, Veronica Martell, Señor Toñito, the Bokara troupe and the Leon de Rousseau troupe. There were the Chaludis, the Rodolpfos, the Reiffs, the Idnavis, Gran Pilona and Kareff Manus and the Fredonia family, and many more.

John's generosity as a talent scout has never been equaled. He even tried acquiring a group of reindeer for his 1948 spec, "'Twas the Night Before Christmas." He got as far as Norway, only to learn the animals he wanted had been quarantined because of an outbreak of foot-and-mouth disease. Santa's sleigh was pulled by a line of antler-bearing pachyderms.

Surprisingly, given the eye-opening evidence now available on a number of new video recordings of actual Ringling performances in the 1940s and 1950s out on the fan market, many top-drawer turns signed by North and his scouts have been either overlooked or underrated in time. These include the likes of zany animal performers and star aerialists (some of whom have already been mentioned) whose wonderful exploits have somehow not survived the collective memory of fans and historians very well. I'll mention only a few of these neglected gems. For starters, the dashing bravado and novel participation of elephant trainer Baptiste Schreiber, who appeared with the show only one season, 1950, and from whom a young Gunther Gebel-Williams is sure to have derived a good measure of his own similarly theatrical style, has been curiously under-reported over the years. Schreiber was sent flying into the air off a teeterboard, activated by one pachyderm, to land on the noggin of another (as Williams would do years later). The massive charges waltzed and strutted through the sawdust, as did their humorously inclined trainer, who appeared to be goading them on. In another inventive twist, the plucky trainer stood over two bulls facing each other, one foot planted on each of their heads, and sank eerily into a semisplit position as the mammoths slowly parted company.

Hammerschmidt's Wonder Apes, featured in the 1952 and 1953 editions on a raised stage, cleverly enacted domestic "human" activities in a wildly amusing vein, although the act's grossly realistic agenda did not charm everybody. Among the very basic household rituals mimicked: the lighting of the trainer's cigarette by one very deft and accommodating chimp seated next to him at the dinner table; the going off to bed by another ape, who first knelt down to pray, then took his potty and, figuring the little bowl might make someone a nice hat, tried it out for size on his head.

Headliners in 1951 and 1952, the Rodry Brothers delivered a chilling work of aerial audacity wherein one member, serving as the catcher from a cradle rigging, hurled his partner through a fast-moving series of forward and backward somersaults and pirouettes between his outstretched arms, the two not connected in any way during the tricks. Even more incredible for this type of act, the pair worked without a net below or any safety wires whatsoever (as did, for that matter, virtually all aerialists, except for the flyers, in those days of perilous integrity).

Another fabulous duo who worked a double-trap act were the Geraldos. Booked for the 1949 and 1950 tours, they executed extremely rare ankle-to-ankle catches among their many thrilling swaps and lifesaving connections that kept them miraculously off the sawdust. A near tragic fall their first season out with Ringling led to the installation, the next year, of a small net below.

Although he was deservedly billed "The Greatest Juggler of All Ages" and given the center spot for the three consecutive seasons he appeared with the show, starting in 1948, the tremendously talented Francis Brunn has, nonetheless, never, it seems, received just acclaim for his rapid-fire, sensationally choreographed performances to the music of Khachaturian's "Saber Dance." Every spellbinding movement in his rhythmically twisting body made it, too, seem like just another prop under his intrepid control. Brunn sustained constant motion. Balls, hoops, and clubs whirled over his head, through his legs. Sometimes one came rolling across his back or along his arms, to be smoothly tossed off hands and feet into other moving designs. The intensely active Brunn created fountains of color. Truly he was, as the ringmaster announced him, "THE NIJINSKY OF THE MAGIC GLOBES!"

Single-trapeze artist La Norma Fox was another star who offered that kind of marvelous fluidity in her own nonstop program. Her loving reach for the audience was as immediately human as was the detached poetic mystery of Pinito Del Oro, who, in stark contrast, moved through her own surreal sphere above as if oblivious to the crowds below quietly watching her in utter amazement. Both aerialists were stunners.

The American circus scene was literally flooded with transatlantic talent booked by John Ringling North. And once these artists were released from their Ringling contracts, many transferred to more lucrative jobs on the indoor Shrine circuit produced by the likes of Orrin Davenport and the Polack Bros. Circus. Many of them worked back-to-back seasons for John North and still made winter dates as well. Like Unus, they could make twice as much money whenever they appeared with another show.

A whole contingent of familiar faces—including La Norma, Claussen's Bears, Peterson's Jockey Dogs, Francis Brunn, and even the Ringling elephants—who were seen during the off-season in such places as Detroit and Indianapolis, played the same cities the following summer under Big Bertha's canvas. So popular were these acts that John could not prevent them from working elsewhere when his red wagons rolled into winter hibernation. His influence was everywhere, especially in the Sarasota circus community, where most of the performers he brought to America eventually settled.

The American Guild of Variety Artists, which held a union contract with the circus, began making waves about the influx of these foreign acts, wanting to limit their number on any program to 40 percent. North resisted, arguing that the primary source of new talent was Europe. Ironically, many of the stars he originally hired were now on the outside, resentful of yet more foreigners being allowed into the country to appear with Ringling. AGVA guidelines failed to materialize into a binding labor law.

John's hectic jaunts abroad were challenged by the extensive paperwork required to get an act out of the country. This, along with the need for an interpreter, is what prompted him to hire Umberto Schichtholz Bedini, the Italian agent he had come to know over the years. Bedini's primary task was to round up all the acts he and John had signed on a typical charge across the Continent and see to it that all the necessary passport and travel arrangements were made through American Express. In 1949, they covered together some twelve thousand miles, touring from southern Spain to the northern tip of Sweden.

Bedini's assistance also freed Johnny to spend more time pursuing his social interests. Miles White remembers much of John's European itinerary consisting of nightclubs and bars. They'd take in a very late dinner, which North ordered ahead. Usually with John then was his girlfriend of the time, Gloria Drew, along with Bedini. Various other guests were invited to join them at table. White recalls the chic merriment and hip good humor of it all. After dinner, they'd go to a club, then maybe another, ending up—when in Paris—at Monsieur's. While violins played, a car with driver stood by to take the guests home, as, one after another, they either tired or passed out. Johnny outlasted them all as night stretched into early morning. He liked to keep the orchestra going, and sometimes he'd send his chauffeur back to the Ritz, where he was staying, to bring some of his music back for the musicians to play. White fondly remembers what jazzy times those were.[20]

Irving Caesar, the noted lyricist who collaborated with John on songs for the 1955 production numbers, was intrigued by his partner's extraordinary lifestyle, although he couldn't overlook its superficial aspects. "I don't think that John had a driving ambition for most things except to live well, which, of course, is an art in itself," Caesar said. "And he had the courage to live well. I take my hat off to him. He was a bon vivant who played at being a polished man of business, a man of affairs, a pleasure-loving fella who did penitence now and then by going to the cures of Europe and justifying it by looking for talent."[21]

There were rare moments when John turned briefly away from the bright lights that obsessed him in his younger years, put his drink aside, and looked straight ahead at something real. One such moment surely occurred in 1946, when, on the night of December 22, he took in a performance of the famed Berlin Scala Revue in Barcelona; its director, Edward Duisberg, was a friend of his. John saw in the chorus a woman of riveting beauty. After the show, he was told by Duisberg that her name was Ida von Zedlitz-Trützschler. At John's suggestion, all of the girls were invited out for drinks. In this way he could be introduced to the young ballerina in the safety of a group and thus avoid offending her with a too-sudden come-on. John was sensitive when need be, and he laid out a delicate romantic foundation wisely and well.

Ida responded on cue, and although she was the only girl in the chorus who could speak some English, she feigned ignorance of the language in John's presence, which added to the mystery of their first meeting. Hampered for lack of words, John broke out into music, singing as many German songs as he knew, according to Ida. She found him "very charming and insistent." The encounter left an indelible impression on both.

They got together again the following March when John caught up with Ida, now performing a solo waltz number with a different revue. He stayed with her for three weeks, attending every night's performance and courting his newfound love afterward. "I learned English," says Ida. "We visited together the best restaurants and were utterly in love with each other."[22]

John had to break away to return to the States for the annual spring rehearsals, but not without the most promising of farewells. "You are different from anybody else I ever knew," he sighed, placing a gentle kiss on her lips. Unus was in their presence on a few occasions and was impressed by the seriousness he felt between them. "I can't say mistress. She helped him a lot. She never was a mistress, because she was a very good girl in the show and I think he treated her pretty nice."[23]

How long the relationship might last was anybody's guess at that point. The pleasure-loving John was prone to any number of dalliances along the road to fame and fortune. Earlier the same year, he announced on Easter Day his intention to wed one Jean Barry McCormick, the daughter of a construction engineer, whom he had met through Rudy Bundy. The romance didn't reach the altar, though, which was not a surprising outcome, given John's growing reluctance to tie himself up in matrimonial knots. In fact, he would never again marry.

A few years later, North met a southern cracker, Gloria Drew, who was selling tickets somewhere in a small-town movie house in Georgia. He succumbed to helpless infatuation, as most men would have over the sight of so blazing a beauty, blessed, some swear, with two eyes each of a different color. John proceeded, gifts and all (for example, one hundred dollar Italian shoes), to set up the twenty-year-old and she took to the arrangement with gleeful abandon, drawn to North's power and purse and more than amenable to the erratic hours he kept. They traveled together across Europe, two carefree sensualists, the one in love with the thrilling immediacy of lust, the other with the accoutrements of wealth.

When Gloria accompanied John on his Continental journeys, ironically she saw very few foreign sights compared to the time she spent at his beck and call, staying up most nights and being too exhausted to enjoy the days. One summer when Miles White was also in North's European party, Gloria announced that she and John would be off the following morning on an act-finding tour. White wondered how the pair would be able to get up so early given the fact they would be out all night. "Oh, no," explained Gloria, "we just stay up."

Once en route, however, they got in their rest. When they set off on one occasion for Amsterdam, White expressed to Gloria what marvelous scenery she could look forward to. "Oh, no," she replied, "John pulls down all the shades and goes to sleep."

Sometimes Drew did venture forth in full daylight—like out the door of the Plaza Dome, where they were staying, to a hairstyling shop a few steps down the boulevard. That's about all she ever is known to have seen of the City of Love. White tried encouraging her to broaden her horizons. He invited her once to visit him, pointing out how easy it would be to find his apartment because it was so close to the Louvre. Gloria still seemed disoriented, having never heard of the Louvre.[24]

She was not as typical of the type of woman John was really attracted to, as some have cynically suggested. She was, though, significantly typical of the life John was then living, when his flirtation with fame and fortune was at its most intense. Drew was, some would say, another adjunct in North's life, more spangles on his résumé, an ornament of success to flaunt along with his exquisite attire and grooming, his fine wines and worldly contacts, his chauffeur-driven evenings into woozy disorientation. "I don't think he gave himself to anybody," observes Stuart Lancaster, "even to his own brother, Henry. I don't think he really equated with anybody. . . . I think he was a loner in the sense that he was all for his ego."[25]

Why do certain people barricade themselves behind such shallow trappings? The stock answer usually leads to a simple word, insecurity. And yet North's life was largely shaped by the bigger-than-life mentality of circus ballyhoo in which, like it or not, he had been raised. His life became a series of grand gestures, synonymous with the sweep of a ringmaster's hand or the strange, fleeting magic of a circus parade passing silently by. And in that surreal sense, everything—well, almost everything—that John did had a rare artistic unity to it. He was truly turning into one of his most intriguing attractions. Original, yes. Explainable, not quite.

Broadway to Sarasota

Back in New York, the party continued. John returned to the Waldorf-Astoria, making sure that window shades were hung in his room to keep the sunlight from disturbing his sleep. At night, he headed for the Turkish baths at the Biltmore, then on to his favorite nightspots—Reuben's, Club 21, where, in Art Concello's words, "he did his act."[1] He frequented an Irish pub, singing along with the band and tapping out the tunes with a spoon against his glass. He could let his hair down without looking too ordinary in the big town.

As he mellowed into the night, he had little to say of importance about anything. Circus? A subject seldom raised except when he might briefly describe a new act he signed that held particular interest for him.

At Reuben's, home of the famous sandwich, John drank brandy alexanders. With acquaintances at hand, he ordered a dozen or so bottles of Helickin, delivered in a silver bucket. A few laughs. A few stories to tell. Chatter and intrigue. Entrances and exits to observe. All very glib and smart. John's circle included a wild, eclectic mix of characters, and to say that he socialized well with members of his production staff, many of them of the gay persuasion, is to note how open and nonjudgmental he was. After all, he was too bohemian himself to be intolerant of eccentricities in others. He respected creativity wherever he found it—indeed, with the same adoration he felt toward the well-honed skills of a juggler or equilibrist. Fun-loving Gloria Drew, John's current mistress, was adaptable in the group. At the world premiere of Agnes De Mille's *Fall River Legend* at the American Ballet Theatre in New York, Drew made a dashing entrance down the aisle arm in arm with Miles White, who had designed the costumes. Phil Hall, who attended the opening-night bash, recalls what a grand impression the two made, the youthful White as handsome as he could be, Gloria with her long blond hair flowing freely. "The most gorgeous couple you ever saw."[2]

It was a party without an end, punctuated by the fresh morning air that greeted John when he returned to his hotel to sleep while most of the world worked. He refused to stay awake during the daylight hours, although he might—before retiring—plunk himself down at a piano and sound the notes of a new tune taking shape in his mind. He also liked running around his suite in the nude, according to Dan Gordon Judge, the lawyer representing Edith and Robert Ringling's interests, who had many dealings with John.[3]

Not everyone in John's employ saw these all-night charades as a fringe benefit. They could become tiresome fast. Art Concello, not known around the show for frequenting many bars with his boss, has confessed that possibly the most difficult thing about working for John were his frequent invitations for companionship. He says that "you learned how to duck out of sight when you saw him coming."[4]

Perhaps because he did not want to be bothered, maybe because he held them in such high regard, John invested unconditional trust in the people he hired to shape and direct his shows. Murray Anderson declared him a breeze to work for. "A man of great courage . . . John left me completely unmolested in my work. I introduced many innovations, but all of them, however, within the idiom of the circus. North never interfered, but was content to accept most of the credit."[5]

Richard Barstow, who did the choreography for Anderson and took over his job as director in 1952, was tickled to recount how he was hired by North, who contacted him rather than vice versa. "Is this Mr. Barstow?" began John, acting on Murray's suggestion that Barstow might be just right for creating the dance routines.

"That sounds fascinating," answered Barstow to the job query. "However, I've never seen a circus."

An awkward silence followed. "Well, ah, tell me, Mr. Barstow. . . . "

"Call me Richard."

"Richard. Have you ever owned an animal?"

"Yes, I have," said Richard. "I owned a little Scotty dog that I got in Scotland when I was a dancer. I called him Tuffy. I loved the animal."

"You *loved* the animal?"

"Oh, absolutely."

John breathed easier. "Well, then, I'm willing to take a chance if you are."[6]

John's methods were the antithesis of committee rule. He refused his business associates a say in the artistic end of things. Typically, the planning of a new circus program commenced a couple of months after the current edition had opened in New York, usually by the time the show was under canvas in Philadelphia. Informal meetings were conducted, attended by John and maybe Henry, Art Concello, Pat Valdo, Murray Anderson and Miles White, special composer Henry Sullivan, and a few production assistants. Ideas were tossed around, some meeting with silence, others stimulating the group to excitement. John sat by like a benign father figure presiding over a circle of gifted children. He might offer a few ideas of his own. Mostly he just watched as the others jockeyed to win support for their brainstorms. He could delicately sway the consensus with a persuasive sigh or the lack of one. Sometimes an original song might suggest the theme of a number. This happened on occasion when John began supplying the production music, which put the creative staff at the mercy of his variable compositions. A melody would be deemed suitable for the spec, then lyrics would be tacked on.

By this time, John's effort to revamp the overall production format had been pretty well established, so that he was now more content to preserve it than disrupt or advance it. Maybe when he first produced there was more humor in the performance. What he now seemed to favor was a lavish spectacle with a semblance of artistic unity holding everything together. Murray Anderson perfected the workable concept with his theater background. He had staged *Jumbo* for Billy Rose, and he had directed his own moderately successful *Almanac* revues. His finest credit was yet to come: the direction of Leonard Sillman's *New Faces of '52* (which Barstow choreographed), considered to be about the best all-around revue ever done.

Anderson held the most influence at the production meetings, followed by Miles White, with whom he had worked so well. Generally, the opulent specs presented in those years fell into one of several categories: exotic locales, Americana, great days of the calendar, fantasy, or patriotism. In 1948, for example, Barbette created "Monte Carlo," an aerial spectacular that to this day is still raved about. Barbette utilized a multitude of trapeze riggings—each individually hung—which required incredible preparation. There were revolving ladders, foot revolves, loop-to-loops, iron jaws, single traps, and cloud swings—and the performers to do all these things simultaneously. "How the hell they ever got that all together without killing anybody I don't know," remarks Jackie Le Claire. "The logistics of it was unbelievable. That they could have all these things going, there must have been guy wires all over the place. Whereas today, everything goes up at once hooked to a single unit."[7]

White dressed the girls in red and black to approximate the French gambling casino. What was more amazing were the complex aerial skills that Barbette was able to pass along, in a relatively short period of time, to the showgirls, many of whom had never seen a circus before in their lives. Mary Jane Miller, who adored the temperamental genius, remembers him as a remarkable teacher. "He could get you to do things you never thought you could do."

Once in a while they veered off the beaten path into alien territory, such as the primordial "Jungle Drums," a rousing elephant romp that brought the 1950 edition to a close. It had a haunting score built around the title song, composed by Henry Sullivan, with dramatic arrangements by Sammy Grossman. The number, filled with ominous swirling counter-melodies, was delivered by Merle Evans and the band with pounding force. "Jungle Drums" suggested a bold departure—perhaps into the realms of terror and suspense—which, unfortunately, was not further explored in subsequent programs.

John was lucky to have such talent. He would sometimes put out a simple request to push a particular performer or idea, as when he once told Dick Barstow, then staging the show, "Do something for Pinito." That was 1954, and Barstow designed a whole number around Pinito Del Oro, "Rocket to the Moon." He had her entering the arena in a fire-emitting rocket. The doors opened, and she emerged from the cockpit sitting on her trapeze bar, which was then hoisted aloft. The surreal Spanish star guarded her pristine image, avoiding the sunshine as much as Johnny seemed to avoid it, so that when she threw her cape aside in the air, her entire body resembled a statue of white marble. The visual poetry was mesmerizing. Del Oro owned the solo spot for seven consecutive seasons, each spent in the center of an aerial extravaganza.

Altogether, the four customary production numbers (spec, aerial ballet, dressage, and finale) were a mixed bag. The notion of there being a single theme for each performance was press agentry. There is little evidence that the staff ever tried relating all the numbers to a single concept, something readily confirmed by White. And yet, interestingly, there are years when one can detect connective threads. In 1950, all of the pageants transported audiences to far-off settings: "When Dreams Come True," "Seville," "Old Vienna," and "Jungle Drums." In 1952, the four offerings—"Mardi Gras," "Butterfly Lullaby," "The Good Old Times," and "Gold Dollar Moon"—evoked the magic of open-air festivities. The 1953 edition favored a nostalgic looking back on old America— "Minnehaha," "Candy Land," "Derby Day Honeymoon," and "Americana, U.S.A."—while those produced the following season cast a view on worlds beyond our national borders with "Fiesta," "Dreamland," "Rocket to the Moon," and "U.N."

What sort of message, if any, did Mr. North have in mind? Certainly it was not a realistic one, nor did he pay tribute to the biblical or historical epics, topics addressed by his uncles and their rivals in days gone by. John dwelt in the never-never land of pretty faces and places, as one might expect from a man detached from the real world and caught up in his own escapist pleasures. Perhaps the boldest thing he ever produced was the risqué horse show for the New York World's Fair back in 1939, nudity intended. And that was a commercial flop. Ten years later, ten years older, John was satisfied to stress beauty and enchantment in sentimentally rich doses, with the female figure placed high on a pedestal.

He filled the big top with color it had rarely known. His friend Ernest Hemingway penned a lovely piece for the circus magazine which contains these now oft-quoted lines: "The circus is the only ageless delight that you can buy for money. . . . It is the only spectacle I know that, while you watch it, gives the quality of a truly happy dream."[8] One of the songs Johnny composed for the 1954 show, with lyrics by E. Ray Goetz, sums up the fanciful thrust of it all:

> Someday, there is a dreamland
> Crowded with memories and dreams to be
> Somewhere, a cake and ice cream land
> Holds all life's treasures for you and me!

John may have felt intimidated in the presence of so many gifted creators, he had such respect for their talents. In bringing them all together, he did what his brother, Henry, believes to be the producer's main function.[9] In fact, he was so trusting, according to White, that he had little idea what the whole thing was about until he saw the costume sketches. And then he would examine them—wherever he happened to be when Miles caught up with him, at the baths, at some club— with scarce critical comment, more like a simple soul in a museum accepting each painting on the wall as worthy of respect.

White spent long weeks laying out the entire show with elaborate color charts. Now famous with Broadway credits, when White first worked for North as an assistant to Norman Bel Geddes, he won his approval to costume the entire performance act by act, something that had never been done before. This gave the designer complete control over every hue seen by the audience. It was really Miles White, therefore, who gave the circus whatever artistic unity it possessed. And his work was much admired by North. White gift-wrapped the show in unstinting radiance and splendor. His designs bore a brilliant imagination, so exotic and theatrical, at the same time so true to the subject at hand. The novel shapes alone of many of White's costumes lent a festive, animate air. He dazzled the eye with rare, surprising color schemes. His vision to paint the world in fresh, unexpected hues seemed at times limitless. In essence, the circus is pure visual enchantment, and Miles White celebrated this magical fact with more taste, style, pizzazz, artistic truth, and sheer imagination than any other designer before or since who has created for the big top.

Broadway to Sarasota: Anderson and all the others took the train down to Florida in late February for spring rehearsals. And what a zany cross section of humanity converged on winter quarters, from surly roustabouts to tall female models imported from New York agencies for production work. Some of the glamorous girls fled the scene immediately; many didn't last out the season. No wonder the show required, by contract, even its top stars—name performers like La Norma Fox—to appear in spec. They could be counted on to complete the tour. Among the celebrity contributors present was composer Henry ("Hank") Sullivan, who wore a ton of face powder and carried an umbrella to shield it from the sun, and who went on about his operetta, based on the life of Robert Burns, which he hoped some rich lady would finance.

There was, of course, Richard Barstow, keeping his own outrageous ego in check lest he offend Murray Anderson, who hoarded the center of attention with his melodramatic directing style and his devilish penchant for nicknaming everyone in sight. There were Anderson's assistants, among them at one time or another Phil Hall, Concello's relatively sane friend, and "Peaceful Allen," former manager of the rare-book department at Macy's in New York, who had taken over for another precious New Yorker, Tommy Farrow, now departed, and who palled around with Miles White.

Fey was the word. One evening, Miles and Peaceful needed quick transportation down to Miami. Betty King of the King Sisters was getting married, and Miles, who had created some of her costumes, was invited. He and Allen went out to winter quarters in search of wheels and were directed to, of all places, the cookhouse. The old green meat truck was available. The two laughing sports took off in it and a few hours later pulled up in front of a posh Miami hotel, the Fontainebleau, to the amazement and amusement of reporters covering the nuptials. Stepping into the gala throng came the unassuming Allen and the impeccably attired White, with kerchief flung around his neck, from the Ringling Bros. and Barnum & Bailey meat department. Their diesel-powered entrance made the local papers.[10]

In 1951, they rehearsed four new numbers: "Circus Serenade," which incorporated Walt Disney characters; "Picnic in the Park," the equestrian romp based on White's idea to do something set in Queen Antoinette's court in Versailles; "Luawana," the aerial ballet; and the finale, "Popcorn and Lemonade." Anderson (lyrics) and Sullivan (music) contributed wonderful new songs for three of the productions, while "Lovely Luawana Lady," composed for the web routine by the new team of North and Goetz, had a lilting South Seas beat. In toto, the original melodies composed that year rank as the best ever for a single Ringling edition.

After six weeks of long and grinding walk-throughs in the sun, dictated with sadistic glee (some felt) by John Murray Anderson blowing away into the microphone, the show was loaded up for the new tour. The freshly painted trains were blessed with holy water by a Catholic priest; then they began their clanging and banging up the mainline for New York City. Given only forty-eight hours' rehearsal time at Madison Square Garden, Anderson, growing more irritable by the minute, likened it to "rush hour in the subway."[11] Miles White worked feverishly around the clock, supervising costume fittings and the last-minute alterations. Indeed, no phase of the production held John's attention as much as the costumes. When the cast came out wearing them for the first time and gathered in the center ring for inspection, John stood by with quiet fascination.

Not all of White's creations—some very subtle, others flamboyantly eccentric—proved practical for the people who had to perform in them. In this regard, comical results sometimes ensued. Lorna Nifong, who was hired in 1949 to twirl a baton in the big finale "The Glorious Fourth," found herself decked out in a gigantic veil hanging from a huge hat with ostrich feathers. Not only that, hooked onto her dress were tails that draped down between her legs. She was mortified over the thought of twirling anything successfully through this getup. She spotted North standing nearby and went up to him, unafraid. "This is atrocious, Mr. North! I can't work in this thing!" "Have you got your baton?" he asked. "No," she replied, "it's back in the dressing room." John handed Nifong his walking cane and said, "Here, show me." The cane, once active in Nifong's hands, became hopelessly entangled in the long tails. John called over Miles White. "I want this fixed immediately. She can't use it."[12]

Riggings were hung and rehung, acts respotted and regrouped, first-of-May showgirls dissuaded from deserting the tempermental director. In cool contrast to all the commotion, once rehearsals were under way, John North usually took it all in from a rather solitary position. Sometimes he stood alone in one of the walkways connecting the performers' entrance doors with the arena. At other times he might find a seat halfway up in the arena. "He would like to look down on his kingdom," as Dick Barstow put it, fondly recalling his boss's calm, supportive manner. "He might come down from his perch," in Barstow's words, to air a reservation. North broached whatever he wanted to say very diplomatically, clearing his throat and speaking in low tones. "Well, ah, Richard, I think we should have a little more light over there."[13]

Never to be underestimated were the deft programming skills of Pat Valdo, who had been around long before John Murray Anderson and crew arrived and who would outlast them all. It was Valdo more than anyone else who laid out the lineup of acts, who nut-and-bolted everything together in the practical sense. If Anderson and Barstow were the architects, Valdo was the construction superintendent. Having proved his usefulness so many times before, from talent scout to equestrian director, Valdo enjoyed North's and Concello's unstinting confidence. They were actually afraid to take issue with his judgment lest he leave them. As Art says, "if Pat Valdo did it, we'd say, 'We like it.' It was always good."[14]

Once again the critics mostly liked it, too, although, in reviewing the 1951 edition, some of them focused on the production elements in a questioning frame of mind. Observed Herb Golden in *Variety:* "John Ringling North has again furthered the evolution of the Ringling Bros. and Barnum & Bailey show from the Barnum and Hagenbeck concepts to that of a Billy Rose.... The emphasis is increasingly away from animals and acrobats to pulchritude and spectacle, the effect being to broaden its appeal."[15] *The Billboard* cast a like viewpoint. Although reporting the show to be "another stupendous and colorful edition," it found the new replacement acts "not, for the most part, as good as their predecessors. . . . The thrills seem subjected to the tinsel and flash of the illusionary creations which favored the stage rather than a sawdust arena."[16]

Business at Madison Square Garden was down slightly that spring. Road business was probably not on a par "with the peak 1948 season," as claimed by management. A more telling indication was an evasive piece that Roland Butler authored for the circus route book, in which he skirted the subject of attendance and gross receipts, spending his prose in praise of a circus under canvas. Butler wrote of magical unloadings at dawn, of exotic aromas and transitory thrills, as if he realized they would not be around much longer. In addition to the increasing amounts of entertainment the circus now faced as it moved into the 1950s (indeed, into the "I Love Lucy" era), there was yet another competitor about to make life even more difficult for the Greatest Show on Earth, a movie titled *The Greatest Show on Earth.*

Photographed by De Mille

Ever since he set out in 1938 to "make the circus a more valuable property," John had brought in an impressive array of movers and shakers from other fields: Norman Bel Geddes from the industrial sphere; Stravinsky and Balanchine from ballet; Anderson and White from Broadway. He okayed televised airings of the show until, with the rapid increase of television sets in American households, it looked like he might be giving it away. He then brought the lure of television *to* the circus instead by booking Howdy Doodie into the sideshow at the outset of the 1950 tour. Try this. Try that. John courted the influence of almost every other form of entertainment save Hollywood, still to make its mark on the Big Show.

As early as 1943, John Murray Anderson had suggested to Robert Ringling the idea of a motion picture bearing the show's famous title and was encouraged to pursue a treatment. He interested movie promoter Gil Boag, who engaged Lowell Thomas to compile a biography of the Ringling brothers. The book was never published and nothing came of it.[1] In 1948, after North regained control of the circus, Anderson revived the idea. North and Concello signed an option with David O. Selznick (of *Gone with the Wind* fame) to produce a movie. Selznick set a five million dollar budget and planned to begin shooting in early 1949. His option gave him six months' time to prepare a treatment acceptable to the circus, which he was unable to do. Concello refused to renew the option. By that time, Cecil B. De Mille was expressing keen interest, first having sought Johnny out during the 1948 New York run.

Who knows how many other film companies had put in their bids. The circus made a tremendous splash in Los Angeles that summer when it hosted an opening-night benefit for St. John's Hospital Guild, seats going for upwards of one hundred dollars each. More than two hundred film stars turned out, nearly drowning the lot in a sea of celebrity goo and glitter. (During spec, populated with dozens of familiar faces, columnist Sheila Graham hacked viciously away over a typewriter inside a lion's den while Bing Crosby and Frank Sinatra shook the bars from without.) Seven years since the show last played L.A., this one took the town by a whirl. Many directors would have killed for the rights to make it the star attraction in a big-budget movie. De Mille and the circus were made for each other.

The journey from conception to finished film took well over three years, and it was probably worth all the agonizing time spent trying to do it right. Even if the screenplay is overdone, the depth that De Mille achieved in his portrayal of the circus itself (its logistical operations and remarkable showmanship) has proved most enduring.

The director joined the circus in Chicago in 1949 for a two-week visit to begin research. With him came a Lotus Land entourage, of course, consisting of, among others, Gladys Rosson, his Girl Friday; screenwriter Fred Frank; and a budding thirteen-year-old grandaughter, Cecelia De Mille Calvin. They were met at the La Salle Street Station by Phil Hall and delivered to Art Concello, the man on the lot—not John North—with whom De Mille would be dealing. Hall was amazed at Concello's refusal to be intimidated. "He talked the same to De Mille as he talked to North, and De Mille put up with it. He would say, 'Goddamn it, C. B., we can't do it that way! We'll do it this way!' "[2]

De Mille spent his sixty-sixth birthday with the show in Madison, Wisconsin, where he was hoisted to the top of the tent in a bosun's chair from which, for a good hour, he peered down on the action to consider camera angles. He rode the Jomar as Henry North's guest and regaled everybody with stories of his young days as a Shakespearean actor playing in many of the smaller towns the circus now visited.

One rainy morning, De Mille surveyed a very muddy lot, pathetically surrounded by immobile trucks and wagons—the roustabouts standing idly by, the canvas not yet spread out—and concluded the date was lost. He returned to the train. Early that afternoon came a strong knock on the door from Concello.

"Aren't you going down to see the show?"

"You're giving a show *there*?"

"Well, damn it all, yes! Of course we are, C. B.!"

They had somehow gotten the tents up over the soggy terrain and spread plenty of sawdust on the track. They played to a packed house.[3] De Mille's respect for the survivalist spirit of circus troupers deepened, and he began to see in Concello the model for his central character: the iron-willed, no-heart boss driven to keep the show going. He had plenty of fun hyping his ongoing research and the supposed struggles of the story department to develop a treatment worthy of the subject. De Mille said he wanted to achieve a "stream of civilization" story. He expressed himself thoughtfully in a piece he wrote for the 1950 circus magazine: "I found the circus the most unifying force in American life. . . . The circus is emphatically American in that it rejects the concept that any one class of Americans is naturally hostile to any other class. I looked upon the circus as a micro-cosm in which all peoples and all governments may find an example of the enormous strength that can lie in cooperation, tolerance and unity. . . . That, to me, is the circus, truly the greatest show on earth."[4]

He was back with the show in 1950, still prowling around for inspiration and subject matter. While Paramount crews began shooting preliminary stills, background shots, and audience reactions, De Mille and his writers wrestled with any number of likely scenarios, finally settling upon a melodrama that contained about as many plots as the big top had poles. At the heart of the story is a rivalry between two aerialists, played by Cornel Wilde and Betty Hutton. She loses her center-ring spot when Wilde is booked at the last minute to—surprise!—guarantee box office and stave off the dreaded creditors.

A stodgy subplot, involving gangsters who run a crooked midway "joint," was not welcomed by North or Concello. In fact, they fought unsuccessfully to have it removed from the script, fearing its odious implications. Then there is the mad, brooding elephant trainer, obsessed with his female assistant, played by Gloria Grahame, who strings him along sadistically, film noir style, while savoring the memory of an affair with the Great Sebastian (Cornel Wilde) and conniving to recharge it.

Lovable James Stewart plays a doctor hiding out behind clownface, on the run from the law for the murder of his terminally ill wife, an act of compassion to spare her the pain. Charlton Heston landed the role of the tough circus boss, who seems bent on keeping everyone in a constant state of unrest. This makes him ever the more attractive to the patronizing Betty Hutton, who prevails with sweet, masochistic charm to win him over. A barrel of clichés, yes, but somehow it all worked, maybe because back in 1952 the world was a more romantic place.

De Mille's casting decisions were good ones by typical Hollywood standards, and he drew from the circus personnel for many minor parts. Johnny North got a chance to play himself in an early scene in which he confers with his business associates over a pressing issue: whether to keep the show out for a full season or bring it home after the lucrative New York and Boston dates. How prophetically sensitive those screenwriters were to a real-life problem of mounting importance!

The principal shooting began at winter quarters on January 31, 1951. Wagons were converted into dressing rooms. A special cook tent was erected for the film crews. The grounds swarmed with actors and acrobats. And when John Murray Anderson arrived a few weeks later to begin rehearsing the actual circus program, the tension between him and De Mille only added to the off-camera drama.

Even though he had suggested making such a movie in the first place, Anderson now wanted no part of it. Ego is the source of a thousand contradictions. The presence of De Mille and company reminded him of how indifferently he had been treated by Hollywood when he once spent six weeks there on contract and sat around in a big office with two telephones that never rang. On this set, Anderson had some say because his contract with Ringling prevented it from using his production numbers in any other context. So Paramount was forced to pay Anderson a special fee for the use of his work in the picture. Firsthand observers state that he and that other director avoided contact. (Although the film depicts the bustling preseason activity at winter quarters, not included are any of Anderson's rehearsals. A shame.) One evening, while standing in line at Morrison's Cafeteria, Anderson finally had a nickname for his rival. "I've got it! DeMilestone around my neck!"[5]

Concello resented De Mille, too, thinking he was getting too much from the circus for too little (a $250,000 advance against 10 percent of the gross receipts). He exacted all kinds of extra fees from Paramount for technical advice, and some of it he passed along to loyal hands. Concello charged De Mille a hefty sum for figuring out a way to film a scene in which Cornel Wilde misses a trapeze bar and falls to the ground. He had a large hole dug in the ring, then covered it with a safety net. On top of that he spread leaves and dirt. Before he allowed them to shoot, he took a practice dive himself—in his street clothes. When Concello struck the fake earth, an unexpected surge of muddy water shot up all around him, and he crawled off the net like a soldier out of the winter trenches. Applause and laughter greeted him.

"Okay, C. B.," he shouted, his face covered with liquid dirt, "pump out the water in there, put more leaves down and you can shoot."[6]

Irony abounds in the acting realm. Of course, Wilde had a double (Fay Alexander) take the tragic fall for him. Wilde was even terrified when he got more than a couple of feet off the ground. He and De Mille nearly came to blows over the director's impatience with his timidity on the set. There was an angry exchange of words during which De Mille berated Wilde for acting so scared on the rigging, and the actor took it as an assault on his craft.[7] Though Wilde had not been De Mille's first choice to play the part, what he gave his abusive director in the end is possibly the film's finest performance, flawless in every frame. It is a true feather in Wilde's acting cap that he somehow came off as so believable and unaffected when others around him—Hutton and Heston in the lead—wreaked of excessive melodrama.

In contrast to Wilde's fear of flying, circus style, Betty Hutton took to the air with zeal when first coached in the fundamentals by Antoinette Concello. Flyer "Bones" Brown constructed special rigging for Hutton's closeups, and La Norma Fox, one of De Mille's favorites (she tried doing all the crazy things he thought up, most of them impractical), did most of the doubling for her long shots. La Norma's young son, Gilbert, was offered the part of a circus boy greeting Sebastian upon his return from the hospital—by shooting a cap gun in his face. Gilbert couldn't pull the trigger, he had grown so fond of Wilde, who, along with Jimmy Stewart, was with him during his first real-life haircut.[8]

Pinito Del Oro refused to do any doubling for Hutton (whose act was so unrealistically diversified that no circus aerialist alive could have done all those tricks). What repulsed Pinito was the thought of covering her black hair with a blond wig. Antoinette claims, however, that Del Oro does appear in some long shots. In any event, North's press agents tried making hay of Pinito's refusal to take part by fostering the notion that North kept her from appearing in the film.[9]

De Mille pampered his favorite stars, giving them fresh half-dollars whenever they got a few feet off the ground or spoke their lines right. He showed his more brutal side to the circus performers. Daisy Hall was one of four showgirls rounded up by Antoinette Concello to appear in the open-air-web routine at the end of the picture. They were forced through a cruel repetition of eleven takes despite Antoinette's warning to De Mille not to push the girls beyond six. "He didn't give a damn," says Daisy. "We were all bleeding. Our feet were all burned. Sally Marlow finally fainted. We all had terrible rope burns. We had to go to the commissary and get bandaged." At least they were in perfect shape for the train-wreck scene, next to be filmed. "I don't think he cared about people. He wanted a result. He was a slave driver."[10]

Maybe De Mille saw himself as the headstrong character he was coaching Heston to play. Maybe a little of Art Concello was rubbing off on him. De Mille's intensity did not unruffle Johnny North, however, when he came around for the shooting of his scenes. John's cool charm translated well before the cameras, and he impressed his director by remembering all his lines on the first take. Johnny's girlfriend at the time, Gloria Drew, was given—no doubt as a favor—one line to utter: "Sebastion, you're back!" Gloria and her flowing curly hair came off with bubbling innocence.

De Mille had virtually no control over the content or direction of the circus performance itself. Basically, the film is a faithful record of what Ringling audiences actually saw in 1951—except, that is, for enhanced lighting effects and superior studio-recorded musical arrangements. Most of the show was filmed under canvas during the Philadelphia and Washington stands. Customers were informed that a ticket purchase constituted permission to be filmed. This was thought to have caused record turnouts in Philly, everyone wanting to be caught by the camera's eye. Paramount added extra lighting equipment, some of which the circus bought and used regularly thereafter. There were glitches, as when a strange green tint showed up on some of the processed film. To justify it, they added a special scene just to show a light man fitting a green tint over one of the follow spots.

Victor Young's shimmering score captured the spirit of the Merle Evans music, and he reorchestrated the production songs to achieve greater sonority and gusto (tapes of the original show music as played by the Ringling band during 1951 sound passive by comparison). All of the Sullivan and Anderson songs—"Circus Serenade," "Picnic in the Park," and "Popcorn and Lemonade"—are knockouts, and formed the melodic heart of the sound-track album issued by RCA Victor. John's one contribution, "Lovely Luawana Lady," is an asset, too. Young himself composed two superb numbers, "Be a Jumping Jack," and the movie's title song, which quickly became probably the most popular circus theme ever written.

Another of De Mille's concerns was the look and sound of the ringmaster. He placed a handsome actor near the performer's entrance and made him a figure audiences could relate to, rather than some anonymous unseen voice from afar occasionally announcing an act. De Mille's man in red did wonderful justice to the opening salutation, "CHILDREN... OF... ALLLLLLLLL... AGES! JOHN RINGLING NORTH WELCOMES YOU TO THE GREATEST SHOW ON EARTH!" He introduced all the displays in a pleasing manner.

Not included in the final cut (a curious omission) are extended shots of the menagerie, nor did the cameras pan the cookhouse and dining tent, a fascinating aspect of circus life. Also left on the cutting-room floor were several outstanding aerial turns on the bill that year, among them sway-pole thriller Leoni; the Great Morituris in the Globe of Death; the Man in the Moon; and the exceptional Rodry Brothers. Presumably, their tricks would have diverted from the focus placed on the two rival aerialists (Wilde and Hutton) and all the things they did. One face who did show up—only for the film—was Hopalong Cassidy, who had appeared with Cole Bros. Circus during 1950 and whom Paramount booked independently as an added attraction for the main spec, "Circus Serenade."

The animated finale, "Popcorn and Lemonade," a great, great number, was a sad victim of economics, although its wonderful theme song made it to the RCA album. According to Miles White, John Murray Anderson, who received royalties for his work that was filmed, wanted too much money for the "Popcorn" sequence, so De Mille passed it over. A second shame.

It was to be the last edition of the circus staged by Anderson, the person most responsible for helping John evolve the new format. Anderson and Concello never got along too well, each being equally high strung. Concello never really believed that Anderson needed the six-week rehearsal period, upon which he had insisted and for which he was paid twenty thousand dollars. Concello suspected that he and his Manhattan cohorts relished the extra time in the Florida sunshine away from the cold New York springs. The two eventually reached an impasse, and Concello informed Anderson that if he couldn't put the numbers together in three weeks to forget it. Murray wouldn't budge, so Art took it upon himself to make a change, notifying John in his usual bossy manner, "We ain't gonna use Anderson anymore. We can get Barstow to do the job for half or one-third the price."[11]

The film was premiered in Sarasota on January 31, 1952, exactly one year to the day after shooting had commenced. The circus folk loved it, as did the critics up in New York, who greeted the Gotham opening with a chorus of nearly uniform raves. "This huge motion picture of the big top is the dandiest ever put on screen," declared the *New York Times*, praising it in particular for "the brilliance with which it portrays the circus and all its movement." The *Daily Mirror* rightfully guessed that it would "shatter every record in the history of the screen and will probably hang up grosses that will never again be equalled," while the *Journal American* judged it as simply "the greatest piece of entertainment that C. B. De Mille had turned out in years of making colossal movies."[12]

Trade pundits wise to the big top were less willing to turn cartwheels. Writing in *The Billboard*, James McHugh, though recognizing that "anyone who enjoys the circus will revel in the technicolor portrayal of the Big One," branded De Mille's treatment "a hodgepodge of every imaginable fiction device, or, perhaps more properly, cliché." He lambasted the mid-way grift scene, suggesting it "should be enough to make the Ringling brothers turn over in their graves" and wondering how much it might "endanger a valuable property and reputation it has taken years to build."[13] McHugh raised a good question, for one thing is certain: it didn't appear to help business any for the real-life version of the circus.

The Greatest Show on Earth was a box-office smash, racking up all-time high grosses and attendance records around the country. Today's students of cinema may easily dismiss the contrived, overly melodramatic story. Heston's unrelenting meanspiritedness is excessive to an almost laughable degree. In its day, the movie worked wonderfully, and it remains an adequately suspenseful treat for first-time viewers. One thing time has not tarnished are the sarcastic asides delivered by both Gloria Grahame and Dorothy Lamour, still very funny. And the scenes of the tents being set up and torn down are likely to enthrall people for years to come. Also for the viewing are tantalizing glimpses of the Concello seat wagons in various stages of assembly, of the interior of a women's sleeper, and of a Geddes-designed midway. The train wreck is a classic, and the ending, however hokey, stirs the emotions with its resolute show-must-go-on attitude.

Shots of the performance itself have stood the test of time. "Picnic in the Park" fills the tent with a festive air: horses and carriages in grand commotion, then a parade of fast-entering liberty horses, down the track and into the rings. "Circus Serenade" lifts the rapture of a storybook to lyrical heights. Most of the marvelous acts John booked that year are preserved on film forever. A long shot from the front end of the tent frames all three flying trapeze troupes in simultaneous flight.

The sublime poetry of a three-ring circus was never more beautifully photographed.

De Mille's triumph was something to behold. Scores of moviegoers stayed in the theater—or returned—to see the film a second or third time. It won two Academy Awards in 1952, one for best screenplay, the other for best movie, beating out (today's film buffs can't fathom it) *High Noon* and the movie musical classic *Singing in the Rain*. Maybe it was De Mille's time for recognition instead of Gene Kelly's. At the awards ceremony, the crusty director praised all the circus personnel and audiences for bravery displayed during the arduous filming. This certainly marked a high point in De Mille's career, as it did in the rising fortunes of John Ringling North, whose name was never more magical. John's scene in the movie added another layer of charisma to his glamorous image. One critic commented: "He should play juve roles—that's how handsome he photographs."[14]

When Ringling Bros. and Barnum & Bailey Circus opened at Madison Square Garden in 1952, shortly after its movie version had premiered, John was given tribute for his annual charity benefits. According to reports, he "rose for an extremely brief acknowledgement in the best of taste," accepting the honor "in the name of all of us with the circus . . . happy to participate in this great cause."[15]

He was never more in demand. John scaled the summit of his great success with quiet charm, the aloof impressario showing up on such programs as CBS-TV's "Celebrity Time." The budding songwriter's "Lovely Luawana Lady" was getting national airplay, and other tunes of his (future hits, maybe?) were being sung for the first time at the circus. John walked into clubs. Eyes turned. The music played and he was a part of it, part of the center of the center of the center. He had been preparing for these moments all his life. The previous summer, he and Gloria, then galavanting around Europe, made hay of their modest screen credits. Reporters were told that the circus mogul was in the market for fifty new acts and that the beautiful blonde at his side was, well—did you not know—"the screen star, Gloria Drew." Really?

Yes, really. Johnny was on top of the mountain, the reality of his achievements obscured by the illusion of success. Nearly everything he saw seemed easily below him, easily within grasp. He could scarcely foresee the inevitable descent on the other side. He was too busy walking on air.

His Own Music

I see a beautiful rainbow
Laughing at clouds in the sky
And the sun smiling through
Says to me and to you
"Bid your cares and your worries goodbye!"
I see in that beautiful rainbow
The flags of all nations unfurled
I hear song and mirth
I see peace on earth
In that wonderful, beautiful, marvelous, glorious
Rainbow around the world![1]

These words by Irving Caesar to a tune by John Ringling North pretty well reflect the Pollyanna attitude of most of the songs written for the circus specs the next few years. John's music for the number is amply enthusiastic, the overreaching melody line characteristic of so much that he composed.

As much a dabbler in music as were his uncles Charles and Alf. T., who also wrote original scores for parts of the show, John yet achieved a semblance of credibility with his very professional "Lovely Luawana Lady." The song luckily rode the great success of De Mille's film, in which it was sung, and the subsequent RCA album, which gave it coast-to-coast exposure. Robert Lewis Taylor, in his puffy profile piece on John in the *New Yorker*, mentioned Cole Porter as having "spoken very highly" of North's music. He reported that Johnny's quarterly ASCAP royalties had advanced in recent years from $2.77 to $13.00 and were expected to go somewhat higher still, thanks to the song's becoming "nationally popular."[2] However, Sid Herman of Famous Music, the song's publisher, rebuts such a claim, saying, "It was far from a hit. It got very little airplay. They did not go out and try promoting it."[3] Another song John wrote in later years, "Those Maracas from Caracas," also was termed a hit by brother Henry in his book *Circus Kings*. Again, the allusion to songwriting success could not be substantiated when the publisher, in this instance Frank Music, was consulted. The firm's representative, Joseph Weiss, was unable even to locate a record of the work among a spate of obscure North tunes, written with another collaborator, Tony Velona, the firm had on file.[4]

Dilettante or not, John had been composing melodies ever since he was a schoolboy back in Baraboo, and the lure of trying them out on circus audiences was irresistible. Moreover, the departure in 1951 of stager John Murray Anderson, who with Henry Sullivan had created the original show music, left the door wide open for a new team. Indeed, Anderson's exit could well have been caused in part by friction between him and John over the latter's desire for more musical input.

Anyway, John appointed himself and his partner, E. Ray Goetz, to fill the void. Goetz had been actively involved for years in popular music and musical theater. He produced Cole Porter's first two Broadway hits and applied countless words to countless tunes in a largely undistinguished career redeemed by one big pop standard, "For Me and My Gal." Working with Goetz, John turned out a passel of mostly pedestrian tunes, though none quite or nearly as bad as the hackneyed, if not thoroughly uninspired, lyrics provided by his partner: "Someday today will be the good old times / If you will climb each rainbow when it climbs / And cheer what's here / Then someday you will say / God bless this yesterday!" or "Lovely Luawana Lady / When your hopes and dreams grow fadey / Don't you ever be afraid he won't come back to you."[5]

The two got together late evenings over a piano, sometimes in John's private car, the Jomar, John banging out with a couple of expressive fingers a new melody of his own or maybe something he remembered from the past, Ray gesturing dramatically as he searched his shallow creative pool for words to match. Piloted by John's simplistic dream of conquering "The Hit Parade," how shackled they must have felt by having to address such asexual circus themes as Mexican horse exhibitions and fairy tales of yore.

North and Goetz offered four original songs in 1952. All were basically effective in context, thanks mostly to John's rambunctious melodies and to the equally assertive renditions given them by musical director Merle Evans and the booming baritone vocalist, Harold Ronk, who had joined the circus only the year before. "The Good Old Times," a typically reaching North number, added considerable spirit to the parade, as did the songs John wrote for other specs the following three seasons, "Gone Are the Days," "Dreamland," and "Birthdays." All were rich in stirring refrains.

Other 1952 production music included "Mardi Gras," a rousing but superficial galop; "Gold Dollar Moon," another rhythmic piece short on substance; and the exquisitely lovely "Butterfly Lullaby," played as a backdrop for the aerial ballet and possibly the most expressive tune John ever composed. The notes stay close together, creating an intimacy of feeling he usually avoided. While the score could hardly match the excellent Sullivan and Anderson contributions of the previous season, it did surpass what that team had delivered in both 1949 and 1950, and it struck some of the critics as being plausibly passable. *Variety*'s Leonard Traube found John's music on the "schmaltzy" side, calling the new show tunes "catchy, if not distinguished." Commenting on "Mardi Gras," he wrote, "The North-Goetz song aids the gay atmosphere building"; of "Butterfly Lullaby," he remarked, "Harold Ronk vocals the theme song with nostalgic delicacy."[6]

The new Ringling songwriters were off to a credible start, although what followed did not smack of progress. In 1953, except for "Gone Are the Days" (with a better-than-average Goetz lyric), the other numbers were lackluster. "Minnehaha" was atmospheric and time consuming; "Derby Day Honeymoon" was a plodding workout on the ears; "Americana" was a largely undetectable melody. Altogether, the score was more a drag than a push. Then came 1954 and yet more mildly irritating duds: "Fiesta," composed in Chicago in the Ambassador Hotel's Pump Room, where it should have stayed; "Rocket to the Moon," a number that died on the launching pad; a rather bouncy closer, "U.N."; and the one fine song, "Dreamland," which redeemed the year's abysmal offerings.

The deeper John reached into his musical trunk, the less he came up with. It was probably a joking press agent who wrote in the circus magazine, detailing the extensive preparations for that year's edition, that "veteran bandmaster Merle Evans insists on extra rehearsals to do full justice to the lyrics of E. Ray Goetz."[7] Johnny had reached a creative dead end with his wordsmith. How ironic, considering that most teams get better rather than worse the longer they stay together. By now, the reviews were politely (it would seem) avoiding any mention of their offerings. The only thing that saved these numbers were the aggressive arrangements supplied by Samuel Grossman, associated with "The Hit Parade," whom John had hired back in 1947, and the spirited, not-always-on-key vocals of Harold Ronk, who sang only spasmodically well on his way to becoming truly one of the great ringmasters of all time.

Grossman embellished the production music—as he had done when Sullivan wrote it—with popular songs and Broadway standards appropriate to the setting. By format, the original song would be sung through once, followed by a medley of familiar refrains, then reprised as the parade came to a close. Merle Evans usually topped off the finish with a rousing, climactic fanfare (nobody could write them like he did). Evans tolerated the North originals, never much of a fan. Getting a handle each spring on the new production scores was not easy for him. Evans and Grossman reported to a New York studio, where the latter would spend long, grueling hours drumming the new music into the bandleader's brain so that he could impart it to his musicians. Evans much preferred faster tempos, such as "Jungle Drums," or pulsing ballads.

John needed a better lyric writer whether he wanted one or not, and with Goetz passing on to the hereafter, he was able to change partners without difficulty. He went to the top of the heap by hooking up with Irving Caesar, a preeminent lyricist who worked alongside the best of them, having written "Swanee" with Gershwin, such hit shows as *No, No, Nanette* with Vincent Youmans, and a string of standards: "Crazy Rhythm," "Just a Gigolo," "Is It True What They Say about Dixie?" "Tea for Two," "I Want to Be Happy," and more. Caesar, in turn, was charmed by the prospects of creating songs that would be sung to millions of circus lovers in cities all over the country, particularly in the grandiose setting of Madison Square Garden.

"John had these melodies, a few tunes that he had more or less savored for some time," explains Caesar, "so he was very happy to find that I could find words for them." The two worked late at night at John's Waldorf-Astoria suite. "He had this wonderful apartment. He always played host with the right wines. He had dinner on several occasions. They were dinners of opulence and affluence. And he had the chauffeur-driven car, and one likes to work with that kind." When John's new collaborator went down to Sarasota for spring rehearsals, he was treated just as well. "They put me up in the Ringling Hotel and made a big to-do about my being down there."[8]

Caesar came up with words for a number of John's tunes, which he was told would be used for the various production numbers. One turned out to be "Mama's in the Park," which brought fifty-five elephants into the picture. Another was for the aerial ensemble, "On Honolulu Bay." "Three Cheers for Holidays" and "Birthdays" paced the main spec, and "Rainbow around the World" the finale. With Irving, John created his best all-around score, far better than what he had done the previous two seasons in fizzling tandem with Goetz, and it contained the most effective circus number he ever wrote, "Impossible."

The creation of "Impossible" marked the one time when music followed words. Caesar pulled the finished lyric out of his trunk of unpublished material. He had previously fitted it to the German hit "Auf Wiedersehen," believing at the time he was about to acquire the American publishing rights to the song (he operated his own publishing company). The deal fell through, leaving Caesar with a good lyric in search of a melody. It seemed so right for the circus with its list of adjectives—impossible, incredible, remarkable—that John was given a copy and encouraged to compose a tune, which he did easily and with inspiration. "It was quite spontaneous," recalls Caesar. "He sort of paraphrased the German setting, which is all right, which is a good example of his flexibility."[9]

The song was perfectly placed in the aerial spec, just at the moment when the surreal form of Pinito Del Oro began moving hypnotically through the air high over center ring. Everything about the number, from the arrangement to its dynamic juxtaposition with Del Oro's act, was a stroke of pure, spine-tingling circus craft. It was reprised three times in the program: slowly while Josephine Berosini ascended an inclined wire up to her rigging, in march tempo for the liberty-horse display, and in waltz time during the flying-trapeze turns.

The other North-Caesar songs were at least proficient. "Birthdays," a tag ending on the "Holidays" spec, was a sentimental rouser. "Mama's in the Park" had a catchy soft-shoe beat. "On Honolulu Bay," similar in form to "Lovely Luawana Lady," was recorded by Mitch Miller, and "Impossible" made it onto wax by way of the Sammy Kaye orchestra, *The Billboard* rewarding it with a respectable though noncommital review. Neither tune achieved the elusive hit status John longed for. Indeed, he was so confident of his 1955 score that he had two huge simulated record turntables placed in the end rings up in New York and Boston a half-hour before each performance. The original music was played over and over while the audience convened, and then again in the overture. Still, not enough people left the arena whistling any of it to cause a stampede at the record stores. Sheet music published by Irving Caesar Music at 1619 Broadway remained on the shelves, as did the forty-fives cut by Sammy Kaye and Mitch Miller.

John had the makings of a good composer, and some of his songs worked very well in the circus programs. He lacked the musical education and technical skills necessary to harness and manipulate his native talents to greater effect. Caesar sensed insufficient ambition: "John wasn't a good pianist. As a matter of fact, he was a very poor pianist. I'd say he had the kind of talent that might occasionally produce a good song, but I don't call that a songwriting talent. A songwriting talent to me means a talent that can write a song, that can lend itself to write any kind of a song at any time."[10]

Nor was John much driven beyond his simplistic desire to produce a hit. He had only himself to account to. "I don't think he had hard work in his inventory," states Caesar, who is nonetheless proud of what he did with John. "I think we achieved a certain intimacy even in the circus with these songs. I think a song like 'Impossible' did it, and 'Mama's in the Park,' too." Speaking of "Rainbow around the World" ("a beautiful song"), he recalls how the tune was first presented to him in Dixieland form. He wrote a "Swanee"-type set of words which the two were high on, believing they had a number that a singer like Sammy Davis, Jr., then playing at the Apollo in New York, might record. (John had been an early fan of Sammy, he would tell others years later, and he had been one of those to help the singer along when Sammy was only a brilliant unknown.) The lyrics to the North-Caesar song went like this:

> Why do I miss Mississippi?
> Listen and I'll tell you why.
> There's a miss that I miss
> That I once used to kiss.
> (You know I'd tell you no lie.)
> That slick little chick down in Vicksburg,
> I'm going to find her a guy.
> Cause if I don't find my miss in Mississippi . . .
> Mississippi, I hip, I hip,
> Mississippi, goodbye![11]

John made an appointment for he and Irving to visit Sammy Davis backstage. Came the moment and John, sounding semi-immersed in a hangover, phoned Irving. "Can you go over there and tell him I can't make it? I'll try to call him. Present him the song, Irv. . . . See if he can do something with it." Caesar went over by himself. After about an hour of waiting in the wings, he went outside to kill some time and picked up a copy of the evening *Telegram*. A big, bold front-page headline announced that three blacks had been murdered in Mississippi by members of the Ku Klux Klan. Irving suddenly had grave second thoughts about approaching Davis.

"It certainly was not time to sing a song, 'Why do I miss Mississippi? Listen, and I'll tell you why.'"

Just the same, he returned to the theater, not about to stand up Davis, then in the formative stages of a promising career. Caesar finally reached him through the usual sea of hangers-on and would-be agents. "John sends his best regards, Sammy. He was detained in, ah, some meeting at the Garden. Oh, by the way, we have a little song you can look at sometime when you have a chance. No hurry."

"Sure, I will," said Davis, turning to the next person in line.

In fact, Caesar says he buried the lead sheet under some towels in Sammy's dressing room, too embarrassed to hand it to him personally. "I beat a hasty retreat, hoping that he didn't see the title before I got out of the theater!"[12] Davis, a liberal black, might have understood but surely would have not recorded. Hushed by the hand of history, the melody was turned into a march and given the "Rainbow" lyric. Had it been introduced in its original version thirty or forty years earlier, maybe it would now be a standard.

John's failure to show for the Sammy Davis appointment typified his lackadaisical attitude toward much of what he did. Perhaps he was not comfortable with Caesar's folksy "Mississippi" lyric and its allusions to the Old South, yet it was a more specific verse than most of the synthetically nowhere lyrics provided by his previous partner, E. Ray Goetz. John displayed little growth as a songwriter while he turned out one good-feeling number after another. Of course, he was writing for the circus, which was not in the business of spreading gloom or provoking deep philosophical insights. And John's music was vulnerable, as all music is, to the words placed next to it. A refrain of substance can easily be trivialized, if not suppressed, under a "happy" lyric. He and Goetz produced a fine little gem in "Gone Are the Days," the kind of a number—like songs introduced in college revues and flop Broadway shows—that never receives the recognition it deserves.

Another tune of John's, "The Moon and My Love and Me," which he wrote and/or put into use a few years later, dances on a gentle refrain, each note tiptoeing gracefully to the next. Rooted in the genteel sensibilities of an older American South, it is both charming and detached. If the composer preferred drifting through nostalgia and fantasy, his collaborators evidently complied, never trying or being allowed to push one of his tunes out of never-never land into a more realistic sphere.

Few of the songs were ideally performed at the circus. In the first years when original music was featured, the show sometimes settled on mediocre vocalists, or the ringmaster might inherit the chore in default. Efforts were made to secure professional singers, especially for the New York run. William Tabbert once served a brief stint at the Ringling mike before landing a breakthrough role in the Rodgers and Hammerstein hit *South Pacific*.

Anyway, John was now a participant himself, and he relished the role. When the parade passed by, it bore the imprint of his music. Most of his friends and employees quite naturally offered the confirming praise he expected. Even years later they are reluctant to say much one way or the other. Where do you think his music will be placed? Answers Rudy Bundy, himself a professional musician with some composing credits of his own, "It probably won't be used any more than mine."[13] Others, less kind, dismiss it all in haste.

Concello, around the show continuously, could not escape the music of his boss, and at one point he challenged Johnny on its questionable value to the show. They were at Reuben's one night with Phil Hall, circa 1953, when the topic of original show music came up.

"All right, Phil," began Art, chomping on his long, long cigar. "You're the music guy around here."

John picked up his drink nervously.

"Tell me, Phil. Now, you just listen a moment, John. Wouldn't it be better if the main song in the spec was a song that Bing Crosby sang and one the audience knew?"

John set his glass down on the table.

"Because," continued Concello, "John writes these songs, and my contention is that no one's ever heard them, so there's not going to be any code of recognition."

Hall was caught in the middle. He didn't wish to offend Johnny's music, nor did he wish to disappoint his friend Art.

"Well, of course," Hall replied, clearing his throat. "I can see what you're saying, Art. But, on the other hand, all shows have their own tunes."[14]

John hadn't much to add. This sobering exchange, however rationally motivated, certainly did not ease the mounting friction between the two cocky partners who ran the Greatest Show on Earth, the one from afar and the other close up. Art Concello. The words cut to the quick. Was he really needed that much anymore? North wondered.

Gone Are the Days

Whatever John felt about Concello, there can be no argument that he gave him enormous power and was incredibly differential to him. This is best demonstrated by an incident Phil Hall observed when he went out to winter quarters one day in the spring of 1953 to see Art. He discovered him in a heated exchange of words with John over the latter's desire to have his private car, the Jomar, attached to the circus train again that year. It had been off the road the previous tour and Art was not in an accommodating mood.

"You just can't take your car out this season!"

"But, Art, you know I have to have my car."

"It's too expensive. There's no room on the train. We can't do it."[1]

And they didn't. Here was the owner and president of the circus being overruled by his own general manager. It was the price that John paid for Art's services. At the semiannual board of directors meetings, held each spring in New York and during the summer in Chicago, when one of the minority stockholders asked John a question, he or she would be directed to Art for the answer. It was a flat-out routine. John just sat there; Art did the talking.[2]

During their honeymoon years, North and Concello operated this way. John was too busy running around Europe and frequenting nightclubs. He had little reason to question Art's management so long as the show made enough money to support his lavish lifestyle and pay for all the new Miles White costumes. Whatever frictions there were between the two were handily repressed until business started sliding, a gradual decline at first followed by an ominous continuing drop. By 1952, the circus not only was competing against De Mille's film version of itself (packing movie houses everywhere), it also faced the rising popularity of television and other modern diversions. The country's entertainment patterns were changing. Naturally, it was Art who fretted the most, since he was the one given the task—by John—of bringing back a good statement at season's end. Records show that attendance kept slipping.

Could they simply blame it all on TV? The answer is never that easy. The key to a successful engagement in any city is dependant on a wide range of variables, from the amount of advertising undertaken to the time of the year to the location of the lot. Always important factors are weather conditions, the attractions offered, word of mouth. How many circuses have been there first? Is the city's economy in good health? There are intangibles that complicate things even worse. While Texas almost always guaranteed the Ringling circus—indeed, just about any circus—strong turnouts, Chicago could never be counted on for anything but its own fickleness.

The publicity factor was extremely important, and yet the greatest amounts of advertising alone will not guarantee turnaway business. When Gargantua was in his heyday, storming back and forth in his cage next to the one that contained his would-be mate M'Toto, he alone did not automatically draw huge crowds in every stand, despite the myth that he "saved" the circus. He alone did not spell the difference between a profitable tour or a losing one, any more than air-conditioning the big top did, or the opulent parades John introduced into the performances. All of these factors together spelled the difference in collaboration with general economic conditions and the ever-changing tastes of the public.

When Gargantua died, incredibly, on the very last day of the 1949 season (what a trouper!), John still had Unus to ballyhoo. He had his magnificent productions to tout, as he did a host of imported European stars. For a couple of years, he had the glamorous presence of De Mille and the Paramount crews on his lot, another source of advertisement for the show's timeless appeal. At the same time, John remained true to his own producing concepts, elaborated upon by his brother, Henry, to a *Variety* reporter at the outset of the 1950 season, when the year's total revenues were projected to reach $6 million. Said Henry, the fine business they were enjoing could be attributed to John's "yearly drive" for new acts, the lavish theatrical trappings, and the sex-appeal factor they had been stressing. "We're trying to outmode that bugaboo in all circuses, that 'what's the use of going again, I saw it last year' attitude. We think we've succeeded to a considerable degree by our constant efforts to get new acts and the large amounts of money we spend to re-dress the show each season."[3]

By the same token, the new look given the circus by the North brothers could soon become an old, predictable look through repetition of format. Getting into show business is difficult enough; staying in it is murder. By focusing the public's attention on the idea of novelty and spectacle, John conditioned his audiences to be more demanding, thereby increasing the challenges he faced each year. What could he do to keep their interest? It was nearly impossible to come up with startling new acts or bold new production concepts year after year. No given art or entertainment form can reinvent itself so often. When the circus business started declining, was it the fault of a once-fresh format suddenly looking not so fresh? Or the inevitable outcome of changing American lifestyles and the advent of the boob tube?

After John allowed two complete televised performances of the circus on CBS in 1948, he shied away from any further such tie-ins. He told a *Billboard* correspondent that he was jittery about doing it again because there were too many TV sets in houses.[4] In the *Variety* article in which Henry was quoted, he indicated they had gotten some "fabulous offers" from television networks, but none was big enough "to merit the box-office chance we feel we might be taking." Instead, the Norths decided to concentrate on pushing for appearances by the staff on talk and game shows. Mary Jane Miller, for example, showed up on "What's My Line?" and was all too quickly—the strong look of her hands and the timing—pegged by Dorothy Kilgallen.

While patronage declined, expenses soared. North and Concello were forever dogged by labor demands and skyrocketing transportation fees. They continually dragged their feet with the American Guild of Variety Artists, with which they theoretically held a contract, hoping at every negotiating phase to avoid a further drain on the books. In 1950, out of exasperation trying to deal with North, Henry Dunn, the guild's national administrative secretary, branded his surly attitudes "no longer a challenge to AGVA but a challenge to organized labor."[5] Shortly afterward, the circus forked over a check for six thousand nine hundred dollars as payment of dues for the 260 performers on its payroll. And still Dunn was working without a contract. The circus agreed that if one was not signed by the end of the Madison Square Garden run, union negotiators would be allowed to travel on the train for as long as it took to come to terms. As so often had been the case, the AGVA proceeded with a letter of agreement signed by Ringling. In 1952, Concello notified the union of advice from his own legal counsel to refrain from instructing his personnel to join. The circus attorneys had discovered a loophole they could use in their defense. North and Concello never gave organized labor a birthday cake.

Rail transportation was another costly item. In 1950, the circus spent nearly half a million dollars moving itself over the tracks. This represented an astounding 111 percent increase in a five-year period. Art got John's approval in 1951 to cut the train down to seventy cars and confine the tour within 15,000 miles (exceeded by 932 miles). The anticipated total rail fees were $335,000—still more than the circus put out in 1947, when it carried thirty-eight more cars on the train.

The differing manner in which John and Art tended to address these problems reflected the classic differences between them. John opted for more extravagant programs, believing they would draw larger crowds; Art pressed for further cutbacks in equipment and personnel, convinced that the only salvation lay in reducing expenses. This put the two on a potential collision course not obvious to everyone at first.

Art did everything he could to find alternate ways of presenting essentially the same kind of circus on a smaller scale. Max Weldy set up a costume factory in Sarasota, where seamstresses cost a lot less than the high prices they had been paying to the independent Ladies' Garment Workers' Union up in New York.[6] In addition to eliminating cars from the train, in 1951 Concello incorporated the menagerie into the front end of an expanded five-pole big top. The ingenious move was not without precedent, *The Billboard* reporting it a throwback to pre–Civil War circuses, when animal cages were spotted inside the main tent. The shrunken configuration eliminated two seat wagons, reducing capacity by nearly a thousand chairs. And patrons were now assaulted by a variety of animal aromas wafting in over a thin canvas partition that separated the zoo from the performance area.

Art accepted the diminishing crowds that came with the new era, realizing the circus no longer dominated the entertainment scene. At the same time, he made the physical layout more comfortable and aesthetically inviting. He and John did not revive the air-conditioning wagons as they had announced they would do at the outset of the 1948 season. Instead, they utilized another, noncostly method of diffusing the heat on hot summer days: loose canvas flaps were placed over netted sections at the top of the tent. Called air vents, they reduced temperatures by as much as twenty degrees.

They carpeted the seat-wagon aisles. And in 1952, two large wagons outfitted with portable restroom facilities, called comfort stations, were spotted at the edge of the animal-display area. A substitute for the older canvas latrines, they were well maintained and proved to be a hit with customers. Art invented every labor-saving device imaginable, from lighter-weight plastic-coated aluminum cable (of less diameter than rope) to power winches that hoisted the big top's twenty-one tons of cloth into the air. Everything to trim the work force and make the show less vulnerable to cheap itinerant labor.

Art showed what a fine innovater he could be when he gave the midway a dazzling face-lift and outdid even Norman Bel Geddes. First, he had all four ticket wagons painted purple and placed in front of the marquee, a definite break with tradition. He redressed the sideshow fronts with illuminated shadow boxes containing blown-up photographs, soon damaged by rough weather. Bill Ballantine, a Ringling clown and free-lance writer, wanted to paint them over in gaudier colors, so he approached the general manager.

"I thought you were a writer," said Art.

"I'm an artist, too," replied Bill.

"Okay, Bill, the job is yours."[7]

Just like that, Ballantine had the assignment. He drew on the styles of several of his favorite artists in creating a unique concept. His vivid hues swirled with expressionistic flair. The spirit of circus prevailed. Ballantine and his two assistants, Ralph Hunter of Detroit and William Tracy of Sarasota, installed a large lattice marquee—in collapsable sections—over the four ticket wagons, triumphally lettered with the circus's famous name. Altogether, Ballantine's inspired artwork transformed the midway into—as Roland Butler so aptly described it—"a screaming riot of color." The fine toast offered by Butler in his 1953 route-book piece is more than deserved: "His eye-seizing painting of the side show attractions, in huge Victorian rococo shadow box frames, originated by Art Concello, were nothing ever before seen on this continent. Extending across the tops of the brilliantly bedecked ticket wagons at the main entrance was a highly ornate 50-foot scrolled panel, peaked with pennants. This striking midway innovation, emblazoned with every hue of the spectrum, made circus-goers' eyes pop and warmed the welcome to wonderland."[8]

Art experimented with new modes of promotion and presentation.

The Cow Palace engagement in 1948 had been such a success (thousands turned away each night) that the circus not only repeated the date the next year but added two other indoor stops along the route: Saint Louis, Missouri, and San Antonio, Texas. The avowed purpose was to see how fast they could get the show "in and out" of new buildings springing up around the country. The press department acknowledged the stints as "further manifestations of the indoor trend."

Another big tentless engagement added in 1949 was the Sports Palace in Havana, Cuba, where the circus opened for several years thereafter just before Christmas. The best acts were sent over, along with the production frills and floats, adapted to a one-ring format to fit the arena. The inaugural show, as Jackie Le Claire remembers, "just wowed 'em. They had those fantastic production numbers, and La Norma and Unus knocked 'em on their ass."9 The annual visit turned a profit. Within a few years, however, rising political unrest in Cuba (foreshadowing the Castro revolution) posed too many risks and Havana was dropped.

Where was the circus in America headed, with so many new arenas now dotting the urban landscape? An important article in *The Billboard*, "Is the Big Top Disappearing?" took up the issue with foresight. Its author, Tom Parkinson, revealed that the Ringling show had tried securing more indoor dates in 1949. He stressed the cost- and labor-cutting advantages inherent in auditorium bookings. Lighting and seats were generally superior; so were safety and fire-protection factors. More circuses, the Cole show included, were starting to play all their dates indoors. Parkinson reported that the Ringling management was now more or less set on appearing under hardtops wherever possible while playing the remainder of its dates beneath the traditional canvas roof. He wrote, "It may be as simple as leaving most rolling stock and tops in quarters, to move the show indoors."10

That North and Concello pursued such a policy with clear-cut intent is not so clear. Ringling Bros. and Barnum & Bailey, the nation's most beloved entertainment giant, did not at first face these indoor options with a set agenda for shucking aside its romantic canvas trappings, not anywhere near. It appeared to be wandering, almost unconsciously, into the uncertain future, half-aware of the need to adapt, half-clinging to its rich traditions. All great institutions suffer from such schizophrenia.

Another new form of promotion Art and John experimented with was the use of sponsors. For the Ringling show, which had long survived outside the realm of civic and charity tie-ins, the move marked a radical and rather sad departure. The show had already been pitching block ticket sales to various industrial concerns, among them the Firestone Tire Company of Akron, Ohio. In these instances, sometimes the entire performance was bought out by a company as a gift to its employees, without the odious taint of a charity pitch. In 1951, manager Frank McClosky and general agent Waldo Tupper tried out a couple of sponsored dates in Augusta, Georgia, and Daytona Beach, Florida. Both were so successful that the auspices at each stand invited Ringling back the following year.

So in 1952 there was the impetus to set up a string of sponsored dates, be they under the good graces of the local police or firemen's association, the Shriners, or the Moose or the Elks. The stated policy was "to make good business better." In fact, had the tent been filling up all along, it is doubtful such a strategy ever would have been undertaken. Promotion manager Paul Eagles sent four agents ahead to follow up on a flood of queries from prospective community groups wanting to beat the drum for the circus and share in the profits.

The contract offered gave the sponsor 20 percent of the net proceeds, exclusive of any and all amusement taxes, over and above twenty thousand dollars in ticket sales. In return, the sponsor agreed to secure suitable grounds, all the required permits and licenses (presumably free of all the sundry payoffs that had routinely been extracted from the Ringling agents), adequate police and fire protection, and water. It agreed "to use its best efforts to further the sale of tickets and to secure publicity, including furnishing 20 letters requesting free space for display of posters and window lithos." The circus provided the insurance and its usual lavish, star-studded performance.

Ideally, this package promised the circus freedom from having to give away so many free tickets and under-the-table bribes and more political access to prime lots closer to the center of town. Eagles and his staff were instantly effective in signing up the necessary sponsors. Virtually all the dates for the first half of the canvas tour were put under auspices. A box-office bonanza did not materialize, however. To the contrary, Ringling officials were so disappointed by the mediocre returns that they decided to book the second half of the tour on a fifty-fifty basis, half of it sponsored and half "cold," so they could compare the results.

Roland Butler lamented the meager publicity efforts of the outsiders. Possibly in anticipation of this, Concello had had a sixteen-page flier, replete with action-filled photos, printed that year. Mass-distributed through the U.S. mails to the cities booked in advance of circus day, it didn't make a great deal of difference, either. Some towns delivered full houses; a lot of them delivered far less. In the cities where local sponsoring officials stood nervously by, waiting for large crowds that didn't materialize, Concello was nervous, too. He felt embarrassed having to face the sponsor, who had tried but lost, and he often volunteered to reimburse the sponsor for expenses incurred, even though the contract did not stipulate so magnanimous a gesture.

Such was the case, for example, in Reading, Pennsylvania, where the American Legion did not even earn back (through two half-full houses) the $700 it had put up to bring the circus to town. At another dismal date in Albany, New York, the Association of Commerce was outspoken in its praise of the Ringling management, which had given it a check for $1,500 to cover the cost of lot, license, and water fees—all sponsor expenses, technically. At least one-third of the auspices groups did not recoup their investment, and many were routinely helped out of debt by Concello's sympathetic staff. Some eked out a small profit from control of parking facilities. In Chicago, where the circus played to thirty-five thousand people under the graces of a coalition of churches (raising money for an old-age home), the sponsor received but a paltry $750 check for its efforts.

Yet by midseason *The Billboard* reported the circus to be satisfied with the new setup and planning to continue its use the following year. Concello was obviously not the source consulted. He was never at ease with the arrangement. (Years later, he remains evasive on the subject, refusing to acknowledge that such a practice ever took place at all.) Nor had the sponsored dates proved to be a boon to business. Mostly they were an embarrassment. And with Concello against the policy, it had little future. He met with John and Henry in a postseason confab over the policy and they decided to abandon it. "The plan generally proved a bloomer," reported the trades. "Sponsors for the most part were hard pressed to make a buck."[11]

Those were some of the things Art tried. As for John, he was, as always, obviously content to spend more money on more acts and more costumes, hoping the public would now and then turn out in overwhelming droves to acclaim his latest offering. It worked less frequently as the show moved into the 1950s, and yet John's extravagance knew no limits. When he went with the show to Cuba, he sent over his Cadillac and his personal chinaware, had his royal box at the Sports Palace decorated in red velvet, and invited into it any number of celebrities from near and far who happened to be around, including President Batista and Fidel Castro, the future pro-

Communist dictator. Ernest Hemingway, his literary flame fairly extinguished, spent many hours in Havana bars with John.

By now, North had turned away from the bombast of the Gargantua era into a more aesthetic phase. Although, to be fair, the sideshow still boasted such earthly oddities as Ted Evans, "New Giant Import"; Frances O'Connor, "The Armless Wonder"; or Ted Warner, the tattooed artist whose mouth was even decorated, proclaimed a "human picture gallery." The main program, though, had evolved into something more closely akin to Broadway than to Barnum with its emphasis on artistry over the sham deformity of contrivance in which P. T., never really a circus producer, had specialized. Johnny North, a very different breed, had moved the circus closer to a spectacle of unity and depth. In 1952, he and Miles White hosted a modeling surprise on elephants, "The Greatest Fashion Show on Earth," sponsored by *Look* magazine. Under White's supervision, the work of such American designers as John Frederics, Omar Kiam of Ben Reig, Adrian, Clare Potter, Hattie Carnegie, and Nettie Rosenstein was displayed by twelve "gorgeously garbed girls" astride a like number of willing pachyderms. The program dubbed it "A Prodigious Panoramic Processional Pageant of Topflight American-Designed Clothes."[12]

Costume-happy John and Miles set sail for Paris shortly after opening night, the one to scout for more new acts and the other for every available sequin in sight. The American outlets had fallen short of the necessary shiny bobs needed to satisfy the Ringling costume mills. White returned with many new designs presewn in flat sections, ready for final assembly and fitting in Sarasota.

John returned with an ample number of entertaining new acts. In the 1952 and 1953 editions, he favored his audiences with the likes of Dieter Tasso, a crack slack-wire juggler who tossed a series of cups and saucers into a stack on his head; sway-pole exponent Tell Teigen; the Camillo Mayer troupe of high-wire walkers, who prepared a meal for themselves on high; whirlwind acrobats the Sons of the Midnight Sun, and roller-skating wizards the Heirolls. Who else? Aerial first-timers included the Montons, Nina Karpowa, Greta Frisk, the Pivotos, the Renellys, and the Morlings. There were the Maxims, contortionists, and the plate-spinning Alcettys. The Great Linares worked the tightwire. Harry and Long presented comedy gymnastics. Also numbered among new acrobatic troupes were the Ricoris, Fenis-Ferroni Duo, the Six Frielanis, the Rassos and the Bisbinis, the Riggettis, and the Abbott Girls. Animal novelties included Oscar Konyot's Lions, Hammerschmidt's Wonder Apes, and Tassi's Vagabond

Canines. John signed a German motorcycle maniac, Arno Nickhold, who worked inside a bottomless "wall of death." Tragically true to its billing, the wall of death accidentally opened at the wrong moment, and Nickhold went careening out to his demise below, shortly before he was scheduled to open with Ringling in 1952.

John took his chance on occasion with offbeat offerings. The one attraction in which he placed his deepest faith, ordering a ballyhoo comparable to Gargantua's, was a mere lad of five or six known then as Baby Mistin, whom he had come across at a circus in Stockholm. The child played the xylophone in a charming and confident manner. John was captivated on the spot. He signed his next feature attraction and set the Ringling hype machines into motion. Somewhere in the translation to center-ring star, some of Mistin's charm got lost. Maybe it was a mistake to rename him Mister Mistin, Jr., which detracted from the image of early childhood that had so enamored him with European audiences. Richard Barstow once quipped, "I wonder if he was a little boy. I think he was someone's grandfather reincarnated."[13]

Mistin landed the cover of the circus magazine. He was depicted in a drab childlike watercolor, possibly his own work. Inside, following Ernest Hemingway's deft contribution, "The Circus," came an article by Roland Butler, "Monsters to Mistin," in which the five-year-old child prodigy was given star focus. Mistin, readers learned, weighed thirty-six pounds and stood thirty-six inches tall. He spoke five languages fluently and practiced from one to two hours daily. "He loves toys, ice cream, soda pop, and hates to go to bed," reported Butler.[14] The tot made his official debut with a Belgian circus in Brussels, his hometown, "at the unbelievable age of two." His billing as Display 7 in the program:

PRODIGIOUSLY PROCLAIMED PHENOMENON
John Ringling North's
Latest and Greatest Importation
The Tiny Musical Prodigy Who Has Astounded Millions
in Europe, Asia and Africa
MISTER MISTIN, JR.
THE CHILD WONDER OF THE WORLD
First Time in America

In his debut at Madison Square Garden on April 1, 1953, Mistin did not quite astound. He merely pleased. In a kind *Variety* review, Leonard Traube sensed a degree of showmanship not discernible to everyone:

The jury will probably be deliberating all season on the merit, appropriateness, and impact of Mister Mistin, a Belgian moppet whose age is given as five but who may be a year or two older. This Brussels sprout, who operates in an electrifying way upon a xylophone, is given the kind of staging and buildup that only the big bertha of circuses could fabricate with any degree of credibility. Under other auspices the act would be considered the acme of corniness, but at New York's Madison Square Garden, amid a vast expanse with its multifarious trappings, it comes off before a hushed audience—jampacked to its 15,000 capacity—as one of the biggest tricks in modern circusiana. . . .

The sight of a small lad playing the warhorse "Poet and Peasant" overture on a slowly-revolving high platform in the center ring is a spectacle of sorts, and the preem crowd responded with a characteristic ovation at the finish of the piece. . . . The kid is in full command: he has been coached to milk the audience, boxing the compass extensively while so doing and probably going beyond the script in this regard. He speaks English well, for the few words he has to say. John Ringling North has gone all-out in the newspaper advertising and billing with faith in the attraction's pull. How this treatment may affect the regular troupes, who have spent years in perfecting their routines, will no doubt be evidenced as the season progresses."[15]

Other scribes reacted less promisingly, The Billboard declaring, in a generally negative review of the circus, that Mister Mistin was only "so-so." On recorded tapes of the show, Mistin comes off as a quiet charmer with his perky little presence and precise musicianship. He pulled strong sustaining applause sprinkled with cheers. Art Concello, not a fan of the act, conceded that it went over "fairly well."[16] And Richard Barstow, among the decidedly enthusiastic, praises North for his openness to new ideas in big top entertainment: "Everybody said, 'Oh, my God, what is this doing in the circus?' Well, I think that's rather exciting. He was a riot, he was a rotten little boy. You'd give him guns and things and he'd shoot you. He was a great showman."[17]

Whatever anybody felt, the act lasted only a single season—the most telling of critiques, although certain presentations, such as Mistin's, are basically novelties that don't hold up the second time around. (The lad's ring time was edited down from fifteen minutes to eight.) Looking at him critically, what Mistin lacked was the air of mystery that could play on the public's imagination. Whereas Gargantua evoked fearful visions of destruction as "the world's most terrifying living creature," whereas Unus challenged the supernatural with his illusory one-finger stand, Mistin, by contrast, was merely a very good, very young xylophonist. He was too honest a manifestation of his own natural talent to suggest phenomenal powers. He was simply too real.

The 1953 Mistin tour, with cutbacks ordered by Concello in the advance billposting brigades, did not turn back the elusive downward spiral in attendance. The Garden engagement, which drew a healthy nine hundred thousand souls, was termed "the first boost in attendance since 1949," thanks in part to one hundred radio and television appearances arranged by the press department during the all-important Gotham run. Could they have been so lucky on the under-canvas circuit? In his year-end route-book report, Roland Butler, who had showered his verbiage on Mistin in the circus magazine, had not a word to say about him now. Nor did he call the season's patronage "splendid" or anything close as he had done the year before. Butler made passing reference to some three million people having seen the show that season, a far cry from the four million souls who crowded the midway annually through the mid 1940s. By then, the show had collected $1.3 million in royalties from Paramount Pictures for its participation in the hit De Mille movie, and it was still struggling to stay out of red ink. Gone were the days, so it seemed.

Neither North nor Concello had been able to recapture the huge, profitable crowds. Still, Johnny resisted Art's campaign to reduce the size of the show even more—a growing source of friction between the two. The conflict was only symptomatic of other factors that changed the North-Concello relationship significantly. By this time, John had cleared his debts with Art, to whom he now felt naturally less obligated. He had also cleared the corporation of the remaining Hartford-fire claims. And both Aunt Edith and Cousin Robert—always a potential source of antagonism to John's management style—had by now passed away, Robert in 1950 and Edith in late 1953. So John was freer than ever from .the restraints and favors of others.

He became less willing to let Concello bully him around, to the ridiculous point of deciding whether or not he could travel on the train in his private car. John could also now afford to distrust Art in a way he had not been able to before. There were always rumors that Concello was bent on gaining control of the circus. Whether or not this bothered John, surely he wondered how much money he was losing to the various ticket-selling rackets that Art condoned and collected on. There were plenty of reasons John could muster up to justify distancing himself from his power-hungry general manager. And the reasons went far beyond the mere diversion of money away from the red wagon. Toward the end of the 1953 tour, a shooting incident that linked Concello to Maggie Smith, a Ringling showgirl, was reported in *The Billboard*. Initially, the police were informed that Smith had been shot while she was walking alongside the circus train and that she did not know who fired at her. Later, she changed her story to coincide with Concello's account. The gun was his, he told police officers, explaining that he had "accidentally fired the shot which injured the girl." He said they were in the pie car, where he was playing with the .25-caliber gun, which went off by mistake. Smith agreed it had been an accident.[18] Considered by insiders as the upshot of a lover's quarrel, the incident was a dangerous example of Concello's tactless infidelities to his wife, Antoinette. A divorce followed. Art and Maggie enjoyed a long-term relationship and eventually married.

Reason by reason, John mounted his own personal case against Art's usefulness. Now, he decided to take on Concello's irritating frugality. In 1953, against Art's wishes, Ringling Bros. and Barnum & Bailey was still a gargantuan enterprise, its forty-odd tents encompassing seventy-four thousand yards of canvas and billowing out over fourteen acres. The show traveled 18,907 miles on thirty-seven different railroad lines. One thousand two hundred eighty-nine employees representing thirty-five nationalities consumed three thousand five hundred meals daily in the cookhouse. In all, 2,252 tons of hay was purchased during the tour, 207,000 pounds of horsemeat devoured by the carnivores. The lot required fifteen diesel plants to produce the necessary energy, 24,700 feet of cable to carry the current. Seventy-two miles of rope was used in the mammoth circus setup.[19] Ticket prices were in line with those charged for Broadway musicals. Still, the circus took in scarcely more money than it put out.

Art wanted to curtail expenses drastically. He argued for slashing twenty more cars off the train. According to Art, John wanted the very opposite: let's add ten cars and make it bigger and better than ever. The partners held a conference with each other less than two weeks after the train rolled into the Sarasota barns. Resisting John's strange expansionist zeal, Art tried pointing out politely, "I don't think I can handle it with ten more cars, a hundred more men." John taunted Art's budgetary concerns, boasting in heated tones, "Hell, I'll go down with the greatest show on earth rather than some skimpy nickel-and-dime-store version!" Art became defensive. "Okay," he said, tired of it all. "If you wanta make it bigger, you come on back here and *you* operate it."[20] And with that he rose, ready to exit. John made no effort to stop him.

On Thursday afternoon, December 3, 1953, North and Concello parted company. Art wrote out an official resignation and placed it on John's desk: "You can do better without me. As of today, I'm finished." The only reason given by *The Billboard* was a supposed disagreement between the two over the upcoming Havana engagement, Art wanting to skip it because of rising political unrest in Cuba.

When Art Concello walked away, leaving John solely in charge, in effect he opened the floodgates on the most bizarre chapter in Ringling circus history. If only De Mille could have started the cameras rolling now, he would have recorded a spectacular real-life drama. Writers not needed.

Ringling personnel director Pat Valdo, left, actor Charlton Heston, one of the stars of Cecil B. De Mille's movie *The Greatest Show on Earth*, North, and circus choreographer Richard Barstow. (Photo by Ted Sato)

North, backstage with Marlene Dietrich, guest ringmistress at the 1953 New York opening, a gala benefit for the United Cerebral Palsy Fund. (Photo by Ted Sato)

The 1955 spectacular, "Holidays." (Photo by Ted Sato)

"Americana," the 1953 finale. (Photo by Ted Sato)

Backstage at Madison Square Garden in 1954: floats and costumes by Miles White were as eagerly awaited as the newest star performers. (Photo by Ted Sato, from the collection of Timothy Noël Tegge)

Paul Jung and a show-girl in the circus back-yard. (Photo by Ted Sato)

Lou Jacobs, one of the very few clowns ever to enjoy a solo spot on the Ringling program, seen here in his classic car-into-gas-station routine. (From the collection of Timothy Noël Tegge)

Otto Griebling, favored by most fans over Emmett Kelly, takes his own selected "roll call" out in the seats during a preshow warm-up in the indoor era. (From the collection of Timothy Noël Tegge)

Antoinette Concello, the first woman to complete the triple, flew with visible enjoyment. In later years, she directed many of the aerial ballets. (From the collection of Timothy Noël Tegge)

Flying trapeze star Tito Gaona, a personal favorite of North's. (From the collection of Timothy Noël Tegge)

North, at the piano, with his good friend Rudy Bundy, in the M'Toto Room of Sarasota's John Ringling Hotel, circa 1950. (Rudy Bundy Collection)

Ida and John, who lived together for nearly thirty years, in 1958 at Venedig. (Courtesy of Countess Ida von Zedlitz-Trützschler)

North and one of his great loves, actress Dody Heath, in 1954. (Dody Heath Soames Collection)

The Norths at Northbrook: John, right, with Henry, who is holding his grandson, John Ringling North III. Henry's son, John Ringling North II, looks on in the background. (Courtesy of John Ringling North II)

North relaxes in his prime years during the mid-1950s. (Photo by Ted Sato)

A Stab at Tomorrow

Despite Art's contention that the only issue which separated him from John was the number of cars on the train—he wanting to cut it by twenty, John wanting to add ten—the size of the train increased by *one* car the following season, John's Jomar. In fact, nothing much changed. Frank McClosky moved up to assume the general manager's position vacated by Art, and virtually all the other key department heads remained on board with the one notable exception of Tuffy Genders, a Concello loyalist who had supervised the front door. John replaced him with his old pal, Rudy Bundy, with whom he again grew close after severing ties with Art.

John and Rudy had shared much together with their common love of music, and Rudy represented a valuable friend who could be trusted in a high management post. John invited Rudy to visit him in Havana at Christmastime in 1953 when the circus was playing there. They renewed their friendship, and John got Rudy's band back at the M'Toto Room in the Ringling Hotel. He also talked Rudy, once again, into working for the show. Rudy was made superintendent of the front door, which gave John tighter control over the omnipresent potential for the ticket-selling violations that had flourished under Concello's sneeze mob. Rudy was approached right off the bat by Frank McClosky. "Let's work something out," he proposed, but Bundy refused to become part of any illegal schemes. "We were never great friends after that," he explains.[1]

The flacks made a big to-do about the Jomar's going back on the rails after a two-year hiatus. A circus-magazine story titled "The Jomar Rolls Again" promised circusgoers a view of Ringling royalty: "The Jomar doubtless lies today in the railway yards of your city with one of the sections of the Ringling Bros. and Barnum & Bailey circus train. It is Mr. North's home, his castle. As head of the Greatest Show on Earth, he, of course, has an office on it. His command is in the No. 1 office wagon on the circus lot."[2]

The organization remained more intact than turned over at this deceptively stable point, and the 1954 New York opening, a gala benefit for the United Cerebral Palsy Fund that raised eighty thousand dollars, went over fabulously. Among those attending was Art Concello, there ostensibly to oversee his flying acts, which still held a Ringling contract. There were more than two hundred photographers and enough celebrities to make the "Dreamland" spec, in which they all guest-paraded, look more like a Hollywood roll call.

Besides John's normal set of opulent, eye-popping pageants, staged with gusto by Richard Barstow, the program offered a host of attractive new thrillers: aerial contortionist the Great Logano; the Rixos, who worked opposite ends of a ladder horizontally balanced on a trapeze bar; slack-wire dynamo Luis Munoz; and ground acrobats Evy and Everto, the Four Radinos, the Wendanis, Burton and Son, the Tumbling Whirlwinds, Yong Sisters and Brothers, and the Bully Trio. High-wire walker Josephine Berosini was a real looker with a sly style all her own, whose act *Variety* described "a sort of controlled nightmare of audience apprehension." The Four Nocks, Swiss sway-pole daredevils, generated excitement with midair exchanges atop sixty-foot spars, brought to a riveting conclusion as each slid down a pole, headfirst, in a swift, breathtaking descent.

Another surprise hit of the show was Victor Julian's (to quote the program) "Globally Celebrated Trained Dogs." They pranced whimsically about the ring in all sorts of humanlike getups, the satirical effects being hilarious now and then. Unus, absent from the show for three seasons, was brought back "by insistent popular demand." John evidently had learned his lesson with the disappointing Mister Mistin, Jr. Audiences wanted the mystery of incredible feats. Unus certainly delivered, as did so many of the other top artists.

Miles White fashioned an exotic feast of costume delights. Barbette, last seen at Ringling in 1948 with his marvelous "Monte Carlo" aerial ballet, returned to direct a captivating new work, "Rocket to the Moon." In the splashy finale, "U.N.," scores of showgirls entered with drums, pounding out a simple primitive beat. Merle Evans and the band followed down the track. Long, rolled-up ribbons bearing the designs of various national flags unraveled to the ground.

The show received much-deserved praise from the press watchers, Robert Coleman in the *Daily Mirror* calling it "North's masterpiece . . . the best version of the Greatest Show on Earth that he has produced so far." Wrote Jim McHugh for *The Billboard*: "North has expertly bridged all aged levels in packaging this year's extravaganza. The production is replete with novelties, including imports more worthy of note than in the last couple of years, sufficiently working animals, wild and domestic, to satisfy all tastes, long-legged beauties in sufficiently scant and form-accenting costumes to keep male members awake and interested, and some thrill turns which are about the best featured by the circus in several years."[3]

John was in high gear once more. His stylish image became lionized by Maxwell Coplan's now-famous photograph of him, which was printed in the circus magazine that year for the first time. He is seen wearing a derby hat and a somber pin-striped coat, one hand clasping a set of gloves at the end of a cane, a cigarette and holder in his mouth, the thin shaft of smoke rising from it as subtle as the expression of well-being and quiet control on his handsome face. Attending the picture was an elegant blurb: "Heads Circus World." The adjoining page had a story by brother Henry, "Put the Show on the Road," while the lead article, "Circus," carried the byline of another literary giant on friendly terms with the North brothers, John Steinbeck.

Another boost to North's magical reputation was Robert Lewis Taylor's sketch on him for the *New Yorker*. The piece came out during the New York engagement, and appeared a few years later, along with other Ringling profiles, in Taylor's wonderfully witty but overfancified tome *Center Ring*.

John was so pleased with the bullish reception accorded his 1954 effort that he took out an ad in *The Billboard* to trumpet his sentiments: "John Ringling North has received the Broadway titan's cherished accolade: 'The Perfect Show.' . . . John Ringling North brings the 1954 edition of the Greatest Show on Earth to the entire nation with humility; yet with the natural and not-to-be-denied pride of acknowledged achievement."[4]

What delighted the critics did not fill all of the Madison Square Garden seats, however. Not that the circus publicists didn't put their best feet forward. William Fields, a top-flight Broadway press agent on the Ringling payroll, masterminded an advertising tie-in with a Macy's print campaign, resulting in more than two hundred full pages of exposure in the metropolitan dailys with the slogan "See Ringling Bros. Circus for the Greatest

Show on Earth—see Macy's for the Greatest Sale on Earth." Circus background music was used on Macy's radio commercials. The department
store mailed ad copy bearing the circus name to more than six hundred
thousand subscribers. Experts estimated that it amounted to hundreds
of thousands of dollars' worth of free advertising space, and all the circus
had to put out in return were five hundred free ducats for a dress-rehearsal
performance the night before opening. Incredibly, Fields had faced resistance to the tie-in when he first discussed it with his employers.

Not everyone responded to the Macy's ads as was optimistically expected.
The Garden run drew a respectable eight hundred thousand paying
customers, discouragingly fewer than the nearly one million people who
patronized the show's Gotham stand through the late 1940s. It was,
nonetheless, a good-enough sendoff for John, now on his own away from
Concello. That spring, in a final wrapping up of the Hartford-fire litigation,
he agreed to pay the receiver one hundred thousand dollars for his
accumulated services. John hoped to bring the big top back to Hartford
that summer on the tenth anniversary of the tragic blaze, believing it
would be a fine symbolic gesture of healing and forgiveness. Despite some
goodwill displayed on both sides over the idea, Ringling agents were
unable to secure the necessary permits. City officials claimed they simply
could not foresee being able to handle the traffic problems. It is more
likely that they were afraid the sight of Ringling canvas against the city
skyline would reopen old wounds and prove politically troublesome.
Never again did the circus pitch its tents in Hartford, although in later
years it played the Hartford arena.

There were many other places to play, and John encouraged his routing
agents to try out new towns. His creative spirit recharged, he faced the
future with the same bold openness to change and adaptation he had
when he first took over the circus in the late 1930s. He seemed to
recognize the failed Mister Mistin ballyhoo by turning back in a more
traditional mode. The return of Unus and the engagement of such acts as
the Nocks and Berosini exemplified John's renewed respect for the power
of strong, visibly compelling attractions.

He sent his foreign-rarities scout, McCormick Steele, into the depths of
Africa after a tusker reportedly larger than Jumbo. Steele failed to work
the magic, nor was he able to round up a group of natives amenable to
Stateside exhibition or another troupe of the platter-lipped Ubangis such
as the sort the show had crassly exploited twenty-five years earlier. Steele
also tried, in vain, too, to book a tribe of Ituri Forest Pygmies in the Congo.

However, in the process, he purchased a very rare okapi—reported to be one of only six in captivity—from an Ituri Forest trapper. And he acquired a number of baby pachyderms for John, who was going elephant mad.

Back in New York, Dick Barstow received a phone call around three o'clock one morning.

"Ah, Dick," said John on the other end, a little hazy, "ah, what are you doing?"

"Well, I was in bed, John."

"Come over. I have something that I must tell you."

"Can't you tell me in the morning?"

"No, Richard!"

Barstow got out of bed, dressed and went over to the Waldorf-Astoria. He wandered up to the desk, fatigued.

"I'm here to see Mr. North."

"He's in the steam room, sir."

Barstow went downstairs, exchanged his clothes for a loose towel, and joined the hip crowd sweating it out. He discovered his boss sitting with a couple of prominent people and was offered a bottle of imported beer.

"I would like, maybe, a cup of coffee."

"Sure."

"Now, Richard," said John, "I've got something for you. A gift."

"Oh, what is it?"

"I have fifty-five elephants for you!"

"Oh, my God," replied Barstow, waking up fast.

"That's the largest performing herd in the world, Richard!"

John's director was flabbergasted. He could hardly handle thirty of them at one time.

"Fifty-five elephants?"

"That's right."

"Well, you know what you can do with them."

The two got to laughing. Behind it all, of course, Johnny was dead serious, and that's how "Mama's in the Park" was born, in a discussion at the Waldorf steam room, when the piece was originally titled "Strolling in the Park." Barstow came up with the concept of dressing the girls as cancan dancers, the clowns as Keystone Kops, of a park bum played by sad-faced Emmett Kelly. He cast the bigger bulls as mothers pushing the little ones around in carriages.[5]

John had no intention of making the show less epic and more cost conscious, even though that year he had hired an efficiency expert with

New York credits, William Conant, to poke around the office and see what expenditures could be trimmed. While Conant was saving the show hundreds of dollars, North was spending thousands more on elephants, the transportation for which would require additional cars on the train, another bloated expense. The 1954 tour winningly in progress—termed at one point by Frank McClosky "the best since 1950," with capacity and turnaway houses registered in a record-breaking nine-day Chicago run—it did anything but curb John's flamboyant bent. He was driven like a gambler, driven to produce a show the public simply could not resist. How could people resist the promised spectacle of fifty-five elephants parading around the hippodrome track? Given the increasing number of entertainment options competing for their dollar, they could and they did.

What John did believe, correctly so, was that there must be new ways for presenting and promoting the circus, and to this end he addressed his energies, fostering the most creative and volatile period in Ringling history. John moved ahead with little absolute knowledge of his own, rather with his usual confident receptiveness to the ideas of others, no matter how extreme, especially from those outside the circus world.

One of the most pressing questions on his mind was how to make the most effective use of television. In 1954, TV shows were booking jugglers and clowns by the cartload, bringing the image of sawdust magic directly into the living rooms of America. "The circus is less circusy after tv," observed an editor at *Variety*, arguing that television had a crippling effect on circus business. "It is a fact that customers of every age and stripe are visibly jaded by such blurbs as, 'And now, ladies and gentlemen, for the first time in America!', when they saw that act or something similar on 'Toast of the Town,' 'Big Top,' or 'Comedy Hour.' "[6]

Like every other circus owner, John had to deal with the perplexing issue. How to exploit TV without becoming its victim. How to tease the public onto the midway without appeasing its curiosity in front of a flickering nineteen-inch screen.

Another issue was how to advertise. In an era when circuses started looking passé, would they do better to dispose of their old posters and adopt a more modern style, say, similar to movie ads, thus fostering the image of success by association? In his search for the answers, John made a number of rather rash, rather daring appointments, some impromptu, to bring fresh blood into the operation. His first major reshuffling was the controversial hiring of Edward Knoblaugh, a former Associated Press and International News Service foreign correspondent, to the newly created post of director of public relations. When Knoblaugh was offered the assignment, he admitted to knowing nothing about the circus. John was delighted. "That's just what I want, somebody with a new approach."[7]

To make way for Knoblaugh, John in effect pushed Roland Butler, the show's veteran publicity boss, off to the side, limiting his functions to the placement of news and radio advertising. The move devastated Butler, for even though he expressed respect for the new PR director, within a few months he submitted his resignation, announcing that he and his wife wanted some time to take a vacation before retiring in Florida to set up a printing business. Knoblaugh is sure to have offended Butler with his stated policy against using old-time press agentry cluttered with adjectives and grandiose distortions of fact. He announced that his press books would contain realistically written articles conforming to "concise journalistic models."

Knoblaugh told *The Billboard*'s Guy Livingston, "We are going to put out news stories that will sell to editors on their own merits as news." He wanted the show to extend itself beyond a conservative audience. "We are going to appeal more to foreign groups, or rather racial groups. In New York, we did a lot with Latin groups, and with colored groups."[8] Women's sections, he said, had been underestimated by the Ringling toutmasters. And he made friendly overtures to the Circus Fans Association of America, which North and Concello had not been courting of late. Copies of the first route card for 1954 were mailed to all members of the organization with a warm message: "To you, a valued friend. . . . As we embark upon this, our 84th season, we of the Greatest Show on Earth pause to extend to you . . . a cordial invitation to make yourself at home on our lot . . . whenever, wherever and as often as you visit. . . . Our equestrian director, official host to members of the association, awaits the opportunity to extend a personal greeting when you visit." The gesture was thought to signify a new and more congenial attitude on the part of management.

John's next surprise appointment was Hollywood agent Milton Pickman to the position of promotional director. Pickman, whose brother was a key executive at Paramount Studios, had been instrumental in getting North and De Mille together on the film deal. He was president of his own newly formed motion-picture producing company, as well as an agent for General Foods, which was interested in sponsoring a telecast of the circus in 1955. Pickman had lots of marketing ideas to offer John, such as selling rights to use the Ringling name for the merchandising of toys, clothes, foods, and various other products.

Pickman urged John to consider televising the circus, not the entire performance, as had been done in 1948, but in the more tantalizing format of a special highlights program. John was in a listening mood. His contract with De Mille prohibited the circus from being filmed for TV or movies until 1960, and Pickman, with connections at Paramount through his brother, might be able to waive the restriction. John was also drawn to the one hundred thousand dollar fee offered by General Foods for the right to sponsor the projected spring telecast in 1955, although, as it turned out, after Pickman collected a 10 percent commission and the show spent another twenty thousand dollars on unanticipated preparation expenses, there was a scant seventy thousand dollars remaining. John was dealing with an operator. Paramount relented, and Ringling signed the TV deal.

Then came a more daring suggestion from Pickman, which John also embraced, though not without first suffering the pained reactions and prophecies of doom from members of his staff during a tense discussion of the issue on a cold January afternoon in Sarasota: why not do away with outdoor billposting and spend all the money, instead, on larger news ads, some even in color, and on TV commercials? Pickman was nearly lynched by the dissenters. F. A. Boudinot, Ringling's general agent, who managed the advance billposting crews that traveled ahead in three sections, was stunned. So was Bev Kelley, who argued that outdoor advertising was too powerful and distinctive a medium to give up, as were the colorful news ads. Oddly, Kelley actually refused the larger amounts of money the proposed new policy would give him to spend on television blurbs, saying it was unnecessary.

John compromised a little, agreeing to a 75 percent cut in the outdoor budget, which spelled the retirement from the road of the last advance-advertising railroad car and the elimination of some twenty-five billposters from the force. Boudinot was handed a couple of trucks and five or six guys to help him hang a few lithos around. He soon quit in disgust. Los Angeles–based Paul Eagles, who had worked for the show intermittently, primarily as a booking agent, took over in Boudinot's place.

John's easy acceptance of the Pickman plan amounted to a bombshell, setting the circus world off in a storm of protest. Overzealous reporting by *The Billboard* only added fuel to the fire: "The plan, which won North's approval, virtually kills the show's outdoor advertising, the means by which the entire circus business was built. . . . It will be the first time that major Ringling features will not be billed with special posters."[9] Every move North made was now being watched with mounting disbelief by veteran troupers and industry analysts. Suddenly, he wasn't just a crazy eccentric or innovator. The name John Ringling North started to take on a sour taste. Old-timers especially saw him as a real threat to revered traditions.

Next to be hired into the Ringling hierarchy was an amiable-enough chap—not another Hollywood hack, exactly, or a journalist averse to circus syntax—no, just the affable and not particularly talented Michael Burke, a friend of Henry through their wartime escapades attached to the Office of Strategic Services. The two had participated in some heroic Italian actions, once capturing an Italian admiral and later recovering some invaluable top-secret equipment. Out of it all, each had earned a Silver Star "for gallantry with complete disregard for his personal safety."

Burke projected a fighting image in whatever he did. Before his naval stint, the native New Yorker had been a college football star, earning All-America honors as a halfback at Pennsylvania. After the war, he took on a variety of jobs, from technical adviser and contract author at the Hollywood studios to consultant to the U.S. High Commissioner in Occupied Germany, never distinguishing himself in much of anything, yet never flopping out, either. (He would later become president of both the New York Yankees and Madison Square Garden, positions he held with diplomatic savvy during losing phases of those respective organizations.) When he ran into Johnny North one night in New York at the 21, Burke was between assignments and receptive to any and all offers.

John was in the market for a new general manager. As Burke tells it, "he wanted someone in there to represent ownership that he could trust completely."[10] John implied all kinds of wonderful things to Michael, leading him to believe the management post included responsibility for his vast real estate holdings and oil interests. Furthermore, if Michael accepted the job and played his cards right, a substantial legacy for his family might be left in John's will.

"You're our brother," said John, according to Burke's recollection of the historic discussion as published in his autobiography, *Outrageous Good Fortune.*[11]

Like Knoblaugh, Burke admitted that he hadn't a clue about the circus business. That pleased John even more. "You've been training for it all your life. You just haven't known it." There were a lot of things Burke didn't know until he had accepted the position with mixed feelings. One of the most sobering revelations of all was that the circus was nearly a

half-million dollars in debt. "I was curious why North had never mentioned this," he says. He was also curious about why, as it turned out, the
oil and land holdings were excluded from his supervision. Burke tried
making an organization chart and discovered to his dismay that all department heads reported directly to one person: Frank McClosky, who drew a
modest annual salary of fifteen thousand dollars, yet drove a fancy Cadillac
and flashed wads of large bills from his pocket.

One ominous discovery after another: Burke was horrified to learn, just
when the show was loading up for its spring trek to New York City, that its
bank account held a total of three thousand dollars. The rail fees alone
amounted to forty thousand dollars, and bill collectors were banging on
the doors, some intimating court action. Burke drove hurriedly over to
Bird Key, where John was visiting his mother. He protested the bill of
goods he had been sold.

"What do I do now?"

"That's why I hired you, El Burkello," replied Johnny, blasé as ever.
"You're a resourceful fellow."[12]

Burke used the payment from General Foods for the upcoming telecast
to keep the creditors from throwing rocks and calling up hungry attorneys.
He got Madison Square Garden to lend the circus the forty thousand
dollars needed for the rail haul as an advance against ticket sales. Then he
was informed by Gen. John Reed Kilpatrick, the Garden president, and
Ned Irish, his manager, that rent for the following season, not yet under
contract, would be raised from six thousand dollars to ten thousand
dollars a day, not counting such extras as air conditioning, an additional
two hundred dollars a day when the circus wanted it turned on.

North and Burke railed against these outrageous rental increases, which
threatened to push an already narrow profit margin ($100,000 on a gross
of $1,800,000) into oblivion. Back in 1950, when the current contract that
was about to expire had been up for renegotiation, John had hinted at
disposing of the Garden stand altogether. Later that year, both parties
again came to terms, although the Ringling side was said to have accepted
them with bitter resignation. Now came these new increases, and John
once again ranted and raved that he might just go elsewhere. He publicized to the hilt his consideration of other options in the hope it would
make Kilpatrick and Irish more reasonable.

North and Burke talked to Robert Moses, New York park commissioner,
about playing under canvas in Central Park. Moses was not thrilled. Burke
wondered out loud in a session with New York Giants owner Horace

Stoneham how the circus might go over at the Polo Grounds under a canopy of some sort spread over the infield. Kaiser Aluminum engineers provided estimates, and the press was pampered with information. The idea of playing New York in the great outdoors added impetus to the development of a more advanced big top, one without poles and capable of being heated and cooled by the latest technology. So many economic factors made it seem a viable alternative.

While the current efficiency expert (they came and went with cost-inducing inefficiency) tinkered over the tiniest expenditures, John ordered the addition of ten cars to the train, mainly to transport his huge herd of fifty-five elephants and the canvas and poles for a separate menagerie tent. The animal display area was once again divorced from the big top. This provided room for the reinstatement of the two seat wagons that had been dropped when Concello merged the two tents into one and raised the seating capacity to slightly more than nine thousand.

John stuck with his vision of a bigger and better show. He even spoke seriously about air-conditioning the tent, as he had done in the late 1930s, with specially equipped wagons. A new design was developed to force cool air through the sides of the tent and down over the seats rather than through vents in the canvas roof as before. The scheme was never implemented, though, nor did North's prized okapi attraction make it into the expanded Ringling fold. It was kept under quarantine by the U.S. Department of Agriculture and later traded to a Chicago zoo.

The 1955 edition of Ringling Bros. and Barnum & Bailey Circus opened on the wings of a record-breaking advance sale and was given the usual critical huzzahs. It was a splendid program with a set of gorgeous, brilliantly conceived and executed production parades: "Holidays," "On Honolulu Bay," "Mama's in the Park," "Rainbow around the World." Miles White outdid himself with his costumes, all very appropriate and enchanting. Some of them graced the pages of *Life* magazine in a color spread on the opening, "New Shine for the Circus."[13] And there was ample talent to please all ages. John's new imports included Della Canestrelli, who worked an elevated rolling-globe act; Attalina on the low wire; the Oliveras on horizontal bars; The Seguras on springboards. There was stylish juggling by the Adonos; trick unicycle riding by the Naukos; whip spinning and paper shredding by the Cordons. Unus was back, as were the Nocks on their swaying spars, Pinito Del Oro, Josephine Berosini, and the usual trio of flying-return troupes, the Palacios earning the center ring with their graceful maneuvers. Takeo Usui, another first-time-in-America presentation (billed "Nipponese Genius Extraordinary"), surprised the crowds with a stand-up backward slide, without pole, down an inclined wire. *Billboard* appraised the production numbers as "ranking with the best ever," while judging the overall spread "a close facsimile of last year."

The gala benefit, this time staged by Michael Todd, brought Marilyn Monroe into the arena on the back of a pink elephant during the "Holidays" pageant, populated with a plethora of other famous faces, too. Milton Berle, the guest ringmaster, sent the crowd prematurely to its feet and toward the exit doors by announcing at the end of the first half, concluded around 11 P.M., "Thank you very much, folks, and goodnight." By that time, North had presented more circus than most shows offer during an entire program. Harold Ronk grabbed the microphone from a confused Berle and called the audience back. "The show's only half-over, ladies and gentlemen! Show's only-half over! Intermission, please!"14

The televised airing, sponsored by General Foods, of the previous night's final dress went off well. A still-running tradition was inaugurated that night when a TV announcer uttered the words, "The one and only JELL-O! Jell-o, America's favorite gelatin dessert, who tonight introduces the exciting new flavor Apple Jell-o, proudly presents the most eagerly awaited spectacle of the year! For the first time on national television, John Ringling North's production of the Greatest Show on Earth!"

John cohosted the show with John Daly and came across in a kindly, formal, and slightly monotonic manner. The two achieved a nice rapport as they chatted, in voice-over form, about the various performers.

Not a cheerleader for the acts, considering John's comments on face value, his favorite was definitely the aerial spec "On Honolulu Bay" and its star, Pinito Del Oro. "One of the great moments of the circus," he sighed. "There's nothing like it in the world." John's admiration for Del Oro was evident. "Look at her eyes in this close-up," he remarked. "They say that Pinito's balance is achieved by self-hypnosis; she has to put herself in a trance."

When Unus appeared to perform his one-finger stand, Daly challenged the boss: "Come clean, John. How on earth does he do that?" Replied North, "Believe me, I wish I knew. It's one of the most popular guessing games in the circus. But so far, no luck." They interviewed Josephine Berosini backstage before she did her high-wire walk. "The most dangerous part of the act?" asked Daly. "Grasshoppers," said Berosini, explaining how they got tangled in the wires on hot summer lots when the big top was being erected.[15] The pleasant format set a standard and style that has been followed ever since as the circus continues to televise annual highlights each spring in an hourlong special, using guest celebrity hosts. ·

The new ads were an arresting blend of circusiana and Hollywood artwork. They played up the production elements, heralding two of the North and Caesar offerings, "Impossible" and "On Honolulu Bay," as "hit songs" that could be heard at the circus. Johnny was in high form, having turned out with Irving Caesar his best score. Two of the tunes were on wax; a trip to "The Hit Parade" seemed as promising a possibility for John as it had ever been. He made guest appearances on, among other outlets, Rudy Vallee's radio show and Igo Caini's RCA TV program.

The circus racked up new record-high New York grosses. That gave John good reason to trust his producing instincts. He continued turning traditions upside down when the show embarked on its canvas tour, as if what he had already done was not enough for one season, let alone a generation. He decided to abandon the half-price kids' ducats, linking it to another first for the Ringling circus: all-reserved seating in the general-admission sections. Up to that time, holders of the cheapest accommodations sat anywhere they wanted—or could find a place—on simple unnumbered planks. The new policy was prompted by Michael Burke's goal to hold cheating ticket sellers and ushers more accountable. By establishing specific seat locations, North and Burke eliminated the possibility of the staff's admitting an indiscriminate number of people into the grandstands through the rehashing of tickets.

Yet another bold departure was the drastic curtailment of press passes allowed the show's publicity department, although a similar cutback, not nearly so harsh, had been ordered by Concello when he was in charge. The Ringling agents ordinarily handed out upwards of ten thousand comps during the New York run alone, in return for which they usually garnered tons of free publicity and kept a lot of the critics and feature reporters more enthusiastic than otherwise might have been the case. In protest, they now claimed their effectiveness would be seriously hampered. These flacks were experts at capturing the public's attention, so when they cried—more or less out loud—over North's cutbacks, it only added to the mounting hostility against his radical Ringling revolution. Dissenters gathered in increasing numbers on the sidelines.

What made everybody angry in concert was the firing of F. Beverly ("Bev") Kelley, a gentleman if ever there was one, from his post as director of radio and television. He had served the show over the years with dignity and imagination. A fine writer, Kelley placed a couple of his stories about circus life in two different issues of *National Geographic*. He had gotten the Ringling circus band, led by Merle Evans, on several editions of the "Fitch Bandwagon" radio program. He had coauthored with Emmett Kelly his best-selling biography, *Clown*. Kelley had arranged numerous radio and TV appearances for dozens, more likely hundreds of Ringling performers and personalities, John North included. Kelley's termination, surely one of the most ill-handled moves that John ever went along with, was justified by management on the basis that his duties were being amalgamated with those assigned to two other press agents.

Milton Pickman, it was assumed, instigated the action. Michael Burke confirmed it with incredible tactlessness, intimating that the Ringling press staff was "versatile enough" to include broadcasting publicity. And if it proved otherwise, he added, the show would have to "look elsewhere for new blood."[16]

That last remark went down with the Ringling press agents like a guillotine on the tooth fairy. William Fields, the well-known Broadway tub-thumper, lashed out at Burke's comments and at what he termed a number of "dizzy directives" by management in a courageous letter to *The Billboard*:

> Now this is pretty tough talk from an individual who may or, to do him full justice, may not be aware of the fact that the Ringling press staff is the most pitifully paid group of publicists operating in the amusement field. With the one likely exception of department head Edward Knoblaugh, not a single man on the staff of this show receives even the minimum wage designated by the press agents union of which they are members.
>
> No more effective choice of words could have been found in this management representative for the complete erasure of whatever little morale still exists on this show, minimum morale not alone on the press staff but widespread throughout all operational avenues of Ringling Bros. and Barnum & Bailey Circus. . . . And in this same connection may I remind Mr. Burke that since the start of the 1955 circus season a few short months ago more department executives and top assistants have resigned or been fired from RBB&B in four months than ever occurred previously in any given decade."[17]

Fields's rebuke was echoed in a statement of concern by Hal Oliver, business agent for the Association of Theatrical Agents and Managers, AFL. While acknowledging Kelley's departure as legally acceptable and stressing that relations between the union and the circus had been good over the years, Oliver considered it proper to take North to task for his talk about looking elsewhere. He told a *Billboard* reporter he had sent North a telegram warning him against such action and that the union would fight any moves by the circus to hire nonunion personnel. "These amateurs don't stop to ask questions. We have no complaint when they try to use some old-fashioned and outmoded exploitation stunt which never did the movies any good, but we don't want anything done which will affect our people."[18]

North and Burke relented a little. They hired three more publicists and gave their press department back some of the comps they had taken away. They ordered a slight increase in outdoor advertising to demonstrate an adultlike flexibility.

All the while, Burke had on his mind a much more sweeping reform: eradication of the sneeze mob, that circle of grifting opportunists who persisted in running the petty rackets that robbed the show of revenue. John gave the ethics agenda his blessing, although in the end he was prodded along more by Burke's reformist zeal than by his own outrage. Most of all, it promised tighter accountability in the sale of tickets. Box-office revenue stood to gain.

Burke first had to convince Frank McClosky, who kept the mob going after he got Concello's job, that he, Burke, was not a figurehead but an actual executive empowered to implement North's policies. He encountered snickering hostility. "Their attitude was, this first-of-May was not going to come in and tell us how to run the circus." That didn't much bother Burke, who persisted. "These rackets have got to go," he warned the general manager, directly under him in authority. Shortly afterward, Burke was warned by "Blackie," a member of the prop crew, to watch out for his life because the regular gang could easily erase his unwanted presence by releasing in his path, at the opportune moment, a loose quarter pole.

Nothing would hush or stop Michael Burke, a fighter at heart with a burning sense of big-top reform. In his book, Burke recounts blatant examples of theft as he observed them firsthand:

> A number of people were allowed to bilk the show as long as they paid the sneeze for their bilking privileges.... Receipts were a joke. The lot superintendent bought the horsemeat for the wild animals; by a curious coincidence he was the fellow who *sold* the horsemeat. The sneeze directly controlled the dice, whiskey, and beer rackets, forbidden by show policy and by law.... Beer was sold to the captive people on the circus train at a five hundred percent profit.... More brazen was the printing of duplicate tickets. After a time my eye grew quite good at estimating the house, and from time

to time, when the final night's figure was tallied by the treasurer in the ticket wagon and was reported to me, I was surprised at how much I had overestimated. I was puzzled until the night I saw the first two rows around the tent fully occupied and, on a hunch, went to the ticket wagon and checked the racks. Our official tickets were still there, unbroken."[19]

In reality, the circus management had long tolerated these relatively innocent forms of graft, which never victimized the customer. Because fewer ticket sales were reported to the front office, there was less amusement tax to pay the government. And the show could dole out low wages by offering its underpaid staff the compensations they earned from the rackets it quite willingly—and conveniently—turned its back on. With tradition on his side, McClosky argued that it would be impossible to keep the show moving without the services of these men who counted on lucrative under-the-table earnings. John is reported to have protested that if they couldn't turn a profit on the up and up, that they had better well get out of the business.[20] The issue did nothing to calm his growing doubts about running a huge tented circus in a world that seemed increasingly less friendly to it.

Although McClosky agreed to crack down on grifting at one point, he didn't. He had seen so many strange faces arrive and depart from the outside world that he probably thought if he could outlast Burke, he could outlast the reform campaign that Burke, more than North, was trying to push. By the middle of the 1955 season, nothing had changed.

Burke reported his disgust to John by telephone, informing him that McClosky and his men were not cooperating. John opted to meet with them first, face to face, during the show's upcoming Chicago stand. Burke recalls how McClosky turned up drunk out of his mind at the Ambassador East Hotel, where he and John were to confer, and couldn't even seat himself in a chair without falling onto the floor first, a wordless coward. John made up his mind then and there to get rid of McClosky and his two top managers, Willis Lawson (a friend of John) and Walter Kernan, the latter also known as Walter Forbes. Reluctant to face a man at the end of his usefulness, North assigned Burke the unpleasant task, giving him instructions to hold off on the heave-ho for a few days. Maybe things would improve. They didn't.

Up on the lot in Saint Paul, Minnesota, about a week later, Burke called the three into the red wagon just before the evening show. The message was terse: "You guys paid no heed to me. In order to survive, you guys have to go."

They scoffed at the thought.

"I want you off the show tonight. Goodbye, gang, pack up and leave."

They tried to warn Burke that without them the show wouldn't go anywhere.

"I want you off the lot," he reiterated, "off the train before midnight."[21]

McClosky, Lawson, and Kernan then handed in their resignations, already prepared, and walked away.

Rudy Bundy was standing at the front door when Kernan exited past him, hollering back, "Okay, fink, see what *you* can do with it!"[22]

A few minutes later, just after the evening show had commenced, Robert Dover, the equestrian director, came running up to Burke. "No one's striking the animal cages! Nobody's in the prop tent!"

Burke raced around to the backyard, where he discovered that the property boss, Bob Reynolds, had taken his crew off the lot out of loyalty to McClosky. Inside, a clown walkaround had been in extended progress for so long the audience was growing irritable. Burke took the microphone in hand. "I'm sorry, ladies and gentlemen, I'm sorry. Due to forces out of our control, we're not going to be able to put on a show tonight."

He was assailed by boos and jeers.

"Please! Please! Anybody who wants their money back can stop by the ticket wagon on your way out. Or your ticket will admit you to tomorrow's show in Minneapolis, God willing."

The tent emptied in a pouring rain. Some of the roustabouts gravitated around the unstruck cage in the center ring, where bits of information were exchanged. They learned of how the deposed bosses had vengefully proceeded to rally as many department heads as they could into crippling inaction. More startling was the news that Edward ("Whitey") Versteeg, the superintendent of the light department, had been ordered to throw the electricity, something he had the decency not to do.

It kept raining on the dark, ghostly tent. The circus world of Ringling Bros. and Barnum & Bailey stood ominously still in the storm, its future sadly uncertain. For a couple of hours, nobody knew what was about to happen. The wind and rain blew freely against the deserted canvas structure, unchecked by human hands.

The Big Top Falls

One of the few trouping pros who remained on the Saint Paul lot was Noyelles Burkhart. He had been with Ringling for about six years after a productive career in Cole Bros. Circus management. Burkhart is a no-nonsense person, decisive to a frightening degree. He started in the business as a lad on the pie car of Hagenbeck-Wallace Circus, managed by Jess Adkins. He worked his way up through the pass-exchange booth to front-door superintendent to the man who ran the day-to-day operations of Cole Bros. from 1940 through 1949, when it was sold to Arthur Wirtz. Burkhart then accepted Art Concello's offer to work for Ringling as its legal adjuster, succeeding the retiring Herbert Duval.

Noyelles Burkhart is one of the people who was left with no affection whatsoever for North. Although he granted an extensive interview for this book, in which he justified his hostilities, Burkhart subsequently refused to be quoted directly. During the conversation, he recounted several instances when he was called upon to get the circus out of trouble but he was not fully backed by management. This was during a freaky period in the mid-1950s after Concello had gone and when North was riding the train (in circus parlance, running the show). There was the time in Kennewick, Washington, when one of the elephants got loose and went rampaging over a two-mile course through residential gardens and backyards, knocking down fences and trumpeting its way through clotheslines in its path. People with property-damage complaints lined up at the red wagon on the midway as if they were there to buy tickets. Burkhart feared that some of them might try to get an injunction against the show, which could have kept it from moving out of town that night. To avert this, he talked a local circus fan into acting as a special representative of the circus in handling the mounting claims. The fan would assess each, reach a settlement figure with the claimant, and have a signed release form forwarded to North for payment. After about thirty or forty damage awards had been made, North flatly refused to honor any more. Burkhart was flabbergasted.

Another upsetting incident occurred around Waco, Texas, when federal tax agents went through the train looking for the head porter, Charles Burslem, suspected of bootlegging, and inadvertently discovered private stock in the compartment occupied by Unus, whom they arrested, along with several porters. Viva Unus, in tears, approached Burkhart between shows with news that her husband was behind bars. Burkhart hurried down to the jail and whipped out the personal bankroll he carried with him for such emergencies. He offered to pay the sheriff the necessary fines to have the men released. Each cost him two hundred dollars. Burkhart was reimbursed by all but Unus. He took up the matter with the show comptroller, James Powers, who referred it to North for approval. North refused to reimburse Burkhart, to his utter astonishment. Burkhart had to threaten legal action against his employer before he finally recovered the funds he had advanced from his own pocket.

Another time, when the circus was down in New Orleans facing resistance from a Shrine Circus date, Burkhart learned that an officer of the corporation would be needed in court the following morning to sign some papers. There were two officers traveling on the train at that time, North and James Ringling. Burkhart decided the matter warranted North's attention first, so he went down to the railroad yards and banged on the door of the Jomar. The porter informed him that North had given orders not to be disturbed before midnight. Burkhart, refusing to step off the platform, insisted on a meeting with the boss in a tone of voice that demanded immediate response. He got John's ear, and James Ringling was given the courtroom date.

Indeed, John needed that kind of action-oriented person—like Burkhart, like Concello—who would not be intimidated by his lofty bohemian airs. He certainly needed that kind of a person on the Saint Paul lot after McClosky, Lawson, and Kernan were fired and the show stood still in a heavy rainstorm. Young Michael Burke was unable to rally the depleted crews into action. About 11 P.M., John arrived on the grounds and made an appearance inside the big top, his nose not very high in the air, with Burkhart at his side. Outraged over the inaction he observed, Burkhart became obsessed with getting the show off the lot. He seized temporary control, recalling the air of authority he once exerted when he ran Cole Bros. He remembered that the ringstock boss, who had gone back to the train, had worked for him on the Cole show. Burkhart told one of the drivers to go down to the train and tell the guy to get his ringstock boys and bring them back to the lot. And he said to make it clear that the orders were coming from *Burkhart*.[1]

It wasn't too long—around midnight—before a busload of men showed up at the lot, followed by more busloads of more men, including performers like Unus. They swung into action, knocking the quarter poles out from under billowing canvas, slamming chairs into flat, folded tiers against the wagon sides, tractoring the wagons out of the tent, then letting the huge, rain-drenched spread collapse, like a popped mushroom, onto the cold, damp earth below. The sections were unlaced in the pelting downpour, rolled up and hoisted onto the trucks, the trucks driven off through the dark, sloshy maze back to the runs. The clanging noises and shouting voices shot through the windy air with breathtaking vitality, ghostly figures hurrying about to stash things away in trunks and wagons, hurrying to get the show on the road to tomorrow's town. John stood silently by, saying not but a few words to Michael Burke. Burkhart was in charge that night.

By 1:10 A.M., the job was done. A few hours later, the train crossed the Mississippi into Minneapolis. And the next day's matinee began at 2:25 P.M. Burkhart remembers John thanking him that day. More than this, he also remembers it as the only time that North ever talked to him. The pivotal role he played that dramatic night in Saint Paul will live on as one of the great moments in circus-trouping history. Today's fans have only the videos of yesteryear to remind them of what extraordinary efforts were required by management and labor working together to keep the show moving, the tents in the air over a new lot every day.

Although John surely was becoming more erratic, contrary to a popular misconception he was not an absentee owner those precarious days. He was either on the lot or close at hand in the States should his presence be required. So concerned was he with the flimsy state of things that he canceled a couple of European talent-finding trips. In Minneapolis he conversed with reporters, explaining that the fired employees were "more interested in privileges" (rackets) than running the show in an acceptable, businesslike way. He diplomatically took *The Billboard* to task for its coverage of the Chicago date: "There have been only three engagements in Chicago in the entire history of the circus which exceeded this year's business, and of those three, only last year's business (1954) exceeded this year's business by more than a few thousand dollars. This dates back to the 19th century, from the 1880's on to the present time."[2]

He held on-the-spot conferences with his dwindling staff to analyze the new policies and redress mistakes. More outdoor posters went up. More press passes were handed out. All kinds of interesting ideas for improving the show's appeal were tried. One of the biggest problems was John's impatience. Many of the new procedures his staff tried out were progressive and sound; they just needed more time than half a season—or a couple of months—in which to prove themselves. For example, there was an all-too-brief period when one end section of seating was designated for adults only, the other for parents and kids. Once effectively advertised and known, the move might have drawn additional customers wishing to enjoy the show away from the distraction of tiny tots running up and down the aisles.

Henry North had rejoined the show before the so-called Minneapolis massacre as a goodwill ambassador, a task he performed with exemplary grace. He and John were anxious to counter the negative press and fortify the ranks against union organizers, now back on the scene. In Richmond, California, the two brothers were seen on the lot together, hosting visitors in a small tent erected at the edge of the midway. There were rumors of yet more baby elephants being recruited to join the horrendous herd. Business was good, and had been.

The next day, in San Francisco, John entertained reporters in his suite at the Saint Francis Hotel with his winning smile, a few soft-shoe steps, and a rare message of optimism in the face of a pending Teamsters strike. "Rain or shine, movies or television, it's still the greatest show on earth, and everybody loves the circus."[3]

No amount of optimism could offset a growing impression that the show was in deep trouble, its future in the balance. From a prophetic editorial in the *San Francisco Chronicle*, "Say It Ain't True, Jo-Jo," came this:

> The Greatest Show on Earth moves into San Francisco tomorrow after a lapse of two years and this time it comes trailing clouds of passing glory and uneasy intimations of greatly changing times. . . . What disquiets us is not that it arrives in no apparent aura of pent-up juvenile anticipation about to erupt; or that it will get down to business with no street parade overture of carved and gilded wagons, and sultans aboard swaying pachyderms, and sighing steam calliopes, nor yet that it will pitch no big top on a fresh

and fragrant multi-acre bed of sawdust and shavings, but will display its marvels under the solid roof of the Cow Palace. . . . Those are old, familiar circus adjuncts long since swept away by the tides that erode yesterday's splendor, and we have become reconciled to their absence. Our unease springs from the nagging rumor that this may well be the last time around for the Greatest Show on Earth—that the circus has been hounded from the American scene by a conglomeration of things that have evolved a new order in which the inhabitants prefer other amusements to circuses. . . . This is, we suppose, part of the price that must be paid for progress. If the new order in its swift advance tramples down the marvels of the three-ring circus, who is to stop it? Not us, certainly—but we can mourn a little.[4]

The show was more vulnerable than it had ever been to the insidious tactics of labor organizers. Michael Burke had been paid a visit back in Denver by a Teamsters Union representative, Harry Karsh, tersely notifying him outside the Jomar door that Jimmy Hoffa wanted to sign a contract with the show. Burke, who suspected that the spurned McClosky had gone to Hoffa in revenge, looked upon Karsh and his two bodyguards with disinterest.

The uninvited visitor persisted. "Jimmy wants me to talk to you about it."

"That would be a very short conversation," replied Burke, "because we really don't want the circus organized."

"It's a big union, Mr. Burke."

"We're not interested, Mr. Karsh. Now do you mind?"

"What'ya trying to say?"

"I think you're old enough to understand."

"Hey, now, you. I've been to no damn Ivy League school, but are you telling me to fuck myself?"

"If that's the way you want to phrase it," said Burke, "that's okay with me."

Karsh stormed down the steps. "You'll hear from us!" And they did.[5]

Karsh checked into the Saint Francis Hotel, too, where he was joined by Joe ("Killer") Kane (last heard from in these pages when he, then a Ringling usher, protected Daisy Hall from her boyfriend gone mad, another ex-con). Kane had since been kicked off the circus and had set out to organize its workingmen, partly in retaliation and partly, others suspect, in collusion with the avenging designs of the ousted sneeze mob. He had first set up picket lines through the Ohio, Indiana, and Illinois stands, fronting the AFL Retail Clerks Union. Now he was more logically affiliated with

Karsh's Carnival and Allied Workers Union 447, which had recently signed up Royal American Shows, the largest railroad carnival in the country.

The Ringling show was now haunted by its infamous past. Karsh and Killer Kane picketed the San Francisco engagement, first at the downtown department store in which advance tickets were sold (the sale was discontinued to avoid embarrassing the merchants), then at the Cow Palace. Given the town's pro-union makeup (Harry Bridges and his longshoremen made sure of that), the circus parade got rained on by a chilly reception.

There was even an earthquake on Labor Day, the last day of a four-day stand which had drawn pitifully small crowds. When the wagons were packed and ready to rumble out of the Cow Palace, a solid line of two thousand teamsters and longshoremen blocked the driveways. Michael Burke, former football star, bristled at the barricade. Karsh and Kane refused to relent. Lloyd Morgan signaled the driver in the first truck to pull out. The pickets stood firm. Burke secured road clearance from the sheriff and they still refused to give way. His Irish temper boiling over, Burke told his drivers, "Roll up your windows, lock the doors, and step on it!"[6]

The first truck charged through the line, and protesters scattered in all directions. One tractor driver was knocked off his seat, the transmission stalled. A crew of about thirty canvas men, rumored to be armed with tent stakes, pulled up on a flatbed. More deputy sheriffs arrived to help escort the wagons down to the Geneva Avenue rail yards. The show struggled out of town.

John, who had stayed away from the Cow Palace, maintained a good front, however troubled he may have been by all the problems. Back on the East Coast, Madison Square Garden officials, at odds with him over a new contract, were courting other prospective producers. One of them was Art Concello, all over the country pursuing deals for himself and now and then stopping on the Ringling lot to pay a social visit. Lawsuits by disgruntled, unpaid support services sprang up, one by the Monroe Greenthal Ad Agency (which had been replaced by another agency) for the amount of $82,774. When the show moved down to Los Angeles, pickets ringed the lot and effectively scared off thousands of customers.

If only De Mille could have photographed the drama swirling around this circus. There were rumors of an early closing, rumors of an extended season of indoor dates. Jimmy Dorsey might play the midway under a special tent for dancing, they said. Winter quarters was going to be turned into another Disneyland, with Frank Lloyd Wright designing the face-lift. In John's anxiety for instant results, he treated his employees with little sensitivity, shuffling them around like so many disposable pawns in a game without discernible rules. He failed to realize that all ideas depend on human beings to implement and that, lacking a cohesive staff, the best new policy under the sun has little chance for success. He moved too fast for his own good, and the morale of the company plummeted. The circus played to fewer people in 1955 (only two million according to Burke's book). Henry North reported that the season operating expenses amounted to six million dollars; the gross was a million short of that figure.

John canceled his annual salary, not so sacrificial a gesture, for his oil and real estate interests were paying off nicely. The next season looked to be even worse, with Jimmy Hoffa threatening to "put you guys out of business." When North and Burke went down to Miami to see Hoffa during the winter, they tried explaining how economically crippling a union contract would be. John pointed out that they did use Teamsters Union drivers for the New York date. Burke added, "Our people see no advantage in being Teamster members or paying Teamster dues." Hoffa showed no mercy, roaring, "*Your* people! Who gives a goddamn about *your* people. We're just a couple of parties making a deal. Don't give me any crap about *your* people!"[7]

John's "people," an interchangeable crowd at that. Some were let go. John finally came to his senses over Milton Pickman, a costly innovator with little sense of humanity. "Some of his ideas were good," says Burke, "but this was a struggling circus business and not an opulent motion picture operation, and some of his ideas of spending money were not in keeping with the amount of money we had to spend."[8] Henry North is less tolerant: "He sold himself to my brother as being a wizard in practically anything, and I think he knew nil about circus publicity. And, of course, my brother came around to the same feeling."[9] John called up Burke one night. "I'd like you to fire him."

Ed Knoblaugh, another fatality, probably didn't deserve the shoddy treatment he is thought to have received. When the journalist went to Havana in the winter of 1955 to discuss his contract with John, he was given the cold shoulder. It upset him so much that a cerebral hemorrhage he suffered shortly afterward has been linked to the incident. Gravely ill, Knoblaugh was flown back to his home in Illinois, never given another chance to discuss continued employment.[10]

While John's side of the Knoblaugh affair is not known (possibly

Knoblaugh's flight to Cuba was out of place to begin with), a clear trend comes through in this and other such examples of the cold-blooded insensitivity John could show to a person he had no further use for, or whose agreements with him he chose to ignore. John was definitely not above misleading people with promises he either did not intend to keep or later decided to renege on. And when he no longer desired their assistance, he couldn't fire them face to face. Others were given the unpleasant task. John pushed his unethical behavior to the limits. The lawsuits he sometimes faced as a result didn't bother him. He was the unscrupulous operator he has been accused of being by people like Noyelles Burkhart. At the same time, John had to deal with a lot of characters just as obstinate and underhanded as he could be. Certainly, Concello was one. And despite their fallings-out, some of these men returned to work for North again.

On the other hand, John rarely, if ever, treated a single member of his production staff in the same deceitful manner as he often did those on the management, promotion, and operation teams. Name them: Pat Valdo, Dick and Edith Barstow, Miles White, Merle Evans, Harold Ronk, Bob Dover. With rare exceptions, these and others who helped design and prepare the actual circus performances were virtually immune to the expedient side of John that others were made to suffer. And when some of these production people departed the Ringling payroll during the winter of 1955, it was they, not North, who instigated their terminations. Among a spate of faces who walked, Merle Evans led the cheerless parade. He felt, rightly so, too apprehensive about the season ahead. Vocalist Harold Ronk walked, too, as did elephant handler Hugo Schmidt. There were voluntary desertions in other departments as well. Treasurer Theo Forstall left, followed out the door by the latest controller, James Powers, who was replaced by a *third* chief accountant in as many seasons.

Then came a surprising and welcome influx of old-timers, headed by the press agent of press agents, Roland Butler, whose latest term of employment—"to put the department back the way it used to be"—started on December 21, 1955, and ended, following disputes over his contract and rate of pay, on January 24, 1956. By the show's next visit to New York City, all the old flacks were gone, the department managed by Zac Freedman and staffed with such newer names as the gifted Norman Carroll (who quit in late March and came back a week later) and Ringling's first female publicist, Lorella ValMery.

Over the next few months, George Smith, who had once managed the show, made it back to the fold, assisting Paul Eagles, the general agent, until Eagles resigned, at which time Smith assumed his duties. Floyd King, a sprightly old duffer well versed in old-time advertising, joined up around about that time for a brief spin through the revolving Ringling door. So did Howard Bary, another ballyhoo pro from the recent past. John held no grudge about a man's previous affiliation if he could use him again, not even George Smith, so strongly associated with the Robert Ringling era, whom the North brothers had fired for drinking problems in 1942.

New blood. Old blood. The 1956 edition was a graphic reflection of how significantly things had changed. It had a totally new sound, a totally new look. John talked the French Impressionist Vertés into designing the costumes, and this led to a curious billing war with Richard Barstow over the prominent type size guaranteed Vertés in his agreement. Barstow claimed it violated his contract, which offered him alone the largest type, second only to North's listing. Dick's sister, Edith, who choreographed the show, stuck up for him in a defiant manner. "Dick won't do the show under these circumstances," she said. "Get somebody else." Attorneys got into the picture and billed a lot of hours without resolving the dispute. Finally, Edith came up with a bright idea, introducing a new credit, "Staged and directed by Richard and Edith Barstow," to appear in box form the same size as John's credit. Underneath it would come the directing and designing credits in smaller type size, Vertés garnering as much ink as Barstow.[11]

The artist had to go along with it. In fact, he had to put up with a lot. As told by Barstow, Max Weldy, still in charge of costume construction, hated the Vertés designs. "Vertés designed flowing things that didn't flow." Indeed, the skimpy, cost-saving executions suggest a contempt on Weldy's part. One of them was a pink dress worn by a group of showgirls in the spec which bore, in the amused recall of some, a J. C. Penney label. Neither did the imaginative float ideas, also conceived by Vertés, escape the sabotage of frugality. Chuck Burnes, though he considered the show to be quite "terrific," describes the payoff float in the principal parade, "Say It with Flowers," as resembling "a big hunk of concrete." Explains Burnes: "It had an elevator inside it. It was supposed to be the marriage of wheat and barley, something like that. There were two people in wheat and barley costumes. They'd come up and wave, and then the thing would put them back down inside."[12]

"Ringling Rock 'n' Roll," a pachyderm production, had all the assurance that "Flowers" lacked. It had a driving original title song for which Barstow, a talented lyricist, supplied the words. It had exotically foreboding costumes, inspired by movies that McCormick Steele had taken of the Zulu tribe he came close to booking. (He pulled out at the last minute when he learned how long their act would take. "Once they get off their ceremonies," Steele reported back, "the Zulus never break the routine for three days, and we felt the circus couldn't stand still just for this.") Vertés wanted the elephants to wear raffia blankets. He received a letter in his Paris studio from Weldy: "Terribly sorry but we can't use raffia for the elephant skirts in the jungle number, as you have requested. They love to eat raffia, and if we gave them skirts made of it, they'd be naked by the time they got out of the arena."[13]

Vertés created some beautiful costumes in a manner more subtle than lavish. A lovely painting of his made the cover of the circus magazine, and inside he contributed a warm piece, "I Like the Circus." John was lucky to get Vertés. It's too bad the artist couldn't have worked for him at a better time.

Barbette, absent the previous year, came back to direct the aerial spec, "Mexicanorama," and to stage a novel finale, "Hoop Dee Doo." The new bandleader, Izzy Cervone, added violins to the music, turning it slightly away from the old march-and-galop gusto. The popular songs of Frank Loesser, woven infectiously through the score, added considerably to the show's appeal. Preston Lambert, a handsome, fine-voiced baritone, took over the announcing and singing chores and was another asset. Most of the acts were holdovers from recent tours, John being too consumed by domestic problems to get over to Europe for talent bookings. Different music, different costumes, a new ringmaster—they gave the circus quite a different personality, somewhat more resilient and accessible than before.

All the loose ends were neatly tied together by Pat Valdo, one of the very few people who had survived every Ringling regime. Michael Burke still had to get in his two cents' worth on opening night, when it seemed as if the show (too long as usual) would never end. Burke asked Barstow, "Can't you speed the music up?" Barstow, dumbfounded over such a suggestion, replied, "Well, no! My girls would just be dancing too fast!"[14]

The New York premiere was a sad shadow of past opening nights, noticeably lacking in celebrities. Proceeds were pledged to the Police Fund, likely a move to keep in good graces with the law-enforcement sector. The Teamsters were outside picketing the Garden, and the circus needed all the protection possible. Hoffa had made good on his threat, first dispatching his rabble-rousers to harass CBS television crews in Sarasota during the filming of a Christmas special hosted by Charlton Heston. Now at the Garden, entrances were blocked, and a small minority of the performers were refusing to cross the lines. The show was weak in spirit, its press department depleted of the reliable old faces whose mere entrance into newsrooms was met with lots of endearing attention. The new gang did the best job they could. They scored at least one publicity coup with a clown audition. The Barstows judged the participants, and the winner was given a temporary job with the circus. It drew so much media interest that plans were made to stage similar auditions in each city along the route.

The more serious-minded critics found much to applaud. "The fine and tinsled daring nonsense a circus should be," wrote Michael James in the *New York Times*, finding the Vertés-designed productions "all very pretty, frilly and delicate, and not at all the robust and gilded foolishness that was so much fun for so many in the past."[15] *Variety* observed a questionable shift to the "Park Avenue crowd," while *The Billboard*'s Jim McHugh thought it to be basically still a very good show in the now-predictable North format.

Lackluster overall press coverage, however, combined with the force of union pickets outside, cast a pall over the box office. Houses were terribly sparse at a time when John's rent had skyrocketed. The new five-year contract he signed with the Garden gave it a substantially larger cut of the gross, which had caused the arena's manager, Ned Irish, to boast, "He has no occasion to rejoice over the terms."[16] An impromptu business session called by North turned into a marathon affair, going from 8 P.M. one evening until 8 A.M. the next morning. The staff was in a frenzy trying to figure out ways to improve business and hold firm against the strikers.

John was not facing Ralph Whitehead, the old Shakespearean actor whose fledgling union, the American Federation of Actors, it had been so easy for him to outwit and foil in the late 1930s. He was now facing Jimmy Hoffa and the Teamsters and the American Guild of Variety Artists, which joined the picket lines and staged a rival circus up in Boston. The union show didn't lure big crowds, but it put another crimp in Ringling's business. John refused to budge, all the while maintaining that "not enough people" wanted to join. To be sure, his was not the only circus under pressure to organize. At least two of the other twenty-one-odd tenters on the road that year—Clyde Beatty and King Bros.—were put to the same test. Neither buckled under to union demands and both closed prematurely, each declaring a form of bankruptcy.

Once her tents went up for the canvas tour, foundering Big Bertha was an easy target for Hoffa's saboteurs. The hoodlums slashed tires, dumped sugar into fuel tanks, cut power winches. They joined as truck drivers and abandoned their vehicles in obscure locations. Nonunion drivers were beaten up. The antagonists threw bricks onto the back lot and dropped them from overpasses onto the circus fleet as it passed below. In Philadelphia, the entire route from the showgrounds to the train yards was lined with policemen every twenty feet or so. In the Canton, Ohio, rail yards when a section of the train was maliciously bumped by an engine, numerous individuals on board were thrown to the floor.

Inexperienced help was another hindrance. Roustabouts received a couple of bucks from the union for quitting, only to hire back so they could quit again and collect another two dollars. Twelve elephant stampedes erupted, always when the younger bulls charged around the track at the end of "Ringling Rock 'n' Roll" (a conditioned reflex they had learned from the previous year's "Mama's in the Park" number) and the older bulls tried subduing them for lack of human control. Marcella, the elephant Chuck Burnes rode, would invariably stop and put her head down, as if to say, "Get off, Chuck. Got something to do!"[17]

Late matinees were commonplace. Some towns saw only one performance. In Geneva, New York, a storm ripped through the big top and turned it to shreds. Luckily, only eight hundred people were in the tent when it happened and only fifteen suffered minor injuries. A couple of days later, the previous year's tent arrived from Sarasota as a replacement. In Meadville, Pennsylvania, the show gave the first seatless performance in its history. Nobody knew why the seat wagons were left on the flatcars. In Youngstown, Ohio, circus officials had to fight with local authorities for the use of a lot they had legally booked, occupied the day they arrived by revival tents, the preacher having rented it from another source.

Adversity was so prevalent it is a wonder there were no deaths. Still, through it all, a semblance of the trouping spirit prevailed. Michael Burke spoke of a projected benefits and bonuses package for the personnel. John took out a booth at the Industrial Recreation Association convention in New York to pitch block sales and performance buyouts. A new style suspension-pole tent housing the menagerie was tried out in the early stands. On the Fourth of July, the circus hosted its annual employee picnic. Singer Dick Todd, traveling as a guest of the show, served as master of ceremonies. Burke made a goodwill speech. John Staley prepared a bountiful feast in the cookhouse. The festive celebration included the performers doing takeoffs on each other's acts (Justino Loyal earned big laughs with his Pinito Del Oro spoof) and a wild stake-driving contest, won by the property crew. If only the entire operation could have moved with the proficiency demonstrated by those stake drivers on that hot patriotic afternoon!

Outside that fragile little world, the adversarial forces of time and change were casting a dark shadow on the days ahead. "It was a bloody mess," recalls Michael Burke, who himself was victimized by the opposition in Buffalo, New York, when he was arrested and sent to jail on charges of labor violations. He believed the charges were trumped up by a local justice acting under "Hoffa's spell." Released the next day, by the time he made it back to the show, it was too late, as it had always been during Burke's earnest tenure. The myriad problems faced by the Greatest Show on Earth simply overwhelmed its shrinking staff.

John came on the lot in Alliance, Ohio, and turned to his best friend, Rudy Bundy, in the last hours. John had taken part in a directors meeting two weeks earlier in New York, where a number of options were weighed, and he had come to the show to make further staff changes and reduce daily operating nut by three thousand dollars. Ten cars were to be eliminated from the train. However, when John took a walk with Rudy through the big top between performances, he was so dismayed by the trashy condition of the seats—an eyesore of disorder and neglect—that he changed his mind.

"Rudy, we've got to close this thing down."

Later that night, en route to Pittsburgh, Pennsylvania, John got off the train during one of its stops to call Dan Gordon Judge, the attorney for the minority stockholders, and advise him of his decision. John also called his brother, Henry, then living in Rome. Back aboard the Jomar, he sat down at his desk with pencil and pad and proceeded to write out a note, his handwriting distorted in places by the pitch of the car as it jolted down the tracks from side to side. Rudy watched quietly while American circus history took its most dramatic turn. When John was done, he handed Rudy the note. "Here, when you get up tomorrow morning, no matter what time it is, why, give this to the press." The message read: "The tented circus as it now exists is, in my opinion, a thing of the past. We are considering plans for the future which involve an almost completely mechanically controlled exhibition. The all-new 87th presentation of Ringling Bros. Barnum & Bailey Combined Shows will open as usual on April 3, 1957, at Madison Square Garden in New York and will play the 1957 season in other air-conditioned arenas all over the United States."[18]

The next morning, Rudy made copies of the document and kept the original for himself, which he still has. He handed them to the show's press agent for immediate distribution to national news outlets. Message of the closing trickled down through the staff, some first hearing about it on the radio. Between shows, Bob Dover called everyone together outside the wardrobe tent. "I guess you've heard," he began. "This is the last show. The train will be leaving for Sarasota. If you don't want to go to Sarasota, you can stay here."

"It was very depressing," recalls Chuck Burnes. "Some performers were crying, especially the ones who had just come over to join the show for the first time from Europe, and suddenly, this huge show was closing."[19]

The last performance under the big top—jam-packed with about twelve thousand souls—commenced around ten o'clock that evening. It was the kind of a straw house that harkened back to John's best producing years, the sort of a scene he had sought through so many unkind twists of fate to recapture. And he wasn't even there. Ironically, it was the occasion more than the circus that had drawn the massive turnout. One old-timer quipped, "Hell, they could go on for a couple of years playing 'Farewell' performances to crowds like this!" Maybe the best of all promotional angles, in fact, had been passed over. Dozens of photographers crowded the hippodrome track. Flashbulbs popped off like fireworks. Tearful circus fans scooped up sawdust and sand from the rings to save and sell. When the last act was over, the band played "Auld Lange Syne."

That marked the end of an era, and it brought to a close the most turbulent and, in some ways, creatively fascinating period in Ringling history. John had not gone to the lot to witness the last show. He remained isolated in his private car, surrounded by private policemen, haunted by the lonely feeling of failure. The ride back to Florida was much like a protracted funeral procession, each passing mile bringing the circus—and John—closer to the inevitable finale. While circus fans prayed that it wasn't really so, prayed that the tents would rise once again, the man in charge faced the future with somber resignation. He knew that the adaptation to an all-indoor show posed plenty of vexing challenges.

Rudy did the best he could to soothe his friend's deflated spirit. At one stretch in the journey, they talked about what would become of the circus train. "I'd like to buy one of the coaches," said Rudy, "maybe turn it into my own private car." John replied, "The way things are going, there ought to be more than enough cars to go around."[20] He eventually gave Rudy the Jomar.

John had been forced at last (some say by fate, others by his own bumbling mismanagement) to accept the new realities. All of his previous dabblings in arena presentation, as well as the many new promotional angles that were experimented with, would now come together into a more logical mix to provide a formula for the future. From this moment on, John never looked back. He had done his damndest to keep the show on the road in all its gargantuan splendor, just as he had boasted to Art Concello he would do when the two parted company. Indeed, he had gone down with the Greatest Show on Earth.

Once a Circus King

John remained locked inside the Jomar as the train rattled slowly southward to Sarasota, pelted by rainshowers and shunted onto sidings now and then while freight trains loaded with profitable goods for urgent destinations whizzed by. He slept not at all, yet stayed up in his pajamas the whole journey. He drank bourbon. John's refusal to see reporters along the way—to see anybody else for that matter—intensified speculation concerning his next moves.

The trains arrived in Sarasota amid an outpouring of teary-eyed public support and sympathy: "WELCOME HOME CIRCUS" placards were in the air everywhere. Chamber of Commerce officials were on hand. How ironic that Merle Evans, who had quit his Ringling post less than a year before, now led a makeshift band through spirited circus refrains. Some people broke down and wept. News reporters egged on the disillusioned for juicy quotes. Killer Kane, also in town, boasted to journalists of the union's success in bringing the circus to a humbling, profitless halt.

And still no sight of John Ringling North, a circus king now in virtual exile in his own sinking kingdom. He stayed fairly isolated, a shaken man, for the next two or three weeks. It is doubtful that he could have foreseen the tidal wave of animosity his historic decision would cause, most of it aimed directly at him.

Striking the Ringling Bros. and Barnum & Bailey tents for good was tantamount to declaring an end to Christmas or the Fourth of July. Ringling epitomized a great Yankee institution, a kind of living historical monument on the move. As Jackie Le Claire has reflected, "when you worked for the Ringling show, you were propagandized and brainwashed that there was nothing else in the world but Ringling Bros."[1]

And so was the public. Ringling's press agents had spent many years building up the lore of the Greatest Show on Earth and keeping it vividly alive in the public's consciousness. They courted and coddled the newsrooms of America, big or small. They spread good cheer with passes. They made circus day *the* event of the year. Even the sight of the Ringling trains passing majestically through one town on the way to another evoked rapt attention. "There were always people at every cross street when the train went through," recalls Chuck Burnes with watery eyes, "always looking at the train, waving at the people, looking for whatever they could see. And then you'd get into the town, and there'd be tons of people waiting, and their eyes would just follow you when you got off the train to go somewhere. And you know they were wondering: 'Is that a clown?' or 'Is he a trapeze artist?' or 'Does she ride horseback?' 'Look! What do they do? Who are they?' It was the most important thing to happen in those towns, and lots of times the newspapers would say, the circus train will pass through town at such and such a time on its way to . . . and the people would be out just to look at the trains go by."[2]

Never mind that the Clyde Beatty Circus had, that same ill-fated season, filed for bankruptcy. Never mind that two other shows also went broke in 1956. Sadly typical of the times were six King Bros. Circus trucks stranded off to the side of a road near Stroudsburg, Pennsylvania, next to a sign: "DONATIONS APPRECIATED." One did not accept the same fate for the Ringling show with anywhere near the same understanding. Not the Big One. Not Big Bertha. The show's sudden, confusing plunge into a tentless future evoked as many angry and irrational responses as it did impartial ones. Scenes of the final performance under the big top flashed across television screens. Newspaper editorials assayed the sad passing of a slice of Americana, most reporting it to be the inevitable outcome of changing times. Cartoonists put their usual bite aside to appreciate the pathos. One showed a lad brushing away his tears as he held a magazine titled "Circus to Close," a little dog standing next to him. In the background, a great procession of clowns and elephants, giraffes, and gilded wagons passed out of sight forever. Another cartoonist, Hungen Ford, depicted Uncle Sam tipping his hat to a big top in the clouds; a gravestone beneath bore the inscription "Here Lies Ringling Bros. and Barnum & Bailey Circus."

Traumatic events demand a scapegoat, and John was the instant candidate. Almost overnight, his credibility and stature—at an all-time high only four years earlier with the release of De Mille's picture—plummeted to an all-time low. The chaotic events leading up to Pittsburgh gave his critics all the ammunition they needed. Even the trades reacted with ambivalent logic. *Variety* first cited bad business as the reason the show closed and blamed it on North's "Hollywoodized format." Later it acknowledged "tough luck, bad weather, labor troubles and obsolescence" as key factors, predicting the new indoor operation would give North "a chance to make more money with less expenses."[3] *The Billboard* hammered away at North's mismanagement, and one of its editors, Herb Dotten, took John's cavalier showmanship to task in an open letter:

> Somewhere along the line, your interest must have flagged. You lost sight of the fact that the circus was for children and for others young in heart. You sexed up the show and you in turn gave it the Broadway and Hollywood treatment. Then you began to take a dim view of some of your key people in almost every department. . . . Morale on the show broke down as you shucked aside first one, then another of the men who had been with the show for a long time. . . . Out went billing. Out, too, went circus press agents who were widely esteemed among newspapers, radio and tv people. . . . Indoor circuses have hewed consistently to the traditional circus pattern. There is little emphasis on sex. There is much accent on those things calculated to delight children and their elders who are young in heart. I cite these things because I would hate to see another field of show business hurt.[4]

Little wonder that John stayed in isolation for so long. A horde of detractors came out from under the wagons to prepare his coffin. Reporters clung to their every word, eager to promote a scandal. Overstatement thrived. Bev Kelley, Ringling's esteemed publicist, shared his frustrations with one scribe (making such comments as "amateurs killed the big top"), then shortly afterward authored a very fine account for NEA in which he examined the plight of the circus with superb objectivity: "It must be remembered that John North has some circus milestones to his credit, too. For he brought to the scene the greatest wild animal crowd-puller since Barnum's Jumbo when he found Gargantua, the giant gorilla. He spent vast sums on wardrobe and made the circus beautiful to behold beyond the dreams of the old time operators. He bought the biggest herd of elephants (55) ever to appear on tour with a circus. Only time will find his proper place in the kaleidoscope pattern that is the circus in America."[5]

The tumult that began in the trades poured over into the popular press, where hack reporters had a field day. None was more one-sided than Phil Santora, who whipped up a scandal-ridden three-part series, "The Big Top Flop; Circus Folk Blast Owner North," for the *New York Daily News*. He interviewed the bitter. James Haley told him that John was rarely around the lot and that his "Broadway revue" version of the circus tripled its production costs. "The circus under canvas is an earthy, lusty sort of thing," said Haley, "and circus people—most of them Europeans—are morally clean people. But the Hollywood influence came in and with it all sorts of queer ducks."

Aubrey Haley told Santora, "John fired good circus acts, and he replaced them with pretty girls." An old-timer added: "An act that couldn't have made a side ring with the old circus was now featured in the center ring." Rather incredible assertions, considering that John generally engaged the finest circus stars available. (In a 1963 *New York Times* story listing some of the world's best circus acts, six of the eight troupes chosen had all been presented at one time or another by John.)

Santora got the kind of quote he wanted from John Sullivan, who ran the Circus Hall of Fame in Sarasota: "Who the hell is John North that he can put an end to a great American tradition? It has to be under canvas. It has to have the cotton candy, the sideshows, the menagerie, the clowns, the smell of roasting peanuts, the pink lemonade—all the trimmings. . . . Anyone who would abolish that part of the circus would shave off Lincoln's beard or paint moustaches on the Mona Lisa."

The article spelled out the backyard rackets and payoffs, claiming they victimized innocent circus performers. To the contrary, a few of those performers interviewed for this book do not recall feeling ill at ease during those precarious days. The mandatory tips (for such things as a bucket of fresh water) were a customary part of the business, they say. As for the petty rackets, Santora failed to mention that North and Burke had actually tried purging the show of these when they fired their three top managers in Saint Paul, a move that jeopardized the show's organizational stability and led to its downfall. There was no way a journalist of Santora's ilk would give John North credit for anything. His story concluded with a glossy description of the "good old days," including the erroneous notion that John Ringling was firmly in command until the day he died.[6]

Had John closed the circus at the end of a normal tour followed by a formal announcement that henceforth it would play indoors, he would have encountered considerably less criticism. Its dramatic demise in the middle of the year—the trains clanging back to Sarasota early—is what gave the story meat. And most of the reporters who hurried into Florida to cover the event cared not that North had said the show would open as usual the following spring in Madison Square Garden. Because the tents would not go up again, they tended to imply that the show would not go out again.

What killed the circus? Lack of good business was not the prime culprit. There can be no arguing, however, that the turnover-plagued organization became ill equipped to make the dates on time, thus failing to accommodate the thousands of potential matinee customers who stood on vacant lots with money to spend, waiting for the tents to go up. A stronger staff might have countered the union resistance and the normal obstacles, such as bum weather and bad lots. As it was, working conditions became ominously unsafe, and North's decision to close was a prudent one. In fact, he would have been negligent not to do so.

The more burning question raised by circus fans was—and still is—had the show been properly staffed and managed, how long could it have survived under canvas? Probably not very long in its unwieldy size. In a sharply reduced scale, such as Art Concello had once advocated, maybe for a long time. Concello concedes he might have been able to keep the same size show on the road for six or seven more years.[7] Beyond that, skyrocketing rail transportation fees and the increasing unwillingness of railroads to move the circus trains in a timely fashion over a series of one-day stands would have spelled an end to the Ringling enterprise as it was then known. Michael Burke writes in his book: "It was a delusion to think that a three-ring circus playing under a big canvas tent, traveling the country in an eighty car train, was viable in 1956. It simply was not."[8]

John had to choose, then, whether to cut back in size and risk looking too much like the smaller tent shows on the road, such as Mills Bros. or Clyde Beatty, or play indoor arenas where he could maintain a traditional Ringling program commensurate with public expectations. Once he accepted the latter option, the decision was easy to make. He finally broke out of his brooding silence by granting a telephone interview to Abel Green, the editor of *Variety*. Much of what he said bears repeating, for rarely did he pour out his soul so articulately, revealing both pride in his accomplishments and a wise sense of history:

> Fundamentally, the circus has operated in its lavish style because of cheap manpower and lots of it. Well, we haven't it today anymore. In 1942, our railroad haulage bill was $115,000, in 1956 it was $600,000, and even

though the eastern and southern railroads gave me a 26 percent discount, what is that compared to a 400 percent increase? We do well in New York at Madison Square Garden, in both Boston and San Francisco indoors and in no time that $25,000-a-day nut that we have gets drained. You can't take in 25G a day any more and why operate just to meet the overhead? That's why the portable big top idea is just as spurious as all the "expertizing" about "overglamorizing" etc. Furthermore, I'll tell you a surprising thing or three which the short-memory, Monday-morning-quarterbacks forget or just don't know. And if they're ignorant, that's all the more reason we should not take them seriously.

Back in 1915, my favorite uncle (John Ringling) told me that my other uncles and kin had told him just about the same thing "what was wrong" as we have it today. Because in 1915 the Metropolitan Opera ballet master, Ottokar Bartik, under the then Gatti-Cazzazza regime, had staged our ballets and did so for four seasons. We had 120 girls, again in the same appeal-to-the-kids spectacles like the Cinderella story, or Rumpelstilsken or whatever. Who said pretty girls were ever a liability to any showbiz venture? Uncle John said that at the time that if he "had listened to anybody we'd be out of business in six months. Run the show as your best instincts tell you. Your judgement is as good, and should be better, because this is your property and your responsibility. Never mind listening to all those small show experts who brag how they personally carried the water to the elephants. If all of them ever did all the bulls in the world would be so waterlogged none of them could ever perform. It's like the 400 original Florodora Sextet girls I have personally met so far. If it weren't for the Big Top some of the small shows wouldn't have a prayer, so keep it that way, Johnny."

Strangely enough, the 1956 circus, as an attraction, garnered perhaps the best press of any Ringling show in decades, and this was from real experts whose job it is to appraise and evaluate, not the disgruntled few press agents who used to be allied with us and no longer are.

On the defensive, John beat the drum for some of his undisputable past accomplishments: "In the same period that we had Frank Buck and Gargantua, we had Charles Le Maire, who did the costumes for Florenz Ziegfeld, do 'em for us; John Murray Anderson, who staged for all of the top Broadway entrepreneurs, produced the Big Top for us; and Norman Bel Geddes, who designed for the Theatre Guild dittoed for the Ringling show. So you see we had pretty girls then, too, and lots of hoopla and glamor—and we did a terrific business! What's wrong with dozens of lookers on ropes in precision formation, playing xylophones or whatever?

Of the future he said: "We closed because it was good business not to try and outsmart the law of diminishing returns. The moment labor and other factors started to make us 'the latest show on earth' was when I thought it wise to return to winter quarters. . . . The fact that this is smart showmanship and sound business, to prepare ourselves for the new scheme of things, playing less of the 'death trail' and more under hardtops; the fact this is plain common sense for us to do so seems to be ignored."[9]

Although North's words held the sway of reason, they could hardly begin to offset the public-relations disaster he had brought upon himself. The air of confidence he exuded to *Variety* did not stay with him long. One day he was high on his decisions, the next day he sulked in his fear of all the unknowns that lay ahead. And not very far outside his door were his relatives, with their mounting reservations over the depressing thought of a Ringling circus without tents. At the forefront of family dissent stood Stuart Lancaster, who now admits to never having been around the circus other than to take in a performance on rare occasions. When the big top fell that summer, Lancaster, a talented actor and director, was gliding through the dream world of subsidized theater in Sarasota's Palm Tree Playhouse, an Equity house he had established. He ran the operation with massive amounts of money (upwards of eight hundred thousand dollars over the years) doled out to him by his mother, Hester Ringling Sanford. A schoolteacher like her late mother, Edith Ringling, Hester encouraged Stuart in the theatrical arts, preferring them to the less-respected form of entertainment known as circus, Ringling or otherwise. And she pretty well figured that the well-heeled existence they enjoyed would go on forever, thanks to the legacies left them from Charles Ringling's will.

When the circus trains pulled into Sarasota that ill-fated summer of 1956, Stuart was moved by the sight of people crying. "The trains stopped, all the people got off and wandered away, into the crowd. It was a very emotional thing. That's when I got interested. I kept saying, 'Well, this can't happen.' I just assumed that the Ringling Circus was something that would go on forever. It was a feeling, suddenly you realized the pride in the feeling—well, this *is* a big thing in America. It can't be. That's when I got over involved."

Stuart spent a lot of time at winter quarters the next few weeks, watching and wondering and asking questions. He was chilled by the answers. He walked through the train and was appalled by stench and decay. "I never saw such garbage, I mean, all the cars were completely rotten and falling apart. You saw the bunks where the roustabouts lived. It was just filthy in there because nobody was doing anything. They just let the stuff sit. The few people that worked there were stealing right and left. All that wonderful equipment was just all run down and the grass wasn't cut. It was a picture of degradation."

From what he was told, he pieced together a sketchy portrait of John North's controversial lifestyle: "He began to spend less and less time overseeing the operation of the circus, and more and more time in Europe, ostensibly seeing acts and sending them back, and finally becoming sort of an international playboy, and he didn't oversee the circus at all. I think it's really tragic what happened. I think he started out very well, in spite of being manipulative and ruthless and getting control of it in the way he did. . . . Maybe he got too much power too quickly, and it went to his head. . . . They said, John North got the circus, but the circus never got him."

Lancaster gained a sense of the corruption that had vexed the show for years, and he started seeing himself as its potential savior, as the person destined to right the wrongs and put the show back on the tracks and back under the tents where it belonged. Stuart picked up a telephone and had the long-distance operator call his mother, who was traveling in Germany at the time. He rang up $150 worth of telephone charges, broaching a subject his mother had never much savored: the idea of her son's becoming the family's next circus scion. That's how the forty-niner movement was born. And if Hester Sanford was slow in joining her son's parade, it is no wonder, for she had long displayed the same ambivalent attitude toward the circus that most of her relatives—going back to August and Salome Ringling—had. Hester went along with Stuart's wishes, and she eventually became a strong advocate herself for a recall of the errant North in charge.

The Lancasters began to develop the grounds for a mismanagement suit. "It didn't seem that John was really running a business the way it should be run," recollects Stuart. "I went from person to person. I had to talk to them at great length to gain their confidence. They told me all kinds of stuff that would just curl your hair, about the amount of skimming, about people who went to work as an usher, who were driving a Chevrolet one year, and after one season with the circus they bought a huge home in Sarasota, had three Cadillac cars. Everybody was stealing from everybody else. The collapse of the circus didn't have to take place. It took place because it wasn't properly managed. Maybe the same result would have happened, it finally would have folded, but it would have folded under better conditions."[10]

Stuart Lancaster consulted with attorneys. He and his mother tried to persuade Dan Gordon Judge, trustee of the Charles Ringling estate, of which they were beneficiaries, to take legal action against North, but Judge dragged his feet. North's first reaction to all this was a manipulated effort to placate Stuart. He invited him to the Jomar for drinks one night and spent most of the evening warning Stuart about Judge. They also talked about what might be done to save the tented circus, a subject that meant more to the guest than it did to the host. Stuart remembers, however, finding John in a foundering mood (this was only a few weeks after the Pittsburgh closing), reaching for a solution to his bad fortune.

"He didn't seem to have any definite ideas as to which way he wanted to go with this," says Lancaster. Maybe John hoped to silence the Lancaster campaign by seducing his prospective rival with the illusion of family ties. While he plied Stuart with more liquor, John kept assuring him, "I'm on the other side of the family, Stuart, but I'm just warning you for your own good about Judge, because blood is thicker than water, and you're Hester's son. Watch out. Judge can't be trusted."[11]

Probably it was a camouflage. The Lancasters continued pressing Judge to file suit against North, and Judge continued to resist, holding firm to his authority, which, it is said, set him in complete charge of everything. The Charles Ringling will is such a prime example of what flagrant power an attorney can wield over the fortunes of an estate that a Florida law school once spent a whole summer dissecting it.[12]

John had Stuart appointed to the board of directors, another attempt to silence him. John even went so far as to offer his wrangling relations $1,750,000 for their stock interest in the show. They didn't accept. What the Lancasters really wanted was the right to examine the books, something the court finally ordered. Stuart set up a workbench with his brother, Charles, an engineer, and the two tinkered with an alternate logistics plan whereby the circus (under canvas if they ran it) would be moved both on railcars and overland trucks.

While the Lancasters clung to the impractical past as they developed a scenario for wresting control of the show, North grappled with the new order of things, to which he had theoretically committed himself. Uncertain exactly how to proceed, he listened to a lot of people with all kinds of ideas. There was no lack of advice offered him, for free and for a fee, and of offers to buy the circus, from such diverse figures as Mike Todd, Billy

Graham, and even Liberace. John listened to them all. He huddled in
New York with sports promoter Bill Veeck, who reportedly wanted to
reinstate the tents. They were joined by Art Concello, rumored to be the
man who would run it for Veeck. Nothing came of the offer, except that
North and Concello were talking again.

In early September, John announced in one of his upbeat moods that
he was flying abroad for "a European quickie" to see what his booking
agent, Umberto Bedini, had "whipped up." He told a trade reporter, "The
American public wants three rings. It favors the excitement of almost too
much to see and digest, but that is the essence of the Greatest Show on
Earth." A month later, an item appeared in *Variety* to the wonderful effect
that the tents would again be used in 1957, with the indoor plan put back
until the 1958 tour.[13] By the following week, however, John made big
news by rehiring Concello to manage the show, and the only thing they
talked about was adapting it to play arenas, stadiums, ballparks, and
fairgrounds.

According to Concello, John pursued him all over town, finally catch-
ing up with him at the Plaza Restaurant, where he and a mutual friend,
department store owner Bud Montgomery, were dining. "Artie, how are
you!" beamed Johnny. "It's good to see you!"

Art expressed his sympathy for John's recent troubles.

"Damn it, Artie, you were right! I shouldn't have gone to eighty cars."

Also according to Concello—who insists he did not relish the thought
of trying to revive a circus $1.8 million in debt—his help was not easily
recaptured. He would go to his private car at night to find John sitting
outside in his Cadillac, waiting and waiting. "Jesus, Artie! I'm sick! I know
you're the only guy that can put this show in buildings and make it go."

Art strung John along for a while, determined to get the best terms
possible before he would agree to come back. Given Concello's well-
reported activities during the previous two years, however—forever making deals to own or operate other circuses, which invariably fizzled out—there
is every reason to believe that he was more obsessed than North with the
challenge of turning the circus's bad fortunes around. Even so, Art put up
a good bluff, pretending indifference when his former boss needed him
most. He was offered a 10 percent stock interest in the show and vast
autonomy over its operations. Concello was satisfied and the two were
partners once more, much to John's relief. It has been long surmised that
North would have thrown in the towel had Concello not rejoined him.

This meant that Michael Burke, still technically on the payroll, had to go. By Concello's account, Burke, who was in New York when the tents had been folded in Pittsburgh, came down to Sarasota asking for six months' pay. When John heard of the request, he told Art, "Go out and fire the son of a bitch." Burke got as far as the door to the Jomar, there to be told by Art, "Mike, you're kidding yourself."[14]

Burke explained in his own words what happened to him in his book *Outrageous Good Fortune*, a tome that cannot always be trusted (Burke was *not* on the show when the tents were struck in Pittsburgh, nor did North attend the final performance "standing in his private box," as Burke recounts). Burke writes of discussing his termination with John when faced with the news of Concello's return. "He comes. I go." They reached an amicable agreement, according to Burke, whereby he would continue to receive his regular salary for six months, paid weekly, in the form of severance pay. He left Sarasota with the first check, which turned out to be the last. Burke brought up the matter in New York with the show's treasurer, George Woods, whom he remembered once accusing John of being "a God damned chiseler." Woods told Burke, "I'm with you on this," but he was unable to reverse John's change of heart. "Occasionally I wondered how Johnny felt leaving me, his 'brother,' hanging in midair with a wife, children, no income, and no bank account. At the time I thought it was an act of world class shitiness."[15]

Whatever John's true feelings about Burke's management skills were, he never aired them. What he needed very badly at the pivotal moment in his circus career was a strong hands-on executive with solid circus-logistics experience, one who could guide the show through the precarious transition it faced. He needed Art Concello, not just to glue the organization back together, but to restore his own psychological well-being.

And yet John could never quite acknowledge publicly how important Art was to him. When he was asked about the circumstances of their getting back together, John's reply revealed more emotion (and more anxiety, too) than anything else he said during his interview for this book. "Oh, I ran into him. I needed him to . . . ah, figure out . . . how to fix up the special rigging for outdoor dates."[16] Equally telling were John's dismissive gestures as he spoke, aimed at minimizing the true importance of it all. Outside Art's presence, John seemed reluctant to give him his full due. In fact, Concello was important enough during North's most trying hours that he earned the title of executive director, a seat on the board of directors, and the 10 percent stock interest.

The two pulled together a basically familiar North-style circus for the

1957 New York opening. The Barstows were back, as was Miles White with an adequate number of picturesque costumes. Most of the acts had already been seen in Ringling rings, about half of them the previous year. Few were new to these shores. There were four new production numbers, in keeping with John's format—the "Coronation of Mother Goose" spec; the web number, "Cherry Blossom Time"; a horse fair, "Saratoga Racing Ball Of 1913"; and the colorful closer, "Carnival in Venezuela."

Maggie Smith was made the aerial director, replacing Barbette. Galla Shawn took over in the aerial ballet for Pinito Del Oro. John wrote more original music, this time with a new collaborator, Tony Velona. Their initial batch of ditties—the result, according to press agents, of "almost a year's hard work"—were mostly lightweight and forgettable. The lead number, "Open the Window Wide," was a turgid, tuneless intrusion that admitted little sunshine (as the lyric feebly promised) into the proceedings. Back to the basics, not really, except for the band's having dispensed with the stringed instruments and Harold Ronk's rejoining to provide some boomingly good intros. Maybe the show had a little more of its older pizzazz and crackle. It was somewhat less lavish.

The circus made peace with AGVA, and the opening went off without hitches or glitches. The New York critics offered praise (they wanted North to succeed), and the Garden run netted a nifty $1.8 million—topped only by the record 1955 receipts. At the end of the tour, the show played Mexico City, where eager crowds lined up to buy tickets. The arrangements that had been made with the building originally booked for the event fell through. The circus played in bullrings instead. "We lost $75,000 down there," says Rudy Bundy, "but that's not a great loss."[17]

John stuck to his creative instincts as Uncle John had once urged him to do. He merely took his concept of circus indoors. Producing the kind of a performance that had kept him famous and successful for so many years became a habit of security. Besides, most of his energies were now focused on the monumental task of developing a viable yearly route of indoor dates. John was in the unique position of having to prove himself all over again. All the while, he was troubled by the voices of discontent that chipped away at his image and would haunt him through the early 1960s with their condemnation of his management. Numbered among them was the clown and writer Bill Ballantine, who, when not on North's payroll, took cheap shots at North's policies in lurid tabloids. One of his articles, "How They Loused Up the Circus," appeared in a 1962 issue of *Saga*. The ambivalent Ballantine, writing on the "Broadway vulgarization" of the show, stated: "John Ringling North had a ball while tried and true old-timers went out behind the big top and threw up."[18]

North's key antagonists, of course, were the minority Ringling stockholders, back in action with a threat to have him legally removed from his position and the circus put back under canvas. For a time, John either lost his radical, innovative spirit or suppressed it in order to survive. At the same moment he came to his better business senses, the daring artist within him faded from view. In a curious way, the passing of the big top had taken John's heart with it, as it did so many others, be they innocent Indiana or Iowa circus buffs or worldly journalists irrationally moved to attack the man who uttered the fateful words, "The tented circus is, in my opinion, a thing of the past."

Greatest Show on Asphalt

By turning the show back to Art Concello, John made definite compromises. Art's frugality in addressing the $1.8 million deficit simply would not allow John his usual extravagance in booking a flood of new acts from abroad and gift-wrapping them all in unstinting opulence. The programs offered the first indoor years—at least through the early 1960s—were scaled-down versions of a now-typical North performance. Art trimmed the payroll to less than 300 people (including 175 performers), the daily nut to $8,000, about a third of what it had been. Of course, more savings were realized in the elimination of the train, tents, and seats.

What suffered the most was atmosphere. Miles White had insisted upon lemon-yellow mats to cover the arena floor, and they were a stunning sight to behold. But soiling as quickly as they did, they proved hopelessly impractical, so Concello substituted in their place drab green mats (he called them "grassy green")—nothing compared to the colorful ring carpets and various shades of tinted sawdust the circus had sported in previous years. Overhead, the new aerial support frames (another Concello first) were a network of interlocking bars between two standard flying-trapeze riggings. They were easily hung in auditoriums or mounted on support posts in ballparks and fairgrounds. The equipment now moved overland in trucks, the performers in house trailers, the elephants in two railcars.

If the new utilitarian look lacked even a semblance of the old tent-days ambience, the abbreviated production numbers and parades failed to compensate much, especially when presented down the racetrack in front of a fairgrounds grandstand or around the bases of the old ballpark. The production staff had less money to work with, and Miles White, who had designed the circus to greatness, left after the 1957 opus, never to return. According to White, neither he nor the management pursued an extension of his contract. White's chores fell into the klutzy hands of Max Weldy, whose best years were clearly behind him. Weldy's dated designs gave the show a mediocre, second-rate look. Nor did musical director Izzy Cervone strike a very original or refreshing chord with his schmaltzy music-hall sound of Europe in the thirties. And the new songs by North and Velona were on the stiff side. Even Galla Shawn, who replaced Pinito Del Oro as aerial principal, was on the stiff side.

John refrained from stirring things up much—as long as Concello kept the show on the road and his songs were used. Another dependable old hand, Pat Valdo, accumulated more power in the wake of John's declining input. Weldy, well aware of Valdo's clout with the producer, joined forces with him by sharing credit for the production-number ideas. According to Richard Barstow, Valdo contributed almost nothing in this department. Weldy merely took cocredit with Valdo in order to win guaranteed approval from John, who respected Valdo's judgment. So from 1959 on, Valdo and Weldy held the authority to decide on the theme and content of the ensembles, even though Barstow (who returned in 1960 after a two-year absence) still staged them.[1] As for the so-so aerial specs, they were put together by Maggie Smith, Concello's girlfriend.

It was hard to know who deserved praise or blame for the costumes. Max Weldy received program credit for their creation and execution, while each year other names showed up in the "designed by" category. Jose de Zamora was most mentioned. Others were Erte, Bob Willy, and Arnold Dobrin. Such names as Winniford Morton and Crayon were listed as "supervising designer." Whoever was responsible, the variable creations bore no imprint of note. Some, to be sure, were amply colorful; "Carnival around the World," presented in 1959, made a marvelous splash. Another high point was two illuminated flags featured in one of the finales, each purportedly bearing one hundred twenty thousand miniature light bulbs. The costume trappings were pleasing enough, though often not much better than those seen at a typical sponsored indoor circus of the day.

The number of new acts John imported each year dwindled to only a handful. By the early 1960s, an abundance of annual "First Time in America" turns seemed a thing of the past. Among the few newcomers who graced the center ring with flair were the head-walking Kaichi Namba, and Scipilini's Chimps, premiered in 1957. Introduced the next year were teeth-hanging juggler Bert Holt; the Two Suns, an acrobatic hair-hanging duo; the Six Verdus on rolling globes; the Szabos and the Sobrianis (acrobats); wire walkers Manuel Santos and Dely; jugglers Tony Durkin and Kolmedy; aerialist Carmen Del Teide; and perch artists the Canovas. Imported for the 1959 show (a crackling good one directed by Concello himself and loaded with talent and glitzy, fun-filled productions) were the fabulous Stephenson's Dogs from Ireland, one of John's greatest finds ever; tightwire wiz Domi; the Berosinis on risley; the Dior Sisters and the Six Dovers; the Mordells; and Dianna Sisters and Brothers, English equestrians.

American-born and trained Gerard Soules, a mesmerizing single-trap star, made his auspicious debut with Ringling in 1960. Ferry Forst also excited crowds that year with his illusion act. Santos, another fine low-wire walker, joined the Domis and the Steys to present a three-ring panel of simultaneous forward somersaults. A welcome event that season was the return (he had been away for two years) of ringmaster Harold Ronk. Premiering in 1961 were the Three Morles, unicycle jugglers from Germany; the Three Waever Sisters in the air; and the hilarious house-painters routine of Mike Coco, with Billy Livingston and Segura. King Everest came on in 1962 to perform a simulated ski jump—on his hands. By then, the majority of acts were familiar faces and many were in the top-drawer ranks: Unus, Harold Alzana, Stephenson's Dogs, and Gerard Soules, to name a few. They provided the sort of action circus fans never tire of. But the public at large eventually tires of too much repetition.

Henry North has pointed out, rightly so, how much better lighted the circus could be in modern arenas. *Could be.* Not always the case, as when the show played in some dinky, not-so-modern building in a smaller city. The lighting might be inferior and the air conditioning might not work. Each new setup posed a different set of problems, and the performers had to readjust constantly. It was like opening night all over again. The performance was in a continual state of flux, which made it impossible to sustain a polished and fixed program. Worse yet, rather than capitalize on the opportunities at hand to create a more festive atmosphere with bunting, banners, and ring carpets, Ringling refused to carry these embellishments. If ever the circus needed a Norman Bel Geddes (if ever it *didn't* need those drab green floor mats), it was now.

The method of ballyhoo changed drastically, too. The bulk of the dates were initially booked by the circus magazine publisher, Harry Dube, and each city was assigned to an independent promoter whose task it was to place ads in the media, schedule TV appearances, arrange for special tie-ins with local commercial outlets, pitch group sales, and drum up business. Concello contracted out to several promoters in different regions of the country, though he relied principally on the services of Martel Brett of Birmingham, Alabama, who owned a gas company and liked handling a few dates; Harry Leshinsky, a friend of Rudy Bundy out of Charleston, South Carolina; and Irvin and Israel Feld and their Washington, D.C.-based Super Shows Attractions. Other promoters included Ted Bentley Productions, responsible for a Hollywood Bowl date in 1958 that drew as many as twenty-three thousand people to a single show, probably the largest crowd to that time ever to witness a Ringling program; the Barnes Carruthers Agency in Chicago, which worked some fair dates; and Werner Buck's Show Management on the West Coast, responsible for many California stands.

These private contractors paid for the cost of advertising and took a percentage of the gross receipts. Explained Concello to an *Amusement Business* reporter in 1962: "We don't fool with guarantees, either, so every deal is a partnership. If they win, we win, or vice-versa. But the promoter has every incentive to work like the devil because his obligation includes such things as advance expenses, ushers, building rental, etc., all of which comes out of his end."[2]

A few arenas promoted the date themselves. Naturally, the turnouts varied, depending on all the variables of competition, the local economy, publicity, and word of mouth. More significantly, by entrusting the all-important public-relations activities to these promoters, the Ringling organization relinquished much of its power to create and sustain the sort of image it desired. At the same time, North and Concello could draw from a wider variety of promotional angles should they eventually decide to promote the circus themselves or establish a more unified concept of selling it to the public.

The disappointing business realized the first couple of seasons did little to offset the lingering impression of a once-mighty circus now floundering pathetically to reassert itself in a questionable new format. Gone was the sleek silver circus train loaded with red wagons and exotic cages. In its place was a fleet of square, stainless-steel trucks on whose sides the words "Ringling Bros. and Barnum & Bailey" seemed out of place, out of time. Gone were the billowing canvas, the sawdust, and the poles. Now, just a bunch of drab rubber mats. Some venues were downright dreary. Bambi

Burnes recalls a closing night in an outdoor Miami date, last day of the season: "The finale was on. It was pouring rain, with mud up to our knees. Some of us lost our shoes right there on that lot. It was raining so hard, we literally could see only an outline of the grandstand. We could not see the people."[3]

Dismal circumstances such as those and the tepid box-office returns gave the minority stockholders further reason to challenge the chief executive officer of the corporation. In September 1957, Hester Ringling Sanford and her son, Stuart, filed a twenty million dollar mismanagement suit against John North, his brother Henry, and Art Concello. It alleged that North had drained the circus through unauthorized personal expenses and racketeering among personnel. It accused him of closing the show without authority of the board. It alleged that ushers were forced to give kickbacks to hold their jobs, that other employees were coerced into patronizing dice games and the sale of liquor. It characterized John as a "part time president" and Henry as "the vice president in charge of Rome," whose living costs abroad were charged to the circus. Both were accused of "registering in certain hotels" with female companions, their sensual amusement bills routinely paid by Ringling accountants.[4]

One month later, Dan Gordon Judge finally got off his duff and filed a similar suit against North on behalf of the forty-niners in federal court. Hester, still upset with Judge's basic indifference, filed another suit in a circuit court to have him removed as trustee of the estate. She accused him of failure to abide by the terms of the will, which stipulated that the heirs receive annual payments from the four-million-dollar legacy, and of resisting, with hostility, her attempts to bring earlier court action against North. "He only brought it reluctantly," explains Stuart. "He couldn't wait to get it dismissed. He just filed it, that's all."[5]

All of the charges, true or not, cast further aspersions on John's sagging image. No wonder he hired back, in 1958, his three best press agents—Bev Kelley, William Fields, and Frank Braden—to represent him to the public. No wonder the foreword he (or one of them, perhaps) wrote for the 1958 circus magazine went like this:

> One not so fine day about two years ago—July 16, 1956 to be exact—I found myself in a public situation comparable to that of the poor chap falsely accused of having shot Santa Claus. I hadn't shot anyone that day not even a man out of a cannon, but I had packed up our Big Top and sent it and all the rest of our circus back to winter quarters.

Winter quarters in July—a bone chilling decision tinged with sadness on a hot summer's day. Sentimentally and emotionally, it was a hard decision to make, for my whole life had been tied to the Circus. My earliest and happiest memories are of that tinseled world of make-believe. But the make-believe part of the Circus is the happy part enjoyed by our patrons once a year while I found myself faced with the other side of the coin—grim economic immediacy. The daily operation costs of our Circus had mounted inexorably in the changing national economy to the point where we could no longer meet them. If our Circus was to survive, those costs had to be drastically and immediately reduced without in any way affecting the performance.

So, I, with a heavy heart but undiminished faith in the long proven durability of the circus, sent it home so that it might have its well deserved opportunity to greet another spring. And discomfited though I was by the role I then had to play, I hope you—children of all ages who make up our audience will agree with me that it is still the Greatest Show on Earth, bigger and better than ever.[6]

Henry added his own thoughts on the subject in an adjoining story, "Plus ça Change," in which he stressed the need to face the here and now constructively. "Nostalgic memories often provoke yearnings for things past but as all is changed the wise man seeks and finds satisfaction in the present." Maybe so, but Henry resigned that spring, later confessing that he no longer felt humanly needed in the new scaled-down indoor version, not as he once had felt in the old under-canvas days when rostabouts turned to him for sympathy and loans, feuding families for a friendly mediator. "These paternalistic actions were not possible anymore."[7] He found little satisfaction in the present.

Neither did his cousin, Stuart Lancaster, set on returning the circus to the big top, where everyone in his right mind felt it belonged. The forty-niners sought a temporary court injunction restraining North and Concello from selling the train and burning discarded equipment and wagons. They also resisted plans, advanced by North, to tour a unit of the circus in European cities under the Barnum and Bailey title. By the summer of 1958, exactly two years after the tents were struck, the two differing minority stockholders, James and Charles Ringling, who had refused at first to participate in the mismanagement suit (siding, instead, with North and Concello), fell into line with the Lancasters. The forty-niners, now totally united, launched a campaign to arouse public support in their behalf. They issued a colorful press release headlined "A Crusade to Return the Greatest Show on Earth to the American Public . . . Let's Bring

Back the Circus." Petitions were included. Hester, who had resigned her board seat, asked for an expression of public sentiment, likening the Pittsburgh debacle to the 1929 stock-market crash on Black Friday: "Ours is a proud family—proud of the entertainment and excitement that we were privileged to present for the amusement of America's young—and young in heart. We have watched the decline of a great tradition under the present management, while we prepared a national crusade to return the 'Greatest Show on Earth' to the hands of competent, experienced showmen with the know-how to return the circus to the public, using modern techniques and equipment but retaining the vital elements of the show we all so dearly loved."[8]

The "terrific" response they received, according to Stuart, did not stop North and Concello. Nor did Dan Gordon Judge's grudging cooperation help any. And the Lancasters were further stymied by inept legal advice costing them hundreds of thousands of dollars. Their lawyers were as shady as the old Ringling ushers. One ended up in a penitentiary; another two were disbarred. "I got delusions of grandeur," admits Lancaster, looking back with perspective. "I decided I was going to be the big hero, I was going to save the family, save the circus, and I ended up suing not only John North, but Judge, too, which was a stupid mistake. I should have sued one at a time. I knew nothing. I was like 37. I didn't know what I was doing. I had a lot of bad legal advice, so I began to run out of money."[9]

In December 1958, Hester and Stuart withdrew their two lawsuits against North and Judge and let stand the suit Judge had filed against North. It vegetated in a paper mill of pending litigation while the more important emotional campaign began to lose steam.

The circus started making money again, enough to keep the doubting Thomases in abeyance and Concello committed to the new order of things. A three-season downward trend in gross receipts was reversed in 1959. As recorded in Rudy Bundy's ledgers, the year's take was $4,312,000.[10] Better yet, business at Madison Square Garden the following spring reached a hefty $1,932,000, approximately equal to the watershed $2,000,000 mark realized in 1955. It took six more days to do it, but the figure was cosmetically uplifting, and it merited a self-congratulatory half-page ad in *Amusement Business,* in which, ironically, James Ringling, one of the minority stockholders suing North, was listed as the person to contact for booking information!

There is nothing like success to hush a thousand dissenters. In June 1960 the forty-niners quietly dismissed their suit. North and Judge announced in a joint statement, as reported by United Press, that all differences among the owners had been resolved and that the circus family was once again "firmly united in carrying on the operation of the 'Greatest Show on Earth.'" Maybe some of John's relatives were given under-the-table bribes. Maybe they were charmed by news that a Ringling circus train would once again roll down the tracks. It was to be a fifteen-car version, with newly designed tunnel cars transporting a small fleet of silver aluminum wagons. Hester Sanford got her seat back on the board. Stuart retained his, which he all along considered a token appointment to keep him satisfied. "They were hoping I'd stay away." He was amused by John's oblivious attitude once the suit was dropped. "He acted as if nothing ever happened!"[11]

In Los Angeles that summer, the show grossed a delicious $500,000. It played to more than two hundred thousand people and racked up a couple of impressive old-time turnaways. Turnouts in San Francisco and Oakland rose 25 percent from the previous year. The date in Dallas drew seventy thousand patrons in eleven shows. The same erratic season, the circus lost $25,000 in Detroit, a town much committed to the annual Shrine date, which that year was promoted by Al Dobritch. The 1960 tour grossed $4,651,000, still shy of the $5,000,000-plus figure said to have been reached in the best under-canvas years.

The 1961 season extended the winning streak by about a million dollars. Credit another booming New York run and more long lines at the Los Angeles Sports Arena, where Saturday-morning shows were added to handle the rush. More turnaways ensued in the City of Angels, thanks to an exceptional media blitz masterminded by Norman Carroll. He garnered heaps of free coverage: eight television network show appearances, nearly ten full pages of pictures in the dailies, twenty-one feature stories. The publicity coup led to his being named national press chief. In between, there were bum dates, too. In Philadelphia, one matinee pulled fewer than four hundred souls. Rudy Bundy happily informed a reporter from *Amusement Business* at the end of the tour that all past debts were now paid off and the circus held "a substantial cash reserve."[12] Costs were rising about 5 percent a year, he reported. The mood was upbeat.

Strangely, John became less involved as the show moved back into the black. It was never easy for both he and Art to be around at the same time, anyway, they were such strong personalities. They could be compatible drinking and socializing together. On the show, Art guarded his power and didn't like sharing it with anybody else. Even in the production end of things, John participated less and less, relying on Dick Barstow, Pat Valdo, and Max Weldy to perpetuate the format. That left him with his songwriting chores, and they came to a dead end after three seasons of collaborating with Tony Velona.

The marginally tuneful score they provided in 1959, their last year together, did contain a few pleasant surprises: the heretofore mentioned "The Moon and My Love and Me," and a finale rouser, "My Heart Beats in Time to Your Music." Other titles—just for the fun of it—included "You Might Wear a Patch on Your Eye," "That's How Long the Blues Is Gonna Last," "Why'd I Have to Fall in Love with You For?" and a special theme song, "Children of All Ages," that not even Frank Sinatra could have breathed life into. The critics had reached their limit. Wrote Robert J. Landry in *Variety*: "The music is handled loudly and competently by Izzy Cervone, who provides the orchestrations for the singularly unmelodic works of the circus owner's pet composer, himself. One pines for the old circusy tunes like 'March of the Gladiators' instead of 'My Darling Said Yes'. . . and the quick-to-stale 'Children of all Ages.' "[13]

When the circus opened the next year without a single North tune to its name, Irwin Kirby, reviewing in *Amusement Business*, remarked with evident pleasure, "John Ringling North has created none of his specialty music, and this absence is not lamented in any quarter."[14] Kirby reiterated his disdain in the 1961 notice, in which he welcomed the dearth of "John Ringling North inspired melodies." Nonetheless, the final batch of songs written by North and Velona found their way into a popular children's record album cut by Cricket Records. Also included were other parts of the Cervone score, the standard galops and marches. The playful treatment, combining the spiels of the ringmaster with the fast-changing tempos, proved something of a hit with the moppet market. Hardly the kind of validation, though, for which John longed.

There seemed to be no place in the circus for him anymore. He drew more satisfaction from the respect accorded him abroad. There, he didn't have to face a horde of hateful fans, still angry with him for having taken away their big top. There, he was *the* circus king, the mogul who toured the Continent (even if he didn't do so some years) in search of new stars for his famous circus. That it now performed under hard tops mattered little to the Europeans, who had little emotional stake in its history. And so John was able to maintain his act in their midst. It was natural for him to gravitate to where he was wanted.

He turned his attention toward foreign markets, probably more in search of personal acclaim than additional revenue. In 1961, he dispatched a second unit of the show, titled Ringling Bros. and Barnum & Bailey International, to South America for a string of dates, beginning in a sixteen thousand-seat arena in Rio de Janeiro on February 16. Subsequent stops were scheduled for São Paulo, Brazil, and Buenos Aires, Argentina. Carlos Vasquez, who had handled a recent Moscow Circus engagement, took over the promotion, while a number of Ringling regulars—Lloyd Morgan, Justino Loyal, Bob Dover, Richard Barstow, and Maggie Smith—made the trip to help start things up. Raymond Escora fronted the band, and a small clown alley consisted of Jackie Le Claire, Billy McCabe, Ken Dodd, Kinko, and Lou Mirando, among others.

The program offered well-known Ringling headliners. John persuaded Unus to go along, allowing him an open expense account in lieu of the higher salary he wanted.[15] A branch of the famous Cristiani family went along, too. It had been nearly twenty years since they were last seen in the Big Show, and their names added power to the South American marquees. Thirty-five girls were hired locally to fill in the production slots. The run did okay business. Historically significant, it marked the first time that Ringling fielded two units simultaneously bearing its name and distinctive three-ring format. The Ringling brothers had originally operated their show and the Barnum and Bailey title separately, and in 1943, Robert Ringling produced the one-ring "Spangles." Never, though, had the combined Ringling-Barnum title been used on two separate units.

It was rumored that the South American company would return to the States intact and play a "number two route" of towns not played by the regular unit. It was also rumored that efforts were under way to book the company—or a third unit—into such distant lands as Asia and the Soviet Union. In 1962, John and Art signed a contract to play the 1964–65 New York World's Fair with a one-ring circus built around a special story line. All the while, John had been needling Art to assemble an edition of the show for an extended tour of European cities. He had Art flying all over the projected territory to check out available buildings and study logistics problems. His own informal records showed there to be some twenty arenas with at least seventy-five hundred seats. John kept hammering away at the resistant Art, who didn't share the vision.[16]

All of these foreign preoccupations diverted John's creative energies away from the Stateside show, which became staid and stodgy. The same faces appeared year after year. Unus was brought back "by insistent popular demand" several seasons in a row. Between 1960 and 1964, John imported few new acts to speak of. In 1961, the program contained an astounding thirty-two displays, yet only three of the acts were given "first time in America" billing. The typeface designating this fact was so tiny as to suggest management did not wish to draw attention to the scarcity of new attractions. What did distinguish that edition was the return of Merle Evans to the bandstand, to the cheering delight of circus fans. Nobody before or since has quite matched Evans's genius for weaving a variety of musical sources, from classical to pop, into a compelling, action-packed score. Irwin Kirby of *Amusement Business* happily stated, "The show was never better."[17]

A surfeit of familiar faces and predictable production trappings did not, however, impress the paying customer. In 1963, the show attracted many fewer souls in some of its most important stands. Rudy Bundy's records reveal a dramatic drop in gross receipts at Madison Square Garden, down to $1,586,000, and at Los Angeles they were $500,000 below the record take achieved two years earlier. Static magic is not what the public wanted. Other big arena circuses sustained ample patronage despite Ringling's intrusion into the market. Al Dobritch's Detroit date in 1963 turned away thousands at every performance.

Symptomatic of this lackluster period was an equally lackluster TV series, "The Greatest Show on Earth," launched by Desilou Productions in 1964 and starring Jack Palance. The one-hour weekly used film footage of actual Ringling acts for background color. It lasted only one season and has yet to show up in the rerun market.

John North no longer seemed on the cutting edge of innovation. And if he was bothered by the dwindling returns, there is little indication during this period that he took any bold producing actions of his own to reinfuse the show with a brand-new marketing appeal. Of keener interest to him by far was a European tour of the circus, something he had toyed with on and off for the past several years. "You got to do it!" he kept telling Art Concello. As he approached his sixtieth birthday, maybe John thought his showmanship would be acclaimed on the Continent as it once was in America. Concello finally gave in, against his better instincts. The two men moved once again onto a potential collision course.

At Home across the Sea

Whatever interest John still had in the circus, his personal life abroad by now had clearly taken center stage. In fact, he paid very little attention—at first—to the formation of the European unit of the Ringling show, in contrast to earlier years when the big top commanded his fullest energies. Of course, John's format was established and he had the iron-willed Art Concello to watch over things. He seemed more engrossed in the quest for a relationship that would come as close to approximating marriage as he could accept. More and more, he began to deal with his own mortality.

Who was the man behind the myth? Despite a misconception that has been passed down over the years about John's possessing so little feeling for others, about John's being incapable or unwilling to sustain enduring relationships, he was, in fact, a very loyal and romantic individual who valued continuity in his personal and social life. Even then, only a handful of souls—those closest to him on a long-term basis—have any inkling of the man inside the man, and they seem unsure when trying to answer questions about his thoughts and feelings on general subjects.

Rudy Bundy, probably John's best friend, lends the impression of a warm and lasting friendship that was more socially than mentally stimulating. Through all the years—before Rudy ever went to work for John's circus and long after John sold the show and Rudy was no longer an employee—the two stayed in close contact. John called Rudy often with an invitation to visit, whether it meant a short drive in the States or a flight across the ocean. There was the time when John, an avid fan of Chinese cuisine, discovered a fine Oriental restaurant in Miami. He telephoned Rudy to join him for a sampling of the menu and sent his chauffeur up to Sarasota to bring Bundy down for the day. The visit lasted a good week. "I was wearing his underwear before I got back," recalls Rudy.

The two friends spent their time together talking about such things as music, the topic of mutual interest that had brought them together in the first place, and show business. They might discuss politics, too, though Bundy is quick to point out that John "wasn't political."

John's generosity was constant up to the very end, says Rudy, upset by reports to the contrary that have him reaching out to John for financial help for his ailing wife and being given a cold, heartless shoulder. "Never been true," insists Rudy. Typical of how John treated him over the years was a check for eleven thousand dollars that John received from one of his Oklahoma oil interests, which he endorsed and placed firmly in Bundy's hands. "Now, I don't want to hear anything about this," he stated. "It's yours. Take it."[1]

The man who ran the circus mysteriously from afar was not the least bit mysterious or inaccessible to those with whom he associated. His nephew, John Ringling North II, found him even tempered and easy to talk to. Nor was John anywhere near as sexually promiscuous as some writers have intimated. Stuart Lancaster is of the mind that North tended to relate monogamously to women. Arthur Concello strongly confirms this, denying a popular notion that his boss indulged compulsively in one-night stands. In truth, while John may not have observed fidelity in the strict sense of the term, he was clearly a romantic, very much in love with love. So much so that his affair through the early fifties with the simpleminded Gloria Drew seems somewhat atypical of his relationships. Drew drank a lot like John did, but she was unable to conceal her lingering alcoholism under the veneer of chic social merriment. Superficially true to John for as long as he would keep her around, Gloria flirted outside John's presence. She snuggled up to other men on the dance floor when she could get away with it. "She was a real hot number," in the words of Stuart Lancaster, who himself stood in line to fox-trot or tango with Gloria.[2]

When John decided to dump Drew, he went to his cousin, Hester Ringling Sanford, who loved music and who had some cultural connections. "Hester, I wonder if you'd give Gloria some vocal lessons, so she'll have something to fall back on."

"Now, that's a rotten thing to do, Johnny!"

"Yeah, but if she can sing, maybe it'll soften the blow."

Gloria was given a car by her vanishing boyfriend and introduced into the Sanford household down in Sarasota. She took it all in chipper stride. Hester set her up in a guest room. Each morning, the beauty spent almost two hours on her face. She poured out her heart in the singing lessons she was given. Gloria did well enough to land a chorus spot up in the Chautauqua Civic Light Opera Company in upper New York state, during the family's annual summer vacation there. Gloria's career in the arts, subsidized by the Ringlings, was pathetically short lived. She landed back in her own native Georgia, where the bleakness of common life compared to what she had tasted in Johnny's company was the cruelest fate of all. The accounts of her sad, tragic end vary only in the grim details. One has Gloria marrying a gas-station attendant and being shot to death when discovered in bed with a truck driver. Another family recollection holds that she took her own life in ultimate despair by drinking carbolic acid.³

There was apparently little depth in the North-Drew affair, which is probably the reason John dropped her in favor of the next heroine on his romantic stage, Seattle-born Dody Heath. Much better educated and decidedly more independent than Drew, Heath was a working stage actress with a very promising career when John met her in 1954. And in contrast to what little information others have been willing to supply about John's intellectual and cultural interests, Heath has vivid recollections of the man's bright, inquisitive mind, of his vast knowledge on any number of topics, and of his natural appreciation for art. He was a "voracious reader," she recounts, remembering times when North had piles of books nearby. Heath was struck by an encounter she once had with the English doctor Earnest Petrie, who told her that he had "never met an American as well read as John." Indeed, according to verification from North's nephew, John North II, he read "almost every type of book, from Jack Higgins thrillers to classics." John evidenced a keen interest in military history, says Heath, especially in famous military leaders. He could describe in meticulous detail many of the epic battles. And on matters of art, when the two visited the great museums of Paris, John spoke with eloquent knowledge on each and every painting.

John nicknamed Dody "Doodle Bug" and composed a song for her called "Dody." She understood well what lovely music he was capable of composing, and she experienced his considerable artistic sensitivities. So it was depressing for her when she read a one-line entry for John Ringling North in a jet-set *Who's Who:* "Circus producer, with an eye for beautiful women." She showed it to John, expressing how sadly limiting the listing was. John only shrugged his shoulders. He had grown accustomed to a role the media and society (partly at his doing) had assigned him, which distorted and glamorized out of proportion the man he really was.

When John met Dody, she was appearing on the New York stage in the hit *Oh, Men! Oh, Women!* Before that, she had played the part of Hildy in the musical *A Tree Grows in Brooklyn* and had turned in fine performances in two films, one as Miep in *The Diary of Anne Frank*, the other as the scene-stealing Meg Brockie, a man-chasing flirt in Lerner's and Lowe's rhapsodic *Brigadoon*. John North was immediately taken with Heath's stunning looks and her bubbling, playful personality. Since Gloria Drew was still in residence with John at his Waldorf-Astoria Towers suite, not yet out of his life, North took out a suite at the Saint Regis Hotel in order to present to Dody's friends and family (she was of Quaker stock) the spanking image of bachelorhood.

Dody Heath was ambitious, smart, gregarious—and around thirty years younger than North, then in his fifty-first year. Something of a fun-loving spirit herself, Heath was in this sense the ideal match. Although by her account in tempered retrospect the two were a pair of star-crossed lovers. John's strategy for winning Heath over was to profess that marriage to her represented his "last chance to live a normal life," to settle down and actually raise a family. Heath was much too young, and with much too promising an acting future at the time, to be saddled by this overpowering gentleman. He needed to be in control. Whenever, for example, they went out together into another evening, he would typically ask, "Where would you like to go tonight, Dody?" If she suggested the Colony, his follow-up would be, "No, I want to go to 21." And when they got there, North's insecurities were no less evident than his dominating nature. "Don't leave me alone," he would tell Dody, who remembers him as "a very shy man."

They took in Broadway shows like *My Fair Lady* and *Pajama Game*. They were an item at the clubs. Heath tolerated the late hours on occasion, though she rarely stayed up all night, and she wasn't too thrilled with some of North's shadier cronies, the ones who were willing to hobnob till dawn with her new boyfriend. She has fond memories of Art Concello's attendance, now and then, at the table. "They had a history. They had been in the trenches together. John admired Artie's grit and guts." Another late-night North companion was gambler Eric Steiner, whose son North helped put through college.

Most of all, Heath found North to be "a great character . . . a real delight." He wasn't the type to buy expensive gifts, she says, pointing out that his particular generosity came through in his being the perfect host.

She admired his wit and good nature, and she cannot recall his ever bad-mouthing anybody or indulging in petty gossip. He reveled in festive evenings and in being the great storyteller that he was. His flamboyance was in the more subtle style of an earlier era. Nonetheless, Heath's first impression was that of a playboy whom she couldn't imagine settling down into matrimony.

Their courtship was fairly intense and stormy, and was not enriched by North's occasional attempts to sabotage Heath's acting career. By the end of 1954, however, both seemed amenable for a fleeting moment to getting married. John made plans for a wedding in Paris, with author John Steinbeck, then residing in Rome, lined up to be his best man. Another last-minute spat about Dody's role as the next Mrs. North confirmed her worst fears that her life in the theater might be suppressed out of existence. Wedding bells did not ring out at the fashionable chateau secured for the event. Heath asked for another year to think the whole thing over. North said okay. At the end of twelve months, Heath agreed, but now North was on the fence. As 1955 came to a close, he had little time to think about marriage. He was, in fact, sinking into the most vexing and dismal chapter in his career as a show owner. This was the moment when he was virtually at war with Jimmy Hoffa and the Teamsters Union. "For God's sake," he once told Heath as his troubles mounted, "I'm trying to save my circus!"

The relationship was sabotaged to a degree by just that: the labor strikes and the organizational instability that would soon force John to close the show in Pittsburgh and declare an all-indoor future. So by the time he struck the tents for good in 1956, Dody Heath had folded her tents, too, on any further thought of a life with the difficult Mr. North. She distanced herself from the relationship, and she wasn't around with any sympathy for John when his bad fortune with the circus shortly followed. About nine years later, then married to Jack Cushingham, a Hollywood agent, Heath ran into North and the romantic sparks began flying once more. John declared his renewed intention to win her back. He was not so inclined now to let the circus come between him and his love life.

His professional interests were compromised. Indeed, the pressures John felt to uphold his public image as the dashing, up-all-night entrepreneur came into greater conflict with a more basic need he was beginning to feel for a simpler, more conventional marriage-type existence. Heath can see this transition as she looks back in time. When John had visited her out on the West Coast during the fifties when she was busy with film acting, his "greatest joy," as she puts it, was for the two of them to go shopping at the Farmers Market in Los Angeles, return home, and cook their own meal. Later on, they would pop some popcorn. Behind his impressario airs, believes Heath, "he would have made a darling, stay-at-home husband."[4]

That is basically what John became with the most practical and enduring love of his life, Ida Gräfin von Zedlitz-Trützschler, the ballerina he had met and romanced back in 1946. When Ida learned of John's troubles after he closed the show in 1956, she sent him a warm letter of commiseration and invited him back into her life. Ida's overture arrived at the most opportune of moments. John had suffered nothing but defeat and devastation in both his business and personal affairs, and he was elated. He asked Ida to meet him in Copenhagen. The reunion went like a dream, and it gave the two a fresh start on a relationship that now meant much more to John. His growing maturity made the difference. They fell back in love.

"From that moment on," says Ida, "we were together again, as happy as before." They kept the romantic wheels spinning. They dined at the best restaurants, took in operettas and music halls, an occasional symphony concert. They socialized with such friends of John as J. Paul Getty, Sr., and Dr. Jean-Pierre Grether of Switzerland. Ida talks about John's "happy nature," of the spontaneity with which he faced life. "Every day was different. He enjoyed life most intently. He was very social, and he especially admired people who had achieved something in particular." She was charmed by his zest for fine dining. "Whatever he ate, it was with the greatest pleasure. He tried everything and made an extravaganza even of a Bavarian sausage."

To be sure, John still drew the greatest pleasure, according to Ida, from "the circus, the travels, the search for the best artists, the discussions with the directors." Successful opening nights at Madison Square Garden gave him the deepest satisfaction. Ida escorted John on numerous occasions when he attended circuses abroad in search of new acts to sign. "We talked very much if we would take the artist or not, in which place he would be perfect—in the middle ring, or in the right side or in the left side. So it was always very exciting. He was with all his soul absolutely for the circus. We always spent many, many days together till things were done of contracts for the artists. Sometimes we had Mr. Umberto Bedini, and, of course, then John decided, 'Yes, this is the one, absolute, I will have,' and 'Umberto, please do the making of the contracts.'"

In Ida's company, John revealed his true zeal for songwriting, a dedication his lyricist collaborators may not have been around to witness. "The composition of music pieces and melodies was one of the big and strong hobbies of John's," recalls Ida. "He was able to sit and concentrate on a composition for days, days and nights. I used to sing and rehearse his compositions over and over again until he was satisfied with the result."[5]

Ida's growing importance to John is certainly the main reason it was so easy and tempting for him to settle down in Europe. She gave John the marriage he needed but was no longer able to accept. She did this by living with him out of wedlock. They were, as Dody Heath observed them from afar, very much like a middle-class German couple. On more than one occasion when Heath telephoned John, she heard a sizzling sound in the background while John exclaimed, "Oh, we're cooking Chicken Maryland!"[6]

The supreme irony of John's abiding attachment to Ida was how disappointingly ordinary and dull it seemed to some of his closest friends and relatives. It wasn't so easy for them to accept John in the less-glamorous role of a contented homebody. He evidently craved a safe haven away from the world that demanded his costumed appearances. This is what Ida, it would surely appear, gave him so fulfillingly. In her simple, unaffected presence, John was freed from having to present any sort of an impressario facade. He could shuck aside all the pretentious airs and trappings. He could stop the acting, step off the stage, and relax. No wonder John stayed with Ida for the rest of his life. The basic human need for companionship and solace is something he, too, treasured after all, despite all the years he had spent flaunting a·playboy image to the world.

Ida was open minded in her tolerance of John's ongoing friendship with Dody Heath. In fact, when John and Dody resumed seeing each other in later years, Ida and Dody conversed a few times over the telephone in amicable fashion. And if Ida was as much a religious nag with John as some have suggested, she had no trouble allowing his lusty nature full vent. In the words of John North II, commenting on the thought of Ida's preaching to his bohemian uncle, "It wouldn't have done any good if she did."[7]

North and his countess moved into a rented apartment in a small town within seven kilometers of Zurich. Years later, they acquired a second apartment, then eventually moved to Geneva. For a period of time each year, they stayed at the Palace Hotel in Brussels. When that structure was closed for renovation, John and Ida started checking into the Hilton, which they patronized thereafter. John never owned a house during his entire life.

The Ringling Norths were very much a Continental family now. Brother Henry, whom John adored, lived in a Rome apartment. The brothers bought back three hundred of the original one thousand two hundred acres of the Irish estate of their ancestors, Northbrook, in eastern Galway, with the intention of turning it into a homestead for themselves and Henry's son, John North II, who raised cattle on the property. They undertook a massive restoration of the old house, having an architect draw up plans and some evacuation work done for stables, but they didn't proceed any further. They decided the cost would be too high.

As for the Ringling circus about to be launched on the Continent, that was something for Art Concello to figure out. It does seem puzzling that John's high hopes for this new venture did not inspire him to take a more active role in its development, however absorbing his personal preoccupations may have been at the time. Considering that North and Concello basically favored a duplicate version of the current circus they were producing, there is little evidence that much brainstorming took place on any level.

Concello had made about thirty trips abroad over the past three or four years, inspecting arenas and gathering vital information (such as height clearances through the doorways), sometimes with Tuffy Genders, his number-one right hand. In February 1963, they leased a building in Lille, France (where the show was scheduled to open on September 18), for preparation work. Lloyd Morgan was put in charge of the construction of ring curbs and rigging and a fleet of aluminum wagons to transport the show on Continental railroad flatcars. Most of the equipment was built in the French facility. Dacron nets and ropes were imported from Florida.

Art told John how they could get their acts to Europe without having to pay their airfare. Art's shrewd maneuvering took calculated advantage of the special so-called American Circus he had been hired by Morris Chalfen, the ice-show impressario, to take to Moscow. This was part of a cultural exchange program between the United States and the Soviet Union arranged by Chalfen for the sole purpose of allowing him the right to promote the first U.S. appearances ever of the famed Russian circus artists. Most of the acts Art booked for the Moscow-bound American Circus were ones he also wanted for the new Ringling European unit. Once they finished the three-city Soviet tour, they would depart the Chalfen payroll and travel to Lille to become Ringling employees. And since they were already in Europe, Ringling would not have to pay for their airfare over.[8] (Some have misconstrued the American Circus, which Chalfen and Concello organized for Soviet consumption, as being a Ringling-produced product. Technically it wasn't, though it might as well have been since Concello assembled it and relied on name Ringling acts to fill the bill and on Merle Evans to go over with him and teach the Soviets how to play American circus music.)

Another good business move on Concello's part was his use of Chalfen, who had toured his Holiday on Ice abroad since 1950, to line up buildings and local promoters for the Ringling tour. Chalfen told a trade reporter that if he couldn't find the right people in a given city, "I may step in and handle the date myself."

Although Concello can't be faulted for taking the right steps to ensure a smooth physical operation, the show he and North sent to France was not as thoughtfully prepared. "This will be a three-ring circus of the kind long identified with Ringling-Barnum," reported *Amusement Business*, revealing that over a million dollars had been committed to establishing a "permanent and duplicate version of the Big Show for the Continent." What comes into question is whether the current production elements (taken from the skimpy 1962 edition) were worth duplicating—or bringing out of the mothballs, as was the case. Concello displayed no lack of faith in the project when he discussed it with the trade magazine's correspondent. "Lille is perfect. It has the shops we need and plenty of big buildings for rehearsal and storage." He said the structure would be "95 percent European," a separate corporation from the Florida-based company. The show's unique title, Ringling's Barnum and Bailey, was said to have avoided the words "brothers" and "circus" because they translated confusingly in different languages.

"Conditions are right for the move," said Concello, concealing any differences he may have had with North. "The shows over there would love to come into those arenas ahead of us. They'll learn our route in time, anyway. And they'll have to live with us for a long, long time."[9] The Ringling brothers in their day had planned a similar permanent annual invasion of the same territory. In 1919, the year they combined their show with the Barnum and Bailey title, they projected a six-week run at the Olympia in London, to open on December 21, Paris to follow. The tour never materialized.

As the time for rehearsals neared, a growing divisiveness within the Ringling organization proved counterproductive. Maggie Smith, her relationship with Concello deepening, already enjoyed the authority to stage the aerial ballets and furnish the choreography for the specs. Dick Barstow, who still held the director's credit, went along with it reluctantly. Evidently, Smith wanted a bigger hand in all the production, or she and Concello fancied the idea of being the real creative forces behind the European unit. According to Barstow's account, the two of them went off to Europe ostensibly "to do the preliminary things," as they told him, promising to call for his directorial services at the proper time. In fact, while Barstow was back in the States waiting for word, Smith was resurrecting the old production numbers and walking the cast through its paces. She added a charming touch to the finale, in collaboration with Jackie Le Claire, a member of clown alley. Jackie took a position in the center ring and balanced a long umbrella on his forehead, self-absorbed as the closing parade passed by. Suddenly all the spotlights were upon him. He removed the umbrella and looked around. To his surprise, the cast was gone. He took the final bow for the show.[10]

Barstow got restless waiting for the cable telling him to come. He heard they were in Lille rehearsing. He wired Concello and received a reply, "Oh, we're just getting the ball rolling." After about five or six of these transatlantic exchanges, Barstow learned to his shock that the show had opened. A perfunctory wire calling for his participation followed. He was furious, and he blames it partly on John's detachment from the center of things. "I think the first time I really noticed or became aware of this was when they took the circus to Europe."

By the time Barstow arrived on the scene, the show was mired in bad luck. Performers had to make their own hotel arrangements, a blow to morale. During the first week, Lalo Palacio, one of the great flyers and not by any means over the hill, committed suicide for no clear reason. And in Paris, police refused to allow the movement of elephants over a one-mile stretch from the train to the arena until nightfall, fearing a massive traffic jam. Other stringent animal-handling rules forced the circus to drop its performing lions and tigers. Replacement animal acts were brought in, some inferior. Barstow stepped into a tense situation and was greeted by John with relief and surprise.

"Richard, *where* have you been?"

"Where have *I* been?"

"Well, I've been concerned."

"Well, I have been, too."

The director was appalled at what he saw. "They had some dumpy little girls Maggie Smith got from England. The acts were not very good. It was a horrible circus, you can take it from me. I'm the heart of it. There were good acts, but they just weren't coordinated. There were not enough rehearsals."

He stormed up to John after the performance. "Take my name off this thing! I'm going back to America! I don't want any part of this!"

"But Richard!"

"Take my name off!"

"You can't!"

"Want to bet I can't? I can!"

"Richard, wait!" cried John, reaching out as he rarely ever did to anyone. "I know how you feel, but now is the time you got to help me."[11]

Barstow knew it wasn't John's fault that he was called in after the fact. "Okay," he said, fuming in disbelief, "*that* I'll do." He stuck with it for a while, working on the pacing and polish like someone applying a coat of gloss to the *Titanic*. He was not alone in his low opinion of the show. Henry North, who hardly ever spoke an unkind word about anything John was connected with, pulls no punches on this one: "It was an absolute disgrace, and my brother was beside himself. But he managed to, in a few days, book three or four strong acts to get in so we weren't embarrassed when we put the show in Paris."[12] Rudy Bundy wasn't too impressed, either. "It wasn't done right. Neither was Barnum and Bailey when they went there in the 1890s."[13]

Just exactly what wasn't done right remains a mystery of sorts, since there are others—such as Le Claire, who performed in the show, or Ken Dodd, who has viewed filmed portions of the program—who think it was quite fine. The opening in Lille was bound to have looked a bit ragged, for Lille was a tryout town. And the scathing review of it in the English periodical *The World's Fair* comes off suspiciously biased. The writer, Bob Alwyn, panned the debut with such words as "out of date . . . unattractive . . . ludicrous . . . meaningless . . . travesty . . . complete misfire." Alwyn praised some of the top-drawer artists—among them Harold Alzana, the Fredonias, Goldini Sisters, Rogge Sisters, Feris-Ferroni Duo, Galla Shawn, Domis, the Bartschellys, and Stephenson's Dogs—and blasted all the animal numbers, the clowning, and most of the ground and aerial acts. He predicted, barring "a miraculous change," that a planned tour through England the following July would be "just so much waste of time and money."[14]

When Ringling's Barnum and Bailey opened in Paris, however, in a much improved form, it received, according to a write-up in *Business Week*, "moderate praise" from the Parisian critics. The report portrayed the

French, accustomed to a one-ring layout, as being somewhat confused by the three rings and indicated that ticket sales were nonetheless "doing well."[15]

On paper, the program that John sold his European neighbors was a fairly typical Ringling circus of the time, a liberal outpouring of acts into thirty displays. Perhaps it was an overly long bill. In addition to the fine acts endorsed in the *World's Fair* review, there were others, such as Unus, Gerard Soules, and Roberto de Vasconcellos and the Valadors, all tops in their respective fields. Maybe it was the mediocre production turns—"Top Hat, White Tie and Tails," "Around the World in Eight Minutes" (not as interesting as it sounds), and "Elephants and Feathers"—with their pedestrian Max Weldy costumes that looked on the frayed and tired side. Or perhaps it was the bloated impression, in spots, of quantity for quantity's sake that turned people off. John had not gone out of his way to present the brilliantly conceived spectacles (like "Holidays" or "Ringling Rock 'n' Roll") which he had more carefully presided over in years gone by. It wasn't enough to parade a plethora of top talent in a rambling three-ring hodgepodge. More important, this indoor version of Ringling lacked the magical big-top atmosphere dramatized in De Mille's classic film, with which the foreign circusgoers no doubt made comparisons. Like their American counterparts, they, too, had a fondness for the mystique of a canvas enclosure.

The unsettling reception drove John to one of the few temper tantrums he is ever known to have thrown, this by way of Art Concello, who is thought to have been the main source of it. John started blaming Art for all his problems. A real blunder by Art was changing the show's name to Ringling's Barnum and Bailey. According to Rudy Bundy, "if that would have gone through before we were able to catch it, we wouldn't have been able to declare a tax loss on anything, because you have to take it off the right name of the company."[16] John continued harassing Art, in whose personal diary is a recurring entry during that time: "North raising hell."[17] Concello became increasingly uncomfortable around his agitated boss. The two went to dinner one night at John's invitation. Art had to suffer more angry questions and accusations. Wanting out, he told John that he had to get back to the States to prepare the World's Fair edition of the circus. He promised to return in time to take the European unit out of Paris to Ghent. Concello flew back home, unaware he was about to be unemployed again.

John had dinner the next evening with Rudy Bundy, who had just arrived in Europe. "Hell," he said, confiding to his good friend, "I took Art out last night, we had a big dinner, and he said he'd be back to take the show to Ghent. He's about to be fired when he lands in New York. I told Thrun to do it."[18] (Robert Thrun was the corporate secretary.)

Things were not resolved quite so casually. Dick Barstow remembered "a terrible combustion," as he dramatically puts it. The following day, Barstow went looking for Concello at rehearsals and couldn't find him anywhere. Maggie Smith was gone, too, back to England was the word, and Shirley Combs, another English showgirl who assisted Smith, asserted her authority fast. "I'm taking over," she told Barstow, "because Maggie isn't here."

"You're no good to me!" cried the director, whose show had been pieced together by so many hands. "Nobody's any good to me!" He spent a few more days working on the performance. "It was beyond saving," he states. "I told them, 'Take my name off!' [which they didn't] and left."[19] Another one who walked out of frustration was Unus, later admitting he was "dead wrong" to do it.

Concello does not concur that he was let go by Thrun. He remembers trying to rejoin the show en route and being told by Tuffy Genders of the word received through Bundy that his services had been terminated. Concello advised Genders, one of his most loyal assistants, against following him off the lot. Art packed his bags and returned to Sarasota. Ringling still owed him forty thousand dollars in back wages, and he had to file suit against the show to get this money after making two trips to the Venice office and being routinely put off. He was also still contractually obligated, however, to produce the circus at the upcoming New York World's Fair. Harry Dube urgently rang Concello up one day to remind him of this. "Don't talk to me," answered Art, "I'm fired!"

World's Fair officials were soon on his doorstep, demanding a progress report. "I don't work for North anymore," insisted Mr. Concello, amused by the organizational chaos into which the circus was once again drifting. The officials didn't find it at all funny and mentioned the possibility of legal action. "Okay," proposed Concello, "I'll tell you what I can do. You put up $50,000 in escrow. When the first ticket is sold, you release it to me. I'll get the tent made and get the whole thing up and going."[20]

They agreed to that. Concello did what had to be done to get a third unit of Ringling ready for the fair. He signed some acts and placed an order with Leaf Tent, then put a bunch of Indians to work erecting it. The program was another mediocre venture, ill conceived and hastily assembled, a token effort to satisfy a contract. It wasn't helped any, in Rudy Bundy's opinion, by being placed in a faraway corner of the fairgrounds, "where everybody was leaving, going out the back door."

Back in Europe, John kept booking more acts for the European unit, as if quantity alone would earn him the elusive critical respect. In Hamburg, two trucks of liberty horses arrived following an all-night haul and were immediately integrated into the program, causing a sea of fresh manure to descend upon the arena floor. "You never saw so much horseshit in all your life," recalls Jackie Le Claire, relating how it took them about half an hour to clean all the rings before the next act could go on.[21]

John often stayed in the same hotel as the performers, another departure for him. In the evenings, without Art or Rudy around, he would summon Wayne Larey, the performance director, to his table for company. Poor Larey had to sit there half the night listening to John mumble on, and when he would diplomatically rise to leave, John would flash a wad of bills. "Here's a couple of hundred. Give it to them, they'll keep the place open later."

In his insecure state, John was unusually accessible to the company. Before Unus blew the date in Paris, he got John to go along with a raise by hinting he might walk if refused. Then he boasted about it to other performers, who in turn beat a path to North's door seeking similar wage increases. Many were accommodated, which swelled expenses. Business, by most accounts, was very good. Lacking Art's stabilizing influence, though, John slipped back into his moods. He fretted over his million-dollar investment. Dan Judge, representing the forty-niners, was called to Europe for meetings. To close or not to close was the subject. Rudy Bundy feels it was a no-win situation anyway you looked at it. "I think Concello had some deals with Holiday on Ice. Hell, we couldn't have made money if we'd been doing *great* business."[22] (The implication is that Concello shorted North again with kickbacks and hidden fees.)

After courting respectable patronage in Paris, Ghent, Hamburg, Copenhagen, Kiel, Brussels, Rotterdam, Dortmund, and Stuttgart, John decided to call it quits, aborting the final three stops at Zurich, Frankfurt, and London. He took an estimated $175,000 loss. A route-book item about the tour, "All the World Is a Stage . . . for Ringling!" intimated that more Old World cities would be visited on future tours; It stated that everything had been "neatly put away in secure storage at the moment for a new day's opening."[23] John told a reporter from *Amusement Business*: "It's simply a case of learning things about the territory."[24]

The truth is, he abandoned the Continental tour as emotionally as he had launched it. At first John didn't want to announce the early closing until the final night in Stuttgart. Holiday on Ice executives insisted, however, that performers be given a customary two-week notice, to which John reluctantly agreed. He was in no mood to have another aborted midseason ending ballyhooed. It appears he had expected too much too soon, for the modest loss seemed negligible given the healthy business drummed up the first time out. Nor were the mixed reviews sufficient cause to back off in humiliation. John most likely concluded that Europeans would not patronize the American concept beyond the novelty of a first visit. And nobody who has since tried selling three rings outside the United States (including Kenneth Feld, who sent an ill-fated Ringling troupe to Japan in 1987) has proved him wrong. Henry told a reporter from the *New Yorker* shortly after the show closed, "Brother John took the 3-ring circus to Europe, but they didn't go for it."[25]

Most of all, John had to be wondering how future foreign tours might adversely affect his reputation throughout the Old World, which he had come to regard and cherish as a haven away from all the residual ill will he still faced in the United States. Ida has declined to offer any recollections of her own about the European tour or how its early demise affected John's spirits. Evidently, he decided to remain a circus king abroad and to continue to face the critics back in the States. Once again free of Art Concello's restraints, John set out on the lush talent-laden trails of the Continent to recruit a new set of stars and rebuild the Greatest Show on Earth, American version. His quest of passion took him for the first time across the Iron Curtain. And because he had no political axes to grind, as John approached his twilight years he was still willingly able to endure controversy in the daring act of affirming circus art, wherever it might be found.

The Sound of Success

The absence of Art Concello, so dominating a figure, allowed John once again to reassert himself more directly in the creative end of things. And most of the present staff members were men whom he trusted and admired: his best friend, Rudy Bundy, whom he elevated from treasurer to vice-president and special assistant; brother Henry, reappointed a vice-president in 1965; Richard Barstow, the oldest living child prodigy, still in charge of production; Pat Valdo, whom the North brothers had adored from their childhood; other steadfast veterans, including Merle Evans, Harold Ronk, and Max Weldy. Tuffy Genders, ironically once associated with the sneeze mob and a Concello protégé, was retained as general manager even after the latter was let go.

Symbolic of North's return to more active participation was the resumption in 1964 of an annual route book. The new issue took special delight in detailing the now-successful indoor operation. Publicity director Mae Lyons went to work on her employer's image with stories that glorified it to the hilt. "JOHN RINGLING NORTH . . . What A Name!" headlined the lead article, containing such tributes as: "Strangely compatible with his circus interests, John Ringling North lives in full keeping with the exalted position of men of great wealth, great position, great fame and great fortune. His life, most of which these days is spent in Europe, is by any standards—colorful, exciting, important. He has given his generation by the very nature of his living the same well-bred flamboyancy that led international society to welcome—in the generation gone by—Mr. John Ringling (his favorite uncle)."[1] One year he was declared "The Greatest Showman on Earth," the next "Sir Circus!"

More symbolic yet was the authority given Bundy, now the top man on the lot representing the Norths. It was a splendid appointment, for Bundy conducted himself in a gracious manner, allowing the staff comfortable latitude. And since he was so closely associated with John, there could be no doubt who was actually in control. It quite naturally affected John, too, for with his best friend representing him as the executive go-between, he felt fewer inhibitions in applying himself. And that is exactly what the circus needed: a reinfusion of the producing flair John was capable of giving it. Company morale rose appreciably. An exciting new era in Ringling showmanship began to unfold.

Shortly after letting Art go, John telephoned Art's former wife, Antoinette, then raising their son, Randy, in Florida, and invited her back to direct the aerial ballets. He flew her over to Paris and had his chauffeur meet her at the airport. Antoinette has fond remembrances: "We spent half the night talking about old times."[2] John was back in the United States the following spring and making himself more accessible to the press. "It was like old times," reported *Amusement Business*, "as John Ringling North came into Boston prior to the Big One's visit on two successive weekends .... His candid comments on a variety of topics, reprinted in the local newspapers, were bound to help what North anticipated as a record stand this year."[3]

He spoke to members of the fourth estate with rare vigor, explaining why Boston was played on back-to-back weekends with a New Haven stop in between; how the new twenty-two-car train was moved on time; why he was so high on such new acts as Charly Baumann's Tigers and Christine Holt, who juggled while hanging by her hair. "I'm happy about the crowds coming back, especially the children," he said. "I think they've grown tired of television, but anyhow they're right here having a wonderful time."[4]

His creative juices flowing, that summer John went on a booking rampage, rounding up as many new acts (forty) as he did for the then-unprecedented 1947 season. To do this, he ventured for the first time into the so-called Iron Curtain countries of Poland, Hungary, and Czechoslovakia, a veritable untapped world of performing riches. John was well aware of the artistry that abounded in the Communist Bloc nations and well aware of the growing international reputation of the famed Moscow Circus, which made an inaugural visit to the United States in 1963 to ecstatic reviews. The closest John could come to booking an authentic Soviet act was to book its counterpart in one of the satellite countries, where circus troupes were organized and run along similar lines, most of the artists having been taught in specialized state schools.

He engaged the help of Trolle Rhodin, who held connections with Communist circus managers, to act as a talent agent, naming him general European representative. The two were notoriously successful in signing contract after contract. Thus, North was once again able to assert his showmanship in a spectacular fashion by offering his audiences some of the greatest acrobats in the world. The 1965 edition marked the beginning of John's bold Slavic period. There were one hundred eighty-five performers in the cast that year, of which forty came from Poland alone. There was a juggling display containing seven acts: the Four Picards, Amazing Fudi, Miss Lilian, Wolf Trio, Bruski Duo, Jimi the Great, and Miss Helena. There was the Vlady Trio and the Nowinskis, Staubertis and Eva and Blanka. There were the Koslowskis and the Zavattas and the Zepanskis ("Whirlwinds on Wheels"), Hillano's Poodles, Helena Rassy's Pigeons and the Perz Bear Act, the Riveros and Rizard and Zygmunt, the Balzas and the Merbs Duo. The Three Mecners, a superb hand-vaulting troupe, premiered that season, as did the two acts that flanked them, Adams and Jeski and the Lilian Keler Trio. Rhodin's wife, Ingeborg, an outstanding dressage rider, made her auspicious debut over Ringling sawdust. The Weizz Trio and Makar the Sailor Man shared a comedy spot. Adela Smieja and her trained lions joined the Big Show. Edmund Meschke, along with Alicja and Roman Lesniewicz, added their liberty horses to the parade. An exhilarating trio of teeterboard tumblers—the Five Tokaji, the Magios, and the featured Varadys Troupe—earned thundering receptions, which led to the steady importation, season after season, of more springboard artists, each adding novel twists to the popular genre. The overall newness of the 1965 program harkened back to John's best under-canvas days.

The press applauded the results. "Marvelous acts . . . wonderful, unbelievable," wrote Richard Watts for the *New York News*.[5] "A circus can lift the bondage of care . . . so many good acts," agreed the *World Telegram*.[6] "Everything was super about the show," observed Harry Gilroy in the *New York Times*, "including the most ardent fans, who were superanuated . . . often tossing out three startling sets of performers at a time. The 'Wizard of Oz,' a pageant that employs all the colors that humanity and even the pop artists have ever envisioned . . . is spectacular and touched with humor, as when the pretty girl, Dorothy, is caught up in the trunk of an elephant and carried that way around the three rings. . . . All in all, this is a spectacular circus, it seems to have more thrills of dexterity, of daring acrobats, and kindly disposed animals, of flash, dash and crash than ever, and yet it has a light quality. On the basis of this year's show, the old time fans will not be ready to surrender the circus to the kids just yet, even if there is no steam calliope in the opening march."[7] The *Journal American's* Mike Pearl reported overhearing a little girl tell her mother, "I wish this could go on forever," and he commented, "You find yourself hoping that it would, too."[8]

On the West Coast that summer, Cecil Smith of the *Los Angeles Times* dittoed the enthusiasm: "It lived up to the wildest and most extravagant superlatives in the lurid vocabulary of circus press agentry . . . in a changing world it seems the only thing enduring is that Ringling still offers the greatest show on earth."[9]

While acknowledging that the circus was mesmerizing the critics, Irwin Kirby's *Amusement Business* notice posed a few pertinent questions relative to the perennial three-ring debate: "It is too much circus, if such a paradox be possible, because this year's version of the Big One requires as many visits to appreciate as does a world's fair. . . . In John Ringling North's very moments of artistic supremacy, his circus stumbles on its own splendor. No human being can evaluate that many simultaneous presentations (seven on occasion) as North fields groups of acts who deserve center ring status with most circuses and has them casually whistled off, whether or not their turns are completed. . . . But this is a minority expression and does not detract from the show's numerous triumphal aspects."[10]

Came more seasons and still more new faces. In 1966, the juggling display mushroomed to nine acts, included among which were three imports, the Kalmans, Jana and Mirek, and the Alberts. Other difficult-to-pronounce names on the bill included Mogyorosi's Canines, Kochmanski (a Polish riding clown), and the Warpol Trio. Karmelo introduced contortion on a slack wire, Los Belios executed nifty tricks on horizontal bars, the Ferkos Duo and Los Tonitos, somersaulting wire walkers, distinguished themselves with style. Adolf Althoff coached a Siberian tiger onto the back of a cantering horse. The Picards pleased on bicycles. There were three troupes of accomplished teeterboard jumpers: the Eight Halasis, the Six Forays, and the triumphantly returning Varady Troupe, justifiably billed "A circus owner's dream come true, three championship four-high Teeterboard acts simultaneously." Audiences went wild. Another crowd pleaser was the showmanly triple-somersaulting flyer Tito Gaona, making his first engagement with Ringling Bros. and Barnum & Bailey. His much-anticipated act would continue to thrill Ringling circusgoers for fourteen consecutive seasons.

In 1967, another great year, the aerial ballerina Erika Pinske joined up. So did the Metchkarow Troupe and the Danis Quintette, Van Donwen's Seals and Miss Rosanova's Doves, the Eight Salvias and Levski Octette, the Dimitrov Trio and the Ivanov Duo, the Bojilovs and the Jacques Rhodin Chimps. In the air, there were the Bozyks, the Szysmanskis, and the Ivankis. That was the year when the Russian bar act, presented by the Swinging Zdravkos, first delighted America, the year the Petrows, the Marinkas, and the Dobritsch Duo, remarkable perch-pole exponents, introduced "frightening feats atop slimline shafts." More springboard stars arrived, bearing the names Salagis and Boitschanows. Together, these virile spirits, many of them from Eastern Bloc nations, gave the circus a more exuberant, fast-moving edge, and Yankee audiences responded with loud, heartfelt ovations. The abundance of action caused a *New York Times* reviewer to comment, "It is as impossible to give a complete summation of what went on as it would be for a fly perched on a wide screen to summarize the movie."[11]

One might have figured John's producing generosity (so many new acts) would enamor him of the public. Maybe so, but not with the circus community. True to North's record for doing things that—rightly or wrongly—provoked controversy, his latest angle backfired when a lot of former Ringling performers started expressing resentment over the massive influx of acts from the other side of the Iron Curtain. Their grievances were well vented in the pages of *Amusement Business.* One letter writer complained, "It is a fact that the Ringling show goes on without shame with the importation of communist acts."[12] A band of members of the AGVA pushed the union to try restricting the number of imported acts that Ringling could present in a given year. About the only act the AGVA was able to keep out of the country was Sahbrah, a high-diving tiger belonging to a former Ringling trainer, Hans Neumann, said to have been booked "by an American circus" for its 1966 season.

Amusement Business in turn heard from a "corporate officer" of the Ringling hierarchy, asking not to be named, who responded with an overly defensive list of logical reasons for the policy. In conclusion, he wrote, "So the George Hanneford Jr.'s are gone this year. The Stephensons will present their riding act, and they are from England. Kubler went back to Germany with his chimps, but we have Oscar Konyot's chimps with us and he's from Sarasota. The Holts are gone but we brought back Miss Mara, who owns property in Florida, and her brother Tonito. And the Flying Gaonas—weren't they with Beatty-Cole? Are any of these

Communists? . . . It's ludicrous. It's all out of proportion and I don't think I'll make any more comments. But I'll say this. When we stop selling tickets to the public then I'll worry. And when we, as producers, are deprived of the right to assemble our own shows, then we'd all better worry. What ever happened to free enterprise?"[13]

And whatever happened to John Ringling North? The supreme irony of his life may be that his producing accomplishments were somehow subverted by his critics into a legacy of failure. Many fans overlook how really good the last shows produced by John were, and how he had come out of the doldrums to exert himself once again. Perhaps he deserves more credit than he has been given for standing aside during the initial indoor years while allowing Art Concello the authority and free reign needed in order to see the circus through a very difficult transitional period. The act of passive restraint can, in certain situations, be the wisest course of action.

And what had John himself to say about the Communist-acts issue? Apolitical by nature, his thoughts on the matter were conveyed in a 1966 route-book story, a typical waxing-lyrical yarn that took a little time for some serious reflection, too: "As with all impressarios and theatre people through the ages, John Ringling North knows there is no such thing as politics in the entertainment area. Artists are artists the world over, he says, regardless of what may have happened to the individual person's freedom and politics. And, additionally, the Ringling nephew says with a trace of a twinkle, it doesn't hurt us any for the other side to see our way of life."[14]

The show ventured into another touchy area in 1966 when it signed a black aerial apprentice, Priscilla Williams, spotted in Los Angeles at Del Graham's School for Circus Flyers, to appear in production. Williams's high visibility (in a lily-white line of showgirls) brought feature reporters to her side, and she was a good interview. "I'd hate to think I'm the only Negro girl who loves the circus. But it's true, there aren't many Negroes interested in circus work. I honestly don't know of any who have an act that could go on right now. . . . I was getting more pay as a club dancer than I am now, but I believe I'm achieving something of permanent value. I'm pulling down barriers in a quiet way and it gives me a feeling of pride."[15]

John's production staff drew certain inspiration from the new mix of talent and from John's renewed involvement. Antoinette Concello conceived a truly wonderful aerial spec, "Swan Lake," the Tchaikovsky score a fitting theme for the current roster of artists. At the same time, the haphazard way in which the number was prepared reveals what a loose organization John either fostered or allowed to exist. To get Antoinette back in his employ, he had to plow through his own devious front office to find her. First he inquired about her at the Venice quarters and was misleadingly told that she was "ill and unavailable." On a hunch, he called her at her home and was delighted to find her in good voice and spirit. "How are you, sweetheart?" "I'm fine," she answered. "You mean you're all right?" "Yeah, I'm fine." Antoinette figured that one of Art's old cronies, still attached to the show, was put up to the task of keeping John away from her.

Then came the curious costume-designing competition (not intended as such) for "Swan Lake." Antoinette came up with her own set of sketches, oddly circumventing Max Weldy's department, and sent them off to John for approval. As capricious as he was, he gave the designs the "O.K., JRN" rating. Then came Weldy across the ocean with his own ideas drawn out on paper. John politely asked about Antoinette's sketches. Weldy replied he had no idea of their existence, obviously scheming to have them vetoed by John's implied approval of his own. Antoinette pressed the issue gently and prevailed, but not without internal discord and, as she sees it, artistic sabotage at the hands of old Max. "He sort of screwed up the wardrobe."[16]

Another conflict was loads more colorful because it involved the ego of Richard Barstow, who guarded his directorial rights (and rites) with monopolistic fervor. John had agreed to engage Trolle Rhodin's brother, Teddy, touted as one of Europe's best-known choreographers and for years ballet master at the Royal Opera in Stockholm. John called Richard with the news. "I've got an assistant for you, to help you with the dancing." A deadly silence ensued.

"I don't need an assistant," declared Richard.

"This is the brother of Trolle. He is ballet. He knows ballet backward and forward, and we're going to do 'Swan Lake.' "

Richard, who claimed the status of "the world's greatest male toe dancer," reminded John of the fact. "You apparently forget that I studied with the late Pavlova."

"Well, Richard. . . . "

"Yes?"

"I signed him and you've got to use him."

"Fine," said Richard, in a devious frame of mind. "I'll give him something to do. Send him over!"

At rehearsals the next winter, Richard came up against not only Teddy Rhodin, soon to arrive as the new ballet master, but his brother Trolle, already on the premises and strutting around like a director himself. Richard picked up a copy of the local newspaper to find a picture of Rhodin with a blurb, "new director and choreographer." Outraged, he lashed into Henry North, who happened to be around. "Excuse me, Mr. North, what is this?" He flung the paper at Henry. "You don't need me. This is a violation of my agreement."

"But, Dick, wait a minute!"

"For what?"

"He's to be the executive producer or something like that."

Meanwhile, Trolle Rhodin was in the arena giving instructions to the cast. Richard grabbed the microphone out of his hand and tossed it in his face. "Do it! Do it!" he yelled. "I'm leaving for New York *right now!*"

Barstow's grand walkout was aborted by Henry, who offered placating assurances and handed him back exclusive use of the mike. Richard next took on the matter of the "Swan Lake" choreography. Luckily for him, Teddy Rhodin's trip to Florida had been delayed five days. "Five days," thought Richard. "Yes, yes, we'll work that to our advantage." He launched into the dance rehearsals for the ballet's opening segments before the designated choreographer could arrive to stage them himself. "I thought, 'That's the way it goes,'" said Richard, devilishly satisfied in reflection. "We had to get it done. I've been in the business for years. I must say, I felt very rotten. Here you go. So, when he comes in, I left sixteen bars or something open, and he choreographed those bars and walked around like this all day, demonstrating a few basic steps for the girls to do on their way to the webs. That was his first and last year." Barstow survived many more and later drew close to Trolle. "We're dear friends now. I think he felt he was in charge and North told him he was in charge, and he just went ahead and did things."[17]

"Swan Lake" was a masterpiece of circus spectacle, credit belonging to Barstow for his fine ensemble entrances, and to Antoinette for the inspired web routines. Merle Evans scored it with sensitivity. It was a clear production hit, revealing the nuances of a more sophisticated circus. The other 1965 spectacles, "The Wizard of Oz," "Pachyderms and Pulchritude," and the finale, in which the girls wore letter-bearing capes that spelled out John's yearly sign-off message, "Thank You and Au Revoir, John Ringling North," were all appealing assets.

Production numbers in the ensuing seasons sustained the more hip attitude. In 1966, the elephants got a workout in "This Is New—Pussycat." In 1967, "Pachyderms and Pulchritude" was revived in an even livelier format. "Artists and Models" was the French aerial ballet that introduced Erika Pinske. "Alice in Topsy Turvy Land" had an original score by Jimmy Selva and Lynn Olsen, recorded on S and R Records, with a strong title song, "It's a New World." The parade itself, an interesting-enough concept that lacked opulence and charm, was typical of the show's one real weakness those years. The specs were nothing like the ones North had produced in the tent days. In his *New York Times* review, Frank Shepherd, who loved the "outrageously daredevil acts," wasn't nearly as moved by "Topsy Turvy Land," commenting that it "came off visually, but, again, the script was quite inane, a jazzing up of something that could be done beautifully straight."[18]

Another plus factor those seasons were the novel entrances and exits worked out for the individual acts. An aerial troupe might be in their rigging ready to begin at the moment they were announced. A group of tumblers might come twisting and twirling down the track as they were introduced. Some acts were seen marching off. Others were not. A variety of approaches kept the show surprising and added that much more pizzazz to the self-assured Ringling format. Whom to credit for these transitional moments? Barstow acknowledges, when asked, having more to do with them in earlier years. Rudy Bundy points to Pat Valdo and Bob Dover. To a degree, they were already a Ringling tradition, just more visible indoors with better lighting and no distracting tent poles.

By now, the circus had learned how to exploit the superior lighting and sound systems available in most of the larger auditoriums. For example, a real enhancement were the three illuminated ring curbs, which suddenly glowed as the house lights fell to darkness and the band swung into the overture. The circus was coming into its own again, conjuring up its indestructible magic in a vast new forum. Gerald Nachman, writing in the *Oakland Tribune*, was so moved: "It remains one of the few memories of the past that refuses to fail or fade. It endures, not as a quaint relic but as a roistering and rousing good time."[19]

One could always argue, and many still do, that indoors, the circus lacks the unique atmosphere of the old tent-show days—the smells, the surly-faced roustabouts in the shadows, the titillating menace of the midway with its sordid banner lines, the gruff-voiced vendors. In at least one department related to the performance itself, however, the new indoor setup excelled as never before. It was a superior-sounding circus, thanks in part to better acoustics and amplification and in the greater part to two forceful giants, musical director Merle Evans and ringmaster Harold Ronk. Both benefited immeasurably in the new setting.

Evans now carried just himself, a drummer, and an organist, supplementing this trusty trio with local musicians recruited in each town through the union hall. Certainly in the major metropolitan areas the band that Evans directed far surpassed in quality of musicianship those he had fronted under canvas, when more than a few of the windjammers, willing to endure the long, strenuous outdoor tours, did not always play with the greatest of ease, if they even had it in them. At certain engagements now, Evans actually used some of the best musicians around, musicians who would never think of going out a full season with a circus but who were delighted to sit in a week or two under the baton of Ringling's famed maestro.

Merle Evans was probably the most versatile and circus-sensitive musical director who ever lived. He managed through the late 1960s to keep pace with changing tastes, always embracing a mixture of pop, show, and classical refrains, sprinkled with exciting segues from one rhythm to its opposite, and with stirring fanfares (of his own composition) that helped move the action urgently ahead. Credit also some fine musical arrangements provided those pulsating years by Robert Hutsell.

Harold Ronk, the storybook ringmaster, was every bit as forceful a presence with his classical style of oratory, delivered with a verbal bravado that soared over the band's emphatic beat. First signed in 1951 by North and John Murray Anderson to sing the special production songs, Ronk was later made ringmaster as well and gradually matured into a commanding figure without ever coming across in the stilted vein of the old-time tanbark talker. He ranks up there with Evans in a class all his own, and if he ever comes out of retirement—as he has tantalizingly hinted at—it will be, in the minds of many fans, tantamount to a second coming.

The indoor circus suited Ronk just fine. He had never taken well to dusty lots. He refused to live on the train, driving overland and staying in hotels and motels instead. (One of his predecessors, another Broadway-ambitious singer, took one look at the tiny stateroom assigned him on the train, walked off, and never returned.) As Ronk was directed into a more visible position in the program, usually being spotlighted around center ring during his intros, he developed a more personable rapport with audiences, all the while maintaining a certain mystique once described by

Al Ringling, urging it upon one of his ringmasters, as "elusive yet vital."
Ronk mastered a number of elocutionary techniques in order to avoid
repetition, and he was given latitude in deciding when to announce each
display. He might introduce one act at the beginning of its turn, another
midway through the routine. Such variations further theatricalized the
circus.

Whether they realized it or not, Evans and Ronk were each other's best
collaborators, so complementary were their robust styles. Together, they
created the greatest-sounding show on earth, *ever*. In 1962, Ronk released
a charming album, on the Harmony label, of circus-related songs finely
sung. He did not always sing anywhere near up to his potential in the live
shows, and he tended on occasion to wander off deep into the wings,
sometimes returning too late to make the next announcement. Evans
didn't miss a beat in striking up the next number, with or without Ronk at
the microphone.

In 1967, both of them participated on a London Phase 4 album,
"Circus Spectacular," which became a hot seller. Evans turned out a rather
predictable mix of regular circus galops and marches (one of Russian
origin which he brought back from his stint with the American Circus in
Moscow). Ronk delivered the mock announcements in splendid form,
beginning with the classic "CHILDREN OF ALL AGES! JOHN RINGLING NORTH
WELCOMES YOU TO THE GREATEST SHOW ON EARTH!" He added a few
humorous touches in the vein of spoofing old-fashioned hyperbole. The
record is replete with atmosphere and sound effects and contains one of
Evans's best compositions and a number that can hold its own against any,
"Symphonia March." As well, included on the cut are a couple of Rudy
Bundy originals, the pleasant "If I Had a Dream" and the zesty "I'm Flying
High." Not to leave John out, several of his tunes are presented in medley
form in a "Finale" segment, melodically framed by the Rodgers and Hart
tune "Circus on Parade" at the beginning and Victor Young's "The Greatest
Show on Earth" at the end. "Circus Spectacular" captures all the power
that Merle Evans and Harold Ronk brought to the circus.

What wonderful shows they had to score and announce those years!
Except for the lamentable lack of lavishness in the principal pageants, the
performances produced by John from 1965 through 1968 were among his
very best. Company morale surged. Annual grosses climbed to record-
breaking heights. In 1965, Madison Square Garden revenues topped the
$2-million-dollar mark for the first time. During Easter week, all night
shows were eliminated in favor of two special daily performances, offered

at 10:30 A.M. and 3 P.M. In the Astrodome at Houston, six shows lured 158,886 souls. A Friday-night performance was seen by 43,000. The four-day gross netted $500,000. The season take reached a record $6.5 million.

New Yorkers were so taken by the "Communist" acts that they returned in 1966 to spend $2,638,000 at the box office. Road-end totals in 1966 reached $7,349,000, as faithfully recorded in Rudy Bundy's personal copy of the ledger, which he kept on hand to share with his pal, Johnny North, when called upon for business briefings. (Circus officials told a reporter from *Amusement Business* that the 1966 gross was $8.25 million, from which a $500,000 profit was turned. Box-office receipts accounted for $8 million. The other quarter of a million came from the sale of programs, concessions, and novelties, *The Greatest Show on Earth* movie royalties, and the NBC spring highlights telecast.)[20]

The all-important attendance records were every bit as heartwarming. In 1967, the show played to 4,164,029 people, about as many as it did in the best of the under-canvas years. In Anaheim, California, twelve sellouts in thirteen shows were recorded. By the end of 1968, the annual gross came thrillingly close to the $10-million-dollar mark. The New York crowd alone had doled out over $3 million for tickets despite one of the most grudgingly ignorant reviews ever filed with the *New York Times*, the writer being Clive Barnes, a man who automatically equated a three-ring circus with mediocre acts.

Other critics, such as Gerald Nachman in the *Oakland Tribune*, were ebullient in their praise: "What always strikes me about this circus is its perfect, almost Grecian, symmetry, the work of director Richard Barstow, who not only fills three rings continually to the brim but somehow balances the spectacle by letting the acts in circles one and three equal the act in the center. What great geometric showmanship!"[21]

About the 1968 edition, it can be said that North and company achieved a nearly perfect program, perfect having to do with an attractive balance of acts, the quality of production, smooth transitions between displays, comedy in the right proportion, the overall pacing from start to finish. A memorable circus performance takes on a symmetry all its own, like a tapestry of interlocking colors or the fluid motion of a champion skater's routine. Indeed, great circus art *is* a form of ballet. Whether a particular audiences appreciates this fact, it will unconsciously respond.

The 1968 opus opened with a line of showgirls, dressed as ringmistresses,

marching briskly down the track as Harold Ronk sang, "TAKE A RIDE ON
A BUBBLE, WHETHER EIGHTY YEARS OLD, OR EIGHT! CHILDREN OF ALL
AGES...IT'S CIRCUS TIME!" The original song, a real hummer, was composed by Noel Regney to Dick Barstow's lyrics. Following after the showgirls
came a parade of llamas and elephants, ponies and camels and zebras, all
of them prancing gaily into the rings to commence their routines. Next was
"Ringling Charivari," an exuberant rush of acrobats down one side of the
hippodrome track. They each took turns flipping and twisting and
somersaulting over thick rubber mats. Three of the twenty-seven new
imported acts were featured in the fourth display, titled "Startling Sky-
High Stunts," with the ingenious Hergotti Troupe working over the center
spot from a novel rotating rig.

The masterful foot juggler Ugo Garrido took his turn in the spotlights,
flanked by no less than four other manipulators. Lou Jacobs, one of
America's most endearing clowns, had the entire arena all to himself next.
Then the Four Titos took off on their trampoline, while Sofia Bardutte
and the Eight Salvia offered contrasting feats in the outer rings. Clown
alley commanded the next display with a surfeit of goofy walkaround
items, easy and fun to watch. Horse riders dashed onto the tanbark circles,
and the Four Dunai in the center of it all kept things alive with their
rapid-fire juggling exchanges accomplished atop cantering steeds. The
house darkened. Spotlights converged on the lone figure of old-time
Ringling jester Paul Wenzel struggling with a small fishing line to wrest
from a tiny hole what turned out to be an enormous catch.

The audience sighed warmly while the band moved into the opening
notes of "On a Wonderful Day Like Today," and the showgirls were
pushed down the track in small sleighs. "LADIES AND GENTLEMEN!," began
Ringmaster Ronk, "RINGLING BROS. AND BARNUM & BAILEY PROUDLY
PRESENTS A NEW CONCEPT IN AERIAL BALLET: AN AERIAL EXTRAVAGANZA
FEATURING HIGH ABOVE THE CENTER RING THE INTERNATIONALLY AC-
CLAIMED HILDALYS, IN 'WINTER WONDERLAND!'" The Antoinette Concello-
conceived number premiered a new form of track rigging (devised by
Andre Prince) that rotated the webs in a circular pattern. Energy was
provided by bicycle riders on high. So the women moved around in an
aerial carousel while thousands of released bubbles conjured up a winter-
time setting and Harold Ronk sang "Love Makes the World Go Round."
The effect achieved was pure enchantment.

There were crisp liberty-horse drills. Then came wizards on wheels: the
Seven Boskays, the Three Picards, and the Karputi Quartette. They were

followed by the Zdravkos Big Swing, from which acrobats were catapulted into the air over ribbons and onto a stack of foam rubber pads. The audience took the rides vicariously and roared its approval. Stilt-walking clowns ambled around the track, then the wildly amusing Stephenson's Dogs (coordinated nonstop tricks and errant behavior) literally brought down the house. The classy, intrepid dressage rider, Ingeborg Rhodin, took her elegant turn next. All the while, the outer rings were graced with pleasing action. The first half concluded with the inexcusably dull "Inauguration Ball," a dead-on-arrival pageant that Barstow claims was foisted upon him by Weldy and Valdo. "It was horrible. I had to make something out of those ideas. It was basically one costume, and after you get through waltzing, what is there?"[22] Not very much at all. The wardrobe was Weldy awful, the content as bland as flavorless chewing gum. Too bad the fine San Francisco artist Dong Kingman, who designed that season's lovely circus magazine cover, could not have designed "Inauguration Ball." At least its costumes would have been appealing. Bring on intermission.

The second half began with Erika Pinske spinning delicate aerial maneuvers from a single web. Charly Baumann's gentler approach to the exhibition of performing tigers suited the changing sensibilities of younger patrons. Evy Althoff's Siberian tiger rode peacefully on the back of a horse, appropriately billed "Natural Enemies Declare Truce." How far things had progressed from the shoot-'em-up days of Clyde Beatty! Not too far, though, to deprive the funmakers of their timeless foolishness now and then. The crazy clown wedding was revived that year, and it preceded three troupes of rather extraordinary perch-pole equilibrists, the Two Alexandrows, the Dimtschew Troupe, and the Petrov Duo. Popular tramp clown Otto Griebling followed with a raucous solo, "Hobo Hooliganism." An amusing assemblage of seals and chimps took over the rings, then the mad, mod "Carnaby Street" hit the track with wry pachydermic force. The elephants were decked out as flower children, the gals as "Mod-Maids." The program called it "Way-Out" and "Real-In." Spectators laughed and clapped most of the way through, then cheered on three whirling families of teeterboard daredevils. The springboard teams powered themselves into four- and five-person-high pyramids. Some were wobbly, others perfectly, rousingly upright.

While the nets went up for the flying acts, clown alley once again cavorted around the track, each joey competing for the crowd's attention with some grotesque, quaintly amusing contraption. Tito Gaona swooped through the upper reaches of the house in rare form. He threw a flawless triple. And at the conclusion, just after falling into the net below, he bounced back into the air high enough to land, smugly erect, in a sitting position on the free-swinging trapeze bar! The seats ringing with grateful applause, maestro Evans coached his musicians up the escalating notes of a dramatic fanfare. A chorus of women came marching down the track, each banging out the spirited refrain on tambourines. "WHEN YOU'RE DOWN AND OUT, LIFT UP YOUR HEADS AND SHOUT: IT'S GONNA BE A GREAT DAY!" sang Harold Ronk. The finale, which anticipated the presidential election that year, filled the air with a rare kind of cool patriotic fervor, and it took the crowd by surprise. The entire company assembled on the track in an arm-waving salute to children of all ages. In thundered eighteen elephants, down the hippodrome, around the far corner to the other side, and up on their hind legs in a massive, screeching long mount. Many souls in the audience, who had started their mad rush for the exit portals, were so taken by the simple emotion of the number that they paused for a few moments to offer a standing ovation. It was a fitting climax to John's producing reign, for that 1968 opus of Ringling Bros. and Barnum & Bailey Circus was technically to be his last.

He left the big top on a high and glorious note—not without controversy, either—just as he had entered it back in 1938 when, with a handful of Charles Le Maire costume sketches, he and brother Henry set out to redress the grand opening pageant and make the whole show "swing out." The enchanting "Winter Wonderland," presented thirty years later, was one logical extension of the evolutionary artistic process he had helped set in motion. And it once again proved that, when it came to producing the American three-ring circus, nobody did it better than Uncle John's pet boy.

Incentives to Sell

When the enchantment ends, we move back into the cold night air, back through the menacing shadows of urban decay and unrest that surround many modern arenas. We hurry past flickering neons, past battered store-fronts and all-night liquor outlets, past lifeless strangers piled up against barred windows and at bus stops. We cross intersections against blaring, angry motorists, onto crowded freeways, into the mad stream of civilization rushing forward into an Orwellian nightmare, the music of the last circus parade growing ever more faint in our ears. It was only a dream. . . .

It should never end, we think. Not ever. And the wizards who make the magic should never stop plying their craft. Not ever. Not the jugglers or tumblers, not the buffoons. Not the maestro up on the bandstand or the ringmaster resplendent in red. Not the man who produced it all. Not ever. Only we overlook how similar these people are to us, hounded by the same hopes and fears, cringing as we do to the world beyond the fantasy, to the mean streets that lay laughingly, tauntingly at its spangled edge. In the middle of the 1960s, as a growing number of the populace took to the streets to protest an array of social and political injustices, the relatively innocent world of the circus seemed ever more anachronistic. Midway during a fourteen-day Los Angeles run in 1965, the Big Show was forced to cancel six weekend performances at the Sports Arena in the wake of race riots, which cost it an estimated $200,000 in lost revenue. Touring through urban America became fraught with apprehension. One can only speculate how the worsening social situation hastened John's desire to sell the show eventually. The North brothers had lived abroad for years. In fact, neither one had ever owned a home of his own in this country.

Probably the most difficult question that every famous person faces is when to take the last bow and let the final curtain fall on creativity. In the circus world, more producers than not tend to go on for as many years as they can. Louis Stern, who ran Polack Bros. Circus for decades (in its heyday, one of the finest in America), doled out thousands of dollars of his own money in the last years to keep the show on the road, at an annual loss, so that he could continue sitting at its edge to enjoy the magic and power he had grown accustomed to. None of the Ringling brothers walked away from the big top to retire before his death. John Ringling died while up in New York struggling to finance his way back into the picture. James A. Bailey succumbed to mortality during a brief illness caused by a simple bee sting when he was in his prime operating Barnum and Bailey.

From most accounts, John North was ambivalent about when to let go. One of the most puzzling things he ever did was to have printed in the 1967 circus program magazine a picture of his brother, his nephew John Ringling North II, and his grandnephew John Ringling North III, accompanied by a message he signed intimating that his two namesakes were being trained to take over management of the show: "P. T. Barnum launched his first railroad show and coined our enduring title in 1871—my Ringling uncles embarked on their tinsel and tanbark career in 1884—my first summer with the Circus was that of 1915. It is now time I believe to start looking towards a couple of newer generations represented in the accompanying photo."[1]

So, for a fleeting moment in time, attention was focused on a possible new North heir to the throne. "I felt very good, and had hopes of rejoining the show," says John North II, referring to the photo. In his youth, he had been given strong signals that a life in the circus was his for the asking. "I was encouraged by both of them (father and uncle), and I spent a lot of time with the show when I was growing up. I was always told that I would run the circus until I got married in 1961. When I got married, my father and uncle decided the circus was no place for a married man. My father offered me the job of running their cattle ranch in Ireland, where I still am."[2]

John II admits, however, to never having been seriously trained to take over in Uncle John's footsteps, even though the idea was romantically advanced by Henry North to the *New Yorker* in 1965: "My son can't wait to get to work with the circus, his first love. My big brother and I always knew that someday we'd be running the circus, just as my son knows that he'll be continuing the circus."[3] But outside his press agentry, Henry had little feeling for the new order of things and was probably content to see his son grounded in a more practical profession. "The circus as I knew it doesn't exist anymore," said Henry in later years. "It's just another type of production. It isn't the unique thing that it was, that made it the greatest show on earth, that thrilled everybody in America. No, not as exciting as a hot summer's day in Nebraska under the old six-pole big top with the sun beating down on 16,000 people. . . . Those were the good old days."[4]

Aside from the Norths, there were no strong candidates among the other Ringling heirs to run the show. James Ringling, one of Robert Ringling's two sons, had demonstrated real interest over the years. He was continuously around the lot, at one time assisting lot superintendent Lloyd Morgan, later serving as vice-president and mostly filling up space. Art Concello does not feel that James had the right stuff. Beset by drinking problems, he drifted into bitter alienation from the family, while his brother, Charles ("Choppy"), overcame similar addictions. Choppy and his wife, Sarah, a Sarasota girl, headed for Texas, where they bought up condemned property and renovated old buildings into low-cost rental units.

There was Stuart Lancaster, whose failed mismanagement suit against the Norths left him clearly outside John's favor and deprived him of whatever viable training he might otherwise have received had he wished to fill an executive post. Lancaster, whose built-in grin suggests charming vulnerability, returned to the theater, then went west out to Hollywood, there finding sporadic satisfaction in local legit productions and television soaps. One of his more noted recent roles, according to a fellow actor, his current wife, was a swaggering bum on "General Hospital."[5]

Except for James and Stuart, none of the other Ringling descendants has made much noise about establishing careers within the industry that bears the family name. Many receive annual payments from the four trusts designated by the late Edith Ringling for Robert's two sons, James and Choppy, and Hester's two, Stuart and Charles, and their offspring. A son of Stuart, Michael Dean, has expressed interest in the circus along literary lines. David, the son of Charles and Alice Lancaster, runs his own wood shop in Canada. His sister, Joanna, lives in Boston and is a writer. Among the other various younger family members there are hairdressers and actors and beatniks. The one thing they all seem to have in common (Michael Dean excepted) is that none is interested in the circus.[6]

These Ringlings may suffer from a collective sense of unease over the source of their legacies. Stuart Lancaster feels little family unity over anything: "I think there were no other Ringlings who were interested or cared (in running the show). I guess it's such a mammoth thing that most people were afraid of it. They didn't really want to get involved . . . to go through all that shit. It's just a disintegrated family. I mean, there are Ringlings all over, in Montana someplace, a town out there somewhere called Ringling. . . . Relatives I've never heard of, don't know where they came from. Patricia Ringling. I have no idea who she is. They send out annual reports of the estate. I see all these lists of names and I don't know who half of them are. It wasn't a very close family and I think it was the circus that did it, because everybody was suspicious of everybody else."[7]

(Short of a Kissinger or Carter being called in, the Ringling family wars seem almost permanently unresolvable. Another feud that would rage on, as late as 1990, concerned whether or not to bury the bodies of John and Mable Ringling and Ida North on the Ringling museum grounds. That's what John Ringling had wanted for himself, argued Henry North in opposition to a couple of his bickering relatives, who didn't want Ida North [mother of John and Henry] buried there also, contending she had nothing to do with the circus. Well, neither did Mable Ringling, for that matter. The museum board of trustees voted to allow the burials, provided the family differences could be worked out. In litigation, of course, a ruling in Henry's favor by a Sarasota circuit court judge was later upheld by the Second District Court of Appeals.[8] And in June 1991 all three bodies were finally put to rest on the museum grounds.)

John North had little feeling for these relatives of his. Some say that his strongest incentive for selling was to be free once and for all of the never-ending feuds with them. "Even when John had fifty-one percent," points out Rudy Bundy, "everyone would bring in their special lawyers and go up there to the board meetings in New York. I think that John and Dan Gordon Judge would have everything pretty well set up before we went in for the meeting. And then we had to sit there and watch the rest of the relatives bring in their attorneys and take up time talking."[9]

Retirement was another incentive. Now in his early sixties, John could more than justify bringing his career to an end. He had guided the circus through more turbulent chapters in big-top history than probably any other showman had ever done with any other circus. And it was back on top of the heap, entertaining millions of Americans annually and turning a brisk profit.

He had all the wealth he needed. He had a comfortable life in Europe and a reputation abroad that his foreign neighbors respected and catered to. And he had Ida, in whose beautiful presence he derived a deeper, abiding satisfaction. He often told her, "What would I do if I didn't have you?" And before retiring each night, he nearly always uttered the words, "Ida, I love you."[10]

John's personal life became decidedly more important to him than his circus back across the ocean. His latest burst of showmanship may have been calculated to inflate the show's value for selling purposes, the program magazine message about a new generation of Ringlings running it just another ploy to manipulate larger offers. While John was rebuilding the show, he became an Irish citizen. Were he to sell the circus, he could thus avoid having to pay tax on money earned outside its borders.

The urge to sell had taunted him for years, as far back as 1956 following his closing of the tent show, when he met with Bill Veeck over a possible sale. There were the sessions with Mike Todd and with Jerry Collins, who owned a half-interest in the Clyde Beatty–Cole Bros. Circus and who made overtures for a piece of the Ringling pie. The upward turnaround in the fortunes of the circus in the mid-1960s, combined with renewed critical enthusiasm, brought it back into the buyers' spotlight. At least four or five would-be owners came forward with offers. Most prominently mentioned was a conglomerate consisting of ABC Television and Madison Square Garden, which had recently acquired a majority interest in Morris Chalfen's Holiday on Ice for $1.25 million. Chalfen had earlier tried to purchase the Ringling show, and the ABC–Madison Square Garden group now coveted it, too. Garden President Irving Felt flew to Switzerland in July 1965 to begin talks with John. Ned Irish, another Garden official, later announced that the chance of a sale was "quite remote."

Irish also expressed surprise at the ten-million-dollar price tag John was dangling about. The forty-niners, who had first indicated a willingness to relinquish their stock for a modest two million dollars, now upped the asking price to match North's per-share quote. (The amount he wanted would presumably be divided, he getting his 51 percent, the forty-niners their 49 percent.) The talks went nowhere fast. John was only testing the waters. He told Rudy at one point, "Run the circus as if we're never going to sell it."[11] John was so erratic by nature that he could flip-flop from one alternative to its opposite within seconds.

Then came a flurry of talks with possible buyers, the most persuasive and persistent of whom was Irvin Feld, who, with his brother Israel, had been promoting a portion of the Ringling indoor dates since the 1957 conversion. Irvin was obsessed with the idea of running the circus and turning himself into a publicly perceived show-business giant. The Feld brothers operated the federally owned Carter Barron Amphitheater in Washington, D.C., and ran record outlets in a chain of drugstores. They managed Paul Anka on his initial rise to fame and promoted concert tours for a number of popular singers. They were among the early instigators of payola (offering cash to disc jockeys in return for playing their records), a practice subsequently outlawed.

Feld first approached John in partnership with Broadway producers Feur and Martin. Supposedly a deal was struck, and at one point another Broadway scion, James Nederlander, tried to get involved, too. The agreement apparently fell through because the Felds parted company with Feur and Martin, then returned with a new associate, the super-rich Texan Judge Roy Hofheinz, who built and operated the thirty-eight million dollar Astrodome in which the Houston Astros, another of his pet properties, played. He had enough money to buy all the elephants in the world.

A politician by nature, Irvin Feld buttered up to John North and scored a bundle of brownie points by helping him land an album of his favorite compositions on the RCA label. Arranged by Joe Sherman in the then-popular Tijuana sound and titled "Circus Brass," its release in 1967 coincided with the feverish talks then under way between John and Irvin over a sale. Irvin's role in the album enabled him to connect with John on a personal level. A blurb about the record in the circus magazine says it all:

> During the period when "Circus Brass" was being prepared, Mr. Sherman worked closely with Mr. Feld, who has been associated with the Ringling organization for many years. As a matter of fact, Mr. Feld's promotion company Super Shows, Inc., has been presenting the Ringling Bros. and Barnum & Bailey Circus since 1957 in many of its key city engagements. Just a few weeks before the album was released, Mr. Feld and Mr. Sherman had the pleasure of taking the first record pressed to Mr. North's Zurich, Switzerland headquarters where they played it and received his commendation.[12]

The gesture marked a turning point for the ambitious Irvin Feld. As for the LP, it is a professional effort that at least proved John could compose likable melodies. Most of them, like elevator music, are pleasant to hear, easy to forget once the turntable clicks off. "Dreamland" is the best number, a lovely little tune deserving of wider recognition. The only thing amateur about the record was the jacket copy written by Ringling's national press representative, Bill Doll. Among the errors Doll propounded is the listing of Otto Ringling as the father of the founding brothers. Fact is, the album couldn't begin to compete in sales with the superior London Phase 4 "Circus Spectacular," featuring the music of Merle Evans, released the same year.

"Circus Brass" gave John a sense of self-pride on the musical front and Irvin Feld a door to his heart. An offer was placed on the table. The Felds and Hofheinz, in a partnership as the Hoffeld Corporation, incorporated in Delaware, proposed buying the circus for $8,000,000 in cash, $1,000,000 to be advanced immediately as down payment. Hofheinz pledged $7,500,000 million, the Felds $500,000. John, with his 510 shares of stock, would receive $4,080,000; the Edith Ringling estate, holding 315 shares, $2,520,000; the Robert Ringling estate, with 175 shares, $1,400,000. In addition, John would collect an annual salary of $75,000 for life, Henry $20,000 as long as he stayed on as a vice-president.[13]

In the last moments of decision making, John vacillated as usual, once warning Irvin in a transatlantic call, "Even if you raise the money and come over here, my writing hand is liable not to work."[14] By then, though, he had rationalized away most of his reservations. Henry feels that he and John had gone the distance:

> Our relations were not active in the management of the circus, and never had been adequately, at least in my opinion, and they were never satisfied with the way my brother and I operated it. No matter what we did, it was always the subject of criticism and we had this constant, constant bickering. There was a lack of harmony, and it just became a little too much to suffer indefinitely. And it seemed to us as we were getting older that we'd done the best we could with our profession, that it wasn't worth more aggravation. When you get old, you have to retire sometime anyhow. You can't go on forever. You're not up to it. It's better for younger hands and minds to take it over. So when somebody came along with a good price, we were glad to get out.[15]

Ida, as close to John as anybody, also believes that his biggest worries about running the circus, and the main reason he sold it, were "the 49% shareholders—the never ending quarrels with the Ringling family." She states, "He loved it very much, but he saw that it was not possible to go on, because he had a lot of troubles with the family . . . that he was thinking he was not that young to go on."[16]

John settled for $2 million less than his original asking price. Moreover, the new owners inherited a $2.5 million cash reserve in a Swiss bank, an enormous rebate of sorts that deflated the actual sale value even further. Before he agreed to sign anything, John called up Art Concello across the ocean. "Come over here to Zurich." Art took the next plane out and faced his former boss in a questioning spirit.

"What do you think?" asked John, his face a little taut.

"Good," replied Art.

John looked surprised. "You think I ought to?"

"Do what you want. Don't forget my ten percent."

John was ready to cross that bridge. (Concello's cut was a part of the agreement he had made with North when he had been hired back into management in 1956.) "I want to buy your ten percent now," announced John.

"Okay."

Art believed that John was afraid his (Art's) lawyers might botch up the sale, good reason, then, to remove him from the picture before finalizing any deal with Hofheinz and Feld. He also got the distinct feeling that John might be hoping he would try dissuading him from the sale by offering to run the circus again.[17] Rather unlikely in that John did not seek out Concello in times of prosperity. Probably in Art's presence, though, John felt the pangs of nostalgia and a natural feeling of regret. They had shared so much together. Concello did not offer resistance.

Irvin Feld, standing in the wings, was anxious and ready to go on. One of John's last significant talent finds, the ambitious promoter evidenced the spark of showmanship and a sincere, heartfelt commitment to the Ringling cause. In making known his decision to sell, John told the press his long-standing relations with the Felds and Hofheinz had convinced him of their "concern and dedication to maintain the concept, traditions and artistic standards inherent in the world famous title, the Greatest Show on Earth." The momentous transfer of big-top power was enacted, appropriately, near the ancient ruins of the Circus Maximus, photographically perfect and well covered.

"John Ringling North, who was regarded as an emperor in the circus world," reported *Variety*, "followed history in concluding the sale. With circusy showmanship he closed the deal in the Colosseum, Rome, where the world's greatest spectaculars were staged for the old Roman emperors."[18]

Photographers and flacks—and an unruly lion—tagged along for the historic contract-signing session. Hofheinz had an arm around Israel, Irvin an arm around John, who smiled with a quiet dignity. The others were noticeably more ebullient. In the background, the lion, restrained by an attendant's leash, looked upon the papers spread over a semicrumbled rock-stone formation of the ancient stadium. On November 11, 1967, Ringling Bros. and Barnum & Bailey left family hands. It had been eighty-three years since the five original Ringling brothers presented their first circus under a small six-hundred-seat tent in Baraboo, Wisconsin. The departure of their nephew, John North, from the show world was met by a rather mum reaction. Nobody expressed particular regret to the trades. That John stayed on as producer, reportedly at the request of the new owners, focused attention away—for the time being, at least—from a far more dramatic transition about to take place.

Irvin Feld was prepared to wage his own campaign for immortality, too. And therein lay the seeds for yet another curious attack on John's beleaguered legacy. His chances for a high place in history grew dimmer with each passing chapter.

Lost in the Press Kit

Among the many parallels between the lives of John and his Uncle John, one of the most striking is that both ended up outside the circus and powerless over its future, John Ringling by default, the nephew by design. And both were in a sense betrayed by so-called friendly associates, John Ringling by Sam Gumpertz, who took over the operation of the circus, John North by Irvin Feld, who did a lot to undermine John's legacy with numerous self-serving fabrications. Both Johns were detached from the mainstream of society and caught up in their own eccentric lifestyles. Neither was much loved by the fans. Neither still is.

After the Felds, in concert with Judge Roy Hofheinz, consummated the eight million dollar purchase of Ringling-Barnum, John was asked to continue producing and things were deceptively pro-North at the outset. In fact, a lot of deception had been perpetrated by both sides, as there would continue to be for many years. Soon after the sale, Cy Feuer and Ernie Martin, two leading legit producers, filed a five million dollar suit against the circus, alleging that a joint-purchase agreement between themselves, the Felds, and North had been violated. Feuer and Martin also claimed to have signed a five-year lease agreement with Madison Square Garden, to begin in 1968, another deal allegedly reneged on. Irvin and Israel Feld, they contended, breached the understanding by subsequently combining with Hofheinz to acquire the circus.[1]

(In 1971, the Hofheinz–Feld brothers trio sold the show to Mattel, Inc. for stock valued at an astounding forty-seven million dollars. The deal was later challenged by Ringling stockholders, who filed a forty million dollar suit against the Los Angeles toy company for fraudulently overstating its stock value at the time of purchase. A court settlement ruled in the plaintiffs' favor, awarding them damages of thirty million dollars. Feld bought the show back in 1982 from Mattel, its toy business then in a tailspin, beaming to the press, "The good Lord never meant for the circus to be owned by a big corporation.")[2]

John went from Feld's employer to Feld's employee, and without much difficulty. Of course, the 1968 edition was by then formulated, the acts selected and signed, the production numbers set. A comment by Henry to *Amusement Business* lent credence to a status quo scenario: "Nothing is changed except the ownership. As vice president I will be remaining on the show, and my brother continues as producer. There's nothing unusual about people selling their interests and then remaining in association."[3] He made reference to three American ice shows which had undergone similar changes in ownership the past five years.

Feld retained North's entire production staff, headed by stager-director Richard Barstow, and many of them—Barstow, Bob Dover, Harold Ronk, Antoinette Concello, and Trolle Rhodin—stayed on for some years. Merle Evans, for reasons never fully explained (although probably because Irvin Feld tried meddling in his work), called it quits following the 1969 tour.

The show that year was basically another John Ringling North circus. He was again given sole producing credit. If it was a token gesture, it was fairly deserved, for John's key people created and directed the show and it is hard to imagine its looking or sounding much different even if John were still the owner. Max Weldy, who had been around thirty-one years, spent his final season helping Barstow, Evans, and Ronk put over a host of talented new acts. A fair portion of them, as was now the case, came from Iron Curtain countries. The best of the bunch included the comically endearing high-wire walker Pio Nock; from Harlem the unicycle-riding basketball cutups, the King Charles Troupe; sway-pole comedian the Great Fattini; Rudy Lenz's Chimps; more wonderful teeterboard antics from two new troupes, the Nine Slavovi and the Nine Kovachevi; and the most memorable of all, surely one of the most glamorous and captivating personalities ever to rule a circus ring, Gunther Gebel-Williams.

John had been after Gebel-Williams for some time, unwilling to pay the youthful animal trainer the fee he wanted. It took a different, more persuasive tact, which Irvin Feld brought off with Barnumesque bravado, to land the superstar. Feld booked not only Gebel-Williams, but the entire Circus Williams of which he was a family fixture, including eighteen elephants, seventy-five horses, and fourteen tigers. He built a second touring unit of Ringling around it.

The production format was adhered to without notable change. Antoinette Concello and aerial-rigging innovator Andre Prince once again teamed up to produce another fetching airborne extravaganza, "Garden in the Sky." Gebel-Williams was featured in the elephant bash, "Safari!" The finale was "Be a Clown," the main spec " 'Twas the Night Before Tomorrow." The latter suffered from an overdose of orange-winged costumes passing in solemn procession—another Max Weldy creation not destined for any awards. Dick Barstow, while cursing the unrelieved color scheme, boasts that he brought off a circus first by sending the first clown to the moon, the moon being manufactured in a Sarasota prop shop. In sum, the 1969 program was another very fine one indeed, electrified by the magnetic aura of Gunther Gebel-Williams making his American debut. Each of his several appearances throughout the show was given generous ovations. He was Feld's stunning coup, a source of enormous prestige and publicity for the circus for a good decade.

Quite understandably, John could acknowledge producing credit (even if he hadn't exactly signed Williams), for it was the kind of a show he had fostered all along. No doubt some of the other new acts it contained were some he had already expressed an interest in signing. And after all, he had been retained by the new owners as producer. In his travels during that time, he graciously presented himself in that role, although he preferred recounting the usual charming anecdotes about his world-famous friends. There was the deposed King Farouk, to whom he once sent boxes of cigars annually from Cuba; Prince Rainier III, who visited with John in Sarasota and stayed up until three in the morning playing drums at the M'Toto Room before flying out to Hollywood to reveal his engagement to Grace Kelly. Such were the tales enumerated by North when interviewed by *San Francisco Chronicle* society columnist Albert Morch during two sessions, the first one beginning at midnight at Trader Vic's, the final one concluding the next afternoon at the Hilton over a bottle of Taittinger '61 *blanc de blancs*, John's favorite champagne. He made only passing reference to the circus while dropping name after name, telling stories he had probably told many times before. Some others:

> Nothing compares with the masked ball given in Venice by Don Carlos Beistegui in 1951 at his palazzo on the Grand Canal. It was a spectacle of

dazzling costumes and elegant people—Barbara Hutton, the Aga Khan and the Baroness Guy de Rothschild, among them.[4]

I gave a party for Lucius Beebe and late in the evening we all went down to Madison Square Garden where the circus was playing. There was a pettable tiger named Lady. Lucius scratched Lady's head, but when I looked around he was in the next tiger's cage slapping it. That particular cat was vicious and had seriously mauled several trainers. Nothing happened to Lucius. Perhaps there is something special about bon vivants? It was the same night that Lucius, as we were cabbing homeward, suddenly whipped out two .45-caliber revolvers and fired at Horace Greeley's statue in Gramercy Park.

John went on like a man of the world who had not a care in the world. How long did he figure he would be producing the circus he sold (or getting credit for it)? He had to suspect that Irvin Feld, younger by eighteen years, would eventually want to run things his own way. It wasn't long. By 1969, Irvin began staking out his own claim to the tanbark throne. He contributed a guest piece to *Variety*'s annual anniversary issue, in which he proudly recounted a telephone call he received the previous summer in a Berlin hotel room while scouting acts for the show. "Mr. Feld? My name is Gunther Gebel-Williams. I hear you've been trying to find me."[5]

Somewhere along the way, though—very soon, indeed—Feld became so obsessed with power and fame that his own real achievements weren't enough to satisfy his ego. He went about creating a mythical past in which the Ringling circus, struggling, inferior, and going broke, needed a savior and he came along. His obvious misrepresentations included his having "managed" the circus since the mid-1950s and "decreeing" that it go indoors. All of his erroneous statements (such as the number of performers then as compared to now) were evidently advanced to make his showmanship look superior. And as much as Feld maligned by implication what North had done, in actuality he honored it with the sincerest form of flattery: imitation of the format. Feld proved to be a master of the ballyhoo, and he worked the media with cunning effectiveness. His press kit became quoted without question, not just by journalists, but by trade journals.

All of this took its toll, of course, on John North's tarnished legacy, by this time a faint echo of a long-forgotten era. The Irvin Feld disinformation campaign nailed the coffin shut. In 1984, when *Variety*—a show publication that should have known better—did a big spread on the one hundredth anniversary of Ringling Bros. Circus, a lead story by Joseph Cohen surveying its entire history did not once mention John's name or any of his contributions.[6]

Neither of the North brothers ever appeared very bothered by the Feld press campaign. "Feld was a newcomer on the scene without any circus background," said Henry, "so through publicity and his own efforts, you can't blame him for wanting to create a circus image for himself. And I think he's a very good promoting circus man. He's put on beautiful productions. He took the organization that we sold him and has more or less kept it intact and made some changes, but it's still a damn good show. I enjoy seeing it every year."[7] And John made no apparent efforts to defend his own history. He didn't even bang his head against a wall in the company of close friends. About the strongest thing Rudy Bundy can recall his ever saying on the subject was, "Oh, who cares? Let them do what they please." On another occasion he casually remarked, "The only problem with Irvin Feld is he doesn't tell the truth."[8] For this book, he expressed himself with a question: "Feld says he built up the circus. But if the circus had run down, why was it worth $10 million, with $2.5 million in cash reserve?"[9] That's all he had to say, and with little trace of irritation.

John was enjoying his "mellow years," in Henry's words. He sank most of his profits from the sale into five and a half tons of gold bars at the low price of $35 an ounce. He watched it leap to more than $820 an ounce in a matter of years and made a killing. How did he know that was as high as it would go, his nephew, John, asked him. "I don't know, but I knew." He also raked in millions more from the sale of his Sarasota real-estate holdings to the Arvida Corporation. Oddly enough, John still seemed much more concerned with Irvin Feld's managerial success than with the undermining of his legacy by the Feld press agents. "I hope the circus is doing well," he said, "because Henry and I have salaries for a lifetime."[10]

In retirement, North pursued basically the same amusement agenda that he had for years. Each summer, on the last Saturday in June, he took in the Irish Derby, where over the years he had won more than he had lost. A racing fan since childhood, he would spend several days visiting his nephew, John Ringling North II, at Northbrook, where the latter operated a cattle ranch. John charmed his nephew with the amusing stories—many of famous people—that he had told to numerous friends through the years. "I totally adored my uncle," says the younger John. "I loved his sense of humor. He was tremendous fun to be with." The nephew never could understand his uncle's well-known resistance to going to bed. "I don't know why, but he hated it."[11]

However nocturnal John may have been, he maintained excellent health until the last few years of his life. While staying at Northbrook, he walked into town and back—seven miles each way—every day. He took the walk all dressed up in the attire his nephew recalls him almost always wearing: blue shirt, blue tie, and blue suit. Tagging along was North's chauffeur in the car, an umbrella on board just in case the boss got caught in rainy weather. Around John's stomach was a lead belt, part of a weight-reducing ritual he observed.

In the evening, John took his nephew and his nephew's wife to dinner and kept them up until early the next morning. He loved to talk about horse racing, and he reminisced about the Kentucky Derbies he had played in days gone by. He became animated in describing to his nephew the jobs he had held with the circus, first as a young boy, then later as a young man. He went on about the fun he had selling real estate for his Uncle John Ringling. He spoke now and then of some of the great circus stars he had admired. He mentioned Harold Alzana many times. He talked about how marvelous he thought Gunther Gebel-Williams was, admitting he had never been able to hire the gifted animal trainer because he wouldn't pay Williams the money he wanted.

In his nephew's presence, John revealed a sense of pride in the production numbers for the circus that he had helped to introduce and evolve. He was also proud of the original tunes he wrote for many of them. When anyone expressed the slightest interest in hearing them, John would happily hum his melodies or play them on a piano. Rarely did he remember the words that had been supplied by his lyricists. With each passing drink, his mood lightened and another festive evening of drinks, witty chatter, and music claimed his eternally gregarious spirit. Remembers John II: "He'd get up there and tap-dance if you asked him."

North teeter-tottered eccentrically from generous soul to dedicated tightwad. Indeed, his nephew observed that the richer he became (his gold investment eventually shot up to nearly ninety-three million dollars in value), the harder he tried to keep from spending anything. For economical reasons, North used Aqua Filters—a throwaway cigarette holder designed to last a pack. John doubled the filter's life by cleaning it out with a straight pin he carried in his lapel. And the beautiful gold tie pin he appeared to be wearing with his name engraved upon it was always upside down. "Why?" asked the nephew one day. Answered the uncle: actually, he had lost his real tie pin and it would be far too costly to replace, so he was now using his money clip.

He could be the perfect giver, too. When his Uncle John Ringling's old valet, Manny Wolf, fell on hard times, he gave him five thousand dollars. Frequently, he sent friends who had invited him to dinner two magnums of Dom Perignon. Once he accompanied John II to a department store in Dublin, where the latter intended to buy a suit. After viewing the basic selection, North inquired who the best tailor in the city was. He took his nephew to the gentlemen and paid for three suits to be custom made. Whenever the two went dining, John would ask for the wine list. Reviewing it carefully, he expounded with great knowledge on the best wines and vintages offered, then concluded predictably, "But the house wine is very good and much cheaper. We'll have that." After the meal he tipped the waiter with extreme generosity, and John II was sent to the bar to get the best bottle of brandy in the house.

North had no interest whatsoever in the beef-cattle operation at Northbrook, though Henry never gave up trying to get him more involved. Once when John was due for another visit, Henry called ahead from Switzerland and asked John II to show his uncle all the stock. When John arrived, he was given the message and reacted to it indifferently. The nephew gave it no further thought. A couple of days hence, John emerged from the house, immaculately dressed as usual, and said, "All right, Johnny, let's go!" "Go where?" asked John II. "To see the stock." They spent the ensuing few hours bouncing over the rugged terrain in a jeep. When they had finally taken in everything there was to see, John sighed, "Thank God! Well, that ought to make my little brother happy."[12]

One summer, North stayed about two weeks at Northbrook while he tried, in vain, to remaster what minimal driving skills he possessed and get an Irish license. (He subsequently renewed his Florida license, which he had accidentally allowed to expire.) After keeping an Irish inspector on the edge of the passenger seat for the course of the test, North watched while the man checked off a number of items on the evaluation form, assuming each item checked represented a passing grade. When John was tersely informed that he had failed, he asked, "What part, sir?" Answered his evaluator, "Every part."

The vivacious Dody Heath was sometimes John's guest when he took in the Irish Derby. Their quirky on-again, off-again relationship had somehow survived the years. When the two had resumed seeing each other in 1965, John was so determined to win back Dody, then married, that he pursued her "platonically." She eventually divorced her first husband, and by 1972, when John, according to Heath, was on the verge of making a settlement with Ida to leave her and marry Dody, a cruel twist of fate shattered his faith in their matrimonial prospects. A very risqué note addressed to Heath in care of the American Express office in London mysteriously ended up in John's Zurich mailbox. He was outraged. The couple didn't speak to each other for another couple of years. Then in 1974, John now seventy-one years old, he and Dody managed to hook up for a third go at it. By now the relationship, as described by Heath, had mellowed into "a profound friendship." She was then a struggling theatrical producer in London, and when the British Home Office threatened to have her deported for lack of a permanent residence and sufficient income, she reached out to John for help. He complied very nicely by arranging for her to purchase a flat in London. He also established a special trust fund that guaranteed her monthly payments. This met the requirements of the Home Office.

Certainly, by Heath's account, John was a very generous and loving friend to have helped her out as he did without having placed any amorous demands on his sustaining monetary support. And in the eyes of those who observed them together, the couple had sustained a healthy, vibrant friendship. By the late 1970s, however, when John was now under a doctor's orders to get plenty of conventional rest, he no longer stayed up around the clock. Dody remembers his visiting her in London and the two being seated and waiting—sometimes alone—in a restaurant at 6:30 P.M. In sad contrast to North's late-night revelries of yore, after an early dinner he delivered Dody back to her doorstep and was on his way by ten o'clock. The last time Heath can remember seeing John was in 1981, four years before he died. (She is now married to international film financier Richard Soames.) He did continue writing her his philosophically reaching notes, at one point asking her for her opinion of the hereafter. Did Dody agree with Ida that he would, indeed, endure through time and eternity?[13]

There was something oddly unreal about John's life: he had through the years become so rich and had spent so much time pampering himself on a perpetual vacation. There are no social or political causes he is known to have supported. And although he was hardly philanthropic, North had turned over to various charities the proceeds of several lavish New York openings. In one of the many wills he wrote out, he bequeathed all his money to the Union Bank of Switzerland to be used to help poor people everywhere.

As he grew older, he seemed to struggle inwardly with his own conflicting values. No wonder, as he saw the sun beginning to set on his life, that he spent so many evenings, according to what he told his nephew, tinkering over his will. "Great! I have all these codicils," spoke John with devilish glee. "And I scratch people out, then I write things in. I have a lot of fun." The nephew was warned not to expect a penny. "Look, I like you, Johnny," North once told him, "but I'm not going to leave you a thing, because you're an American citizen. I don't want those bastards getting any of my money."[14]

About every other year, John (who hated to fly) would, partly at his brother's coaxing, make the flight to the States. He reported to the Mayo Clinic in Rochester, Minnesota, for a physical exam, and sometimes he and Henry caught a performance of the circus during its Chicago stand. Usually John would spend a week or so in Sarasota, where he fondly renewed old acquaintances. He stayed up with Rudy Bundy at his house drinking and reminiscing about the old times. The Bundys once added Chita Cristiani and her husband to the dinner table. Chita remembers John's warm, if subtle, references to romantic times of yore. "Those were the days, my friend," he sighed.[15]

John, of course, rarely let a trip to Sarasota go by without looking up Art Concello. He once bunked in Concello's private railcar, humbly insisting on making his own bed, and at other times stayed in Art's guest house. The two sat up half the night drinking. Between sips and between the long silences rife with meaning, they would exchange a few words and allow a shared memory to embrace them with a bond they would never openly admit to.

"You need anything, Art?"

"Nope."

"I got all this money."

"That's good, John."

"You're the only son of a bitch that loaned me money when nobody else would."

Art struggled to accept the compliment, John to make it real.

"And I appreciated it!"

Art took another sip. "Well, damn it all, you needed the money!"

John thought about it more than Art did.

"You need a hundred thousand, two hundred thousand?"

"I'm all right, Johnny."[16]

Rudy Bundy, John's easygoing friend, would drive him down to the Miami airport when Henry stayed behind for extended Stateside travel.

On the other side of the ocean, John retreated deeper into the relationship from which he drew the most comfort and satisfaction. "He always went back to Ida," as John II points out, and as others have invariably agreed. "The best gal I ever knew," John's comment about Ida, is what Rudy Bundy remembers most in discussing the relationship's meaning to John. Except for his annual reunions with Dody Heath in the United Kingdom, John was always with Ida. They entertained Rudy Bundy and his wife, Katie, many times on the Continent when Bundy was over on business, or there simply on John's invitation to visit. The last time John II saw his uncle was in Switzerland when he had dinner with him and Ida. When it came time for the tab to be picked up, Ida reached deep into her purse and paid the bill in cash. John found it quaintly amusing. "Oh, that's very kind of you to take us all out to dinner, Ida." And they laughed.[17]

He had told his nephew several times, the first shortly after he sold the circus, that the only reason he did so was to be free once and for all of the feuding with his relatives. He told John II that if he had been able to buy the minority stockholders out, he never would have given up ownership. John strayed from his retirement resolve at least once, in the mid-1970s, after seeing the show in Chicago with Rudy Bundy and telling him afterward, "We've got to get this thing back." Rudy sat in on informal meetings (Art Concello was there, too). John supposedly had the money from an Englishman who wanted to see the Ringling circus run by Ringlings again. John's buying zeal vanished, however, when he learned of the show's massive indebtedness to the foundering Circus World theme park in Florida, which Irvin Feld had built in the shadows of Disney World.[18] John never made another such attempt to reclaim the circus he once ruled, although Ida is of the opinion that he never fully accepted his separation from it. "He never said it, but I am sure that he regretted it. . . . I can say one hundred percent that he missed it a lot." Chita Cristiani vividly recalls that his "great dream" was to operate the show once more.

The dream was all that John needed, for he lacked the resolve. Had he really wanted to get the circus back, in Henry's estimation he would have done it. And think what he might, in the mid-1970s the Greatest Show on Earth was as aggressively promoted as it ever had been, with Gunther Gebel-Williams at the dazzling forefront of a glamorous and modern Ringling ballyhoo that captured the American public's fancy. From a purely business point of view, the show was far from needing to be rescued or saved.

Ironically, the younger man to whom John had sold it passed away during his lifetime. Irvin Feld's death in September 1984 came at a time when his brightest ideas had already worn stale through repetition and the crowds were dwindling year by year. No circus owner has yet conquered the elusive fluctuations of public taste and patronage. Still, Feld had constructed a remarkable legacy for himself out of one of the most thoroughly effective press kits ever put together. The epitaphs given Feld, rooted partly in the fictions therefrom, were extensive and filled with praise. The *New York Times* eulogized him as "the man who saved the circus," declaring that when he took it over in 1967, "the greatest show on earth it wasn't . . . not with its animals, not with its daredevils, not with its clowns."[19] *Variety* awarded Feld equal honors with front-page coverage.[20] In the end, how ironic that another man took the glory for folding the tents in Pittsburgh and putting the show indoors. Glory? John, the man who actually made the decision, took mostly blame and resentment for it. John's downfall was Irvin's triumph.

Had the obit writers any adjectives left for North when it came his turn to head for The Big Lot? Maybe his Uncle John was waiting up there to compare notes and have a good laugh over life's baffling vicissitudes, about as reliable as a circus press kit.

A Graceful Exit

All we can do is wait until tomorrow and
see if we're remembered.
　　　　　　　　　—Tennessee Williams

How will John Ringling North be remembered fifty years from now, one
hundred years from now? Producers of entertainment all ultimately
distinguish—or discredit—themselves by what they bring before the public and by their success in generating patronage and critical acceptance.
They are the middle people who bridge audience and artist, the promoting facilitators of an event. They discover talent wherever it is to be found,
set up the forum for its presentation, and take the necessary steps to gather
a crowd.

In the sense of what a producer does, he most reveals himself through
his tastes and preferences. This is how we get to know what he is about.
In the most human way, he says, "Come share with me my love (or
admiration) for these particular performers." When it comes to the
more dubious forms of diversion—pornography and pro wrestling, for
example—the individual who arranges them is more aptly titled a promoter. There is a definite line separating a promoter from a producer.
The one will do anything to draw a crowd; the other favors things intrinsically
worthwhile.

In essence, P. T. Barnum was a master promoter, for he arranged the
exhibition of essentially nonartistic attractions. Barnum's unique passion
(a lifelong addiction) came through in the clever hoaxes that played on the

public's fancy. The vast majority of them were outright shams or freaks of nature, at whose bizarre existence the public paid money to gawk.

John North revealed himself primarily as a producer. Of course, the rich traditions of circus entertainment he inherited from his founding uncles pointed him in that direction. He could have moved the show backward in time to the gutsier days of humbug. He could have moved it forward into a more artistically exciting form. He did both. Starting off with Gargantua, like Barnum he turned a curiosity into a supernatural symbol. That he kept the ballyhoo alive for the twelve years Gargantua toured with the circus— by introducing a mate and then by foisting on the loveless couple a pair of adopted offspring—speaks well for John's promotional savvy.

All the while the budding producer in him was shining brightly, too. North engaged an unparalleled number of stellar acts from around the world and presented them to the public in lavish, theatrically wrought programs shaped and paced by some of the best directors and designers of their day. This was John's unique showmanly statement, the tip of his hat to the gifted artists who spend years honing their craft. At their best, the circus days arranged by John enveloped us in a completely aesthetic experience, from a walk down the restyled midways to the spectacles inside the vast blue big top that overflowed in rich, animate color.

Says Phil Hall in praise of the transformation:

> North imported other disciplines into the circus. The circus was not just the circus. And they made the circus a different thing, and there was some criticism of that. But I found it to be terrific. The circus was entertainment. It was not specific, and Americans tend to want to put everything in its place. They don't want changes. They did the same thing with opera. They want it to be this, to be that. That's not what showbusiness is. Showbusiness adopts, it gets more catholic in its tastes. And North did bring Broadway into the situation. And I did hear some criticism. Well, what's wrong with that? They always had the good circus acts, and what they did was to expand the production numbers, and they made them bloody interesting. They really did—and the music and all of it. And I thought that was probably the best thing that happened. There are circus fans who disagree because they still want something back in the 1890s, and that's wonderful, but that's not the way showbusiness runs.[1]

Harold Ronk was inspired by John's imperial mystique:

> He was a man of amazing stature. You could feel his presence whenever he walked in. There was something about his entrance into the room. The

very presence, the way he sat in a chair, when he got out of the chair, the way he turned. I felt I was in the presence of a great impressario. There has been great controversy about what he did, what he didn't do. He always lent this great family touch to the American circus. You always had a feeling that this was a family affair, that there was one man in charge. And with John, even though he was not around it much, when he was there you were aware, and when he wasn't there you were still aware that his magnetism was over the whole thing. I swear there was something about this family that was passed on.[2]

When John started out, the physical movement of the show was another issue he addressed, equally as important as the content of its programs. Every major hurdle he faced in his career was directly related to the big top, be it the 1938 strike that sent the trains home early; his ouster in 1942 following a family feud over whether or not to tour the tents through the war years; the tragic Hartford fire; the skyrocketing cost of rail transportation; the shrinking number of adequate lots to play on; union harassment and sabotage; late arrivals; blowdowns and washouts; mud, mud, and more mud. . . . What, in his opinion, was the toughest challenge he ever faced? John's immediate answer was one word long: "Labor."[3]

The tented circus became an anachronism, and the never-ending struggle to keep it on the road depleted John's energy and resolve and left him outside the public's favor when he decided to close it down in 1956 and go indoors. If there was a turning point in his life, surely it came that fateful summer day in Pittsburgh, Pennsylvania, when he decided to declare the tented circus "a thing of the past."

The public has a short memory. Sadly, most of John's remarkable contributions—as well as his problem-solving stamina—have been forgotten in the wake of Pittsburgh. It was simply too traumatic an event in American circus history not to have a scapegoat, and John was it. All the condemnation he took from the fans and from the trades, and from his own enemies, drove him into a form of exile: away from the circus community in this country, across the Atlantic Ocean to the Old World. There he played out the role of a cultured gentleman of international affairs. He never stopped traveling the Continent or taking in circus performances. Nothing meant so much to him, by Ida's account, as the company of old circus directors with whom he had worked and performers he had booked in years gone by. John was particularly gratified when they expressed their appreciation for the opportunities he had given them to work in America, including, as well, the side jobs of selling popcorn and souvenirs. They now insisted on buying *him* the whiskey drinks, exclaiming, "Now, *we* are the paying one."

In fact, Ida has strong memories of how John kept repeating his yearly travels abroad, as if he were still actually in search of new acts to engage for a circus he still owned and operated. "I can only say that till the very end, also not having the circus, we did the same route looking for artists and we always went to the same places meeting the same directors, in Sweden and Germany, and in Brussels, in Paris. . . . We had wonderful times. And I do think that is what John needed very much after he gave up the circus. . . . Sometimes, people from America came to see us, then all night long—and often till the next day—that was only one theme. It was about in the time of the circus. His enthusiasm, everything came alive."[4]

Throughout most of the 1970s, John made the annual trek down to Monte Carlo each December to visit his friend Prince Rainier and judge another Circus Festival hosted by the prince. A few of the tournaments, which have become the most prestigious of their kind in the world, were televised in the States, and when the judges were introduced at the outset, John's illustrious name and presence was given due recognition. He rose and waved modestly to the cameras. Some of the fans who attended the events remember North's looking like a loner, not particularly aware of anyone, just coming and going in a detached, self-absorbed manner.

When the infirmities of old age finally caught up with him in the last few years of his life, John, who had enjoyed such good health all along, became frightened and subdued. He had poor vision in one eye, and he lived in the irrational fear of going blind. One doctor had warned him that eye surgery would be necessary. His speech became impaired at times. Despite his efforts to keep pace socially, more and more, noticed Ida, "he really changed. . . . He wanted to be alone."[5]

On the day before Thanksgiving 1982, months after he had suffered a stroke (from which, according to Henry, he was impressively on the rebound), John granted an interview for this book. The brothers were in Sarasota, residing in a condominium on one of the keys developed by the Arvida Corporation, which had purchased the property from John's syndicate.

Came the time, at last, to meet *John Ringling North,* and he appeared, as if from out of nowhere—standing all at once smack-dab in the middle of the room in a red dinner jacket, his face aglow with unexpected vigor and a rare twinkle in his eye. On the short side, his frame was neat and spry, his manner perfectly ingratiating at first. The touching rapport between

John and Henry resembled that of a well-matched couple who had grown in harmony over the years. John positioned himself in a sofa on the other side of the room, much like a capricious king on his throne allowing himself to be viewed from afar. Henry sat next to him in another chair, all the while blowing elegant smoke rings into the air and acting ever so protective and proud. Sometimes Henry would add a word or two in the spirit of gently nudging John along with supplementary information.

As the questions were asked, John gradually turned more straight faced and grim, calling to mind the tense expressions a man will exhibit during touchy negotiations. Some of his responses have already been mentioned in these pages. He impressed with his imperial-like gestures, conveying a mind and will as strong as granite, and with his suave reluctance to extend an opinion on any issue beyond a few sparse words.

Would he be amenable to a series of interviews in the days ahead?

He nodded agreeably.

Could a time be set?

The nodding ceased.

At his convenience, of course.

He asked, "Are you going to be over in Europe this winter?"

Well, not exactly, he was told. Plans hadn't been made.

He nodded understandably.

How about a few interviews while he was in Sarasota?

He moved his head slightly up and down, suggesting accommodation, then sideways, showing he could be contrary at any moment, too. What exactly *was* he?

"I'll be in Europe all winter," he repeated, extending a cheerfully impractical invitation.

Might he be amenable, just the same, to some questions in Sarasota?

There was what seemed an impatient pause.

"Well, I'm *here*," he said, like an actor having to raise his own curtain.

And so began the one interview he agreed to. Was there a particular edition of the circus he liked the best?

"I liked what we did in 1942. After we opened, Peter Arno, whose judgment I admired, came up to me and said, 'You did it.'"

Any other famous people he tried involving in the circus?

"I tried to get Salvador Dalí to design the costumes."

Why didn't he?

"He wanted too much money."

His favorite type of act?

He was hesitant to specify a type.

"I like jugglers," he granted.

The main reason he struck the tent show in 1956?

"It was losing money."

Any regrets about moving it indoors?

"Not disappointed about arenas."

Any second thoughts about selling the show?

"It was a good idea to sell."

His favorite ringmaster?

"I liked the ones on the show when my uncles were running it, like Fred Bradna."

Was he satisfied with the Ringling circus he had seen the previous year in Chicago?

"A leading question."

He became a little demonstrative at this point.

"I didn't book an act just for the end ring, but because it *was* a good act."

His eyes warmed up as he told of answering fan letters with a personal notes bearing his autograph, and he expressed pride in having helped retire the $4 million in debts arising out of the Hartford fire claims.

Some of his favorite stars?

"I have a high regard for Tito Gaona."

His thoughts on the caliber of acts then with the circus?

"Some nice perch acts, but they got all those wires and poles helping them."

And so it went. Sometimes, a few words can say a lot, as when John was asked the following: When you were at a circus scouting new talent, what were the particular qualities you looked for in a performer?

He searched his mind for self-understanding. His eyes lit up like a schoolboy with a raised hand.

"Something I haven't seen before."[6]

Something he hadn't seen before. On June 4, 1985, after John had finished shaving in his Brussels suite at the Hilton, getting ready to go out to dinner with Ida at the city's best restaurant, Comme ce Soir, the cable on his electric razor dropped to the floor. He had difficulty finding it and called Ida for help. She responded, stooping to the floor and crawling around in a humorous manner. In her own exact words, "he bent down, laughing at me, because I had found the cable. At this moment, still laughing, he was dead."[7]

A stroke was listed as the cause. The various wills that John had written over the years, now made known, revealed his vacillating alliances to three would-be heirs: his brother, Henry, and the two lasting loves of his life, Ida and Dody. Henry and Dody ended up on the cutting-room floor. It was not a big shock to Dody, who realized that the obscene letter addressed to her which John had mysteriously received in his mailbox was as good a reason as any for his disinheriting her. And she had been left with the trust, anyway.

As for Henry, however hurt he may have felt immediately, the pain was healed in time by his wonderful memories of the lifelong affection for each other that he and John had so warmly shared. "He was ever a loving brother to me and my sister until his unhappy illness that clouded his last two years."

Ida, who never, to anyone's knowledge, disappointed or disillusioned John, who by all accounts appears to have been a completely devoted and loving companion, ended up the sole heir to his fortune, valued at approximately one hundred million dollars. A small memorial service was held in Belgium. John was cremated, and his ashes are with Ida in her Geneva apartment. She eventually made settlements with Henry and Dody, and she helps Rudy Bundy financially from time to time. She sent Dody Heath the large trunk bearing the distinguished initials "J.R.N."[8]

JRN, the once celebrated circus king, made his rather quiet exit to mixed reviews. The obits ranged from acknowledgment to ignorance. Both *Amusement Business* and *Variety* tended to the reprehensible latter, obviously drawing on misinformation supplied them by the Feld organization. In fact, *Variety* went to suspicious—and erroneous—lengths in detailing Irvin Feld's role in the circus. Wasn't this North's turn? There was no credit or praise offered John by the so-called bible of show business, only a cold shoulder for his alleged bad relations with labor. The major news outlets were not so forgetful of the facts. *Time* gave John his due for Gargantua the Great and for moving the circus into the modern era.[9] So did the *New York Times*.[10] Possibly the most well-informed tribute to John was etched by Burt A. Folkhart, writing for the *Los Angeles Times*, who credited him in the positive sense for having "moved the 'Greatest Show on Earth' from tents to stadiums" and who appreciated how he had "also replaced the circus' unrelated acts with thematic programs, once hiring Igor Stravinski to compose a ballet."[11]

Such were his noteworthy achievements. John never set out to write his own memoirs. He was too concealing by nature to undertake so extensive an exposition. He rarely expressed his deeper feelings to anyone on the myriad issues indigenous to the circus he had managed for more than three decades. Those closest to him sensed his general attitudes. He revealed himself mostly in the kind of performances he created. He remained, to his dying day, a curious enigma, really—like a circus parade in an unreachable distance passing mysteriously by. How would he like to be remembered? Says Ida, the woman with whom he was intimately involved for nearly four decades: "as the best director of the Ringling circus."[12]

It may take many years for the entertainment world to grasp fully and appreciate what John did do—more than that, what he stood for. In spirit, he championed the circus as a superior art form worthy of the highest production values. His profound influence continues to inspire the world-wide circus movement. But the echoes of Pittsburgh reverberate still. History has not been kind to the man who took the show out from under the tents—its ideal setting—and into the everyday world of hard-top arenas. There is a greater truth, nonetheless, that lingers brilliantly on in the present tense, so obvious as to be easily overlooked: the huge indoor audiences of today that make Ringling Bros. and Barnum & Bailey still the most widely patronized circus—indeed, perhaps the most widely attended live show in all the world—are a resounding validation of the showmanship, introduced by North more than fifty years ago, that continues to define essentially how Ringling circus performances are conceived and staged. In that triumphal sense, his greatest shows on earth live on. So, too, may his rightfully earned legacy.

Interviews

Richard Barstow, July 6, 1978, New York City
Rudy Bundy, April 18, 1986, Sarasota, Florida
Michael Burke, July 6, 1978, New York City
Noyelles Burkhart, April 19, 1986, Sarasota, Florida
Bambi Burnes, June 24, 1987, Los Angeles
Chuck Burnes, June 24, 1987, Los Angeles
Max Butler, July 1990 (by telephone), Sarasota, Florida
Irving Caesar, July 6, 1978, New York City
Antoinette Concello, September 3, 1979, San Francisco
Arthur Concello, January 11, 1976, April 19 and 20, 1986, and December 6, 1987
    (by telephone), Sarasota, Florida
Art Cooksey, August 15, 1990 (by telephone), La Porte, Indiana
Chita Cristiani, March 6, 1988 (by telephone), Sarasota, Florida
Cosetta Cristiani, November 10, 1987 (by telephone), Sarasota, Florida
Ken Dodd, January 9, 1988 (by telephone), Sarasota, Florida
Merle Evans, August 1975, January 1976, and April 1986, Sarasota, Florida
Nena Evans, August, 1975, Sarasota, Florida
La Norma Fox, April 19, 1986, Sarasota, Florida
Daisy Hall, April 21, 1986, Sarasota, Florida
Phil Hall, April 21, 1986, Sarasota, Florida
Jane Johnson, August, 1975, Sarasota, Florida
Floyd King, January 16, 1976, Macon, Georgia
Alice Ringling Lancaster, April 18, 1986, Sarasota, Florida
Charles Ringling Lancaster, April 18, 1986, Sarasota, Florida
Stuart Lancaster, June 30, 1987, Los Angeles
Jackie Le Claire, April 20, 1986, Sarasota, Florida

Mary Jane Miller, April 22, 1986, Sarasota, Florida

Cyril B. Mills, through correspondence, 1990, England; written answers to questions submitted by the author

Louis Nolan, May 31, 1977, Baraboo, Wisconsin

Henry Ringling North, October 16, 1979, New York City, and November 24, 1982, Sarasota, Florida

John Ringling North, November 24, 1982, Sarasota, Florida

John Ringling North II, August 28, 1990 (by telephone), Ireland; additional information provided in letters to the author

Curtis Page, Sr., January 21, 1978 (by telephone), Baraboo, Wisconsin

William Perry, January 8, 1977, Sarasota, Florida

Harold Ronk, September 2, 1976, San Francisco

Dody Heath Soames, November 13, 1990, Los Angeles

Unus, January 7, 1987 (by telephone), Sarasota, Florida

Karl Wallenda, August 1975, Sarasota, Florida

Miles White, July 7, 1978, New York City, and November 21, 1987 (by telephone), New York City

Countess Ida von Zedlitz-Trützschler, written answers to questions submitted by the author and through interview, March 17, 1990 (by telephone), Geneva, Switzerland

Notes

Chapter 1: In Uncle John's Image

1. Louis Nolan interview.
2. Ibid. Although historians have disputed such a birth ever taking place at the Baraboo winter quarters, an account similar to Nolan's is offered in an unpublished portion of the Henry Ringling North and Alden Hatch typed manuscript for *Circus Kings,* p. 137, located in the archives of the John and Mable Ringling Museum of Art in Sarasota, Florida. The manuscript was examined by the author through the courtesy and cooperation of the museum archivist, Waneta Sage-Cagne.
3. Stuart Lancaster interview.
4. Henry Ringling North and Alden Hatch, *Circus Kings* (Garden City, N.Y.: Doubleday and Company, 1960), p. 131.
5. Ibid., p. 132.
6. Stuart Lancaster interview.
7. Louis Nolan interview.
8. Alice Lancaster interview.
9. Louis Nolan interview.
10. Curtis Page interview.
11. Louis Nolan interview.
12. Ibid.
13. Henry Ringling North interview, October 16, 1979.
14. North and Hatch, *Circus Kings,* p. 155.
15. Curtis Page interview.

Chapter 2: Ringling Roots

1. North and Hatch, *Circus Kings*, p. 201.
2. Floyd King interview.
3. Alfred Ringling, *Life Story of the Ringling Brothers* (Chicago: R. R. Donnelley and Sons, 1900), p. 71.
4. Ibid., p. 26.
5. Ibid., p. 76.
6. Floyd King interview.
7. Curtis Page interview.
8. *Variety*, December 1909 anniversary issue.
9. *Variety*, October 30, 1909.
10. Charles Lancaster interview.

Chapter 3: Heir Unapparent

1. North and Hatch, *Circus Kings*, p. 170.
2. Robert Lewis Taylor, *Center Ring* (Garden City, N.Y.: Doubleday and Company, 1956), p. 45.
3. North and Hatch, *Circus Kings*, pp. 22–24.
4. Curtis Page interview.
5. Letter to the author from John R. Meeske, registrar, Yale University, March 10, 1988.
6. Lewis, *Center Ring*, p. 28.
7. Curtis Page interview.
8. Ringling Bros. and Barnum & Bailey Circus Program Magazine, 1925, p. 4.
9. As quoted in "Follow the Sun," *Chicago Tribune*, October 11, 1987, sec. 12, p. 3.
10. "The Circus King's Gift to Posterity," *Today's Health*, November 1969, p. 42.
11. North and Hatch, *Circus Kings*, p. 112.
12. Henry Ringling North interview, October 16, 1979.
13. Alice Lancaster interview.
14. *Variety*, September 11, 1929.
15. Ibid., November 30, 1930.
16. North and Hatch, *Circus Kings*, p. 189.
17. Henry Ringling North interview, October 16, 1979.
18. Alice Lancaster interview.
19. Stuart Lancaster interview.
20. Floyd King interview.
21. North and Hatch, *Circus Kings*, p. 206.
22. Henry Ringling North interview, October 16, 1979.
23. Charles Lancaster interview.

Chapter 4: Gargantua on Parade

1. Stuart Lancaster interview.
2. Taylor, *Center Ring*, p. 33.
3. *The Billboard*, November 20, 1937.
4. Ibid., October 16, 1937.
5. Ibid., December 25, 1937.
6. Merle Evans interview, August 1975.
7. Ringling Bros. and Barnum & Bailey Circus Program Magazine, 1938, p. 39.
8. *The Billboard*, April 16, 1938.
9. *Variety*, April 13, 1938.

Chapter 5: Shakespeare's Roustabouts

1. Henry Ringling North interview, October 16, 1979.
2. Jackie Le Claire interview.
3. Ringling Bros. and Barnum & Bailey Circus Program Magazine, 1936, p. 24.
4. *The Billboard*, April 23, 1938.
5. Fred Bradna as told to Hartzell Spence, *The Big Top* (New York: Simon and Schuster, 1952), p. 140.
6. Ibid., pp. 42–43.
7. *The Billboard*, May 14, 1938.
8. Ibid., June 18, 1938.
9. Ibid., June 25, 1938.
10. *Variety*, June 29, 1938.
11. *The Billboard*, July 2, 1938.
12. Ibid., July 9, 1938.
13. Ibid., July 16, 1938.
14. Ibid., September 24, 1938.
15. Arthur Concello interview, April 19, 1986.
16. *The Billboard*, December 24, 1938.

Chapter 6: The Lady Who Wouldn't

1. *The Billboard*, August 10, 1940.
2. Chita Cristiani interview. This chapter rests primarily on the recollections of Chita and Cosetta Cristiani. Henry Ringling North acknowledged his brother John's relationship to Chita as "a nice little flirtation" in his October 1979 interview.
3. Richard Hubler, *The Cristianis* (Boston and Toronto: Little, Brown and Company, 1966), p. 240.
4. Cosetta Cristiani interview.
5. North and Hatch, *Circus Kings*, p. 216.

6. Ibid., pp. 201–2.
7. Hubler, *The Cristianis*, p. 242.

Chapter 7: Brotherly Bombast

1. John Murray Anderson as told to and written by Hugh Abercrombie Anderson, *Out without My Rubbers* (New York: Library Publishers, 1954), p. 215.
2. North and Hatch, *Circus Kings*, p. 252.
3. *The Billboard*, February 25, 1939.
4. Jane Johnson interview.
5. Alice Lancaster interview.
6. Jane Johnson interview.
7. *The Billboard*, October 19, 1940.
8. North and Hatch, *Circus Kings*, pp. 212–13.

Chapter 8: Dream Seasons

1. *Variety*, April 12, 1939.
2. *The Billboard*, April 15, 1939.
3. Jane Johnson interview.
4. *The Billboard*, June 24, 1939.
5. Ibid., November 30, 1940.
6. Ringling Bros. and Barnum & Bailey Circus Program Magazine, 1941, p. 4.
7. *Variety*, April 9, 1941.
8. *The Billboard*, April 26, 1941.
9. Ringling Bros. and Barnum & Bailey Circus Program Magazine, 1941, p. 6.
10. *The Billboard*, December 27, 1941.

Chapter 9: Elephants in Tutus

1. *The Billboard*, July 11, 1942.
2. Arthur Concello interview, April 19, 1986.
3. *The Billboard*, March 18, 1939.
4. Taylor, *Center Ring*, p. 41.
5. *The Billboard*, May 27, 1939.
6. Ibid., June 10, 1939.
7. Ibid., January 13, 1940, p. 55.
8. Ibid., January 27, 1940, p. 61.
9. Arthur Concello interview, April 19, 1986.
10. Miles White interview, July 7, 1978. With regard to the issuing of credits in the program magazines for various creative work, Miles White disputes that he ever merely did costume sketches for Geddes, as his credit line reads in the 1942 program, p. 71. Even though the "Costumes Designed by" credits

for the various production numbers in the 1941 and 1942 editions went to a number of individuals—including Geddes, Max Weldy, Winn, and Thomas Becher—White maintains that when he worked for Geddes, it was he who did the actual designing. Of course, when White returned to the show in 1947 after a four-year absence, he thereafter always received exclusive and prime credit for costume design.

11. Anderson and Anderson, *Out Without My Rubbers*, p. 219.
12. Jackie Le Claire interview.
13. John Ringling North interview.
14. Excerpt printed in *The Billboard*, April 25, 1942.
15. *Variety*, April 22, 1942.
16. Excerpt printed in *The Billboard*, April 25, 1942.
17. *New York Times*, April 10, 1942, p. 14.
18. Ibid., April 19, 1942, sec. 8, p. 1.
19. Excerpt printed in *The Billboard*, April 25, 1942.
20. Ibid.
21. *The Billboard*, April 18, 1942.
22. Merle Evans interview, August 1975.

Chapter 10: Into the Net

1. Henry Ringling North letter to George Smith, dated April 6, 1942, from the Pfening Archives, Columbus, Ohio, courtesy of Fred Pfening III.
2. John Ringling North letter to George Smith, dated November 9, 1938, from the Pfening Archives, courtesy of Fred Pfening III.
3. *The Billboard*, June 20, 1942.
4. Jane Johnson interview.
5. *The Billboard*, September 12, 1942.
6. Ringling Bros. and Barnum & Bailey Circus Route Book, 1942.
7. Alice Lancaster interview.
8. Ibid.
9. Stuart Lancaster interview.
10. Alice Lancaster interview.
11. *The Billboard*, February 6, 1943.
12. Henry Ringling North interview, October 16, 1979.
13. Arthur Concello interview, January 11, 1976.
14. North and Hatch, *Circus Kings*, p. 265.
15. *The Billboard*, January 23, 1943.

Chapter 11: A Fire He Didn't Start

1. North and Hatch, *Circus Kings*, p. 254.
2. Rudy Bundy interview.
3. Ibid.
4. Phil and Daisy Hall interview.

5. Ringling Bros. and Barnum & Bailey Circus Program Magazine, 1943, p. 45.
6. The Billboard, April 17, 1943.
7. Miles White interview, November 21, 1987.
8. Jackie Le Claire interview.
9. Mary Jane Miller interview.
10. Merle Evans interview, April, 1986.
11. Stuart Lancaster interview.
12. Jackie Le Claire interview.
13. Alice Lancaster interview.
14. Stuart Lancaster interview.
15. The Billboard, August 12, 1944.
16. Alice Lancaster interview.

Chapter 12: All Eyes on the Courtroom

1. Variety, April 21, 1945. The most cohesive account of this period, fraught with litigation and family politics, is in "Ringling Wrangling: Three Sets of Heirs Squabble for Control of the Circus," Fortune 36 (1947): 114–15.
2. North and Hatch, Circus Kings, p. 275.
3. The Billboard, April 20, 1946.
4. Mary Jane Miller interview.
5. The Billboard, August 10, 1946.
6. Karl Wallenda interview.
7. Excerpts of reviews printed in The Billboard, May 23, 1947.
8. The Billboard, April 19, 1947.
9. Variety, April 16, 1947.
10. The Billboard, May 13, 1947.
11. Ibid., August 16, 1947.
12. Stuart Lancaster interview.
13. Arthur Concello interview, April 19, 1986.
14. The Billboard, November 8, 1947.
15. Art Cooksey interview.

Chapter 13. North and Concello

1. The Billboard, December 12, 1953.
2. Arthur Concello interview, April 19, 1986.
3. Cyril B. Mills letter to the author, dated October 15, 1990.
4. Arthur Concello interview, April 19, 1986.
5. Ringling Bros. and Barnum & Bailey Circus Program Magazine, 1948, p. 8.
6. The Billboard, June 5, 1948.
7. Daisy Hall interview.
8. Mary Jane Miller interview.
9. Rudy Bundy interview.

10. Phil Hall interview.
11. La Norma Fox interview.
12. Mary Jane Miller interview.
13. Arthur Concello interview, January 11, 1976.
14. Phil and Daisy Hall interview.
15. Arthur Concello interview, April 19, 1986.
16. Rudy Bundy interview.
17. Ringling Bros. and Barnum & Bailey Circus Route Book, 1948.

Chapter 14: Jet-Set Johnny

1. Taylor, Center Ring, p. 48.
2. Phil Hall interview.
3. Richard Barstow interview.
4. Phil Hall interview.
5. Taylor, Center Ring, p. 38.
6. Ruark's column, datelined Havana, as printed in the Santa Rosa Press Democrat, late December 1954.
7. Richard Barstow interview.
8. The Billboard, April 23, 1949.
9. Taylor, Center Ring, pp. 159-60.
10. This Week, April 1, 1956, pp. 12-13.
11. Cyril B. Mills letter to the author, October 15, 1990.
12. Max Butler interview.
13. John Ringling North interview.
14. Noyelles Burkhart interview.
15. Jackie Le Claire interview.
16. La Norma Fox interview.
17. Taylor, Center Ring, p. 39. See also Martin Abramson, "The Girl on the Flying Trapeze," American Weekly, May 15, 1955. This brings into serious doubt the validity of Taylor's account of the Del Oro discovery by North in Center Ring, originally published in the New Yorker. And it is, sadly, yet another disillusioning example of how unreliable and fictionalized such literate writing can be.
18. Unus interview.
19. Ringling Bros. and Barnum & Bailey Circus Program Magazine, 1948, p. 76.
20. Miles White interview, July 7, 1978.
21. Irving Caesar interview.
22. From Countess Ida Von Zedlitz-Trützschler's letter to the author, dated October 2, 1987, providing answers to questions.
23. Unus interview.
24. Miles White interview, November 21, 1987.
25. Stuart Lancaster interview.

Chapter 15: Broadway to Sarasota

1. Arthur Concello interview, April 19, 1986.
2. Phil Hall interview.
3. Stuart Lancaster interview.
4. Arthur Concello interview, April 19, 1986.
5. Anderson and Anderson, *Out Without My Rubbers*, pp. 214–15.
6. Richard Barstow interview.
7. Jackie Le Claire interview.
8. Ringling Bros. and Barnum & Bailey Circus Program Magazine, 1953, p. 7.
9. Henry Ringling North interview, November 24, 1982.
10. Phil Hall interview.
11. Anderson and Anderson, *Out Without My Rubbers*, p. 211.
12. Art Cooksey interview.
13. Richard Barstow interview.
14. Arthur Concello interview, April 19, 1986.
15. *Variety*, April 11, 1951.
16. *The Billboard*, April 14, 1951.

Chapter 16: Photographed by De Mille

1. Anderson and Anderson, *Out Without My Rubbers*, pp. 221–22.
2. Phil Hall interview.
3. Arthur Concello interview, January 11, 1976.
4. Ringling Bros. and Barnum & Bailey Circus Program Magazine, 1950, p. 6.
5. Phil Hall interview.
6. La Norma Fox interview.
7. This from an unpublished portion of the North and Hatch typed manuscript for *Circus Kings*, examined by the author at the John and Mable Ringling Museum of Art, courtesy of the museum archivist, Waneta Sage-Cagne.
8. La Norma Fox interview.
9. Ringling Bros. and Barnum & Bailey Circus Program Magazine, 1952, p. 19.
10. Daisy Hall interview.
11. Arthur Concello interview, April 19, 1986.
12. Excerpts printed in *The Billboard*, January 19, 1952.
13. *The Billboard*, January 5, 1952.
14. Excerpt printed in *The Billboard*, January 19, 1952.
15. *The Billboard*, April 5, 1952.

Chapter 17: His Own Music

1. Ringling Bros. and Barnum & Bailey Circus Program Magazine, 1955, p. 76.

2. Taylor, *Center Ring*, p. 44.
3. Author's telephone conversation with Sid Herman, Famous Music, New York City, June 2, 1989.
4. Author's telephone conversation with Joseph Weiss, Frank Music, New York City, June 1, 1989.
5. From tape recordings of actual circus performances, acquired by the author through the courtesy of Dyer R. Reynolds.
6. *Variety*, April 9, 1952.
7. Ringling Bros. and Barnum & Bailey Circus Program Magazine, 1954, p. 22.
8. Irving Caesar interview.
9. Ibid.
10. Ibid.
11. As sung for the author by Irving Caesar during a tape-recorded interview.
12. Irving Caesar interview.
13. Rudy Bundy interview.
14. Phil Hall interview.

Chapter 18: Gone Are the Days

1. Phil Hall interview. It is important to note how debatable the contention is that North never wanted to travel with or be around the show. Concello has certainly advanced this as a primary given in his relationship with North, and fans have largely subscribed to it. There is evidence to the contrary, such as North's desire here to have his private car, the Jomar, on the train, presumably so he could travel in it during at least a part of the cross-country tour in 1953. He is known to have traveled with the circus in earlier years, as he would do so again during much of the 1955 tour. North actually may have stayed away from the show more than he really wanted to out of a sense that Concello did not feel comfortable with him there and wanted to rule the lot completely.
2. William Perry interview.
3. *Variety*, April 19, 1950.
4. *The Billboard*, May 15, 1948.
5. Ibid., April 1, 1950.
6. This from an unpublished portion of the North and Hatch typed manuscript for *Circus Kings*, p. 363, examined by the author at the John and Mable Ringling Museum of Art, courtesy of the museum archivist, Waneta Sage-Cagne.
7. Arthur Concello interview, April 20, 1987.
8. Ringling Bros. and Barnum & Bailey Circus Route Book, 1953, p. 8.
9. Jackie Le Claire interview.
10. *The Billboard*, April 8, 1950.
11. Weekly issues of *The Billboard* provided extensive coverage of the experiment with sponsored dates during the 1952 tour.

12. Ringling Bros. and Barnum & Bailey Circus Program Magazine, 1952, p. 68.
13. Richard Barstow interview.
14. Ringling Bros. and Barnum & Bailey Circus Program Magazine, 1953, p. 9.
15. Variety, April 8, 1953.
16. Arthur Concello interview, April 19, 1986.
17. Richard Barstow interview.
18. The Billboard, October 24, 1953.
19. Ringling Bros. and Barnum & Bailey Circus Route Book, 1953, pp. 5-8.
20. Arthur Concello interview, January 11, 1976.

Chapter 19: A Stab at Tomorrow

1. Rudy Bundy interview.
2. Ringling Bros. and Barnum & Bailey Circus Program Magazine, 1954, p. 13.
3. The Billboard, April 10, 1954.
4. Ibid., April 24, 1954.
5. Richard Barstow interview.
6. Variety, April 7, 1954.
7. The Billboard, May 22, 1954.
8. Ibid.
9. Ibid., January 29, 1955.
10. Michael Burke interview.
11. Michael Burke, Outrageous Good Fortune (Boston: Little, Brown and Company, 1984), p. 173.
12. Ibid., p. 180.
13. Life, June 20, 1955.
14. Phil Hall interview.
15. From a tape recording of the 1955 Ringling-Barnum telecast, courtesy of Ken Dodd, Sarasota, Florida.
16. The Billboard, July 9, 1955.
17. Ibid., July 16, 1955.
18. Ibid.
19. Burke, Outrageous Good Fortune, p. 185.
20. This from an unpublished portion of the North and Hatch typed manuscript for Circus Kings, examined by the author at the John and Mable Ringling Museum of Art, courtesy of the museum archivist, Waneta Sage-Cagne.
21. Michael Burke interview.
22. Rudy Bundy interview.

Chapter 20: The Big Top Falls

1. Noyelles Burkhart interview. Burkhart's claim that he got the show off the Saint Paul lot agrees with a report of the dramatic night in *The Billboard*, August 13, 1955: "North and Noyelles Burkhart, legal adjuster, appeared in the top, and Burkhart rallied the puzzled crews into action."
2. *The Billboard*, August 20, 1955.
3. *San Francisco Chronicle*, September 1, 1955, p. 4.
4. Ibid., editorial page.
5. Michael Burke interview.
6. Burke, *Outrageous Good Fortune*, p. 190.
7. Ibid., p. 197.
8. Michael Burke interview.
9. Henry Ringling North interview, October 16, 1979.
10. Merle Evans interview, August 1975. His wife, Nena, present during much of the interview, offered this sobering account of the Knoblaugh incident as an example of the silent treatment North would give someone he did not want to see or had no further use for. Nena was North's secretary in those years.
11. Richard Barstow interview.
12. Chuck Burnes interview.
13. Ringling Bros. and Barnum & Bailey Circus Program Magazine, 1956, p. 19.
14. Richard Barstow interview.
15. *New York Times*, April 5, 1956, p. 16.
16. *The Billboard*, November 12, 1955.
17. Chuck Burnes interview.
18. Rudy Bundy interview. Bundy alone witnessed John's writing the historic pronouncement declaring an end to the tented circus. In his most difficult moments, John drew closer to either Bundy or Concello.
19. Chuck Burns interview.
20. Rudy Bundy interview.

Chapter 21: Once a Circus King

1. Jackie Le Claire interview.
2. Chuck Burnes interview.
3. *Variety*, July 18, 1956.
4. *The Billboard*, July 28, 1956.
5. "It's Too Soon to Play Taps," NEA story out of San Francisco, printed in the *Sarasota Journal*, August 7, 1956, p. 8.
6. Phil Santora, "The Big Top Flop," *New York Daily News*, August 7, 8, and 9, 1956.
7. Arthur Concello interview, April 20, 1986.
8. Burke, *Outrageous Good Fortune*, p. 204.

9. *Variety*, August 22, 1956.
10. Stuart Lancaster interview.
11. Ibid.
12. Alice Lancaster interview.
13. *Variety*, October 17, 1957.
14. Arthur Concello interview, April 19, 1986.
15. Burke, *Outrageous Good Fortune*, p. 207.
16. John Ringling North interview. Neither North nor Concello ever expressed much admiration for the other's work, at least publicly. When pressed on at least two occasions during his interviews for this book to supply his own personal critique of North's showmanship, Concello would only concede, and rather reluctantly, "The show made money. He must have done something right."
17. Rudy Bundy interview.
18. Ballantine's comments in *Saga*, May 1962 issue, as quoted in *Amusement Business*, April 7, 1962.

Chapter 22: Greatest Show on Asphalt

1. Richard Barstow interview.
2. *Amusement Business*, May 12, 1962, p. 46.
3. Bambi Burnes interview.
4. United Press story, datelined Sarasota, as printed in the *San Francisco Chronicle*, September 6, 1957.
5. Stuart Lancaster interview.
6. Ringling Bros. and Barnum & Bailey Circus Program Magazine, 1958, p. 3.
7. North and Hatch, *Circus Kings*, p. 316.
8. Press release, "Let's Bring Back the Circus," signed by Hester Ringling Sanford, dated July 16, 1958.
9. Stuart Lancaster interview.
10. Rudy Bundy's ledgers, examined by the author.
11. Stuart Lancaster interview.
12. *Amusement Business*, December 8, 1962.
13. *Variety*, April 1, 1959.
14. *Amusement Business*, April 11, 1960.
15. Unus interview.
16. Arthur Concello interview, April 20, 1986.
17. *Amusement Business*, April 10, 1961.

Chapter 23: At Home across the Sea

1. Rudy Bundy interview.
2. Stuart Lancaster interview.
3. Alice Lancaster interview.
4. Dody Heath Soames interview.

5. Written answers from Countess Ida von Zedlitz-Trützschler to questions from the author.
6. Dody Heath Soames interview.
7. John Ringling North II interview.
8. Arthur Concello interview, April 15, 1986.
9. *Amusement Business*, May 18, 1963, p. 34.
10. Jackie Le Claire interview.
11. Richard Barstow interview.
12. Henry Ringling North interview, October 16, 1979.
13. Rudy Bundy interview.
14. Quoted in *Amusement Business*, October 19, 1963.
15. *Business Week*, October 12, 1963, p. 33.
16. Rudy Bundy interview.
17. From Arthur Concello's personal diary, examined by the author.
18. Rudy Bundy interview.
19. Richard Barstow interview.
20. Arthur Concello interview.
21. Jackie Le Claire interview.
22. Rudy Bundy interview.
23. Ringling Bros. and Barnum & Bailey Circus Route Book, 1964, p. 29.
24. *Amusement Business*, April 4, 1964.
25. *New Yorker*, April 10, 1965, pp. 38–39.

Chapter 24: The Sound of Success

1. Ringling Bros. and Barnum & Bailey Circus Route Book, 1964, p. 7.
2. Antoinette Concello interview.
3. *Amusement Business*, May 23, 1964, p. 36.
4. Ibid.
5. Review excerpt in Ringling ad, *New York Times*, April 8, 1965, p. 45.
6. Review excerpt in Ringling ad, *New York Times*, April 6, 1965, p. 33.
7. *New York Times*, April 2, 1965, p. 26.
8. Review excerpt in Ringling ad, *New York Times*, April 9, 1965, p. 19.
9. *Los Angeles Times*, August 13, 1965, pt. 4, p. 10.
10. *Amusement Business*, April 10, 1965.
11. *New York Times*, April 5, 1967, p. 38.
12. *Amusement Business*, February 26, 1966.
13. Ibid., March 12, 1966.
14. Ringling Bros. and Barnum & Bailey Circus Route Book, 1966, p. 7.
15. *San Francisco Chronicle*, September 2, 1967, p. 25.
16. Antoinette Concello interview.
17. Richard Barstow interview.
18. *New York Times*, April 5, 1967, p. 38.
19. *Oakland Tribune*, August 26, 1967, p. 7B.
20. *Amusement Business*, May 13, 1967.

21. *Oakland Tribune*, August 23, 1967.
22. Richard Barstow interview.

Chapter 25: Incentives to Sell

1. Ringling Bros. and Barnum & Bailey Circus Program Magazine, 1967, p. 5.
2. John Ringling North II interview.
3. *The New Yorker*, April 10, 1965, pp. 38–39.
4. Henry Ringling North interview, October 16, 1979.
5. Stuart Lancaster interview.
6. Alice Lancaster interview. She was most helpful in trying to provide a sketch of how life has unfolded for many of the Ringling family descendants.
7. Stuart Lancaster interview.
8. *Circus Report*, October 9, 1989, p. 11, and June 18, 1990, p. 1.
9. Rudy Bundy interview.
10. Written answers from Countess Ida von Zedlitz-Trützschler to the author.
11. Rudy Bundy interview.
12. Ringling Bros. and Barnum & Bailey Circus Program Magazine, 1967, p. 51.
13. *Variety*, November 15, 1967.
14. Ringling Bros. and Barnum & Bailey Circus Program Magazine, 1979, p. 24.
15. Henry Ringling North interview, October 16, 1979.
16. Written answers from Countess Ida von Zedlitz-Trützschler to the author.
17. Arthur Concello interview, April 20, 1986.
18. *Variety*, November 15, 1967.

Chapter 26: Lost in the Press Kit

1. *Variety*, December 6, 1967, p. 49.
2. *San Francisco Chronicle*, March 19, 1982, p. 34.
3. *Amusement Business*, November 25, 1967.
4. *San Francisco Chronicle*, September 21, 1969, p. 2.
5. *Variety*, January 8, 1969.
6. Joe Cohen, "Ringling Circus Stands Test of Time," *Variety*, January 11, 1984, p. 229. For another chilling example of Feld press-kit fictions parading as fact, see also John Culhane's *The American Circus: An Illustrated History* (New York: Henry Holt and Company, 1990). In his account of the show's transition to an indoor operation in 1957, Culhane writes not a single word about the pivotal and controlling role played by Art Concello, hired back by North to manage the entire organization. Rather, Culhane gives Irvin Feld center stage for having gained "exclusive control of booking and promoting the circus." In fact, Feld's Super Shows promoted only a few dates in the early indoor years, and some of these were among the most poorly attended and unprofitable ones.

7. Henry Ringling North interview, November 24, 1982.
8. Rudy Bundy interview.
9. John Ringling North interview.
10. Ibid.
11. John Ringling North II interview.
12. Ibid.
13. Dody Heath Soames interview. It is important here to note that although Heath alluded to having been the recipient over the years of countless letters from North—some very poetic, others philosophical and reaching—none was advanced for examination despite every effort made by this author to be afforded such an opportunity. Heath did make accessible for review a couple of letters she received from North. Neither was poetic or philosophical, and both were written in clear, forceful prose in terms of addressing the relationship in which the two were then heatedly involved.
14. John Ringling North II interview.
15. Chita Cristiani interview.
16. Arthur Concello interview, April 20, 1986.
17. John Ringling North II interview.
18. Rudy Bundy interview.
19. *New York Times*, September 11, 1984.
20. *Daily Variety*, September 7, 1984. The predictable fabrications in this obituary are so blatant as to suggest the Feld organization wrote it.

Chapter 27: A Graceful Exit

1. Phil Hall interview.
2. Harold Ronk interview.
3. John Ringling North interview.
4. Countess Ida von Zedlitz-Trützschler interview, March 17, 1990.
5. Ibid.
6. John Ringling North interview.
7. Written answers from Countess Ida von Zedlitz-Trützschler to the author.
8. Dody Heath Soames interview.
9. *Time*, June 17, 1985, p. 77.
10. *New York Times*, June 7, 1985.
11. *Los Angeles Times*, June 7, 1985, pt. 1, p. 26.
12. Written answers from Countess Ida von Zedlitz-Trützschler to the author.

Big Top Bibliography

The following books cover various aspects of Ringling circus history:

Author's Favorites and Recommended Reading

Clausen, Connie, *I Love You Honey, but the Season's Over* (New York: Holt, Rinehart and Winston, 1961).

May, Earl Chapin, *The Circus from Rome to Ringling* (New York: Dover, 1963).

Fellows, Dexter, and Andrew Freeman, *This Way to the Big Show* (New York: Halcyon House, 1936).

North, Henry Ringling, and Alden Hatch, *Circus Kings* (New York: Doubleday and Company, 1960).

Bradna, Fred, as told to Hartzell Spence, *The Big Top* (New York: Simon and Schuster, 1952).

Taylor, Robert Lewis, *Center Ring* (New York: Doubleday and Company, 1956).

Harlow, Alvin F., *The Ringlings, Wizards of the Circus* (New York: Julian Messner, 1951).

Ringling, Alfred, *Life Story of the Ringling Brothers* (Chicago: R. R. Donnelley and Sons, 1900).

Other Suggested Reading

Fenner, Sandison and Wolcott, *The Circus Lure and Legend* (Englewood Cliffs, N.J.: Prentice-Hall, 1970).

Fox, Charles Philip, *A Ticket to the Circus* (New York: Bramhall House, 1959).

Plowden, Gene, *Gargantua, Circus Star of the Century* (New York: Bonanza Books, 1972).

———, *Those Amazing Ringlings and Their Circus* (Caldwell, Idaho: Caxton Printers, 1967).

Index

A Note on the Author

DAVID LEWIS HAMMARSTROM, an ardent circus fan and former circus press agent, is the author of *Behind the Big Top* (1980) and *Circus Rings around Russia* (1983), as well as a number of articles about the circus in *Variety* and other show publications. He lives in Oakland, California.